Making Ireland Roman

Making Ireland Roman:

Irish Neo-Latin writers and the republic of letters

edited by

JASON HARRIS & KEITH SIDWELL

First published in 2009 by
Cork University Press
Youngline Industrial Estate
Pouladuff Road, Togher
Cork, Ireland

British Library Cataloguing in Publication Data

Making Ireland Roman : Irish Neo-Latin writers and the
republic of letters.
1. Latin literature, Medieval and modern – Ireland – History
and criticism.
I. Harris, Jason, 1977 – II. Sidwell, Keith C.
870.9'9415'09024-dc22

ISBN-13: 9781859184530

Typeset by Tower Books, Ballincollig, Co. Cork
Printed by Gutenberg Press, Malta

www.corkuniversitypress.com

Contents

v

Acknowledgements

The authors would like to thank their colleagues at the Centre for Neo-Latin Studies in University College Cork (UCC) for the assistance, advice and support that they have provided during the course of the last few years. Acknowledgement is also owed and gratefully given to the Irish Research Council for the Humanities and Social Sciences, which funded the research project out of which the present volume has grown by means of an Irish Research Council for the Humanities and Social Sciences Major Project Grant. The project has also been funded by the Irish government through its research funding programmes PRTLI 1 and 3, by Atlantic Philanthropies and by internal sources within UCC. We are greatly appreciative of the recognition and support that such funding entails. In addition, publication of this volume has been facilitated by a grant from the NUI for which we are indeed grateful. We would also like to thank the Collegio San Isidoro in Rome for granting us permission to use the cover image. Finally, there are many who have contributed to the weekly seminars co-ordinated by the Centre for Neo-Latin Studies, and without their efforts the current state of research would not have been attained, nor the present volume written. Many thanks to them for their insights, humour and enthusiasm.

Acknowledgements

Introduction:

Ireland and *Romanitas*

JASON HARRIS and
KEITH SIDWELL

The idea for this volume arose from a larger-scale enterprise, the production of a handbook which would cover the copious printed literature written in Latin by Irish authors of various cultural, religious and political colours during the period *c.* 1500–1750.[1] In the course of the several years it has taken for the project to take final shape (1998 onwards), weekly interdisciplinary seminars at University College Cork (UCC) have brought together Latinists, historians and specialists in early modern Irish and Anglo-Irish literature to study and discuss texts such as Richard Stanihurst's *De Rebus in Hibernia Gestis* (Antwerp, 1584), Stephen White's *Apologia pro innocentibus Hibernis* (manuscript, *c.* 1637), Philip O'Sullivan Beare's *Tenebriomastix* (manuscript, *c.* 1650), Dermot O'Meara's *Ormonius* (London, 1615) and John Lynch's *Alithinologia* (St Malo, 1664). A further consequence of this venture will be a series of textual editions (with translation and commentary) of some of the works studied. Attention is drawn in particular to the forthcoming editions of O'Meara's *Ormonius* by David Edwards and Keith Sidwell and of Stanihurst's *De Rebus in Hibernia Gestis* by John Barry and Hiram Morgan.[2]

The unique access to a body of (at best) neglected and sometimes previously unstudied works that was offered to this cross-section of early modern scholars soon began to generate the beginnings of a new field of historical research. To promote interest in this and to capitalize on work already done by scholars not initially associated with the UCC project (see below for details), it therefore seemed timely to the editors (and especially to Jason Harris, who first mooted the idea) to gather together some pieces by this burgeoning group which could serve as a way of opening to a wider public the importance of this material.

Many of the volume's contributors have, in the course of the seminar's (1998–) and the subsequent project's (1999–) existence, been regular attenders at the seminar. John Barry, David Caulfield, David Edwards,

Jason Harris, Hiram Morgan, Diarmaid Ó Catháin and Keith Sidwell are in this category. As has been stated above, several of these are also associated with forthcoming or planned textual editions of Irish Latin works. Colm Lennon has been an advisor since the project's formal inception, and has read a paper to the seminar. Elizabethanne Boran has long been at the heart of the Ussher project, which is based at Trinity College Dublin, a venture which is parallel to the undertaking at UCC, and has as its focus the production of an edition of the letters of the renowned archbishop of Dublin, James Ussher. Gráinne McLaughlin is the editor on the *Commentarius Rinuccinianus* project, funded by the Department of Arts, Sport and Tourism of the Republic of Ireland and administered by the University of Ulster in Northern Ireland. All of the contributors have either participated in, or benefited from, the efforts of Thomas O'Connor and Marian Lyons's Irish in Europe project, which has helped to place the experience of diaspora at the focus of early modern Irish historical scholarship. The contemporaneous appearance of so many ground-breaking research projects that deal with the intellectual culture of early modern Ireland has helped greatly in providing a sense of purpose and context to the activities of the Centre for Neo-Latin Studies in Cork, and, to borrow a phrase of the seventeenth-century cleric David Rothe, has created a vivid impression that *Hibernia* is *resurgens*.

With the abolition of Latin as a matriculation requirement for university entrance in the Republic of Ireland in 1973 (following at a respectful distance the similar decision in the United Kingdom in 1960) the fortunes of the Romans' language in Ireland have plummeted. This has had consequences, however, not only for the study of classical subjects. For the whole period from antiquity to the end of the eighteenth century was characterized by the employment of Latin as an international medium of discourse between states and among scholars, whatever discipline they professed. Hence, almost at a stroke, and because the artificial support structure required to keep Latin going was not replaced by a similar network of requirements in departments of history, romance languages and other interested parties (such as exists in many continental university systems), the natural association between medieval and early modern history and literature and a knowledge of Latin was also broken. More than thirty years later, the vast majority of our undergraduates and graduate students do not learn Latin, or, if they do, they learn too little and too late for them to be able to deal adequately with material written, as it mostly was, by individuals with a strong grasp of classical style and a deep acquaintance with the classical Latin literature.

For, despite the onset of both literary and scholarly production in the vernacular languages of Europe, it is a fact that up to 1680 most books exhibited at the Frankfurt Book Fair were in Latin; that of those published in Oxford from 1690 to 1710 more than half were in Latin; that 31 per cent of all the entries in *Bibliothèque raisonnée des ouvrages des savants de l'Europe* (1728–40) were in Latin; and that in many European states academic dissertations were written in Latin as a matter of course until the early nineteenth century and sometimes, for example in the Netherlands until the mid-twentieth century.[3] The most remarkable aspect of these facts, of course, is that Latin survived one upheaval which might easily have spelled its doom, the Reformation and Counter-Reformation, before it gradually fell victim to another, the rise of the twin gods of nationalism and utilitarianism, which it was ultimately powerless to resist. This survival happened not merely because those who found themselves on opposing sides of the new intra-Christian religious chasm were already Latinists, or because they still thought that debate might, if not bridge the gap, at least provide a means of saving some individuals from the blight of heresy or wrong belief. It was also the case that the fundamental *material* for the arguments being conducted across the new religious divide was in Latin (and Greek). In any case, and at least partly because Christianity itself was rooted in Latin antiquity, education systems did not have an alternative syllabus ready to hand nor an ideology sufficiently nationalistic and 'progressive' to institute one. Perhaps as importantly, the force of the status quo in inter-state communication was also too great. Reinhold Heidenstein (1553–1620), the official historian of the Polish King Stephen Bathory, wrote as follows in his essay 'The Chancellor' on the role of the Polish chancellor (*Cancellarius sive de dignitate et officio cancellarii regni Poloniae*):

> *Latina lingua tamquam communis omnium gentium Christianarum publico quasi consensu recepta fere ab omnibus est. Repertos tamen aliquando quosdam memini, qui sua etiam lingua ad reges nostros scriberent vicissimque agitatum ut nostra quoque sclavonica eis responderetur, ut cum illi dignitatis gravitatisque suae nimis retinentes viderentur, nos nostrae non omnino etiam neglegentes videremur. Sed maioris partis principum populorumque Christianorum, ut aliis in rebus, ita in hac quoque fortassis consensus spectandus Latinaque oratione utendum.*[4]

The Latin language has been accepted by almost everyone as though by public consent as the common tongue of all the Christian peoples. I recall that at times there have been some who wrote to our kings even in their own language and that it was in turn proposed that they should receive a reply in our own Slavonic tongue, so that when they seemed too conscious of their own position and importance, we should not seem altogether negligent of our own. But in this, as in other matters, one should look to the agreement of the majority of the Christian rulers and peoples and use Latin.

Hence, not only were the international theological debates of the Reformation and Counter-Reformation period conducted, for the most part, in Latin, but a whole reformed system (that of Sweden) could be reconstructed firmly on the foundations of classical learning as late as 1571. Henceforth, and until the eighteenth century, in Sweden as in the rest of Europe, university students learned almost everything, including their mathematics and science, primarily through the medium of Latin.[5] Thus, whenever a vernacular text was aimed at a European audience, it was normally translated *into* Latin. Witness, for example, Galileo's *Dialogo intorno ai due massimi sistemi del mondo*, which was known outside Italy through the Latin edition of 1635. Even *literary* works might be treated thus, as Sir Francis Kynaston's 1635 Latin translation of Chaucer's *Troilus and Criseyde*, Books I and II, demonstrates.[6] It is to this context that the Latin literature of the Irish belongs.

The ethnic, cultural and – from the Reformation – religious divisions within Ireland produced a divided Latin writing and reading community. On the one side of this, the loyalist (for want of a better word) Latin continued in use in much the way it did in England and for many of the same purposes – celebration of the conquest, encomium of crown supporters, praise of the monarch and the forwarding of Protestant theology. The other side used Latin to express both theological dissent from England's Protestantism and to adumbrate to Europeans – especially monarchs – political goals opposed to British control of Ireland. They also employed it in more traditional ways to compose works of religious devotion, of theology and of poetry. However, they were not averse to engaging vociferously with other Catholics in internal debates, over such issues as religious orders and, egregiously, with the Scots over their claim to historical priority in the name *Scotia*, *Scotus* and its attendant saints. For both sides, the medium had the advantage of providing an audience which was not confined to one vernacular language group.

Moreover, Latin conferred high cultural prestige and especially so if written in fashionable, classicizing styles. It is hard, for example, to see quite what merited the effort Stanihurst put into his *De Rebus*, of which the most part is a translation of Giraldus Cambrensis into Ciceronian Latin, if it was not the fact that the founding myth of the Old English in Ireland would be taken more seriously by outsiders in the new *form* imposed upon it by Stanihurst (but also the works of Giraldus Cambrensis, though widely known, had not yet been published). Stylistically, the work is a *tour de force* and its impact would have been consequently the greater among the highly trained and (to their own thinking) discerning members of the *respublica litterarum*, the 'Republic of Letters', as the Latin community was known among its adherents. Nor is it easy to assign a merely utilitarian function to the production of a twelve-page pamphlet of Latin poems, including the diabolically difficult acrostics and anagrammatic acrostics beloved of the baroque era, by the priests of St Isidore's, the Franciscan College in Rome, to celebrate the visit of the minister general of their order to the house in 1672, nor to the (unpublished) collection of epigrams painstakingly composed by Francis O'Molloy, the writer of (among other things) a (published) grammar of Irish in Latin.[7] Much of this was cultural activity, the small change of the educated elites whose training was classical and linguistic and whose free time was often devoted to games which used this accumulated capital to provide intellectual stimulus and amusement for themselves and their group.

The facility of such authors in the Latin tongue, their readiness to play with style, and their assumption that their tricks would be recognized and appreciated reflect the fact that for over a thousand years Latin was one of the principal languages of Ireland, as much as it was of wider Europe. Since the dying days of the Roman Empire, when Christianity was already becoming well established across the Continent, the Latin language had become the medium in which the Catholic Church operated. When Christianity took root in Ireland, Latin came with it and although, as in Anglo-Saxon England, the vernacular still enjoyed major cultural prestige and was used for many literary purposes, nonetheless Irish Latin writers used the official tongue to write in all the specifically Christian genres (hymns, saints' lives, church annals, etc.) and to compose grammars and commentaries, and occasionally poetry.[8] From the advent of humanism and printed texts in Ireland in the sixteenth century until the beginnings of the decline of Latin literacy in the eighteenth, more than one thousand books were published in Latin by Irish authors. In order to convey the idiosyncrasies of Gaelic culture in the language of European scholarship to an international audience, Irish authors had to engage in a process of cultural translation. They had to formulate a vocabulary which represented the unique features of Irish life and politics in a language purified of barbarisms. Many of these authors were Catholic exiles attempting to promote an alternative to the English colonial narrative emanating from domestic scholars. In Ireland itself a reverse process was under way as Protestants attempted to create a learned community from which would emanate a form of classical civility that might reconstitute the basis of Irish society, rendering it more amenable to Protestant reforms and English administration.

In the first half of the seventeenth century a panoply of humanist apologetics for Ireland circulated in the scholarly networks of continental Europe. Whether in print or in manuscript, the writings of Peter Lombard,

Philip O'Sullivan Beare, Luke Wadding, John Lynch, Stephen White, Florence Conry, Henry Fitzsimon, David Rothe, and many others constitute an unprecedented outpouring of humanist scholarship and baroque invective. These authors' books were imbued with the European-wide scholarship and Latinity of humanism but were preoccupied by the specific history of, and political situation in, Ireland. In conjunction with the writings of the Usshers, James Ware and the other Protestant progeny of the new university at Trinity College in Dublin, they constitute a formidable demonstration of the prowess of Irish Latinity.

Two key developments prompted this proliferation of Irish Latin writing: the disastrous collapse of consensus government in Ireland in the course of the sixteenth century, and the appearance in print of the writings of the medieval apologist for the original Norman conquest, Giraldus Cambrensis.[9] The perplexing interlacing of these strands can only be understood within the broader European context of the Renaissance and Reformation; only when the stitches linking them have been diligently unpicked can the full significance of Irish Latin literature be seen.

Irish political life in the later sixteenth century was a brutal contest which was complicated further by both genuine and imagined foreign intervention. The English administration had repeatedly failed to find a stable substitute for the clientage system that had operated under the Kildare ascendancy prior to its collapse in the 1530s. Lacking the financial or military means to enforce centralized government throughout the island, successive governors pursued an inconsistent series of projects to reform the legal and political structure of local fiefdoms. Such an approach (bolstered by a generation of ideologues whose intellectual formation sprang from the humanist revival of Roman imperial law) relied upon the Crown's ability to convince individual magnates, whether of Gaelic or Norman descent, that administrative reform was to their own advantage. At its most lenient, this entailed enticing them or their children with the political self-assurance that primogeniture and royal enfranchisement could offer, compared to the supposed uncertainties of *tanistry* (elective succession). Yet such deals were negotiated amid presages of the violence that would punish recalcitrance – it was a mailed fist that held out writs and concessions to the Irish lords.[10]

However, the Crown's ability to master the multi-dimensional game of Irish magnate rivalry was diminished considerably by inconsistency in its policies, by anxieties about allowing clients to develop into 'overmighty subjects' and by the very real threat of continental European intervention creating a rival clientage system. In the increasingly fraught sphere of post-Reformation international politics, England's political Protestantism, combined with its dangerous tolerance of Atlantic privateering and its geographical potential as a base for ventures to the Baltic and the Netherlands, made it a tempting target for the militant Catholic empire of Philip II of Spain. Ireland seemed to offer the ideal base for an invasion or for sponsoring insurrection, and thus the need for all parties to secure the territory became paramount. While Spain's creditors and empty coffers allowed little scope for a sufficiently large Irish enterprise, the equally impecunious Elizabeth turned to semi-private plantation schemes as an affordable and potentially lucrative way of sustaining and expanding the increasingly expensive military campaigns. The result was that the factional dynamics of Irish magnate rivalry became supercharged with the energy of an international agenda.[11]

The encouragement of magnate rivalry in the context of an increasingly polarized religious situation had incendiary effects. Successive Irish 'rebels', such as Fitzmaurice and O'Neill, could exploit religion as a clarion-call to arms, while the decision to give the plantations a specifically Protestant character, effectively excluding the Old English, contributed to the failure to attract sufficient investment and intensified the hostility with which the schemes were received by displaced locals. Moreover, reconstitution of the Irish legal and political system became synonymous with the extirpation of papism. Catholic centres of worship were ruthlessly suppressed and hundreds of clergymen fled abroad; at the same time, a university was established in Dublin to promote the 'common good' through Protestantism and education in European (i.e. non-Gaelic) civility and customs. Because of the closure of ecclesiastical schools in Ireland, Catholics throughout the country were forced to send their children abroad to be educated. These young scholars entered Irish colleges in Italy, France, Spain, Bohemia and the Spanish Netherlands. All of a sudden, a generation of Irish Catholic students was propelled into the international arena of humanist pedagogy. Irish citizens of the republic of letters were, therefore, the offspring of military conflict.

As the political situation became more volatile, the benefits for local magnates who could keep the peace seemed potentially all the greater. Nevertheless, the brutality of successive English administrations pushed Irish lords into rebellion. When the demands and goals of Hugh O'Neill, the native Irish earl of Tyrone, overstretched the confidence granted him at court, war ensued. From a Crown perspective, the revolt confirmed earlier worries about over-mighty subjects and thoroughly discredited the logic of localized administration by native magnates. Tyrone's ultimate defeat in the Nine Years War was only partially the result of superior military resources at the disposal of the English and rather more due to the tardy, ill-conceived character of foreign support, which in turn energized the English. When Elizabeth died, her legacy to James was an Ireland insufficiently pacified but devoid of significant means for opposition. While James sought to bolster the Protestant constituency in Ireland through both political patronage and territorial plantation, the Old English in Dublin had begun to articulate an ideology of loyalist recusancy. Although the political interests and ideologies of the native Irish, Old English and New English were increasingly divergent at home, the situation abroad was still more complex.

All Irish Catholics educated abroad (whether of native Irish or Old English descent) became imbued with the developing culture of Tridentine religiosity in its various, and mutually competing, forms. While contesting differences between Old English and native Irish Catholics, they advocated uniformity and tried (often without success) to present a united front to the humanist readers of Europe. Fuelling their articulate outpouring of apologetics was the appearance in print of the writings of Giraldus Cambrensis. Giraldus castigated the Irish for their language, culture and religion, while embellishing his accounts of the country with fantastical and often scurrilous legends. Despite their evident unreliability, his writings attracted a wide readership among the scholars of Europe, partly because alternative accounts of Ireland were in short supply, and partly because Giraldus's antiquity and penchant for the marvellous greatly appealed to a culture fascinated by 'curiosities'. Goaded by the sudden and pervasive popularity of these writings, Irish writers felt compelled to defend their country's reputation. Nor did it help when Scottish writers began to claim that medieval 'Scotia' referred to Scotland rather than Ireland, thus denuding Ireland of the 'golden period' of its history and many of its saints (see Chapters 6 and 7). Celebrating one's *patria* was a classical topos widely adopted by humanists across Europe; in Ireland it combined with the nostalgia of exile and the exigencies of Catholic propaganda (for political and religious reforming schemes) to create a national myth of oppression.

Unfortunately for such writers, the Irishman Richard Stanihurst had in 1584 published his text entitled *De Rebus in Hibernia Gestis*, which claimed that the native Irish and Old English were thoroughly distinct racially, culturally and linguistically (see further Chapters 2 and 3 on Stanihurst). Stanihurst coined the term 'Anglo-Hibernus' to refer to his own Old English community, which he presented as much more civilized than its Gaelic counterpart. Stanihurst's neologism crept into Latin usage, providing a categorical blot in the representation of an undifferentiated Irish Catholic populace. Native Irish and Old English authors alike were at pains to reject both the term 'Anglo-Hibernus' and the social distinction it claimed to depict. Stanihurst represents the vested interests of the Old English community within the Pale who were anxious to present themselves as English to the Crown in order to maintain their privileges vis-à-vis the Gaelic lords and to curtail the ascendant New English administrators in Dublin. Throughout the seventeenth century, Stanihurst's Old English critics were easily able to expose his exaggerations and distortions by detailing the level of shared culture among the Gaelic Irish and Old English. Yet the terms of divided loyalty that Stanihurst so deftly expressed refused simply to disappear because they reflected an unyielding dilemma that faced Irish Catholics loyal to the English Crown.

By the 1640s Ireland, like England and Scotland, was riven by civil war. As increasingly hardline Protestants, or Puritans, gained the ascendancy in England and Scotland, the Catholics of Ireland – who formed the majority of the population – became anxious to defend themselves against the threat of persecution. A series of plots and coups in the years 1640–42 led to armed revolt against the English administration in Ireland. Initially successful, the Catholic leaders established a confederacy, claiming to defend their own and King Charles I's interests against the militant English parliament. Crucially, their Catholicism (with its associations of papal appeal) presented an obstacle to the king accepting their help, and the papal nuncio Cardinal Rinuccini, sent to aid the rebels, despaired of the Irish insistence on loyalty to the English king, advocating instead the establishment of an independent Catholic polity. Ultimately, of course, Charles I was executed by the English Parliamentarians, and the insurrection in Ireland was ruthlessly suppressed by Oliver Cromwell. By then Rinuccini had returned to Rome utterly disgusted by what he regarded as the heretical Irish advocacy of royalism at the expense of religious freedom.

In December 1649, with the Catholic Confederacy already fragmented, Rinuccini reported to the pope, explaining what he saw as the ethnic character of religious affiliation in Ireland. He claimed that a distinction could be made between two types of Catholic in Ireland – the native Irish, who are good Catholics, and the Old English, who associate with Protestants, who recognize English common law without regard for the canon law of the Church, and who support the English Protestant monarch because they have become wealthy on the spoils of monasteries in the wake of the English-promoted Reformation in Ireland. Elsewhere Rinuccini stated that the Old English were 'Catholic only in name', and that the papacy in future should not waste its resources on them, patronizing the native Irish instead. These are weighty criticisms of an ostensibly Catholic community; at their core lies an utter rejection of the basic premise that one could be a loyal Catholic subject of the English Protestant king. The ethnic terms in which the critique is couched run counter to the formulations of the Catholic Confederacy itself, which administered an oath to all Catholics, with the specific goal 'to prevent the springing up of national distinctions'. The Confederates refused to tolerate distinctions to be made between the native Irish, Old English and New English, 'upon pain of highest punishment' but rather 'every person or persons whatsoever talking or discoursing, in writing or otherwise of the enemies, shall not call them by the name or names of English or protestants, but shall call them by the names of puritanical or malignant party'.[12] The Confederate leaders evidently believed that the ethnic divisions in Irish Catholicism were merely dormant, but that with a little tact and linguistic sensitivity they would remain so.[13]

The Confederates' painstaking concern for the terms in which they should represent themselves contrasts sharply with the generalizations proposed by Rinuccini. Irish Catholics had long been concerned to represent themselves abroad as a unified group, while frequently doing the opposite for domestic audiences. As stated above, Ireland's Catholic elite had, since the latter decades of the sixteenth century, been educated at colleges and seminaries in Spain, France, Italy and the Low Countries – an education which was supposed to prepare a priesthood for missionary work back home. The Latin writings produced by these exiles are predominantly inclusive in ethnic outlook. Although in practice the Irish colleges were as riven by regional factionalism as society in Ireland itself, authors of both native Irish and Old English descent wrote in honour of a unified *patria* whose Catholic community was undifferentiated by the complexities of ethnic or political nuance. It was, after all, easier to secure foreign aid for a united Irish Catholic cause; hence authors such as John Lynch, Stephen White and Antony Bruodin all sought to reject ethnic categorization of Irish Catholicism, foregrounding the issues of cultural translation that lay at the heart of writing in Latin to a foreign audience.

To some extent, then, it is evidently legitimate to pose the question of how to conceptualize an Irish renaissance that drew upon both the domestic and the international Latin writings of Irishmen concerned about their own identity and its relation to the fate of Ireland. But was this a 'renaissance'? The celebration of *patria*, the recurrent concern of Irish authors with the promulgation of *civilitas*, and the widespread evidence of their eloquent Latinity demonstrate that Irish authors had learned from the innovations of humanist pedagogues in the fifteenth and sixteenth centuries. Yet their notion of civility is complicated by the way it is used to express hostility to heresy and rival political cultures. The recurrent New English claim to further civility in Ireland is employed as a cover or an excuse for savage application of martial law. Conversely, when the Jesuits launched a campaign to promote civility in Ireland in the 1620s and 1630s, they meant Tridentine Catholicism and the reduction of Gaelic cultural idiosyncrasies. To what extent such notions of civility can be characterized as humanist is debatable. Further, the scholarship of most Irish Latin writers was scholastic in focus and expression. While their Latin for the most part is free from solecism, it does not lack medieval neologisms but is commonly devoid of humanist literary playfulness (though for exceptions, see Chapter 8). Nor is there a large corpus of Irish Latin imaginative literature to emulate that of Italy, France or even England. In short, the Irish evidently benefited from the Renaissance, but whether one can speak of an Irish Latin renaissance is a matter that awaits the 'differentiated and interesting evaluation' for which Diarmaid Ó Catháin makes a plea in the article included here (Chapter 1).[14]

In this context, it is worth drawing some attention to the title of this collection. By presenting the notion of 'Making Ireland Roman', we wanted, of course, to echo Canny's much more comprehensive and systematic treatment of efforts to make Ireland British.[15] Yet we also wanted to signal an ambivalence in the concept of *Romanitas* with which many of our authors were working. Whereas domestic writers such as Archbishop Ussher and the poet Dermot O'Meara sought to Romanize Ireland by applying to it the standards of classical civility and erudition, the Catholic exiles sought to make Ireland Roman in a rather different sense, expressing a Tridentine religious agenda in a humanist linguistic register. For both Catholics and Protestants, the cultivation of *patria* was not simply high-minded humanism but a practical attempt to secure patronage and earn personal accolades. Just as ancient Rome weighed heavily on the intellectual endeavours of early modern European scholars, so it carried a rich sense of endowment for both Protestant writers participating in the notion of British imperial *Romanitas* and Catholic writers engaging with the historical and spiritual universalism of the Roman Church. Circumstance has resulted in the absence of any article in this collection on the topic of Jansenism, which has recently been so expertly explored by Thomas O'Connor.[16] His magisterial study will surely prompt further exploration of the complexities of Irish Catholic *Romanitas* in its engagement with Gallicanism and divergent forms of Tridentine devotion. Indeed, *Romanitas*, whether of the ecclesiastical or classical kind, was not a stable category, but a negotiated and often contested mode of articulation. It is worth reflecting that neither the Church of Ireland nor the continental seminaries, both supposed hothouses of a newly educated ministry, managed to meet their cultural goals. While Ireland remained both Catholic in religion and British in administration, the deeper pursuit of *Romanitas* was at best a means to an end for both sides in their attempts to hold on to what were at best partial and contested gains.

The articles gathered together in this collection are organized so as to give some detailed perspective on the context adumbrated above. We begin with Diarmaid Ó Catháin's *tour d'horizon* of both Latin culture in fifteenth- and sixteenth-century Ireland and of Ireland's links to the birthplace of the Renaissance, Italy, in which he provides a fascinating starting point for a reassessment of the effect of that movement upon the furthest western extremities of the Continent of Europe. In Chapters 2 and 3, we take a close look at one of the major Latinists of the later sixteenth century, the Dubliner Richard Stanihurst. John Barry focuses upon his earlier period (up to 1584), arguing for close connections between Derricke's famous *Image of Irelande* and the historical writings (both vernacular and Latin) of Stanihurst. Colm Lennon examines the Stanihurst of a later period, when he was in exile and much more deeply involved in the production of Catholic devotional literature. His correspondence with the great Belgian humanist Justus Lipsius allows us an intimate glance at the operation of the *Respublica Litterarum* and at the ways in which Latinity might facilitate intercourse at a time of religious turmoil. In Chapter 4, we cross the great divide. David Edwards and Keith Sidwell introduce Dermot O'Meara's epic poem on the 10th earl of Ormond, a loyalist and the suppressor of numerous Irish rebellions in the sixteenth century. Here the international language and its high literary culture are seen in political use supporting the English claim to legitimate rule in Ireland. Chapters 5 and 6 take us once more into the literature of the Catholic exile, but lead in two different directions, although the subject of both is the same writer, Philip O'Sullivan Beare. Hiram Morgan first re-evaluates the contribution made to our understanding of the Nine Years (or as O'Sullivan has it, the Fifteen Years) War by the *Compendium*, published in 1621, and aimed politically against the English control of Ireland and towards persuading the Spanish to intervene. Then David Caulfield examines one of O'Sullivan's unpublished polemical works, the *Tenebriomastix*, which takes us into an internal debate among Catholic exiles, concerning the original meaning of the terms *Scotus* and *Scotia*, bitterly fought as a rearguard action by the Irish against the Scots, who had usurped their rightful history. In Chapter 7, we stay with the literature of Catholic exile and deal with another major figure, Stephen White. Jason Harris analyses his two *Apologiae* (one of which has been edited, the other remains unpublished), in particular focusing upon the argumentative and stylistic techniques he employs in his attempted refutation of the politically damaging works of Giraldus and Stanihurst. Chapter 8 concentrates upon another major product of Irish Catholic resistance to English rule, the *Commentarius Rinuccinianus*. However, Gráinne McLaughlin's focus is not so much the overall political thrust of this report but rather the role played by humanistic culture in the production of the invective verses which occasionally brighten its pages. Finally, in Chapter 9, Elizabethanne Boran brings us back to one of the major Protestant figures of Ireland, Archbishop James Ussher, a scholar of European importance and a voluminous writer of Latin. Her paper once more brings us into the wider realm of the *Respublica Litterarum*, and shows in particular how crucial to both sides in the religious debate of the period was the shared culture of learning. Latin continued to unify even as it provided the language of division, a paradox worth contemplating as we attempt to understand the intellectual history of Ireland and of Europe in the early modern period.

In closing, we note that all translations given in this volume are the authors' own, except where another source is specified, and that we have not sought to standardize the style of translation when the author has attempted to reflect the stylistic idiosyncrasies of the original language. Where we have adapted translations from other sources we have marked this in the notes.

1. Some reflexes of Latin learning and of the Renaissance in Ireland
c. 1450–c. 1600

DIARMAID Ó CATHÁIN

The term *Renaissance*, as used by general historians, is ambiguous, sometimes referring to an intellectual movement and at other times to a period of history. The intellectual movement in question is customarily described by such expressions as 'the revival of classical learning' or 'the imitation of Greek and Roman design in the fine arts', while the period designated by the term is usually thought to extend from the mid-fourteenth century to the middle or end of the sixteenth. However, historians have held widely divergent opinions both as to the character of the intellectual movement and the precise boundaries of the period.[1]

Perhaps it is true to say that the Renaissance started in Italy in the fourteenth century and spread gradually outwards across the rest of Europe over a period of some three hundred years, and the elasticity of the term may in part be due to the fact that subsequent writers have identified various manifestations of this influence in different countries over this period.[2]

In literary terms the Renaissance involved a certain interaction with the emerging vernacular languages, as well, of course, as the return to Latin and Greek roots.[3] In the context of Gaelic and Gaelicized Ireland, it is important to bear in mind that the cultural context was significantly different to the European norm. The vernacular was in an entirely different position in Ireland.[4] Ireland had never been a Roman province and it had a long and distinct vernacular literary tradition. Irish literary culture was not mainly based in Greek and Latin lore, although it had absorbed much from ecclesiastical and classical sources and in the medieval period, many Irish clerics, scholars, and doctors made translations of standard European religious, medical and other texts from Latin into Irish. Latin had never been the language of the professions apart from the clergy. The discourse of the poets, the lawyers, and the doctors

14

was in Irish, and their textbooks and treatises on grammar, poetry, law, and medicine were in Irish also.[5] It might then be a mistake to expect to find the Renaissance occurring in Ireland in the same way as in its main centre in Italy, or in other more northern European countries. This is one of the factors which led to what Fr Brendan Bradshaw called 'a *legenda negra* [sic] about Gaelic society which has been going the rounds . . . for a very long time indeed . . .', that Gaelic Ireland remained untouched by the Renaissance.[6]

Bradshaw took Maghnas Ó Domhnaill (†1563) of Donegal, the O'Donnell of his time, as an example. He showed how in his personal life and in his literary exertions Ó Domhnaill revealed himself as a typical representative of the Renaissance. He illustrated Ó Domhnaill's manifold connections with continental Europe and showed how this poet-prince's new, luxurious, manuscript biography in Irish of St Colm Cille (Columba), the patron of the O'Donnells, *Betha Colaim Chille*, written in 1532, reveals many characteristic marks of the Renaissance humanist spirit.[7] Ó Domhnaill (and his assistants), in the course of their wide-ranging research, translated material from the older Latin life and other Latin sources as well as archaic Irish material:

> *Maghnas [Ó] Domhnaill . . . do furail an cuid do bi a Laidin don bethaid-si do cur a n-Gaidhilc, 7 do furail an cuid do bi go gcruaid a n-Gaidilc di do cor a mbuga.*[8]

> Manus O'Donnell . . . bade put into Gaelic the part of this *Life* that was in Latin, and bade make easy the part thereof that was hard Gaelic.

This magnificent manuscript, 'obviously the work of the best scribe available', was written on vellum 'in a beautiful formal hand . . .', and contains 'a full page portrait of St Columcille (in a style which has no precedent in Irish manuscripts)': unusually, it was laid out in paragraph form, perhaps 'influenced by page layout in printed books in O'Donnell's library', and was bound in wooden boards covered in sealskin, with brass decorated anglepieces and hinges.[9] Ó Domhnaill also asserted his own personal involvement in the scholarship in the preface. Bradshaw comments:

> In terms of literary history also, the Betha Colaim Chille must be clas-sified as a distinctively renaissance work . . . In fact what was involved was the renaissance's vindication of the claims of the vernacular as a literary language, if not as a scholarly one . . . In this vernacular form the Latin and Old Irish material – except, in the exceptional case of poetry – was incorporated into the new Life. Manus' concern to

explain all of this in his preface draws attention once more to the noteworthy fact that those features of the Betha Colaim Chille which characterise it as a renaissance work – its lay authorship, its anti-quarian character, its vernacular language – are precisely the features on which Manus comments in the preface. Therefore, not only is the book significant for the way in which it reflects the assimilation of certain features of renaissance scholarship, it also reflects the self-consciously unconventional cast of mind of its author: that readiness to cast off hidebound tradition typical of the renaissance outlook.[10]

Bradshaw considers Ó Domhnaill in the light of Machiavelli's *Prince*, Erasmus' *Education of a Christian Prince* and *The Book of the Courtier* by Baldassare Castiglione, taking Lorenzo de' Medici (1448–91) of Florence as archetype:

> Machiavelli's hard-headed political entrepreneur, Erasmus' scholarly christian ruler, Castiglione's prince-aesthete, all of these, in varying degrees, was Manus O'Donnell.[11]

Maghnas Ó Domhnaill was not an isolated example. Gaelic and Gaelicized Ireland had many links to mainland Europe. There were always manifold trading links between France and Spain and the west, and especially the south, of Ireland. As has often been pointed out, the sea in earlier times was a means of communication rather than a factor that divided. There was a centuries-old tradition of trade with ports such as Bordeaux, La Rochelle, St Malo, Bilbao, Bayonne, Corunna and Lisbon, from which ships plied their wares back and forward to Wexford, Water-ford, Youghal, Cork, Kinsale, Limerick, Galway and other Irish ports of the south and west.[12] These trade routes were strengthened in the course of the fifteenth and sixteenth centuries by circumstances. About 1450 migrating herring became very plentiful in the Irish Sea and off the south and west coasts of Ireland;[13] in the sixteenth century fishery of the herring in these waters was at its height and fleets of foreign fishing boats worked there. Indeed, up to 600 Spanish boats could be found there at a time. These fishermen came ashore to process the fish, and also paid dues which could be substantial to the local chieftains. The presence of these numerous continental boats in pursuit of the herring fisheries brought wealth to the south-west and west of Ireland in the fifteenth century and income to the local chieftains. Timothy O'Neill comments that

> [t]his extra wealth is one explanation for the great renewal of building and refurbishing of monastic houses, friaries and castles that took place at this time, in particular in the Gaelic and gaelicized areas of the western seaboard.[14]

As has been pointed out, the resultant exchanges were not confined to goods and trade but extended to intellectual and religious affairs and indeed 'also extended to architecture, naval engineering, etiquette and even interior décor'.[15] For example, there was such an amount of regular intercourse with the Iberian peninsula that it was reported about the year 1600 that many inhabitants of Baltimore and the Blasket Island area were able to speak Spanish as a second language.[16]

This continental connection was boosted by strong links forged with Spain and the Mediterranean through the success in Ireland of the observant movement in the religious orders in the fifteenth and early sixteenth century. This was a reform movement that unfolded within the various major religious orders before the Reformation. The observant movement among the Franciscans, Augustinians and Dominicans had arrived in Ireland by the 1420s.[17] There was widespread enthusiasm in Gaelic and Gaelicized Ireland for the observants; these reforming friars established their power bases in the south and west and by 1530 had penetrated successfully the Old English strongholds of the towns and cities.[18] To facilitate reform, both the papacy and the central headquarters of the religious orders fostered direct access to Rome in the observant movements, bypassing the existing administrative structures within the orders, which in Ireland were generally under English influence or control. Katherine Walsh states that 'this resulted in a general strengthening of ties between the Western parts of Ireland and the continent, and to an increase in travel between Gaelic Ireland and Renaissance Italy'.[19] As has been observed of the library of the Franciscans in Youghal, County Cork, 'the presence of significant numbers of French and German works in the Youghal library indicates extensive contacts with the continent in the late fifteenth century'.[20] It is known, for instance, that there was a community of Irish students in Seville probably about the end of the fifteenth/beginning of the sixteenth centuries and it is clear, for example, that the number of Irish Franciscans travelling abroad to take university degrees increased throughout the fifteenth century.[21]

The contours of the use of Latin in late medieval Ireland await study and clarification.[22] Over the centuries, demarcation lines seem to have evolved between native learning and Latin learning, Latin learning being Church-driven. It appears that *airchinnigh* (erenachs), administrators of Church lands, occupied an important place in the ecclesiastical structure and that therefore in the families which controlled these lands, Latin learning was necessary and commonly found among the incumbents of the office.[23] Native Irish learning was primarily, in the later Middle Ages, in the hands of hereditary learned lay families, and this situation obtained until the destruction of the Gaelic order in the seventeenth century.[24] The hereditary families who were learned in secular Irish lore often reveal much Latinity also. It seems, for example, to be clear that up to the later part of the sixteenth century Latin was the second language of the educated in Ireland, and the normal medium used by the Irish chiefs in communication with the English and other foreigners.[25] This, of course, was the norm throughout Europe.[26] A parenthetical note in one Irish text expressed it thus:

> Dá gcuirthá a n-iongnadh, a léigtheóir, cionnus do thuig an dias anaithnidh ain-iúil si teangtha a chéile, bíodh a fhios agad to raibhe teanga air siubhal go coitcheann idir na cineadhachaibh, an uair sin . . . amhail mar atá Laidean anois.[27]

> Should you wonder, O reader, how these two strangers and foreigners understood each other's language, know that at that time there was in use between nations a common language . . . just as Latin is now used.

In this context it has been stated that the Irish emerge from the accounts of travellers as being among the best in Europe for their proficiency in Latin about 1600.[28] For example, Count Walter Butler, from Roscrea, who is known in European history as the slayer of Wallenstein in 1634, was able to speak Latin fluently because in his youth he had studied logic and humanities in Carrick-on-Suir under Dr Dermot O'Meara, the author of *Ormonius* (London, 1615).[29]

Individuals are noted regularly in the Irish annals as learned in Latin but they, their cultural milieu and their works, or patronage of works, in Irish, Latin, or both, still remain unexplored. One example of a figure who would repay detailed study of the kind applied by Fr Bradshaw to Ó Domhnaill is Finghín Ó Mathúna (O'Mahony) of Rossbrin, near Baltimore, in west Cork, who died in 1496. The Annals of Connacht recorded his death thus: 'Finghín, feithemh coitcenn congairec einigh et engnamo Iarthair Muman ⁊ an fer fa treighidhe a Laidin ⁊ a mBerla a comaimsir ris . . .' (a popular public guardian of the hospitality and valour of West Munster, a man most accomplished in Latin and English of all his contemporaries.)[30] Finghín was *tánaiste* (second-in-command) and later chief of his family. He lived at Rossbrin Castle, dramatically situated at Rossbrin Cove, a few miles across Roaringwater Bay from Baltimore, in County Cork.[31] This part of the country was visited extensively by the continental fishing fleets mentioned above, and it is most likely that the O'Mahonys enjoyed the economic benefits of the income generated by the foreign boats at the time.[32] It is clear that the area benefited from cultural intercourse also.

The annal entry celebrates Ó Mathúna's learning in Latin and in English. Dr Diarmuid Ó Murchadha describes Finghín as 'one of the foremost scholars of his day in Munster'.[33] As well as being a scholar himself, Ó Mathúna was a patron of scribes and other scholars too. The reference in the annals to his hospitality no doubt alludes to such patronage of the learned class or *aos dána,* scribes, poets and *seanchaithe* (genealogists and specialists in historical lore). One such scribe, Donnchadh Ó Duinnín, in 1465, was transcribing a manuscript which is now a section of the Yellow Book of Lecan at Rossbrin for O'Mahony's houses.[34] Another scribe of the period also worked on the manuscript in another of Ó Mahúna's houses,[35] while Cairbre Ó Cennamhain, a third scribe, completed a medico-philosophical text in Rossbrin in 1478.[36] Dr Ó Murchadha considers it likely that it was about this time that a now-lost manuscript, known as the 'Psalter of Rossbrin', was written or kept at Rossbrin.[37]

A literary work of Finghín Ó Mathúna's was an Irish translation in 1475 of *The Travels of Sir John Mandeville.*[38] The author's original text does not seem to have survived; the earliest copy of his translation is found in a manuscript which made its way to Rennes in France where it is preserved.[39] In the introduction Ó Mathúna makes reference to translating from English, Latin, Greek and Hebrew: '*Óir iss é* [i.e. *Finín*] *do chuir an lebursa a berlai 7 a Laidin, a Greige 7 a hEabra a nGaeidhilge.*' Though the editor of the text thought that the translation was in all likelihood made from English, even such a claim is interesting.[40]

Ó Mathúna 'was also the chosen patron of another learned scholar-historian and alumnus of Oxford, Domhnall Ó Ficheallaigh, who dedicated to Finghín his *Annals of Ireland,* probably the work now referred to as "Mac Carthaigh's book"'.[41] It is not known if any work of Domhnall Ó Ficheallaigh's has survived. The surname 'Ó Fi(th)cheallaigh' is Anglicized variously 'Fihely'/'Fehil(l)y'/'Field', nowadays. This family held the townland of Ballymacrown, beside Baltimore, in west Cork until the seventeenth century and seems to have produced a number of prominent churchmen in the sixteenth century.[42]

A kinsman of this Domhnall Ó Ficheallaigh was one of Ireland's greatest Renaissance scholars, Mauritius de Portu, Muiris Ó Ficheallaigh (Maurice O Fihelly), who flourished at the same time.[43] Muiris Ó Ficheallaigh (*c.* 1460–1513) studied at Oxford and in Italy. He is said to have become superintendent of the press to Octavianus Scotus in Venice, a hugely important centre of Renaissance printing and scholarship, and he was professor of theology at the University of Padua.[44] Ó Ficheallaigh may have been the first Irish author to write for the printing press. He was very highly regarded as a scholar in his time and published at Venice a number of works on Duns Scotus, believing, as many did at the time, that that thinker was of Irish birth. He was for a time provincial of the Irish Conventual Franciscans and was appointed archbishop of Tuam in 1506. He died in Galway in 1513 as he returned to take up his office in Tuam. It was stated that he had with him when he returned to Ireland some more works, yet unpublished, which it is to be presumed were lost in the troubled times which followed.[45]

Another such individual who is mentioned in the annal entries about this time is Thomas, 8th earl of Desmond from 1463 until his untimely death in 1468, and lord deputy of Ireland from 1463 to 1467.[46] The earls of Desmond, in Munster, though not quite as important as their kinsmen, the earls of Kildare in Leinster, were rich and powerful lords ruling over hundreds of thousands of acres. 'Desmond's vast palatinate was in truth a small kingdom which had few equals even among the great earldoms of England.'[47] When Thomas died the chroniclers lamented his passing: '*Ba tigerna erghna eolach i Laitin, i mBerla, et i senscreptraibh Gaoidilge an Tomas sin*' (that Thomas was a discerning Lord, learned in Latin, in English and in old Irish writings).[48] The Annals of Lecan refer to him as surpassing 'bountifullnesse in bestowing good gifts to both laytie, clergy, and to all the learned in Irish, as Antiquaries, poets, Aesdanas of all Irland . . .'[49] I am not aware of any study of the intellectual milieu of this interesting Irish Renaissance magnate and/or of his patronage of scribes and scholars. He was clearly knowledgeable in Latin, English and literary Irish (no mean achievement) and, like Ó Mathúna, a patron of the *aos dána*, the professional learned class, in Irish.[50]

It was doubtless his interest in learning and literature that caused Thomas to secure as a ransom for the release of Éamonn Mac Risteaird (Sir Edmund) Butler, who had been captured by the Fitzgeralds at the Battle of Piltown in 1462, two valuable Irish manuscripts belonging to the Butlers of Ormond, *Saltair mic Ruisderd Buitiler* (The Psalter of Risteard Butler's Son – now part of the manuscript known as Bodleian MS Laud 610) and *Leabur na Carruigi* (the Book of Carrick).[51]

In 1464 Thomas founded and richly endowed St Mary's collegiate church at Youghal, with 'a warden, eight fellows, and eight singing-men, living in collegiate manner and having a common table'.[52] This learned nobleman's most interesting initiative in the present context, however, was undoubtedly his attempt, as lord deputy, to found a university at Drogheda. At a parliament held in 1465, sitting in Drogheda, it was enacted that

> *per ceo que la terre dirland ad nule vniuersite ne study generale deins le mesme le quele ewe voudre causer sibien lencresse de Science richesse et bone gouernance come le avoidaunce de Ryot male gouernance et extorsione deins la dit terre esteauntez Ordeine est establie et gaunte per*

auctorite du dit parliament que soit vne vniuersite a la vile de drogheda en le quele vniuersite poient estre faitz bachelers Maisters et doctours en touts sciencez et facultees sicome ils sount en la vniuersite de Oxenford.[53]

Forasmuch as the land of Ireland has no university or general study[54] within the same, which, [if it] had, would cause as well the increase of knowledge, riches and good government, as the avoidance of riot, misgovernment and extortion within the said land existing; it is ordained, established and granted by authority of the said parliament, that there be a univeristy at the town of Drogheda in which university may be made bachelors, masters and doctors in all sciences and faculties as they are in the university of Oxford.

The 8th earl's involvement in this proposal surely reflects the annalists' characterization of him as a scholar in English, Latin and Irish, and a patron of poets and scholars. It also shows his participation in broader European humanist culture in the fifteenth century which witnessed the foundation of many universities all over Europe.[55] Unfortunately this potentially epoch-making venture came to nothing because in 1468 Thomas was beheaded on the orders of the English government for being intimate with the Gaelic chiefs.[56]

There is ample evidence that the Desmond Fitzgeralds enjoyed a very rich intellectual culture. Thomas's grandfather, Gerald, 3rd earl (†1398), was a highly gifted and cultured man. He has been known to generations of Irish scribes and scholars simply as Gearóid Iarla (Gerald the Earl) because of his fame as a gentleman-poet in Irish. Upwards of thirty poems ascribed to him survive. He struck a new note in Irish with his charming personal poetry, a note that would be continued by aristocratic lay poets (Old Irish and Old English) down to the seventeenth century. He may have written poems in French also.[57]

Maghnas Ó Domhnaill, Finghín Ó Mathúna and Thomas, 8th earl of Desmond, were not the only aristocrats in this mould in Ireland at the time. Further research into these scholar-patrons and others like them, and into the surviving evidence of the networks of patronage at the time, would surely yield interesting material in the present context.

The libraries of Irish monasteries were dispersed by the Reformation, and devastation of records and archives resulted from the troubles of the following centuries. Although we know that there were good libraries in Irish religious houses, no monastic library has survived intact: only one catalogue of such a library is known to survive, and this has only very recently been properly edited and studied.[58] The libraries of the aristocrats fared no better. The O'Donnells, O'Mahonys and Fitzgeralds, earls of Desmond, and by far the greater part of the Old Irish and Old English landed families lost all in the vast confiscations

that followed on resistance and successive revolutions against the impo-
sition of English rule and state Protestantism, and as a consequence,
their records, libraries and inventories were destroyed and are virtually
all lost.[59] In only one instance does information on the library of a pre-
Reformation Irish great house survive, as far as I am aware, and that is
the library of the Fitzgeralds, earls of Kildare, one of the great Anglo-
Norman families of Ireland. Though they were not as thoroughly
Gaelicized as their kinsmen, the earls of Desmond, the Kildare Fitzgeralds freely participated in Irish-language intellectual culture at this
time, as can be seen, for example, from the large number of Irish manuscripts in their library.[60]

Two lists of the Kildare books survive. The shorter of the two appears
to be the earlier and it has been suggested that it dates from the time of
Gearóid Mór, the Great Earl, (†1513) or the early years of Gearóid Óg,
his son (1487–1534). The earlier list contains twenty-four items in Latin,
twenty in Irish, nine in French and seven in English.[61] The second list
was made in 1526. It contains thirty-four items in Latin, thirty-five in
French and twenty-three in English.[62] Irish books are not included in the
1526 list – it may be that the main scribe left this to be completed by
somebody else.[63] Unfortunately these library lists have never been made
the subject of study or analysis, as far as I am aware, and no systematic
attempt to identify the individual works in any language has been undertaken. Even a preliminary review yields interesting results in the present
context, however.

The following are the Latin works as they appear in the 1526 (longer)
list. Where the form of the title in the shorter, earlier, list differs, the form
found there is given in square brackets. Where a work does not appear at
all in the earlier list, a dash in square brackets is inserted [–]. Which are
books and which are manuscripts remains to be clarified.

> *In primis Hugo de Vianna super librum Mathei [Hugo de Vienna super quatuor*
>   *evangelistas]*
> *Hugo de Vienna super spalterium [Hugo de Vienna super spalterium]*
> *Tria volumina operis sancti Anthonii cum tabula [Tria volumina operas sancti*
>   *Anthonii cum glosa]*
> *Tria volumina cronice Anthonini*
> *Quatuor volum[in]a de Lira [Quatuor partes Nicholai de Lyra]*
> *Diallagus sancti Grigorii [Dyalagus sancti Georgii]*[64]
> *Tabula utilissima super Liram [Tabula utilissima super Lyra]*
> *Wirgilius cum glosa [Virgilius cum glosa]*
> *Jacobi Locher philomusi poete epigramata [Jacobi Locher opera poete laureate]*
> *Opus Cornelii Vitelli poete [Opus Cornelii Vitelli poete]*
> *Virgilius cum quatuor commentariis [Virgilius cum quatuor commentis]*

Vocabula juris [–]
Juvenalis cum glosa [*Juvenalis cum glosa*]
Theodosus cum commento [*Theodulus cum commento*]
Boecius de consolacione phylosophye [*Boecius de consolacione philosophie*]
Ortus Sanitatis [–]
Therencius [*Therencius*]
Fasciculus Temporum [*Fascicullus Temporum*]
De diversitate avium [*De diversitate anime*][65]
Liber cronice in pergameno [*Liber cornice in pergameno*]
Liber Alixandre maugne [*Liber Alexandri deauratus*][66]
Ordinale [*Ordinale*]
Summa Angelica [–]
Caliopinus [–]
Ortus vocabulorum et medulla gramatici [–]
Commentaria Sesaris[–]
Vegesius [–]
Uthopia Mori [–]
Hympni Andree poete [–]
Novum Testamentum [–]
Cambrencis de Topogralfia [–]
Laurencius Valla [–]
Biblia [–]
Cronica Cronicorum [–]

The earlier list also contains the following entries which do not appear to
be in the later list:

Vregil [sic][67]
Psalterium deauratum in pergameno
Accidens
Portiforium

In the present context one might note that the English books in the 1526
(later) list include the following:

The sege of Thebes [*The siedge of Thebes*]
Camberens [*Cambrensis*]
The distruccion of Troy [–]
The Enaydos [–]
Troillus [–]
Caton de Senectute & de Amicisia [–][68]

One might similarly note that in the later list of French books are found
the following:[69]

Lez illustracions de Gaule & singularites de Troy [–]
Mandavile [Maundvile in French][70]

Le swong de Virgile [–]
Ercules [–]
Le Methamorphoze [–]
Le graunte Boece [–]
Le ii et iii decade de Titus Livius [–]
Les commentaries de Sesar [–]

Clearly identifiable major classical writers appearing in these Latin lists include Vergil, Juvenal, Terence and Caesar. Significant classical material appears in the English and French lists also, which include Cicero ('Caton de Senectute & de Amicisia'), Ovid ('Le Methamorphoze'), Livy ('Le ii et iii decade de Titus Livius') and Caesar ('Les commentaries de Sesar'). Vergil is particularly well represented, apparently appearing in the English ('The Enaydos' – Caxton's Enaydos?) and French ('Le swong de Virgile') lists, as well as in the original Latin. Some of the works listed in English or French may be translations or possibly editions, or some of them may be medieval reworkings of classical material.[71]

There are religious works of course. One notes the Bible ('Biblia'), the New Testament ('Novum Testamentum'), the psalms ('Psalterium deauratum in pergameno'), as well as a number of what appear to be medieval spiritual writings and commentaries. 'Ordinale' may be identified as a liturgical book.

Among early medieval works appearing are the most important *De consolatione philosophiae* of Boethius (*c.* 480–524) and (as it appears) the *Dialogues* of St Gregory the Great (*c.* 540–604).[72] 'Vegesius' is to be identified as Vegetius, a writer on military tactics, whose *Epitome rei militaris*, also known as *De re militari* (written between AD 383 and 450), it is stated, still exercised significant influence on military thinking in Renaissance times.[73]

'Cambrencis de Topogralphia [sic]' is presumably the *Topography of Ireland* of Giraldus Cambrensis, propagandist of the twelfth-century Norman invasion of Ireland, in its original Latin. The English list of 1526 contains 'Camberens' and among the Irish books in the earlier list is 'Cambrensis', which would appear to refer to an Irish translation of a work by the same author.[74]

There are modern printed religious works in these lists also and it is interesting to note that it seems that a number of the works found here were also held in the library of the Franciscans at Youghal about this time, as revealed in the catalogue compiled between 1491 and 1523, recently edited by Colmán Ó Clabaigh.[75] *Summa Angelica* may refer to a copy of a very popular confessor's manual printed in 1486, the *Summa de casibus conscientiae* of Angelo Carletti of Chiavasso (1411–95), an observant Franciscan.[76] *Tria volumina operis sancti Anthonii cum tabula* [*glosa*] would appear to refer to a work of St Antoninus, a fifteenth-century arch-bishop of Florence, identified by Ó Clabaigh when he refers to the 'probable presence' in the Kildare library of the three volume *Confes-sionale* of St Antoninus (1389–1459).[77] The library contains at least one work of Nicholas of Lyra (*c*.1270–1349): *Quatuor volum[in]a de Lira [Quatuar partes Nicholai de Lyra]*; this may indeed be the same commen-tary on the Bible found in the Youghal library.[78]

A number of works appear to be historical chronicles. While some of these may be manuscripts, *Tria volumina cronice Anthonini* appears be a history of the world or *Chronicon, Opus hystoriarum seu cronicarum,* first printed separately in 1480, also written by St Antoninus, archbishop of Florence from 1446 to 1459, already mentioned, who was a friend and advisor to Cosimo de' Medici (Cosimo the Elder, 1389–1464).[79] *Fasciculus Temporum* may be identified as the work of a Carthusian monk, Werner Rolewinck, first published in Cologne in 1474, 'another chronicle which became very popular towards the end of the fifteenth century . . .'[80]

Some of these works may have been schoolbooks, used for the instruction of children of the house, which are known to have been used in other countries also. *Accidens,* found in the earlier list only, may pos-sibly have been a Latin grammar written in English for teaching purposes, ascribed to John Leland (†1428), entitled *Accedence* or later *Accidence.*[81] *Ortus Vocabulorum* was the title of the first printed English–Latin dictionary, published in 1500, and its main source was an earlier work, here perhaps bound in with it, entitled *Medulla Gram-matice.*[82] *Theodosus cum commento* in the earlier list may be the *Eclogues of Theodolus,* a school textbook popular in various countries in Europe, 'which compared Hebrew history with Greek mythology'.[83]

These lists contain works by some important humanist writers, two of them pioneers in the humanist return to the classical standard in Latin. 'Laurencius Valla' clearly refers to a work of Lorenzo Valla (1407–57), the famous humanist, papal scriptor and secretary.[84] It is perhaps likely that this was a copy of his *Elegantiae Latini sermonis,* completed about 1444, a landmark in the history of writing Latin that is stated to have circulated very widely, defining the break with the medieval tradition.[85] One notes with interest a work by Jakob Locher (1471–1528) in his own lifetime. Locher, called 'philomusus', was a noted humanist, writer and translator in southern Germany/Austria.[86] We also note in the same list, *Uthopia Mori.* This is the *Utopia* of St Thomas More (1478–1535), which has been described as 'the masterpiece of English humanism'.[87] It is interesting again to find this appearing in the Maynooth library during the author's lifetime, and in this case only ten years after its first publication in Louvain in 1516.[88] If 'Caliopinus' in the second list may be read as

'Calepinus', then one might take this as a reference to a very popular multilingual Latin dictionary, the *Dictionarium* of Ambrogio Calepino, first published in Reggio Emilia in 1502 and subsequently reprinted and enlarged repeatedly.[89]

The probable presence of two works by St Antoninus, archbishop of Florence (1446–49) in these lists may be of particular interest in view of the Fitzgerald links with Florence about this time, discussed below. It is curious that no mention is found of a book that was published in Renaissance Italy in 1505, and which was dedicated to Gearóid Mór. We know that in that year, Muiris Ó Ficheallaigh, mentioned above, dedicated one of his works to the Great Earl. Ó Ficheallaigh prefaced his *Enchyridion fidei,* published at Venice in quarto in that year, with a dedicatory address to the Great Earl, as patron. This, in accordance with conventions of the time, would almost certainly have been done with the blessing of the earl himself, and rewarded handsomely by the noble patron.[90] Very likely the communication was (at least partly) through the Kildare friary of the Franciscans. Ó Ficheallaigh was provincial of the conventual Franciscans, as stated above, and we know that the Kildare Franciscan house remained conventual, and did not become observant until 1520.[91]

These booklists reflect the literary culture of the Kildare Fitzgeralds in the time of Gearóid Mór and Gearóid Óg. Mary Ann Lyons has described the library at Maynooth in 1526 as 'remarkably modern' and Fr Mícheál Mac Craith has observed that the second set of lists especially reveals the influence of the Renaissance.[92] The variety of the works, the clear proficiency of people in the household in four languages (at least), Latin, French, Irish and English, and the number of books in each of the languages illustrates the rich nature of the intellectual culture of the Fitzgerald court. The number of what appear to be commentaries on, or editions of, classical texts is perhaps further evidence of Renaissance influence.[93] The very accumulation of such a library is surely a Renaissance reflex.[94] About this time, as Robin Flower pointed out, there was also a renewed interest in the history of Anglo-Norman Ireland and this is most likely connected with the 'all-but kingship of Kildare'.[95] In 1503, Philip Flattisbury of Johnstown, near Naas, compiled the Red Book of Kildare. In 1517 Flattisbury wrote 'diverse chronicles' at the instance of the then earl. As they survive, these seem to be mainly compilations from other annals in Latin with occasional notes in English. A number of manuscripts survive with connections with Flattisbury, containing, it appears, primarily historical/annalistic material.[96] As has been stated, 'There is evident in the patronage of Flattisbury the preservation of family lore and the quest for roots motivated by that historical self-consciousness which marked the development of Renaissance culture in Europe in the fifteenth and sixteenth centuries.'[97]

The Kildare Fitzgerald hegemony was at its height during the time of Gearóid Mór, the 8th earl, and his son, Gearóid Óg. Gearóid Mór was nominated chief governor of Ireland by the English Crown almost continuously from 1478 to his death in 1513. Such was his power and authority that he is considered to have been the effective ruler of Ireland in his own right.[98] Gearóid Óg became lord deputy of Ireland on his father's death. His inheritance left him the richest man in Ireland, and as wealthy as the richest magnates in England. 'The Kildare households at Maynooth, Kilkea and Portlester were lavishly furnished and had long since borne signs of immense wealth, and the vast collection of silver and gold plate held in each castle was the heirloom of generations of Geraldines.'[99] It is perhaps not surprising then that the earlier list of Latin books describes a number of the volumes as *deauratus* (having gilt binding).[100] Gearóid Óg's 'residence was lavishly decorated and furnished'.[101] He used to wear a scarlet cloak, and had a portrait executed by the renowned painter Hans Holbein in 1530. In 1536, as Mary Ann Lyons has pointed out, he was described, in good humanist fashion, as 'the greatest improver of his landis in this land'.[102] The foundation and generous endowment by Gearóid Óg in 1518 of the College of the Blessed Virgin Mary at Maynooth has been described as 'certainly the grandest project in church patronage to have been undertaken by a lay person at that time . . .'[103] In 1521 he rebuilt the old thirteenth-century church of St Mary's 'and refurbished and adapted it in a very beautiful manner to serve as the new college's chapel'.[104]

Gearóid Óg, from the age of six in 1493, was kept at the English court for ten years as a hostage or surety to ensure his father's loyalty to the Crown of England. In 1503 he married Elizabeth Zouche (†1517), daughter of Sir John Zouche of Codnor, in Derbyshire in England, a cousin of Henry VII, and then returned home.[105] As a youth, he would have received some education in England and presumably some exposure to Renaissance ideas while at the English court.

It has been noted that 'the Fitzgerald family, in particular, produced at various times men of culture'.[106] While both the Kildare and Desmond Fitzgeralds shared in the general contacts between Ireland and the Continent, it is surely noteworthy in this context that they enjoyed a particularly interesting and continuing connection with Florence, a city of enormous significance in the Renaissance.

Through medieval times there had been well-established links between Ireland and Italy. By the thirteenth century Italian merchants, especially from Florence and Lucca, were trading with Irish ports.[107] During the Italian Renaissance this trade continued. Irish cloth, particularly serge, was prized in Florence and other Italian cities for luxury clothing.[108] Great quantities of Irish hides seem to have been exported to Pisa and it is recorded, for example, that in one six-month period towards the end of the fifteenth century 34,000 hides were imported, and in another period, 24,000.[109] As one authority has pointed out, apart from trade there were also literary contacts throughout the medieval period. 'The wealth of medieval manuscript material of Irish interest in Italian libraries bears witness to the importance of these contacts.'[110] We know, for example, that an Italian agent for the duke of Ferrara , buying horses in Ireland in the second half of the fifteenth century, brought back with him an 'old book' which is cited by Ponticus Virunnius, a sixteenth-century Italian writer, in his abridgement of British history.[111]

The Fitzgeralds, however, had a unique connection with Florence, which they confidently asserted, and this axis was known and acknowledged in Florence itself also. The Fitzgeralds of Desmond and Kildare believed that they and a noble family of Florence, the Gherardini, shared a common ancestor. According to this origin legend, a follower of Aeneas who had fled from Troy with him to Italy had, after the foundation of Rome, been granted by Aeneas that part of Latium/Etruria where the city of Florence now stands. This tradition recounted that in later times a member of the Gherardini of Florence had gone adventuring to France, and he (or a descendant) had joined William the Conqueror at the time of the Norman invasion of England. From him was sprung the ancestor of all the Irish Fitzgeralds who came to Ireland with the Normans.[112]

This belief in a common Trojan and Florentine origin was part of the Fitzgerald folklore and tradition shared by the earls of Desmond and the earls of Kildare. So, for example, Dominic O'Daly, in his account of the fortunes of the earls of Desmond, *Initium, Incrementa, et Exitus Familiae Geraldinorum Desmoniae* (Lisbon, 1655), commences the story of the family with the departure of Aeneas from Troy. He recounts this as a certain fact ('*compertum est*') and that Aeneas granted to the Fitzgerald ancestor '*pars illa Hetruriae opulentissima, ubi nunc Florentia sita est*' (that most rich region of Hetruria [Etruria]where Florence now stands).[113] In his dedication to the cardinals Anthony and Francis Barberini he refers to this connection with Florence as one well known to his patrons:

> *Crevit siquidem in Hethruria Troianus aliquando pampinus idemque á Florentia florentissimus extendit palmites suos usque ad mare & usque ad flumen propagines eius. Psal. 79. A flumine scilicet Arno pelagoque Mediterraneo Vergiuium ultrà mare processit nobilis & antiqua propago Geraldina ad arctoos Hyberni fines (eos usque scilicet, quos nunquam Romana carbasa batuere, hetrusca vixilla penetrarunt) in quibus quingentorum ferè annorum spatio Kildari Comitibus, ac Desmoni Dinastis floruit ramus iste Florentinus.*[114]

> At a certain time in the land of Hetruria grew a most flourishing vine
> of Troy, and from Florence 'its branches stretched forth unto the sea
> and its boughs unto the river' [Ps. 79]. So from the river Arno and the
> Mediterranean sea, that noble and ancient Geraldine offshoot
> advanced beyond the Irish sea to the northern shores of Ireland (to
> shores that Romans sails never struck, the Etrurian standards pene-
> trated), and where for the space of almost five hundred years this
> Florentine branch flourished among the Earls of Kildare and the
> Dynasts of Desmond.

There is ample evidence that this connection with the Fitzgeralds of
Desmond and Kildare was known and asserted in Florence in the fifteenth and sixteenth centuries also.[115] Antonio Mannini, a member of a
Florentine mercantile family, came to Ireland on business between 1410
and 1413, and was introduced to the then earl of Kildare, Gerald (5th
earl, †1432), who told him about the Florentine connection of the
Fitzgeralds, as Mannini recounted when he returned home.[116] We know
that in October 1413 a group of Irishmen, including a clergyman of the
Fitzgerald family, tentatively identified as Maurice Fitzmaurice, precentor
of the cathedral of Ardfert, County Kerry, passed through Florence, no
doubt on their way to Rome. Maurice, while in Florence, sought out
members of the Gherardini family and recounted the origin story, as was
noted by one of them in a book of records.[117]

We know that in 1440 a young nobleman of the Gherardini of Florence was sent to Ireland. He introduced himself as Giovanni Betti de'
Gherardini and he had come to Ireland on a mission from the city of Florence to seek out his kinsmen. He bore a letter of introduction addressed
to the earl of Desmond, 'Fitzgerald' being rendered in the Latin as 'de
Gherardinis'.[118] The letter was written by Leonardo Bruni, chancellor of
the city of Florence, and official letter-writer on its behalf. Bruni (1370?–
1444), from Arezzo, was a noted humanist, and has been described as
'the first to make translations from Greek into Latin on a grand scale'.[119]
This letter quotes with pride and flattery the tradition that the Fitzgeralds
are sprung from Florence and asserts that if this is indeed so, it is a cause
for the people of Florence to rejoice that even in Ireland, the furthest of
the islands, the Florentines dominate.[120]

> *Domino Jacobo de Gherardinis Comiti Desmoniae. Magnifice Domine*
> *amice Karissime. Si vera est assertio, quae de vobis circumfertur scilicet*
> *vestros progenitores fuisse ab origine Florentinos ex familia nobilissima ac*
> *vetustissima Gherardinorum quae una ex praestantissimis, et praecipuis*
> *nostrae civtatis existit, gaudemus nos quidem immense, ac nobis gratu-*
> *lamur, quod cives nostri non solum in Apulia, et in Graecia, et Ungheria*

magnas dominationes habuerunt, verum et in Hibernia quae est ultima Insularum per vos et vestros Florentini dominantur. O magnam gloriam nostrae civitatis, O singularem benevolentiam Dei erga populum nostrum, ex quo tot proceres, totque dominationes fuerunt per universum orbem terrae diffusi. Profecto gratiae Domino Deo nostro habendae, et agendae sunt pro tot, tantisque beneficiis in civitatem nostram collatis. Nos igitur, magnifice Domine ut longis regionibus distemus, tamen benevolentia, et charitate proximi sumus, offerrimus omnia vobis cum promptitudine animorum. Ad praesens autem proficiscitur ad vos nobilis adolescens Johannes Betti de Gherardinis lator praesentium quem pater mittit ad recognoscendam parentelam, et cognationem vestram. De quo vobis fidem facimus per praesentes litteras nostras, quod iste Johannes qui proficiscitur ad vos et pater ejus Bettius, qui illum mittit, sunt ex stirpe, a patre, et avo, et proavo ex ipsa familia descendentes, quem quidem adolescentem vobis plurimum recommendamus, et quia iter est longum, et distantia magna ne quid suspicationis, aut erroris posit contingere, signa et habitum ipsius Johannis latoris praesentium scribemus. Est enim aetatis viginti trium annorum, magnus supra mediocrem staturam, facie honesta ac boni coloris, habetque cicatricem quasi cruciatam in dextro cornu frontis, et super dorso sinistrae manus cicatricem ab igne. Valete magnifice Domine et a nobis cuncta expectetis, quae a civibus et benevolis debent expectari. – Datum Florentiae die primo Junii, MCCCCXL.[121]

Most magnificent lord and dearest friend. If it is true that your progenitors were Florentines by birth, as it has been told us, and of the most noble and ancient family of the Gherardini, which, even now, is one of the most distinguished of this city, we have ample reason to rejoice and congratulate ourselves that our citizens have not only acquired great lordships in Apulia, Greece, and Hungary, but also in Ireland, which is the most remote island in the world, Florentines rule through you and your family. O great glory of our city! O singular benevolence of God towards our people, from whom have sprung so many nobles and lordships, scattered over the face of the earth. Truly we are bound to give thanks to God for the many and great benefits conferred upon our city. We, therefore, most magnificent lord, though separated from you by great distance, are ever near you in charity and love; we offer you all that we can afford with willingness and promptitude. Just now there departs for your settlements a noble youth, Giovanni Betti de' Gherardini, the bearer of these present letters, whom his father sends to greet his kinsmen. We, therefore, certify by these our letters, that the aforesaid John, who is about to visit you, as well as his father, who is sending him, are descended by the father, grandfather, and greatgrandfather, from the family of the Gherardindi. This youth, with all our heart, we recommend to you; and since the journey is long, and the distance, great, so that no error or suspicion may arise, we will write down the distinguishing features of John, the bearer of our letters. He is aged twenty-three years, above the middle stature, with a countenance of fair complexion and honest look. He has an almost cruciform scar on the right region of the forehead, and on the back of the left hand he bears another wound received from fire. Farewell, most magnificent lord, and expect all that you may desire from our citizens and your well-wishers. Given at Florence, 1 June 1440.

When one considers the wealth of the earls of Desmond at the time, it was not surprising, as Curtis observed, that the republic of Florence should wish to promote its trade with them.[122] The earl of the time was James, 7th earl of Desmond (†1463). A modern scholar has recently written of him:

> . . . he was an astute and powerful leader, ready to engage in warfare to defend his interests, but equally capable of diplomacy. The legacy of James's period of lordship can be seen in stone at Askeaton where he had the castle enlarged and a splendid hall erected, thereby providing himself with a noble, well-defended but comfortable seat where he could receive visitors, entertain his followers and see to the administration of his lands.[123]

This man in the Renaissance mould was in fact a son of Gearóid Iarla, the poet mentioned above. It is likely that the 7th earl also had an interest in matters intellectual in his time, as Thomas, 8th earl, the scholar and founder of the inchoate university at Drogheda, referred to above, was a son of his.[124]

It is most unlikely that this emissary on behalf of the Gherardini and Florence did not also carry letters to the earl of Kildare and visit him in Kildare but I am not aware that any record of such matter survives. We know, however, from Italian sources that in 1507 the Gherardini again addressed letters to Gearóid Mór, the Great Earl. While it does not appear that these letters survive, the text of a letter Gearóid Mór wrote in reply on May of that year is preserved. He thanked them, noted the 'depth of the fraternal love which you bear to your own blood', and told them of the importance of the Kildare and Desmond Fitzgeralds in Ireland. He asked them for records of the family history and offered them anything which his people's skill and industry might procure and especially things not to be found in their country, and in that context he mentioned specifically hawks, falcons, horses or dogs for hunting.[125] Irish falcons, hawks and wolfhounds were sought after for sport and hunting and were regularly sent or given as presents to persons of importance in other countries. Irish hawks, falcons and horses in particular were highly prized in Italy and messengers were sent to buy them in Ireland.[126]

The Florentine humanist, Cristoforo Landino (1425–98), in his *Commentary* on Dante's *Commedia* (1481), proudly refers to the earls of Kildare and Desmond as members of the Gherardini family, and points to them as examples of Florentine success in the world. He is quoted as recalling elsewhere an occasion in the recent past when messengers of theirs came to Florence with presents to acknowledge this family relationship.[127]

Indeed, so well were the Fitzgeralds known in Renaissance Italy that both the earl of Kildare and the earl of Desmond are mentioned by Ariosto in his *Orlando Furioso* (1516):

> *Or guarda gl'Ibernesi; appresso il piano*
> *Sono due squadre; e il Conte di Childera*
> *Mena la prima; e il Conte de Desmonda,*
> *Da' fieri monti ha tratta la seconda.*
>
> *Nello standardo il primo ha un pino ardente;*
> *L'altro nel bianco una vermighia banda.*[128]

> Now, behold the Irish, near the plain
> there are two squadrons: both the Earl of Kildare
> – he leads the first; and the Earl of Desmond
> has led the second from the rugged mountains
>
> The former has on his standard a burning pine
> The latter on white a vermilion band [stripe].

The Irish connection of the Gherardini was also celebrated in a Latin verse in a book on the families of Florence about this time by a disciple of Landino's, Ugolino Verino (1438–1516):

> *Clara Gherardinum domus est haec plurima quondam,*
> *Castella incoluit foecundis Collibus Elsoe,*
> *Insignisque toga sed enim praestantior armis,*
> *Floruit, huius adhuc veneratur Hibernia nomen.*[129]

> Glorious family of the Gherardini,
> whose mansions adorned the hills of Elsa,
> far-famed in the senate, and still more famous for valour,
> Ireland reveres its name still.

The Fitzgerald links with Florence were clearly strong, and they were obviously a matter of interest and comment in Florence as well as in Fitzgerald circles of influence in Ireland.

Gearóid Óg's son, the 10th earl, 'Silken' Thomas or Tomás an tSíoda, was drawn into rebellion against the English Crown. Maynooth was sacked and he and five of his uncles were hanged in 1537. This dealt a bodyblow to the power and influence of the Fitzgeralds from which they never recovered. The heir, Gerald, 11th earl, (†1585), managed to avoid being killed, and was eventually spirited out of the country to the Continent. In due course he succeeded, by political manoeuvring, in re-establishing himself in favour with the English court and he recovered a substantial amount of his property in the early 1550s.[130] The young Fitzgerald heir was taken out of Ireland in 1540.[131] After a period in France he went to Italy, and eventually gravitated to Florence in 1545. According to Richard Stanihurst's Irish material in Holinshed, published during the earl's lifetime, he remained here for about three years, under the protection of Cosimo de' Medici (1519–74), who appointed him master of the horse and awarded him a yearly pension, during his lifetime, or until he should recover his estates.[132] In the circumstances of his background and family, it would not be surprising if this young noble from the Curragh of Kildare were indeed appointed by the de' Medici to the important court position of master of the horse.[133]

It was, in fact, this well-travelled and well-rounded, worldly-wise, young man of the Renaissance, who, as 11th earl, employed Richard Stanihurst as tutor for his son and intended heir about 1571.[134] We might note in passing that in 1584, William Bathe SJ, author of *Janua linguarum* which so influenced Comenius, dedicated to this earl, his granduncle, an early work of his, *A Briefe Introductione to the True Art of Musicke* (London, 1584), which has been described as the earliest original musical textbook in the English language intended for a general readership.[135]

The fame of the 11th earl lived in local folklore in County Kildare down to the twentieth century. In these stories, which even survived the transition into English, he was known as 'The Wizard Earl'. One such folk legend told that the earl, together with his army of warriors, slept underground, awaiting the time when he would be awakened and would lead the Irish to cast off the foreign yoke. Other tales recalled the 11th earl as 'a dealer in magic and spells and occult arts of all sorts'.[136] As a matter of fact, both of these folk motifs also attached in Munster folklore to the Fitzgeralds of Desmond. Dr Dáithí Ó hÓgáin has shown that these stories are versions of folk material which grew up around the messianic Emperor Frederick I, known to scholars as the Barbarossa legend. Ó hÓgáin has stated that the Barbarossa legend had a particular significance in Florence, and probably came to Ireland through the Fitzgerald connections with the Gherardini in Renaissance times. It has been suggested, indeed, that this legend may even have been used for propaganda purposes by the Fitzgeralds.[137] The theory has been put forward too that the reputation for astrology/alchemy which attached to the 11th earl of

Kildare could be folklore accruing around interests acquired 'in Italy of the High Renaissance where he was educated'.[138] Though Vincent Carey has stated that he had not found any sixteenth-century evidence that would associate the 11th earl with alchemy, he speculated that the earl's youth and Florentine education could provide the basis for the association of such matters with his name in folk tradition.[139]

The 11th earl must have become well acquainted with the Gherardini themselves during his time in Florence. He recalled the connection in later life, as is confirmed by the letter of an Italian merchant from London in 1566 in which the businessman refers to the earl as being of the Florentine Gherardini family, and recounts that he had received from the earl 'as a present several sorts of dogs, which he sent to his brother'.[140] And indeed, the Venetian ambassador in London, writing to the Doge in June 1558, referred to the earl as a descendant of the Gherardini family of Florence.[141]

The Florentine connection was known in England – when Henry Howard, earl of Surrey (1517–47), celebrated the beauty of the 'Fair Geraldine', Lady Elizabeth Fitzgerald, sister of the 11th earl, in a Petrarchan sonnet, he wrote:

> From tuscane came my lady's worthy race;
> Fair Florence was sometime her ancient seat.[142]

This sonnet is quoted by Edmund Campion ('made upon Kildares sister, now Lady Clinton') in his *History of Ireland*, written in 1571, when treating of the earls of Kildare. He says, as he introduces them, 'this house was of the nobilitie of Florence, came thence to Normandy', and he recounts briefly the legend of the transition to Wales and then to Ireland. This description is taken over by Stanihurst and repeated by him in his revision of Campion's material which was included in Holinshed's *Chronicles* in 1577.[143] It is clear that Stanihurst became thoroughly familiar with the culture and traditions of the Fitzgerald house during his employment as tutor to the heir, and he surely consulted their books during that time.

In the same work of Holinshed's, Stanihurst refers to a David Duff ('Dubh') Fitzgerald, a kinsman of the earls of Desmond, a lawyer,

> a maker in Irish, not ignorant of musike, skilfull in physike, a good
> and generall craftsman much like to Hippias, surpassing all men in
> the multitude of crafts comming on a time to Pisa to the great triumph
> called Olympicum, ware nothing byt such as was of his owne making;
> his shooes, his pattens, his cloke, his cote, the ring that he did weare,
> with a signet therin veerie perfectlie wrought, were all made by him.

He plaied excellentlie on all kind of instruments, and soong therto his owne verses, which no man could amend. In all parts of logike, rhetorike and philosophie he vanquised all men, and was vanquised of none.[144]

This kinsman of the earls of Desmond, clearly in the mould of the Renaissance courtier described by Jacob Burckhardt, lost his life in 1581 taking part in the rebellion of the earl of Desmond.[145] None of his poems in Irish or Latin are at present identified, but his reputation survived in the folklore and in the literary tradition in Irish. His son, Muiris Mac Dáibhí Dhuibh Mhic Gearailt, was an elegant amateur poet in Irish, and those pieces of his which survive again strike a light, mannered, personal note.[146]

A modern scholar has noted how 'the spread of literacy among the Irish aristocracy during the fifteenth and sixteenth centuries ultimately played a major part in transforming the nature and function of bardic poetry'.[147] In due course, when more detailed studies have been made of the intellectual world of individuals such as Finghín Ó Mathúna, Thomas, 8th earl of Desmond, and others like them, when the Latin sources and the classically inspired material in extant manuscripts and literature in Irish has been examined, and when due attention has been paid to the surviving metalwork, sculpture and architecture of the period, it is likely that a more differentiated and interesting evaluation will emerge of the interaction between Ireland and mainland Europe in Renaissance times.[148]

2. Derricke and Stanihurst:
a dialogue[1]

JOHN BARRY

Richard Stanihurst (1547–1618) was born of a wealthy Dublin family. His father, James, enjoyed the patronage of Sir Henry Sidney and was twice speaker of the parliament in Dublin. Richard was educated at Peter White's grammar school in Kilkenny (1557–62) and afterwards at University College, Oxford (1563–68), before being trained for the legal profession at Lincoln's Inns. At Oxford he became the protégé and friend of Edmund Campion, who encouraged him to publish his study of the Greek Neoplatonist philosopher, Porphyry.[2] Campion visited the Stanihursts in 1570 and, while there, compiled his *Two bokes of the Histories of Ireland*, which became the basis of Richard Stanihurst's 'Description of Ireland' which he contributed to the *Chronicles* of Holinshed.[3] Stanihurst later came under suspicion of treason and, after the execution of Campion in 1580, moved to the Continent where he published his *De Rebus in Hibernia Gestis*, an account of the Norman conquest of Ireland based on the *Topographia Hibernica* and the *Expugnatio Hibernica* of Giraldus Cambrensis.[4]

John Derricke (*fl. c.* 1580) was possibly a member of Sidney's entourage during Sidney's second tenure of office as lord deputy of Ireland (1575–78). He published his *Image of Irelande* in 1581.[5] I went to *Image of Irelande* in search of illustrations for a talk on Stanihurst and the more I looked at Derricke's superb pictures, the more I became convinced that Stanihurst had been looking at them before me, and furthermore that Derricke had been looking at another work by Stanihurst, namely the 'Description of Ireland'.

Derricke's *Image of Irelande* was published in 1581; Stanihurst's 'Description' appeared in 1577 and his *De Rebus* in 1584. The dates make it possible to suggest influence of Stanihurst on Derricke and of Derricke on Stanihurst. More than that, however, the coincidence of choice of subject matter and the diversity of treatment of the same convinced me

36

that we have here a genuine engagement between two authors and three texts – the *Image of Irelande*, 'Description' and *De Rebus* – an intertextuality which can deepen our perception of them all.

This is not to say that Stanihurst and Derricke embarked on a polemic, one against the other. The engagement arose, I believe, simply out of a commercial venture. In the sixteenth century advances in exploration and in cartography combined with increasing nationalism gave a huge boost to the writing of world history and the history of nations, both in the vernacular and in Latin. Reginald Wolfe, master printer, set out to publish a 'universal cosmographie of the whole worlde . . . and particular Histories of every known nation'.[6]

Upon his death he bequeathed the project to Raphael Holinshed. Holinshed narrowed the scope of the project to the histories of England, Scotland and Ireland. He worked himself on expanding Campion's *Two Bokes* and brought the history up to 1509 at which point 'some of those that were to bestow the charges of the impression, procured a learned Gentleman Maister Richard Stanyhurst, to continue it from there forwarde as he saw occasion'.[7]

This quotation tells us two things: one, that in the 1570s Stanihurst was a recognized scholar who was in favour with powerful members of the establishment in England, and two, that Stanihurst was prepared to write, in English, an account of Ireland and the Irish which would not offend the members of that establishment. This young Stanihurst, ambitious for a political career in Ireland, as will be seen, is different from the expatriate Stanihurst who, in 1584, wrote in Latin for a European audience. We can therefore legitimately talk about a dialogue between the earlier 'Description' and the later *De Rebus*.

John Derricke had Irish experience: his depiction of Irish dress and military tactics is accurate and he is even able to insert into his pictures a few words of Irish (Gaelic) such as *ochone* (*ochón*: 'alas') and *shogh* (*seo*: 'here'). As we have said, he probably campaigned with Sidney between 1575 and 1578, and it is easy to imagine him returning to England with a fine portfolio of pictures and every intention of publishing them. Holinshed's *Chronicles* had appeared in 1577 and were a huge success. It is therefore plausible that in writing his *Image* Derricke would be influenced by this and would be inclined to use a text that was already successful and make his images correspond, at least to some extent, with material that was already familiar to his intended audience. Derricke's work was also successful and by the same argument we may deduce that Stanihurst would be influenced by him in his choice of material and in the structuring of his narrative. It is also natural that Protestant Derricke would give a different colour to his account than Stanihurst, and that the older Stanihurst, the expatriate in the Netherlands and largely dependent on the Catholic Spanish authorities, would modify the views of the young Stanihurst who wrote in London and had hopes of a career similar to his father's in Dublin.

We may begin with the *Image of Irelande* and the depiction of the physical appearance of the Irish. Derricke's pictures are accompanied by an entertaining description in rhyming couplets:

> The liuely shape of Irysh karne, most perfect to behold,
> Of man, the master, and the boy, these pictures doe unfolde:
> Wherein is brauely paynted forth, a nat'rall Irish grace,
> > Whose like in ev'ry poynt to vewe, hath seldome stept in place.
> > > *(Image of Irelande*, Plate 1)

Derricke's admiration for the physical appearance of the Irish is evident from both the picture and the verse, whatever his opinion of their moral qualities. This tallies with Stanihurst's 'Description': 'the men are clean of skin, of stature tall; the women are well favoured'.[8] Stanihurst later emphasizes the point, in his description of the Irish in the dedicatory letter of *De Rebus*:

> *si in huius insulæ incolas oculos inferre velis, illi quidem corporis commoditate, ingenij acumine, ceterisque animi ornamentis usque eò præstant, ut nihil eis aut à natura non oblatum, aut ab industria recusatum videatur.*[9]

> If you wish to cast your eyes on the inhabitants of this island, they are outstanding for proportion of body, sharpness of intellect and the

other ornaments of mind; so much so that there seems to be nothing that nature has not given them or that they have not achieved by their own efforts.

Derricke's beautiful verse is structured on his pictures. We read from left to right descriptions of man, master and boy. Stanihurst follows a different pattern in his description of the military organization of the Irish: aristocracy (cavalry), gallowglasses (heavy infantry), kerns (light infantry) and horseboys. Let us follow the sequence of Derricke's picture.

> Mark me the karne that gripes the axe, fast with his murd'ring hand,
> Then shall you say a righter knaue, came neuer in the land. (Plate 1)[10]

This righteous, reforming view of the kerns coincides with Stanihurst's description of them in 1577:

> Kerne signifieth, as noble men of deepe judgement informed me, a shower of hell, because they are taken for no better than rakehells or the devil's blacke guard, by reason of the stinking stir they keep wheresoever they be.[11]

However, even here, we may note that Stanihurst distances himself from his material, attributing the definition to unnamed 'noble men', and if we turn to the Stanihurst of 1584 we find a much less moralizing and rather admiring description of kerns. I cite a couple of passages from *De Rebus* to illustrate my point:

> *Tertius ordo comprehendit alios etiam pedites, ac levis armaturæ machærophoros: ab Hibernicis Karni dicuntur . . . Cetris aut manicis ferreis armati, pugnant: non admodum ponderoso vestitu tecti incedunt.*[12]

> The third rank comprises other footsoldiers, lightarmed swordsmen: by the Irish they are called Kerns [*Karni*] . . . They fight armed with small shields or gauntlets: they go into battle protected by no very heavy armour.

Next in Derricke's picture is 'the master':

> As for the rest, so trimly drest, I speake of them no euill,
> In ech respect, they are detect (as honest as the deuill.)
> As honest as the Pope himselfe, in all their outward actions
> And constant like the wauering winde, in their Imaginations
> > (*Image of Irelande,* Plate 1)

The message is clear: Irish chieftains are not to be trusted. Catholic Stanihurst does not use the same language, but he gives a similar impression of the behaviour of the Irish chiefs in defence of their authority:

neque Anglico sub iure, & imperio esse volunt, nisi quamdiu Angli milites eorum territoria depopulantur. Solent enim, in huiusmodi asperis temporibus, aut metu permoti, in lacus lucósve se abdere; aut se totos dissimulanter (nam præclarè norunt, tempori inservire) ad victorum nutum & voluntatem convertere. ut primùm rursus Angli arma deponunt, isti metu relevati, vetus imperium arripiunt.[13]

They are unwilling to be subject to English law or rule except while English soldiers are laying waste their territories. For they are accustomed in harsh circumstances like this, or when they are prompted by fear, either to hide themselves in lakes or woods or else deceitfully to bow completely to the command and will of the conqueror (for they know very well how to be submissive on occasion). As soon as the English once again lay aside their arms, they resume their former rule, relieved of their fears.

So far I have spoken only of the written word, but my point already begins to emerge: Derricke's choice of material in *Image of Irelande* is influenced by 'Description' and *De Rebus* engages both texts, revealing a shift in Stanihurst's attitude to the Irish. Further, I think it is clear that Stanihurst also responded to the pictures: in *De Rebus* he gives an account of the military organization of the native Irish. The first rank are the horsemen (i.e. the upper class, cf. 'Description', p.114 'the chiefest next the lord'). One of these is referred to by Derricke as 'the master', showing the influence of 'Description' on *Image*). These are also described in *De Rebus* and it is noticeable that the details that Stanihurst chose to describe correspond remarkably to Derricke's image: the 'master' is wearing what is possibly a breastplate and a curtailed version of the 'mantle'. In Stanihurst's comments on the horsemen we find that they *'etiam loricis aut sagis amicti . . . se efferunt . . . ephippia clitellis non dissimilia, subitò occupant'* (even dressed in breastplate or mantle . . . leap up and . . . occupy a horsecover not unlike a saddle).[14] The horseman in the picture is spotless in appearance and this is one of the things Stanihurst chooses to mention: *'ita placidè . . . equitant, ut caligas cœno atque sordibus nullo modo prorsus oblinant'* (so smoothly do they ride . . . that by no means whatever do they besmirch their boots with dirt and filth).[15]

Moving to the horse, we note that the horse-cover is a kind of cushion tied on with a girth-strap. There is no trace of stirrups; again this is one of the things that Stanihurst chooses for comment:

ferreis scalis (quæ à nonnullis, stapides, dicuntur) in equos minimè ascendunt: neq(ue) huiusmodi nugatoria (sic istorum opinio fert) adminicula phaleris adhærescere permittunt.[16]

They do not mount their horses by means of iron steps (which are by some called stirrups): nor do they permit such trifling (as they consider them) aids to be attached to the trappings.

It is notable in Derricke's picture that the horse is a stallion – not a gelding and certainly not a mare – and this is also part of Stanihurst's commentary:

> *Canteriis . . . rarò advehuntur. Equas, ut pariant, tantùm pascunt. Nihil ad equitis æstimationem turpius . . . quàm in equa sedere.*[17]

> They rarely ride geldings . . . They pasture mares only so that they may breed. Nothing is more disgraceful for the reputation of a horseman . . . than to be seated on a mare.

They do not muddy their boots; they do not use stirrups; they must be able to vault onto the horse even when wearing the mantle; they must never be seen seated on a mare: every detail of the appearance and dress of the lord, and the grooming and harness of the horse, that Stanihurst chooses for his narrative is illustrated by Derricke's picture. If we turn our attention to the third figure in Plate 1, 'the boy', we find that Derricke does not expend words on him but he would have been familiar with Stanihurst's description of this kind of personage as a *daltin* 'lackeys serviceable to the grooms or horseboys'.[18] Stanihurst modified this in *De Rebus*, classing the *daltini* on the same level as the horseboys:

> . . . *quos Hiberni, Daltinos, nos Latinè scurras velites, seu servos à pedibus nominare possumus . . . Ad hanc poliendi curam, omnibus corporis nervis incumbunt . . . Etenim hac elegantia, atque equina munditia specialis diligentiæ nomen inveniunt.*[19]

> . . . whom the Irish call *Daltini*, but we, in Latin, can call light-armed squires, or foot-servants . . . They apply themselves to . . . careful grooming with every sinew of their bodies . . . For by this elegance and cleanliness of the horses they gain a name for especial diligence.

A glance at the appearance of the horse in Plate 1 will show that Derricke was also impressed by the work of the horseboys and the *De Rebus* text reads almost like an explication of the image. The impression that Stanihurst had Derricke's book to hand is at this point almost irresistible.

Derricke's Plate 2 is a depiction of a cattle raid. His own verses describe it well:

Here creepes out of Sainct Filchers denne, a packe of prowling mates,
Most hurtfull to the English Pale, and noysome to the states:
Which spare no more their country byrth, than those of th'english
    race,
But yeld to each a lyke good turne, when as they come in place.

(*Image of Irelande*, Plate 2)

It is notable that in his text Derricke is at pains to point out that cattle raiding is carried out indiscriminately, against the English of the pale and the native Irish alike, and that there is an element of revenge in it ('yeld to each a lyke good turne'). From the picture, also, it seems obvious that the victims of this raid are Irish: the man is dressed as a kern, and the woman's head-dress is the same as that of the lady sitting at the feast in Plate 3. He seems to me to be following Stanihurst (even in language):

> To robbe and spoile their enemies they deeme it none offence, nor seeke any meanes to recover their losse but even to watch them the lyke turne.[20]

Stanihurst later expands on this theme, and he seems to be writing with an eye on *Image of Irelande*:

> *si ipsi proceres à quoquam, capitali odio, dissideant, noctem ad prædas non adiungunt, sed exercitum ex sicariis, excursoribus, & servitio confi-ciunt, atqui de inimici ac eius provinciæ bonis, omni totius territorij pecore compulso, luce palàm prædantur; nisi alter, ad arma vocatus, paratus sit, suas rapinarum ministris vires opponere, atque prædonum impetum pugnacissimè propulsare.*[21]

If the lords themselves have a violent quarrel with another they get together an army of scoundrels, brawlers and slaves. They plunder the goods of the enemy and of that province in broad daylight, driving all the cattle of the whole territory before them. This occurs if the other, called to arms, is not ready to oppose his strength to the ministers of plunder and repel the attack of the invaders in a most warlike way.

The language ('brawlers and slaves') echoes Derricke's 'prowling mates', but we note also the mention of 'lords' and that the raiders in Derricke's picture are directed by a lord, viz. the horseman to the right of centre at the back. The man and woman who are the victims of this raid seem to be Irish: the man is dressed as a kern and the woman is dressed (apart from the mantle) like the lady at the feast in Plate 3. They are certainly not 'armed and ready to repel invaders in a warlike way'. We may also point out that just before the passage cited here Stanihurst wrote an account of thatched roofs which are easy to fire. Note also the piper to the left in the foreground of Plate 2: Stanihurst later has a very excellent description of bagpipes.[22] The coincidence of the number of topics chosen for description is already remarkable. Still, it may be objected that these are strange and interesting Irish customs and would serve anyone wishing to titillate the taste of the English public: all this could be mere coincidence.

I come now, however, to a deeper and more subtle intertext which seems to me to make it clear that Stanihurst is actually acknowledging Derricke. This is contained in *Image of Irelande*, Plate 3. After a successful raid, a feast is prepared in the woods:

These theeues attend upon the fire, for seruing up the feast:
And fryer smelfeast sneaking in, doth preace amongst the best.
Who play'th in Romish toyes the Ape, by counterfetting Paull:
For which they doe award him then, the highest roome of all.
    (*Image of Irelande*, Plate 3)

Stanihurst in general has, of course, no truck with this Protestant bigotry: there are several passages in *De Rebus* which show the respect and reverence in which the native Irish hold the clergy.[23] Earlier, in 'Description', he had noted that

> They honour fryers and pilgrims by suffering them to pass quietly and by sparing their mansions, whatsoever outrage they shew to the country beside them.[24]

However, in the dedicatory epistle at the beginning of *De Rebus*, Stanihurst paints a wickedly satiric pen picture of an (in his opinion) uneducated Irish priest, whom he calls Cornelius, who begs his way to Rome in order to gain advancement. According to Stanihurst, this was so common that whenever the Romans met some paltry Irish beggar they used to ask him, 'My lord, do you intend to become a bishop?'[25] Stanihurst then sets up an imaginary interlocutor who enquires what this priest has read:

> *Totámne, amabo, ut alia omittam, sacram litteraturam? Quî potest? Etiámne vetus instrumentum? Magnum, imò verò incredibile opus. Evangelion aliquod integrum? Audio. Epistolas verò Pauli? Quàm vellem numerare eas posset . . . Quid ergo? Dic, oro te, celerius. Ain' tandem? igitur ausculta. Qui Episcopatum desiderat, Bonum opus desiderat. utrum hoc Petrus, vel Paulus scripserit, viderint Theologi. Hæc est summa totius doctrinæ, hoc tantùm Latinitatis habet, hanc sententiam mente sæpius agitare, crebris sermonibus usurpare solet.*[26]

> The whole of sacred scripture? Impossible. The Old Testament? Incredible. One of the Gospels, entire? Keep trying. The epistles of Paul? I wish he could count them . . . What then? Tell me, I beg you. Listen then: WHOSOEVER DESIRES THE OFFICE OF BISHOP DESIRES A GOOD WORK [1 Timothy 3:1]. Whether Peter wrote this, or Paul, let the theologians enquire. This is the sum of all his learning, this is all he has of Latin, this sentence he is accustomed to toss about in his mind, and to bring into frequent use in his conversation.

For the purposes of my argument we must ask what is Cornelius doing? He is in Rome, quoting in a loud voice the only piece of Latin he knows, which is a quotation from St Paul's epistle to Timothy ('whosoever desires, etc.'). The answer can be given in Derricke's words: he 'play'th in

Romish toyes the ape, by counterfeiting Paull'. Stanihurst is responding to Derricke with a satire of his own on the native Irish clergy, with the difference that the satire is based not on race but on class. The choice of subject, the satire on clergy, the mention of Rome and St Paul: the intertextuality is beyond the realm of coincidence.

Yet the engagement goes deeper: Stanihurst is moved to write this satire, moved to write *De Rebus* because he is distressed that people on the Continent derive their image of Ireland from such riff-raff and not from the nobility (such as Patrick Plunkett, Lord Baron Dunsany, Stanihurst's brother-in-law, to whom the dedicatory letter is written) who are notoriously loath to travel:

> *si quam tandem de Hibernia mentionem faciant, eam vel rumusculorum mendaciunculis imprudenter onerant, vel importunis maledictis impudenter figunt . . . Ac mihi quidem in fatalem hanc Hiberniæ . . . calamitatem cum frequenter, tum dolenter intuenti, duæ potissimum rationes obveniunt . . . quarum alteram in procerum socordia, alteram in quorundam scurrarum impudentia positam animadverto.*[27]

> If they [*sc.* foreign scholars] make any mention of Ireland, they either imprudently load it with falsehoods and hearsay, or they impudently pierce it with shafts of distressing abuse . . . And indeed as I ponder, frequently and sadly, upon this damage to Ireland . . . two reasons especially occur to me . . . of which I mark that one lies in the inactivity of the nobility, the other in the impudence of certain buffoons.

I have cited these passages to emphasize that Stanihurst's express purpose is to improve the image of Ireland. I pass over the bard and the harper (Plate 3, foreground, right) although these are also figures which are chosen for extensive comment by Stanihurst; hence let us turn now to another detail in Plate 3, namely the two men on the right, who are warming their bottoms at the fire. This, I think, is a shaft deliberately aimed at Stanihurst by Derricke. Stanihurst's opinion of the education of the native Irish is not high,[28] but he does acknowledge that they had Latin, and that it was fluent even if faulty:

> Without either precept or observation of congruitie they speak Latin like a vulgar tongue, learned in their common schools of leachecraft and law.[29]

Derricke's satiric shot at Stanihurst lies in the fact that the two kerns are speaking Latin, and not only that but speaking Latin hexameters, and not only that but telling about their education!

aspice, spectator, sic me docuere parentes
me quoque maiores omnes, virtute carentes.

              (*Image of Irelande*, Plate 3)

Look, viewer, this is how my parents taught me.
So all my forebears taught me too, lacking virtue.

The second speaker is not as good at verse as the first (whose line recalls Vergil, *Aeneid* 1.392 and Martial 9.73.3). Derricke may, indeed, be gibing at Stanihurst's pride (very visible in *De Rebus*) in his ability to write classical Latin verse. The satire on the *latinitas* of the native Irish does not end there: later in the work (Plate 11) Rory Oge O'Moore is depicted wandering alone in the woods among the wolves, lamenting his fate 'because he sinned in that he moved our noble Queen to ire', and it is notable that not only he but also the wolves speak Latin.[30] And the insertion of Latin is deliberate. It is not that Derricke lacks Irish for such captions: in the verse accompanying Plate 4, when the raiders are repulsed and killed by English soldiers 'the fryer then, that traytrous knave, with Ough Ough hone lament'. Later again, in Plate 7, a messenger hands a note to Sir Henry Sidney: he speaks just one word 'shogh'. Derricke is able to find a phrase in Irish when he needs it: his use of Latin is a part of his reception of Stanihurst.

A final point of connection between these works is that both Stanihurst and Derricke display in their texts an inordinate admiration for Sir Henry Sidney. Sidney was lord deputy of Ireland for two terms, 1565–71 and 1575–78. During the first term there was a parliament in Dublin of which the speaker was our author's father, James Stanihurst. Sidney was on good terms with the parliament and was at least sympathetic to the Stanihursts' aim of 'reconquest through reconciliation and education'; indeed, 'Description' is dedicated to him.[31] Even in exile, Richard Stanihurst records a eulogy of Sidney in Latin elegiac couplets:

Gesta libri referunt multorum clara virorum,
Laudis & in Chartis stigmata fixa manent.
Verùm Sidnæi laudes hæc saxa loquuntur,
Nec iacet in solis gloria tanta libris.
Si libri pereant, homines remanere valebunt,
Si pereant homines, ligna manere queunt.
Lignaque si pereant, non ergo saxa peribunt,
Saxaque si pereant tempore, tempus erit.
Si pereat tempus, minimè consumitur ævum,
Quod cum principio, sed sine fine manet.
Dum libri florent; homines dum vivere possunt;
Dum quoque, cum lignis, saxa manere valent;
Dum remanet tempus, dum denique permanet ævum,
Laus tua, Sidnæi, digna perire nequit.[32]

Books report the famous deeds of men,
And marks of praise are fixed upon the page,
These stones the praise of Sidney still do tell,
Nor lies so great a fame in books alone.
If books do perish, men can still remain,
If men should perish, timbers can remain.
If timbers perish, stones can still survive
If stones decay with time, yet time exists.
If time should end, eternity remains,
Which had a start but is without an end.
While books can flourish and while men can live;
While stones along with timber still can last;
While time remains, eternity endures,
Your well-earned praises, Sidney, cannot die.

Derricke was, as we have said, probably a member of Sidney's retinue in the period 1575–78.[33] This was the term when Sidney 'lived like the general of an invading army in an hostile country, rather than the civil governor of a peaceful and allied province'.[34] Six out of twelve plates in *Image of Irelande* are devoted to depiction of his military prowess and achievements. Plate 10, for instance, which shows Sidney's triumphal return to Dublin after his campaign against the 'traytours that troubled the crowne', is described by the following verses:

When he by conquest thus hath wonne, the honour of the field,
And fame unto our Souveraygnes Courte, report thereof doth yeld
And to conclude when honor braue, his trauells to requight
Hath clothde him with eternall fame, meete for so great a knight
When all these thinges are done and past, then doth he backe reuart
To Dublyn: where he is receiued; with ioy on euery parte.

(*Image of Irelande*, Plate 10)

The eternal fame of Sidney is a theme common to both authors. However, Derricke gloatingly depicts the Sidney of 1575–78, the victor of the massacre of Mullaghmast, the receiver of the surrender of Turlough O'Neill, the enforcer of the policy of the completion of conquest and colonization of Gaelic Ireland, of the exclusion of the families of the Pale from government, and of rule by presidents of provinces. He reflects the reality of English attitudes to Ireland and anticipates the brutal triumphalism of Spenser.[35] Stanihurst, on the other hand, in *De Rebus* looks backwards and remembers the Sidney of 1565–71, the patron of his family, the contributor of £20 towards the establishment of a university in Dublin, the saviour of Campion;[36] in short, the Sidney who would fit in with his dream of an Ireland civilized by education and ruled by a parliament of Palesmen. The dream was dead even as he wrote.

3. The Richard Stanihurst–Justus Lipsius friendship:
scholarship and religion under Spanish Habsburg patronage in the late sixteenth century

COLM LENNON

In the spring of 1592, an exchange of letters took place between Richard Stanihurst, an Irishman temporarily resident in Madrid, and Justus Lipsius, a native of Brabant then living in Liège.[1] Stanihurst had travelled to Spain from the Low Countries (where he had lived for more than a decade) primarily to conduct alchemical experiments in the laboratories of the Escorial under the patronage of King Philip II. Acknowledged by contemporaries as one of the most learned of his generation of scholars from Ireland, Stanihurst had works in print by 1592 on subjects as diverse as Aristotelian logic, Irish history and chorography, Vergil's *Aeneid* (which he translated into English hexameters), and the life of St Patrick.[2] His Flemish correspondent, Justus Lipsius, was famed as one of the leading humanists of late sixteenth-century Europe. A distinguished philologist and historian of the classical world, Lipsius had gained a large following in intellectual circles for his application of the ideas of the Stoic philosophers to the political and religious problems of contemporary society.[3] He published prolifically on a variety of subjects but was perhaps then best known as the author of *De Constantia*, a defining work of the neo-Stoicism of the era, *Politicorum sive Civilis Doctrinae Libri Sex*, addressed principally to the rulers of states, and a definitive edition of the works of the Roman historian, Tacitus.[4]

The letters attest to a warm and long-standing amity between the two men, both accomplished Latin stylists and well versed in the ways of epistolary friendships.[5] The Lipsius–Stanihurst friendship had its origins in the University of Leiden in the early 1580s when the two men, who were exactly of an age, met for the first time. Lipsius was professor of history at the recently founded academy from 1578 to 1591, during which time he adhered publicly to Calvinism. Stanihurst matriculated at Leiden on 29 August 1582 and studied medicine there.[6] Lipsius' testimony to the comradeship forged at that time occurs in the letter to

Stanihurst of 28 March 1592: '*A multis iam annis amicitia nostra coepit, duret in multos annos*' (May our friendship which began many years ago endure for many years to come).[7] A tone of anxious solicitude for the welfare of the other, both physical and emotional, is evident in the letters. The nature of their contact is characterized thus by Stanihurst in his letter of 1 February 1592: '*Verum, mi Lipsi, corporis, non animi erga te discessio est facta*' (Truly, my Lipsius, our separation is a physical one, and not one of our minds).[8] The correspondents adverted to a range of topics of mutual interest. The effects of a confessionally and politically divided Europe bulk large, questions of religious principle and political allegiance weighing heavily on the minds of both men. Their wider circle of fellow humanists and colleagues who shared their concerns is invoked herein in the form of mutual friends enquired of and mentioned solicitously.

The value of a study of the epistolary exchange lies firstly in the glimpse afforded of the lives of the two humanists at a critical juncture for both. The correspondents' career paths down to 1592 had been anything but smooth. Both men were born in 1547, Stanihurst in Dublin and Lipsius at Overijse. Early educational experiences at the hands of Catholic educators shaped them, Stanihurst towards university studies in arts at Oxford, and Lipsius towards classics and law at Louvain. Both were deeply influenced by humanist mentors, Marcus Antonius Muretus in the case of Lipsius and Edmund Campion in Stanihurst's case. An early flowering of scholarly talent led to published works, by Stanihurst in 1570 and by Lipsius in 1569. Thereafter the lives of the two were affected by the politico-religious turbulence of the age. Lipsius' experience of the disorder of the revolt of the Netherlands caused him to change universities and religion several times. He left Louvain for Jena, where he turned Lutheran, and went thence to Calvinist Leiden. In 1592 Lipsius was at the point of committing himself finally to the Catholic Church. As he attempted to resolve the complexities of his position, the encouragement and support of friends such as Stanihurst were critical in the *dénouement* that led to his appointment as professor of history and of Latin at the University of Louvain in later 1592.

Stanihurst's own career expectations had been blighted by political disapproval. He had been schoolmaster to the children of the earl of Kildare in London. His historical contribution to Holinshed's *Chronicles* had fallen foul of the Tudor censors and he was also suspected of counterfeiting because of his alchemical experiments. When he travelled to the Low Countries about the time of Campion's execution in 1581, he resided first in the north at Leiden and then moved south to Dunkirk and Brussels. Stanihurst's religious certitude was forged in the smithy of the Spanish war effort in the southern Netherlands under the dynamic leadership of the governor, Alexander Farnese, to whom he dedicated his biography of St Patrick in 1587. The letter written in February 1592 as his three-year sojourn in Spain began presaged a period of religious confirmation and growing political commitment at the centre of the Spanish Catholic monarchy that was to affect his view of his homeland, and also to provide a climax to his scientific career.

More broadly, the contents of the correspondence reflect the achievements and crises of Christian humanism since the heyday of the friendship between Thomas More and Erasmus in the early part of the century. The Irishman was part of a large network of contacts centred on Justus Lipsius, similar to that with Erasmus as its pivotal figure and More as a prominent member.[9] Generally we may witness herein the harvesting of the fruits of Christian humanism, which acted as a solvent for the friends' studies in philology, philosophy, science and politics. Yet at the core of the Lipsius–Stanihurst interchange lay a crucial issue of concern to the wider scholarly community in the later Renaissance, that of intellectual freedom and enquiry in an era of politico-religious militancy. Both Lipsius and Stanihurst referred to their continuing literary work in the circumstances of a divided Europe. Their discussion of the publication of works of spirituality is freighted with significance in the context of the premium being placed officially on the defence of confessional orthodoxy above all else. They wrote against the backdrop of bitter debates between those humanists who were beset by a 'crisis of doubt' and the proponents of religious certainties who railed against scepticism.[10] By examining the responses of Lipsius and Stanihurst to the predicament, especially through a brief discussion of the import of their spiritual writings, we may gain an insight into the mentality of the humanist when confronted by the claims of the Counter-Reformation to the fruits of scholarship '*ad majorem Dei gloriam*'.

Towards the end of 1591 Stanihurst had stopped at Lipsius' house in Liège *en route* to Spain to be told by a servant that the great man was away. In the letter sent from Madrid in February 1592 Stanihurst expressed his intense sorrow that he had been unable to confer with Lipsius concerning their respective plans. As a token of friendship, Stanihurst treated Lipsius to a racy account of his journey southwards, mentioning the pleasures as well as the perils of the trek through Germany, Italy and Catalonia. Stanihurst's allegory drawn from the experience of near shipwreck in his pointing to the suddenness with which 'false joy' could be overturned by a reversal of fortune, '*in alto tuto velificari, in portu repentino immergi*' (to be sailing safely on the deep, to be submerged unexpectedly in port),[11] elicited a typically Lipsian admonition: '*Agnoscere debes beneficium divinum*' (The beneficence of God must be acknowledged).[12] At no point was Stanihurst explicit about the purpose of his mission to the Spanish court, though he did refer in passing to '*spinosioribus meis studiis*' (my thornier studies)[13] and to the promises and actual largesse that the king lavished upon him. He had been called to the court of Philip II apparently to carry on his experiments in the field of chemical medicine, for which he had gained a substantial reputation in Flanders. In 1587 a report had been drawn up for the Spanish authorities, outlining a series of near-miraculous cures that had been effected by a potion perfected by Stanihurst at Dunkirk.[14] In the Escorial, Stanihurst set to work on his scientific pursuits in the laboratories established by Philip. Although the search for the *elixir vitae* proved elusive, his project did result in an unpublished treatise on alchemy, written in Spanish and dedicated to Philip.[15]

Undoubtedly the highlight of Richard Stanihurst's journey and indeed career was his audience with King Philip II of Spain. In his letter he tried to describe to Lipsius the impact of the meeting upon him, borrowing from Cicero (*De Officiis* 2.48) to exclaim, '*Bone Deus, quanta in potentissimo orbis terrarum Monarcha comitas adfabilitasque sermonis*' (Oh, good God, what easy courtesy of speech from the most powerful monarch in the world!)[16] He continued: '*Narro tamen tibi nihil in vita mea audivi gravius, vidi humanius, novi prudentius. Omnia mihi promittit, etiam opipare praestat*' (I tell you that I have never in all my life heard one more serious, seen one more refined, or known one more prudent. He made promises to me of everything, and indeed fulfilled them sumptuously).[17] Stanihurst's exposure to the court at Madrid confirmed him in what he later referred to as 'Spanish Catholicism'.[18] By this he meant not only engagement with the vibrant Catholic renewal sponsored by the Habsburgs but also commitment to the political objective of a Catholic restoration in the north-western islands of Britain and Ireland through Spanish military assistance. To that latter end he was to devote much of his time in Madrid advising Spanish counsellors on Irish affairs and gathering support among the English and Irish expatriates in Spanish Habsburg lands for the claims of a Spanish successor to Queen Elizabeth. The letter to Lipsius coincided with the beginning of a decade-long period of intensive diplomatic activity on Stanihurst's part.[19]

Lipsius too was on the point of committing himself to a new phase in his career. His allegiance to the politico-religious aims of the Spanish monarchy is expressed in his response to Stanihurst's account of Philip II's liberality. Reviewing the state of northern Europe, with particular reference to the case of Catholics in Protestant states such as Saxony and the Palatinate, Lipsius exclaimed: '*Quae spes afflictae religioni, quae regionibus aliquot et regnis, nisi ab illo Rege quem regit, palam protegit, firmat, auget?*' (What hope is there for stricken religion, what hope for so many territories and king-doms, if not from that king whom He guides, clearly protects, strengthens, increases).[20] Lipsius went on to express the wish that Philip's son, also Philip, would succeed his father as successfully as Alexander of old did another Philip. In lamenting the state of politico-religious affairs in the north, thereby bringing Stanihurst up to date with the news, Lipsius set out the agenda for this involvement of Spanish Habsburg power. He referred to the Low Countries as being shattered, to France as being affected by the 'cancer of intestinal war', and to Germany as witnessing the fearful deaths of good Catholics.[21] A prototype of a German Counter-Reformation potentate is presented in the letters in the form of Julius Echter von Mespelbrunn, bishop of Würzburg, who had offered Stanihurst and his party hospitality as they passed through his territory. Julius was described by the Irishman as *'certus, pius at politicus'* ([a prelate wholly] res-olute, devout and politic), thus combining the ecclesiastical and secular attributes requisite for ruling and reforming his statelet.[22] Stanihurst added that *'dum politicum scribo . . . non uti huius aevi Machiavelliani, qui publica scelera politicis velis obtendunt'*(when I write 'politic' . . . I do not use the word as the Machiavellians of this age do, who cover up public crimes under the veils of politics), thus implicitly acknowledging the overall, if qualified, con-demnation of Machiavellianism in Lipsius' *Politicorum . . . Libri Sex.*[23]

In presenting to Lipsius a portrait of the ideal Counter-Reformation statesman-bishop, Stanihurst was very conscious of the newly affirmed Catholic stance of his correspondent. The Irishman was a member of the support system of leading Catholics who for the previous ten months had been buttressing the Belgian's resolve to be reconciled with Rome. The way was being paved for the re-entry of Lipsius into the academic life of the southern Netherlands as an intellectual figurehead. Mentioning the mixed emotions that the name of Lipsius elicited in Spain and elsewhere, Stanihurst wrote: *'dolere quod ibi tam diu esses, ubi eras; laetari, quod ibi iam nunc sis, ubi es'* (sorrowful feelings are evoked because you were for so long where you were, joyful because you are now where you are).[24] Lipsius acknowledged, *'et fateor caussas suspicionum viris bonis fuisse, dum apud deteriores haesimus, quos quia iam relinquimus, desiisse quoque illos spero'* (I confess that good men had cause to be suspicious of me while we dallied with unregenerate people, but I hope that those suspicions have been dissipated now that we have desisted).[25] As one of the Catholic per-suaders of Lipsius at the crucial juncture of his withdrawal from Leiden in 1591, Stanihurst would have been most gratified to read of his corre-spondent's determination to purge himself of the residue of his past, *'non vita et factis solum, sed et scriptis'* (not just by my life and actions, but also by my writings).[26]

In that context, Justus Lipsius was strongly urged by Richard Stanihurst in his letter of February 1592 to publish an oration of his in praise of the Blessed Virgin that Stanihurst had heard delivered in Liège the previous summer.[27] The exhortation was made on behalf of many, including Stanihurst, who were enrolled in the Sodality of the Blessed Virgin in Liège, Lipsius also being a member. According to his own later testimony, Lipsius had joined the Sodality in Liège, a branch of the highly successful Marian confraternity organized by the Society of Jesus throughout Catholic Europe, as soon as he was permitted to do so.[28] As of 29 March 1592, however, Lipsius was reluctant to let the oration go to the press. He had never published anything in that genre, he argued, nor was he certain that the oration merited being seen in the public light in terms of its method and style. Nevertheless, Lipsius agreed to be guided by Stanihurst's advice and the judgement of his friends.[29]

The interchange on the subject of the publication of works of spirituality affords an opportunity to assess the friends' contribution in this respect, and its place in their literary canon. Albeit a slight enough reference by Lipsius, the light shed upon his personal devotional life is rare enough for it to warrant assessment in this wider context. While the oration in praise of the Blessed Virgin of 1591 remained unprinted, Lipsius went on to publish three works that had a spiritual theme. The first of these was the quasi-religious study, *De Cruce Libri Tres*, published in Antwerp in 1592, which traced the history of crucifixion from classical to Christian times. Two works of Marian devotion by Lipsius did appear in the last years of his life: *Diva Virgo Hallensis* (1605) and *Diva Sichemiensis sive Aspricollis* (1606), both printed in Antwerp. Each recorded the miracles that were wrought in the distant and recent past at these popular shrines of the Virgin in Belgium. Unlike that of Lipsius, only part of whose literary output after 1592 was of a spiritual nature, Stanihurst's entire published *oeuvre* thereafter was devoted to religious matters. Two works on the Eucharist appeared in print, *Psalmi, Litaniae et Orationes, quae coram Augistissimam Eucharistam Perapposite Recitari Possunt* (1598) and *Hebdomada Eucharistica* (1614), as well as one of Marian devotion, *Hebdomada Mariana ex orthodoxis Catholicae Romanae ecclesiae patribus collecta* (1609). In addition, in response to an attack on the apostolic tradition by his nephew, Stanihurst produced in 1615 a defence of the Roman Catholic church entitled *Brevis Praemunitio pro Futura Concertatione cum Jacobo Usserio*. Thus, in their distinctive ways, both men made their own contributions to the advancement of the Catholic renewal.

The reticence displayed by Justus Lipsius in March 1592 towards publishing works of spirituality proved to be justified in view of the reactions of contemporaries and later commentators. Later that year, another correspondent, Janus Lernutius, wrote to Lipsius from London, expressing his surprise at the news that the great humanist had given an oration in praise of the Blessed Virgin. While he was supportive, Lernutius found himself having to defend Lipsius for his action, and especially for the choice of a Jesuit college as the location for the address.[30] In the years that followed, Lipsius was accused by his Protestant critics of becoming a slave to the Jesuits.[31] His erstwhile humanist admirers, including Julius Scaliger, for example, considered that his intellectual independence had been compromised.[32] While his book on crucifixion might be regarded at least as a continuation of his classical scholarship into the Christian era, the works on the miracles associated with the shrines of the Virgin in Halle and Montaigu elicited scorn and derision. Soon after their publication, virulent attacks on the Marian works appeared in print in Latin and Flemish from two Dutch Calvinist ministers, Albert van Oosterwijck and Peter Denaise, a Scot, George Thomson, and an Englishman, William Crashaw.[33] The thrust of their criticism is the idolatrous nature of Lipsius' treatment of the shrines, and the cynicism of the attempt to whip up devotion through the countenancing of the validity of seemingly miraculous occurrences, such as cures and deliverances.

The dismissal of Lipsius' spiritual writings by these contemporary controversialists, understandable in the context of the theological welter of the early seventeenth century, is reflected in the reaction of modern writers. There is an acceptance among the latter of the contemptuous reaction to *De Cruce*, *Diva Virgo Hallensis* and *Diva Sichemiensis* on the grounds of their inconsistency with the rest of the Lipsian corpus.[34] It is certainly clear that Lipsius was anxious at the time of his reconciliation with Rome to place his scholarship and pedagogy at the disposal of the Catholic Church. The grounds for this were self-preservation. The insecurity of his position in the zealotry of the Spanish Netherlands was manifested in the contentious reception of his work on civil governance, *Politicorum . . . Libri Sex*. Condemned by Dirck Coornhert, a seasoned Dutch controversialist, for its rejection of freedom of individual conscience, the book nevertheless also fell foul of the Roman censors for its countenancing of privately held dissenting views within the Erastian state, and spent some time on the *Index Librorum Prohibitorum*.[35] It would not be surprising in these circumstances to find Lipsius stressing his Catholic orthodoxy in works of popular devotion that pandered to his spiritual directors in the Society of Jesus. Moreover, his patronage by the Archdukes Albert and Isabella, under whom he enjoyed the distinction of being *Historiographicus regius*, was most gratifying to the image-conscious humanist. Lipsius' *Diva Sichemiensis* may be regarded as a contribution to the intense devotion of the archdukes to the shrine of the Virgin, then being developed as a major place of pilgrimage in the southern Netherlands.[36]

As to Justus Lipsius' own devotional life, we get very few indications, even from the spiritual writings. It is true, as one critic states, that 'a man shall seldom find in his books . . . the very name of Christ'.[37] Yet in his *De Cruce Libri Tres,* Lipsius interweaves his discussion of many aspects of the crucifixion of Jesus Christ with an analysis of the use of the cross as an instrument of torture and death throughout history. There is herein a skilful blending of the secular and sacred sources, the text being shot through with hundreds of quotations in the Lipsian manner. In an allocution to the reader, Lipsius adverts to the unwonted tenor of the book and defends his eclectic approach to his studies: 'Remember me as a Christian, that is, a priest of peace.'[38] This is echoed in his prefatory apology for straying into Marian studies in *Diva Virgo Hallensis* when he describes himself as a 'Christian of pure and longstanding practice', and exclaims: 'What else would I do if, as well as adoring the Deity [Numen], I did not also celebrate it [in books]?'[39] In response to a Dutch critic of his reliability because of his changes of confession, Lipsius defended his fundamental religious constancy. While admitting that he may have been transient in his adoption of certain rituals and worship during his absence from Belgium, he admitted his errors and declared himself to be stronger and better for recognizing them.[40] While there is no real personal religiosity of tone in the books on Marian shrines, Lipsius did nevertheless describe his devotion to the Virgin: 'From my early adulthood I have loved the Blessed Virgin, cultivating a devotion to her and placing myself under her patronage and protection in all the dangers and troubles of my life.'[41] He also alluded to his membership of the Marian sodality run by the Society of Jesus, and he traced the history of a forerunner of this confraternity in the form of a Sodality of the Blessed Virgin founded in the fifteenth century.[42]

It is clear from everything that Lipsius wrote that religious convictions were for him to be privately nurtured and not necessarily publicly proclaimed. Accordingly, his reluctance to go to print with the oration of 1591 and the awkward defensiveness of his spiritual works thereafter may be understood in this light. In his strongly statist work, *Politicorum . . . Libri Sex,* Lipsius argued for the regulation of religion by the ruler and the persecution of public dissenters from the state creed.[43] But he did contend that private dissidents, or those who 'sinned' in private, should be left unmolested by the regime. This was, in the prevailing atmosphere of the ideologically divided Netherlands, a bold stance, and indeed a cause of the listing of his work on the *Index.*[44] Although his neo-Stoicism as propounded in *De Constantia* prescribed detachment from the religious strife and divisions of the age, Lipsius felt compelled in the *Politica* to write for the guidance of princes and rulers, and had, of necessity, to treat of the role of religion in the state. His enemies, including Coornhert, goaded Lipsius down to 1590 into declaring to which of the two broad confessional groupings he belonged, but the Belgian refused to do so until after his domicile in the Spanish territories had been established.[45]

Lipsius shared with Richard Stanihurst the same printer, Christopher Plantin of Antwerp, whose famous press produced most of their published works. Besides being a highly successful businessman, Plantin was himself a poet and philosopher, whose premises in the Vrijdagmarkt provided Lipsius with a refuge during times of harassment.[46] The printer was also chameleon-like in religious matters, being a leading member of a secret sect, the Family of Love, which was indifferent to the outward forms of Christianity and allowed its adherents to conform to the rites of the dominant religion.[47] Plantin had shifted his printing operation to Leiden while Lipsius and Stanihurst were there in the early 1580s. Lipsius had joined the Family of Love, being attracted by the flexibility offered in the rapidly changing circumstances of the late sixteenth-century Netherlands.[48] He found the religious venom of the era distasteful and passed easily from one religious allegiance to another. His Familism justified for him his dissimulation while living in a Calvinist milieu at Leiden, and when he returned to Brabant he could claim, as he did in *Diva Sichemiensis*, that, though he might have assumed the worship of his adopted place of residence, his fundamental religious beliefs were unchanging. In his last years, and posthumously, his Catholic friends such as Philip Rubens, Balthasar Moretus and Johannes Woverius vaunted his commitment to the Roman Church, and Lipsius would have been happy to acquiesce. His essential theological indifferentism was covered up in the process.[49] But what makes the correspondence of 1592 with Stanihurst of interest is not only the early indication after his flight from Leiden of the need to commit publicly to the doctrinal position of the state religion, but also the place of the Blessed Virgin in his inner life of piety. The later works suggest that, despite his distaste for making his feelings public, he nevertheless felt obliged to write on religious themes in gratitude for his honoured position in Brussels and Louvain, and perhaps also in order to bolster the state religion of the southern Netherlands.

For Richard Stanihurst, the period after 1592 until his death in 1618 was characterized also by attachment to the Catholic Church and the Spanish establishment in the Netherlands. His career as a chemical physician may not have flourished beyond 1595 but he was fully engaged thereafter in diplomacy in respect of Spanish policy towards the islands of Britain and Ireland until 1601. In the aftermath of the Spanish enterprise in Ireland of that year, Stanihurst detached himself from active politics and, on becoming a widower for the second time, joined the Society of Jesus about 1605. He spent his last ten years as court chaplain to the archducal couple until his death in 1618.[50]

Like his friend Lipsius, who died in 1606, Stanihurst devoted his scholarly talents to the promotion of Counter-Reformation devotion and he also shared with him the benefit of being published by the great Plantin-Moretus house. Yet there is nothing of the Family of Love about Stanihurst's approach to religion after 1586. In that year he became a pensioner of the Spanish Crown and in the following one he wrote his *De Vita Sancti Patricii*, dedicating it to Alexander Farnese, duke of Parma, and champion of the cause of militant Catholicism in the Netherlands. Even his scientific work was dedicated to Philip II, 'the oppressor of the infidels, the defender of the Catholic religion, and destroyer of the abominable Lutherans and Calvinists', in the interests of vindicating true alchemy as a legitimate pursuit for a good Catholic.[51] In his subsequent religious writings, the tone was characterized by the ardour of the Tridentine *dévot*. Like Justus Lipsius, Stanihurst came to occupy an official position at the court of the archdukes, that of chaplain to Albert and Isabella. To the latter, also a *dévotée* of the Blessed Virgin, the *Hebdomada Mariana* was dedicated (as had been the *Diva Sichemiensis* of Lipsius). An unpublished treatise, entitled *Margarita Mariana*, was dedicated in the name of the Jesuit-run Sodality of the Virgin Mary of which Lipsius and Stanihurst were members.[52] Perhaps the most evident example of Stanihurst's applying of his formidable scholarship to the advancement of the Counter-Reformation came in the *Brevis Praemunitio pro Futura Concertatione cum Jacobo Usserio,* a robust defence of the apostolic tradition within the Roman Catholic Church against the attacks upon it of his nephew, James Ussher.

The few letters that we have examined comprise a miniature of the impressive edifice of the Lipsian correspondence, and yet they afford a suggestive glimpse of the ideas of two friends interacting at critical points in their careers. For Lipsius we have testimony to a willingness in principle to countenance publication of a work of Marian devotion in conjunction with his new-found commitment to the Catholic Church. Although the work discussed was not printed, the exchange concerning religious writings can nevertheless usefully inform the debate about the place of the spiritual works in the Lipsian canon. For Stanihurst there is the evidence of his being part of an international humanist network that transcended the Irish community from which he came. Furthermore, the Erasmian-style devotion of the followers of Lipsius and their desire to spread his praises wherever they went posits a telling comparison between the two great Netherlandish humanists of the sixteenth century. In that connection, perhaps, a brief assessment of the intellectual milieu of Lipsius and Stanihurst as Catholic writers may help to elucidate the *terminus ad quem* of the crisis for Christian humanists, including Erasmus and Thomas More, in the early Reformation period.

4. 'The Tipperary Hero':

Dermot O'Meara's
Ormonius (1615)[1]

KEITH SIDWELL and
DAVID EDWARDS

Dermot O'Meara (*fl.* 1610), though perhaps better known as a medic, published a five-book hexameter poem on the military achievements of the great Irish nobleman 'Black' Thomas Butler, 10th earl of Ormond, with the London publisher Thomas Snodham in 1615, shortly after the death of the poem's subject. O'Meara (or Meara, as he prints his name, in Latinized form) advertised himself on the title page as '*Hybernus et insignissimae Oxoniensis Academiae quondam alumnus*' (An Irishman and sometime pupil of Oxford University).[2] The book begins with two dedicatory letters, the first to Walter Butler, the new (11th) earl of Ormond, and the second to Ormonius himself:

> *Illustrissimo Heroi ac Domino D. Thomae Butlero, Ormoniae et Osoriae Comiti, Viscomiti de Thurles, Baroni de Arcklo, regni Hyberniae Archithesaurario, Comitatus Tiperariae Palatini Domino, Insignissimi periscelidos ordinis Equiti, et Regiae Maiestati in Hibernia sacrioribus a Consiliis.*[3]

> To the most illustrious hero, Thomas Butler, my Lord Earl of Ormond and Ossory, Viscount Thurles, Baron of Arklow, High Treasurer of the Kingdom of Ireland, Lord of the County Palatine of Tipperary, Knight of the Garter and privy councillor to His Majesty the King in Ireland.

It ends with three shorter poems by O'Meara: a dirge (in sixty-six elegiac verses), an anagrammatic acrostic (in fourteen elegiac couplets) and, finally, a brief chronological poem (in six hexameters).

It is likely that the book had some commercial success. At any rate corrections made to the *Epicedion*, the acrostic and the chronological poem and the addition of an *errata* page in two copies seem to suggest a second edition, though the text of the *Ormonius* itself was not corrected.[4] It certainly became well known to contemporaries. It caused controversy among the Munster Fitzgeralds, as might have been expected, given the

praise that was lavished on Ormond in the text of the poem for his punitive actions against them during the reign of Elizabeth I. The Fitzgeralds'
anger is demonstrated by the (prose) reply later made by Dominic O'Daly
in the *Initium, incrementa, et exitus Familiae Geraldinorum Desmoniae
Comitum, Palatinorum Kyrriae in Hybernia, ac persecutionis haereticorum
descriptio,* which was published in Lisbon in 1655.[5] On the other hand, in
1664 John Lynch in his *Alithinologia* quoted the poem to support a historical argument, and it was also recorded in Harris's catalogue of Irish
writing, published between 1739 and 1746.[6] Since the eighteenth
century, however, it has been almost totally neglected, a victim – like
Stanihurst's *De Rebus in Hibernia Gestis* – of rather different political
visions of Ireland that emerged in the nineteenth and twentieth centuries.[7] Even after the Gaelic literary scholar James Carney published a
summary of its content in 1945, as an example of the Gaelic Latin tradition, it has continued to lie in obscurity.[8]

The poem repays study, both from the literary and the historical perspective: from the former since O'Meara's poetic capacities are not
nugatory (though his linguistic debts may sometimes seem to a modern
reader rather too close to the borderlines of plagiarism for comfort), and
because he has adapted his classical Latin models to a specifically Gaelic
literary form; from the latter because the poem provides details of
Ormond's military campaigns which are not otherwise recorded, and
because a study of the poem's representation of the events it chooses to
record provides significant insights into an aspect of life in early Stuart
Ireland that remains imperfectly understood – the struggle of native loyalists like the Butlers to adapt to a rapid loss of influence.

The poem's subject

The subject of the poem, 'Black' Thomas Butler, was born in southern
Ireland in 1531.[9] As the eldest son of James Butler, 9th earl of Ormond
and earl of Ossory, and Joan Fitzgerald, daughter of the 11th earl of
Desmond, he was heir to the greatest aristocratic inheritance in the
country, with lands and seigneurial rights reaching into eight counties.
The chief seat of his family, and the place where he grew up, was
Kilkenny Castle, a large fortress overlooking Kilkenny town, on the banks
of the River Nore.

In 1544 Thomas was sent to England by his parents to be educated at
the royal court, where he became a schoolmate of the future king,
Edward VI.[10] In one sense, his despatch to London was only in keeping
with family tradition. The Butlers, like many of the inhabitants of
southern and eastern Ireland, were of ancient English stock. Since the

first arrival of their ancestors in the country in the late twelfth century they had remained in close contact with England, and through their ties to the monarchy they had significantly expanded their Irish power base, gaining a string of grants and concessions of which the palatine liberty – or independent jurisdiction – of Tipperary was perhaps the greatest.[11] In another sense, however, the young earl's departure for the royal court was noteworthy. For much of the previous seventy or eighty years the Butler lineage in Ireland had been drifting further and further from royal control, and as Crown authority had retreated, their main territories, spread across Counties Tipperary, Kilkenny and Carlow, had become less and less like English shires, more and more like something rather different, culturally hybrid areas where Gaelic customs and practices had come to share parity with English ones.[12] In fact, young Earl Thomas was himself living proof of the extent to which the Butlers had been partly Gaelicized. Not merely familiar with the Gaelic language, he spoke it fluently, having been fostered with local Gaelic dynasties such as the O'Mores earlier in his childhood.[13] Accordingly, by sending him to London, his parents seem to have intended to reassure the Tudor monarchy that the earldom of Ormond was committed, long-term, to the government policy of re-Anglicization. This did not mean, however, that they wanted him to lose contact with Gaelic ways; of the personal servants known to have accompanied the earl to England some of the most important were Gaelic.[14] Like others of his ancestors, therefore, he was to be a two-faced earl, able to appear English to the English and Irish to the Irish; the only difference between him and some of his more recent forebears was that now that the English Crown was reasserting its authority in Ireland, there was potentially much more to be gained by his investing in the family's Englishness than previously.

The earl's English upbringing proved to be the defining experience of his life. Instead of staying at court for two or three years (as originally planned), owing to changing family and political circumstances, he had to remain in London for the greater part of ten years, only returning home in the autumn of 1554.[15] By the time of his return he had become far more familiar with English royalty and government, and far better adapted to English cultural mores, than any other Irish nobleman of his generation. He had also mastered skills of political survival that would serve him the rest of his life, not least the ability to keep hidden his religious identity at a time of violent religious change. Known personally not just to Edward VI (1547–53), a Protestant king, but also to the Catholic Mary I (1553–8) and the future Elizabeth I, another Protestant (1558–1603), he managed to impress each in turn as a model Anglo-Irish lord, proud of the power and semi-independence of his family but willing to serve the Crown. Just months before his return to Ireland he had seized the opportunity to exhibit his potential usefulness, distinguishing himself as a military commander in London when helping to defend the new monarch, Queen Mary – England's first female sovereign – against an army of Protestant rebels led by the East Anglian knight, Sir Thomas Wyatt.[16] Through service came influence. On the earl's arrival in Ireland it was understood that henceforth he would be allowed to assume a prominent role in the extension of English government throughout the country.

Understood, but not necessarily accepted: for many English officials in Ireland the enhancement of Crown power was achievable only by drastically reducing the power of Irish lords. In their eyes, Ormond's closeness to the monarchy, and the influence it gained him, was an unwelcome complication that tended to diminish official authority. Throughout his life Earl Thomas would have to rely on royal backing to overcome the constant hostility of Crown officials in Ireland – in other words, to look to Whitehall instead of Dublin. Yet there were limits to his Anglo-centrism. The better to impress the monarchy of his political value, he needed not just to make his territories conform more closely to an English model, but also to display his familiarity with and influence over the Gaelic and Gaelicized lords who continued to control much of the country. In this sense being two-faced was one of his strongest cards. Despite the suspicion that it inevitably aroused, he played it repeatedly in the years ahead, often with telling effect, using his contacts in the native lordships to secure allies for the Crown, to dampen down the fires of local conflict and to isolate and if necessary kill rebel leaders and their supporters.

Ormond enjoyed much greater royal influence after Queen Mary's death in 1558. Mary's successor, Elizabeth I, having admired him since his youth, regarded Ormond as one of her premier nobles, and from the very beginning of her long reign he was encouraged to visit England whenever possible to participate in court life. During two periods in particular he enjoyed extraordinary prominence at the Elizabethan court – the first during the later 1560s, when briefly he rivalled the earl of Leicester for the position of royal favourite; the second (and more important) during the Armada crisis of the late 1580s, when the queen admitted him to the inner ring of her closest counsellors, seeking his advice on how to organize England's defences against the Spanish menace. In Ireland, despite the sniping of senior English administrators, Elizabeth indulged Ormond enormously. Soon after her accession she appointed him lord treasurer of the kingdom for life, a largely honorific office – it had little to do with royal finance – the real value of which was that it entitled the earl to permanent membership of the Irish Privy Council, the main executive body responsible for overseeing government business in the country. As such, the earl was usually able to gain prior warning of a policy initiative that might prove detrimental to his interests, and to challenge it by appealing over the head of the English viceroy directly to the queen or her chief ministers in London. As often as not – and the embarrassment of successive viceroys notwithstanding – throughout Elizabeth's reign his objections were upheld, and repeatedly Crown policy in Ireland was modified to suit his wishes.

His success proved highly divisive. For traditional enemies of his family, especially the Fitzgeralds of Desmond, the extent to which Queen Elizabeth was prepared to favour his cause over theirs was a major factor in provoking them into rebellion. Alternatively, for the hard-pressed loyalist communities of southern and eastern Ireland, over time he seemed to be the one Irish lord capable of representing and defending their localist brand of loyalism, by frustrating the implementation of unpopular government policies by challenging them from within. Then again, for English officials the energies he all-too-obviously devoted to enhancing his own interests and those of his growing number of followers led them to accuse him of undermining the service of the state.

Despite some serious setbacks – chiefly the growing unreliability of some members of his family, who rebelled three times – the queen rarely lost faith in him. She repeatedly trusted him to take charge of important campaigns and to act as a counterweight to her leading English officers, and much to their annoyance she allowed him to deal with the rebel Butlers himself (he crushed each revolt in turn, executing many). More than once it was rumoured that Ormond was a candidate for the Irish viceroyalty, and although Elizabeth stopped short of awarding him the highest post, preferring to appoint Englishmen, she nonetheless granted him more power than any Irishman since the 1530s. In 1583 she made him civil and military governor of Munster, and in 1597 (with a Spanish invasion seemingly looming) lieutenant-general, or commander-in-chief, of the all the Crown forces in Ireland.

Such was the royal reliance on Ormond's military abilities that his career is ultimately synonymous with the Tudor/Elizabethan conquest of Ireland. For almost fifty years, from his first major campaign in 1556 until the onset of blindness forced him into retirement in 1601, he played a leading part in the extension and defence of English rule in the country. At one time or another he and his forces came face to face with almost every major rebel of the period – Shane O'Neill, Sorley Boy MacDonnell, James Fitzmaurice Fitzgerald, Rory Oge O'More, Roland Eustace, Viscount Baltinglass, Feagh McHugh O'Byrne, Gerald Fitzgerald, earl of Desmond, and Hugh O'Neill, earl of Tyrone. Revealingly, he never suffered defeat. A brave but essentially cautious leader, Ormond understood better than any other royal commander that war in Ireland was about frustrating the enemy, confining his movements, and curtailing his access to supplies and reinforcements, rather than risking everything by confronting him in open battle. The recklessness of some of the English captains infuriated the earl, as did their propensity to attack well-affected native groups (at least one of the Butler rebellions with which he had to contend stemmed from overt provocation by English officers). From the 1570s onwards each of the campaigns in which he was involved was hampered by the mounting bitterness between the earl and his English captains. This antipathy did not prevent him helping to secure the Crown's two greatest victories of the later sixteenth century, against the Desmond Fitzgeralds in 1583 and the earl of Tyrone and his Confederates after 1594.[17] It did prevent him, however, gaining proper recognition for his achievements. Ultimately, it was his need for recognition that lay behind the production of our poem, *Ormonius*.

To this day historians usually only acknowledge Ormond's role in the defeat of Desmond, passing over his role against Tyrone. Largely this is because his importance in destroying Desmond is undeniable, a clear matter of record. But it is also partly due to Ormond's success in having his role against Desmond commemorated. In 1584, just months after his men found Desmond hiding in a cabin in the Kerry mountains and beheaded him, the English writer, Thomas Churchyard, produced a pamphlet celebrating his achievement, *A Scourge for Rebels*, which was published in London; in all likelihood Ormond or his English-based representatives had hired Churchyard to write it.[18] Moreover, at about the same time the earl had his Irish supporters gather at Kilkenny Castle to sign a declaration addressed to the queen praising him for his great victory. He had the declaration formally enrolled among the official documents of state.[19] His central role in defeating Desmond was similarly remembered in the Irish parliament two years later, when his supporters presented a petition outlining his services that had to be read into the record.[20]

However, his achievements against Tyrone were not nearly so well recorded. Crucially, despite having laid the foundations for English victory after 1594 by securing the south – the obvious target for any Spanish invasion – and keeping Tyrone confined to the north, the onset of blindness in 1601 deprived him of the chance to be in at the climax of the conflict. The only part he played at the Battle of Kinsale was in the background, far from the action, hosting a special council of war at Kilkenny prior to the English commander Lord Mountjoy's departure for the battlefield.[21] Hardly surprisingly, following Mountjoy's triumph over Tyrone and the Spaniards, the flood of chronicles and pamphlets that flowed from English printing presses immediately afterwards said nothing about the 'Black' earl of Ormond.[22] His health declining, he was unable to travel to Dublin to stake his claim to a share of the glory; awareness of his role faded.

The death of Elizabeth I in 1603 sealed Earl Thomas's fate. Although the new monarch, the first of the Stuarts, James I, was quick to offer warm assurances of favour, in truth there was no place for the aged Butler lord in the new régime. From the very start the English official class with whom Ormond had quarrelled for so many years dominated Jacobean Ireland. The new king, a Scot, needed their support far more than he did the earl's; suddenly, with the country conquered, Ormond and his family had become expendable. Although Earl Thomas managed to retain sufficient personal status to receive occasional government appointments, his blindness, advanced age, and growing physical frailty meant he could easily be bypassed.

The situation was much worse for his kinsmen. Even more than the Elizabethan régime the government of James I was able to make the reduction of noble autonomy in Ireland central to its programme. It was also able as never before to make Protestantism the religion of power, by insisting on religious conformity. Hence the reduced status offered to Ormond's heirs, his nephews Theobald Butler, Viscount Tully and Walter Butler of Kilcash (Earl Thomas's son had died in 1590). Although Theobald appeared to embrace Protestantism, and as such should have been promoted to a prominent state position, senior Crown officials ensured he remained stuck in the provinces by pointing to the rebelliousness of his branch of the Butlers during Queen Elizabeth's reign. No such charge could be levelled at Walter of Kilcash, who emerged as Ormond's heir-apparent in 1613 following Theobald's sudden death. Walter's father – Ormond's brother John – had fought loyally against rebels early in Elizabeth's reign, and late in her reign Walter himself had earned much praise (and a knighthood) for his service against Tyrone and other insurgents – service for which he still bore the scars, having received a bad leg wound, and been made lame, during a clash with rebels in Tipperary. Yet Walter too received little favour from the Jacobean authorities, his open commitment to Counter-Reformation Catholicism a source of mounting official criticism and outright obstruction.[23]

The government's treatment of his heirs greatly worried old Earl Thomas. For centuries the English monarchy had supported and nurtured the power of the Butlers in southern Ireland in return for their loyalty and usefulness. Now all that seemed to have changed. With the country conquered, and royal power finally dominant, the Crown was apparently determined to make no more concessions to the great regional lineages, and to rule more directly through English and Protestant officials. To reverse this trend, the earl calculated, the Crown needed to be reminded that whatever their religious affiliations, the great majority of the Butlers of Ormond had remained steadfast, and still did; even more so, it needed to remember that under Earl Thomas's command they had played a major role in making the English conquest possible. The fact that the earl had grown so old added considerably to the urgency of the situation; soon he would die. Unless the Crown was convinced of the importance of his family, and of its continuing value to the state, all his efforts during Elizabeth's reign would have been in vain. His successor might face the prospect of losing much that had been gained over the years.

And so it was in order to arrest the Butlers' declining reputation and to help restore the family to its rightful glory as Ireland's premier noble dynasty that in the final years of his life Ormond turned to literature and to his Gaelic servant, the Tipperary physician Dermot O'Meara. The earl could have chosen another writer from within his circle to undertake the task: for example, Elias Shee, a minor poet who (like O'Meara) had spent time at Oxford University,[24] or else Robert Rothe, the earl's seneschal, who would write a valuable memoir of the earl after his death.[25] We must assume that it was O'Meara's proficiency in Latin that got him the nod. Despite the rise of the vernacular in the wake of the Renaissance and Reformation, Latin was still very much the international language in the early seventeenth century. More particularly, given that Ireland was increasingly a colonial region, with thousands of new settlers arriving from England, lowland Scotland and Wales (and some even coming from continental Europe), Latin was the chief language of communication between the new colonial elite and the traditional native lords, and would remain so until such time as either the new settlers learned Gaelic or more Irish learned English. To reach the widest possible audience, accessible to English, Scottish, Welsh, Irish and also European readers, the poem that Ormond commissioned had to be written in Latin. His target may, however, have been more specific: the king had been a pupil of the most renowned Scottish Latinist of his generation, the dramatist and poet George Buchanan, and would certainly have been able to read, understand and appreciate a Latin epic.

The poem had also to be historical and biographical. Only by giving a detailed chronology – literally, a chronicle in verse – of each of the campaigns in which Ormond and his forces had earned distinction could the historical record of the Tudor conquest be corrected in the Butlers' favour, and wrested away from the monopolizing grasp of the English military and their propagandists. At the same time, however, the poem would have to refrain from challenging too overtly the English version of the recent past, since to do so would mean re-igniting fierce arguments with officialdom.

Accordingly the key task of *Ormonius* was a relatively simple one: to per-
suade its readers of the earl of Ormond's place in history. The poem was
intended to demonstrate that, of all the Crown's servants, only the earl had
served through the entire duration of the Elizabethan wars, from their
beginnings until (almost) the end, gaining victory after victory for his
monarch. So far, so good: but there was more. Springing from a perspective
that in its own way was as skewed and partisan as anything the English
had produced, the poem was to be 'historical' only insofar as this was
useful. Ormond's life story was to be presented as nothing less than the
story of the conquest: the 'true' story, the story of those who, under his
leadership, had 'really' secured English victory – the Butlers and their allies.
Tellingly, English military commanders would be noticeable mainly by
their absence from the text. Likewise, of all the viceroys to have ruled in
Ireland since the 1550s just one would be honourably mentioned (*Ormonius* 2.255–6) – Ormond's great friend and patron, Thomas Radcliffe, 3rd
earl of Sussex (viceroy 1556–64, †1583), who had first set Ormond on his
path to glory by entrusting him with senior military command.

Of course, Ormond would have known that, to say the least, this was
unlikely to be well received by the English official elite that had taken
control of Jacobean Ireland, many of whom had served in the later Elizabethan wars and identified strongly with a very different version of events.
Clearly, they were not the poem's target audience. Instead there is reason
to believe that Ormond hoped the poem's message of Butler loyalism and
military heroism would appeal to a far more important constituency,
namely King James himself and all the nobles and gentry of England, Scotland and Ireland who had a vested interest in ensuring that the new
Stuart/Anglo-Scottish régime was established on a firm and lasting footing
throughout each of its three kingdoms. It was presumably to register its
relevance to early seventeenth-century concerns about security in the
'wild' northern regions of the Stuart dominions, in Ulster and the Western
Isles and the Highlands, that the poem afforded such a curious level of
prominence to Ormond's northern campaigning. While it is true that Earl
Thomas had seen service in almost every part of Ireland before 1600, by
far the greatest part of his soldiering – and his most successful soldiering
– had been located across the southern half of the country. Despite this,
Ormonius would go out of its way to portray the earl as a tamer of the
north. No less than half of Book 2 deals with his harrying of Shane
O'Neill, exploits that no self-respecting historian would consider significant. Similarly, the whole of Book 3 is devoted to an exhaustive
celebration of Ormond's adventures against the MacDonnells of Ulster and
the Isles in 1558, especially his devastation of Rathlin, and Book 5 opens
with his return to Antrim in 1584.[26]

Such disproportionate coverage of the north only makes sense as a deliberate construct to obtain favour with a readership no longer greatly concerned by the threat of rebellion in southern Ireland, but still on edge over the potential of Ulster and the Isles to destabilize the fledgling Stuart state.[27] Two of the most important decisions taken by King James after his accession involved northern security – first his efforts after 1605 to impose greater government control over the Western Isles, culminating in the Statutes of Iona of 1609 and, most famously, the Ulster Plantation of 1610.[28] Yet even with these initiatives under way the 'wild' north still represented a major security risk for several years afterwards, and English apprehension was exacerbated by constant tales of Tyrone's impending return from his European exile with an invasion force, and fears that he might link up with disaffected members of the MacDonnells. Decoded, the message that *Ormonius* was intended to spread was that so long as there was 'wildness' in the Crown's dominions, revolt was likely, and given the long record of Earl Thomas and his family as defenders of the Crown and vanquishers of rebellion there was no more reliable source of state security than the Butlers. The dynasty was not yet obsolescent; far from it. Its loyalism and military traditions represented the surest foundation of lasting political stability. By relying on and honouring its current head, Earl Thomas, the Crown had overcome its enemies in Ireland in the recent past; by relying on and honouring his successor, it would be best equipped to overcome its enemies in the future. As an expression of native loyalist concern over creeping disempowerment and dislocation under the Stuarts, and the belief that the situation was still retrievable through an appeal to history, *Ormonius* is without parallel.

The poem's composition and publication

As revealed by the dedicatory epistle addressed to Earl Thomas that is situated at the start of the book,[29] O'Meara had finished writing the poem while Ormond was still alive – that is, sometime before the earl's death on 22 November 1614. In the same epistle O'Meara also states that he had been working on the text for four years or so before its completion, indicating that he must have commenced writing in 1609, when Ormond was still occasionally active, and not yet fully retired, confined to his Carrick mansion as an invalid. To judge from the truncated character of its final book, Book 5, the writing progressed at a fairly leisurely pace until some crisis or other – almost certainly the onset of the earl's final illness – intervened and caused O'Meara to hurry up. In the rush he was apparently forced to cut short his treatment of the earl's heroics during the Nine Years War – a cruel irony, given Ormond's special desire to have his services against Tyrone fully recognized.

The second dedicatory epistle, addressed to Earl Thomas's successor, Earl Walter, explains just how far advanced the process of printing had been when Thomas had passed away: *'cum adhuc in Tipographi manibus meae chartulae existerent, necdum penitus essent a prelo sublatae, ter maximus ille Heros vitalis aurae usura privatur'* (when my drafts were still in the hands of the printer and had not yet been completely taken from the press, that thrice-greatest Hero was deprived of the use of the life-giving air).

It is very likely that *Ormonius* rolled off Snodham's printing press in time for Earl Thomas's funeral, which took place at St Canice's Cathedral in Kilkenny in May 1615. Everyone involved in the production – Snodham, O'Meara and Earl Walter – would have wanted the book ready for sale by then. Because of his once high status, and especially his membership of the Order of the Garter, Ormond's funeral was one of the major social and political events of the year, and not just in Ireland but throughout the British Isles. Extant records show that it was attended by representatives of the senior English nobility and by members of the governments of the three Stuart kingdoms.[30]

Genre

Before discussing the structure and content of the poem, a few preliminary remarks are in order regarding the genre in which O'Meara chose to write. Surviving ancient epic – which, as we shall see, is of paramount importance in the language and construction of the work – does not (at least directly) deal with living contemporary figures. Vergil's *Aeneid* delved into the distant past and only by implication occasionally sought to refer across to Augustus: it did not set out to relate Augustus' story. Lucan's *De bello civili* dealt with the – by then – long-dead Caesar and Pompey, and Silius Italicus' *Punica* dwelt lengthily upon the war of Hannibal against Rome. Statius wandered back into the mythical age in his *Achilleid* and *Thebaid*. The classical Romans had certainly celebrated contemporaries – Rabirius wrote of Augustus' rise to power and Cicero wrote autobiographical poems (*On My Consulship* and *On My Times*): but none of these survived antiquity. It is the later panegyric and propagandistic tradition represented by the fourth-century poet Claudian (for example, in his *On the Consulship of Stilicho* and *On the Getic War*) and the sixth-century Corippus (whose epic *Johannis* deals with the victory against the Moors of Justinian's contemporary general of that name [AD 546–48], and who composed a panegyric *In Praise of Justinian* [c. AD 567]) that provided models for medieval and early modern works where living individuals and their achievements were epicized. Medieval Latin epic took up this habit of heroizing contemporaries. The early ninth-century poem *Karolus Rex et Leo Papa* dealt with Charlemagne's relationship with Pope Leo III, the pontiff who had crowned him emperor on Christmas Day 800.[31] Despite the lack of ancient models from the classical era, the Latin epic celebrating a powerful individual during his own lifetime became an important genre during the early Renaissance. Examples are numerous. Two will suffice: Matthaeus Zuppardus' *Alfonseis* (1455–7), written for King Alfonso V of Aragon, and Joannes Raduanus' *Radivilias* (Vilnius, 1592), in which the deeds of the Lithuanian hero Nicholas Radvila are praised.[32] One must strongly suspect that O'Meara had read poems of this sort and was at one level concerned to place both himself and his subject in a contemporary, as well as a classical, European tradition. But at present we simply do not know what was available to him or which – if any – were the catalysts. His primary linguistic and structural inspiration is still very clearly ancient epic, especially Vergil, Silius Italicus and Claudian.

There are, however, two complications, one relating to the *classical* genre and the other to the poem's use of a *Gaelic* poetic genre. Let us deal first with the classical models. The opening of the *Ormonius* reads:

> *Quos casus, quae fata tulit, quibus artibus altum,*
> *Conspicuumque decus . . .*

> What accidents, what fates he bore, and by
> What arts the high conspicuous honour won . . .

This is not an odd way to open an epic poem. Vergil's *Aeneid* (one of O'Meara's vital inspirations for Book 1) asks at 1.8f:

> *Musa, mihi causas memora, quo numine laeso*
> *quidve dolens regina deum tot volvere casus*
> *insignem pietate virum, tot adire labores*
> *impulerit*

> Muse, tell me why, what deity was harmed,
> What so aggrieved the queen of gods she drove
> A man renowned for *pietas* to unroll
> So many accidents, to face so many toils.

And there are other reminiscences of epic. At line 6, '*Dicere fert animus*', we hear a clear echo of Ovid *Metamorphoses* 1.1:

> *In noua fert animus mutatas dicere formas*
> *Corpora*

My mind is fain to sing of bodies changed
Into new forms . . .

After the proem, at lines 14–15, where the real action begins, we read:

Prima Caledoniis fuerant exercita campis
Arma viri . . .

The man's armed prowess had been exercised
First on the Caledonian plains . . .

Line 15 is an obvious allusion to Vergil, *Aeneid* 1.1:

Arma uirumque cano . . .

Arms and the man I sing . . .

For the resonance of the opening, though, we must turn not to ancient epic but to ancient didactic. The first lines of Vergil's *Georgics* read:

Quid faciat laetas segetes, quo sidere terram
Vertere . . .
Conueniat, quae cura boum, qui cultus habendo
Sit pecori, apibus quanta experientia parcis,
Hinc canere incipiam.

What makes the crops delight, and when it's right
To turn the sod . . . how one should tend the bulls,
What sort of way to keep one's flock, and what
Experience is required for thrifty bees,
Starting from here I shall begin to sing.

The series of three indirect questions in O'Meara (even if – under the influence of Plautine syntax and the lack of reliable information in contemporary grammars – he uses the indicative *tulit*), introduced by *quos*, *quae* and *quibus*, followed by a formula for composition (here the Ovidian *dicere fert animus*) strongly suggests that he is patterning his poem's prooemium upon Vergil's didactic. There is a further twist to this discovery. The opening lines of Fracastoro's poem *Syphilis* read (1–5; 10–12):

Qui casus rerum varii, quae semina morbum
Insuetum, nec longa ulli per saecula visum
Attulerint: nostra qui tempestate per omnem
Europam, partimque Asiae, Libyaeque per urbes
Saeviit . . .
Hinc canere, et longe secretas quaerere causas
Aera per liquidum, et vasti per sydera Olympi
Incipiam.

> What various accidents in things, what seeds
> Bore the disease, in ages past unseen,
> Which raged throughout all of Europe in our time,
> In parts of Asia and in Libya's towns . . .
> Starting from here to sing, and to enquire
> The secret causes, through the liquid air
> And through the stars of vast Olympus, I
> Shall now begin.

Fracastoro's poem was published in 1530 and soon became very well known. The pattern of indirect questions, dependent upon *hinc canere . . . incipiam*, mark Fracastoro's model very clearly as Vergil's *Georgics*. Though the subject matter is hardly pastoral, Syphilis is in fact a shepherd, and the medical aims of the poem are tricked out with the trappings of bucolic. As a doctor himself and a more than competent versifier, O'Meara cannot but have known of Fracastoro's didactic poem. The deliberate use he makes of Vergil's *arma uirum* in line 15 (*arma uiri*) and the appropriateness of the allusion to change as a theme of his treatment of Ormond in line 6 (*dicere fert animus*) make it likely that he intended to echo the opening words of *Syphilis* (*qui casus*) in his first line (*quos casus*). It seems fairly clear that O'Meara is using the echo to mark himself out as a poetic doctor, following a distinguished predecessor, only with a theme more like that of Caspar Bruschius' *Idyllion historicum* (a versified history of German dioceses).[33]

The poem is in five books. This number probably has no bearing on the identification of the poem's genre. In the Latin didactic canon, Vergil's *Georgics* had four books, Lucretius' *De rerum natura* six, and Fracastoro's *Syphilis* three, while in epic Vergil's *Aeneid* had twelve, Statius' *Thebaid* the same number, Lucan's *De bello civili* ten, Silius Italicus' *Punica* seventeen and Valerius Flaccus' *Argonautica* eight. Neo-Latin epics also vary considerably in this regard.[34] O'Meara may simply have written until he reached the end of his story, though it is hard to believe that anyone would embark on such a large-scale enterprise without serious planning and an eye on some earlier model. Still, the lack of a classical model (which one might have expected) inclines us to suspect that O'Meara originally planned a sixth book (as in Lucretius). This impression is reinforced by the fact that in Book 5 the poem's treatment of Ormond's central role during the Nine Years War is clearly heavily truncated (see further below).

At any rate, it is clear that O'Meara's opening generic statement tends to classify his work as *didactic*, but with a mixture of two types of *epic* material – the theme of inconstancy and change (from Ovid) and that of warfare from Vergil. This is in fact what we might expect at this period, when the clear differentiation made by modern scholars between didactic and epic based on the presence of an addressee in particular was unknown. As Helander has argued, neo-Latin writers were focused primarily on successful praise of their patrons rather than on imitating antiquity *per se*.[35] A confirmation of this may be the further consideration that the *matter* of the poem does not fit any known category of ancient epic-didactic. It is true, of course, that war, the poem's theme, finds pride of place in the *Aeneid*, in Silius Italicus' *Punica* and in Corippus' *Iohannis*. However, O'Meara does not give an account of any whole war, only of those campaigns conducted entirely by Ormond or in which his subject wished to be depicted as playing a leading role. No ancient, medieval or even early modern Latin writer operated thus. Happily, the reason for this unique approach is easily found. In the Gaelic bardic tradition there was a specific type of song that listed and praised the patron's *military* achievements, the *caithréim* or 'battle career'. Furthermore, it is known that 'Black' Thomas Butler had Gaelic poets compose such works to commemorate many of his martial achievements[36] – achievements which are otherwise mentioned, though in much greater detail, only in the *Ormonius*.[37] This is not, in fact, the only way in which *Ormonius* was a specifically *Irish* poem, despite its being dressed in classical Latin. As we shall see below, O'Meara was capable of usurping at least one other Gaelic literary device. This combination of classical and Gaelic literary forms and motifs makes the poem quite unique. It was not, however, isolated from current developments in European Latin writing. Rather, it was symptomatic of the neo-Latin poetry of the early modern period that attempted to import ethnic poetic traditions into the learned language.[38]

The final thing to say about the genre of *Ormonius'* is somewhat more mundane, but is nonetheless critical for understanding why it was written at all. By electing to represent Earl Thomas's life and achievements through the medium of military epic, it managed to avoid having to comment on politics or religion. In military epic the emphasis is always on the fighting and heroism, on the skin and bone and steel of combat, and rarely permits space for treatment of the underlying reasons for conflict. It is easy to understand how, after 1610, in a kingdom controlled by a new English colonial elite committed to Protestantism, this would have suited Earl Thomas, the ageing head of an older colonial dynasty that was heavily devoted to Catholicism. Although being celebrated through military epic meant that some of his greatest achievements would have to be overlooked (such as his managing to compel Elizabeth I to dilute various inflammatory policies, or his suppression of rebellion and prevention of religious conflict in his territories), nonetheless it enabled him the distinct advantage of having his life recorded in a way that was conveniently one-dimensional. Heroic epic privileged military prowess, a skill that was timeless, universal and indeed deemed an absolute virtue, over another, political guile, that was rather more divisive.

The introductory epistles

There are two main themes in the dedicatory epistles. The first is the idea that the noble deeds of great men like Earl Thomas act as a stimulus to young people to follow in their footsteps and that only literature and, more specifically, poetry, can provide that stimulus effectively, through art. The second theme is the fear of envy and rebuke from others that drives the poet to require the protection of a great patron – first Earl Thomas, then (after 'Black' Tom's death) Earl Walter.

Of these themes, the first is a version of the general Renaissance trend towards the use of literature as moral guide. Educators such as Vergerio and Battista Guarino were among the transmitters of this Petrarchan attitude to the north, through their theoretical treatises.[39] Coupled with it is the standard ancient notion that it is the poet who confers immortality. O'Meara himself cites Horace, *Odes* IV.9.25–8 (slightly misquoting) to make this point in the letter to Earl Thomas.[40]

The fear of envy and rebuke, on the other hand, while also a commonplace of literary publication, may actually have reflected something quite specific to O'Meara's situation. He certainly expressed his fears bluntly. In the second letter, he mentions both critics ('Aristarchuses') and satirists ('Archilochi') as his great bugbears. It is unlikely that he was concerned by other writers close to Ormond, such as Shee or Rothe, mentioned above. More likely, the source of his unease derived from either of two groups (even, perhaps, from both) – from pro-Geraldine poets, who could be expected to react angrily to his celebration of Ormond's role in the destruction of their leaders; or else from those soldiers and officials in the English government in Ireland who had always sought to obstruct Ormond and the Butlers, and had much to lose if the earl's version of the Elizabethan wars gained wide currency. A third group, the academics who studied, wrote and were the *arbitri elegantiae* of Latin poetry might well have been in his mind, considering how closely he sometimes runs to Horace's description of the borrowing of others' plumage (*Epistles* 1.3.18–20).

The third letter is addressed to the reader. Its purpose seems to be to justify the use of poetic form to relate what is basically a piece of historical narrative. The problem is posed because in Renaissance theory (derived among other places from Cicero's *De Oratore*, Aristotle's *Poetics* and Lucian's *How to Write History*), the task of history is to tell the unvarnished truth about specific events, while that of poetry is to use fiction to tell more general truths about the world. O'Meara is helped by Horace's dictum from the *Ars Poetica* (333): *et prodesse volunt et delectare poetae* (poets wish both to be of use and to delight), for which he uses the text of Servius (as opposed to the disjunctive *aut . . . aut* 'either . . . or' favoured by modern editions). The historical narrative, he insists, serves the cause of usefulness, while the poetic fictions serve the purpose of arousing the spirits of the young to serve king and country, because they reveal the divine underpinning which caused the historical events to happen. In particular, the poetic fictions amount to showing that (1) kings are gods on earth and must be obeyed; (2) hence whatever successes their subjects have must derive from the will of heaven; and (3) *e contra*, revolution is motivated by the powers of darkness. Thus the narrative teaches readers what Ormond actually did, while the poetic *figmenta* demonstrate how actions taken in support of king (or queen) and country are supported by the unseen apparatus of divine intervention, couched (in this argument, as in the poem) in strictly classical terms. Renaissance readers were encouraged to understand the classical gods allegorically and Vergil's *Aeneid* was a central text in the early formation of the young *literati* of the period. While the justification given by O'Meara might seem slightly bizarre to us, it would ring many comfortable bells for his intended public, and thereby underpin the poem's political purpose to rehabilitate Ormond and the Butlers as the Crown's greatest representatives in Ireland.[41]

The arguments

Before the poem begins, the printed text provides an *argumentum* for each book. Book 1 concerns only one topic, the rebellion in England of the Kentish knight, Thomas Wyatt, a Protestant whose fear of Queen Mary's Catholicism caused him to revolt in 1554. Book 2 deals with two events: (1) the relief by Ormond of the siege of Dun Imulmihil and the confirmation of Conor O'Brien as 3rd earl of Thomond; and (2) the suppression of the rebellion of Shane O'Neill in Ulster. Book 3 relates the threat posed to Ulster by the Hebridean MacDonnells and Ormond's punitive expedition to Rathlin Island in 1558 in the wake of their defeat at Glenarm. Book 4 is more diffuse. It begins in 1560 with the earl of Desmond's attack on Butler territory on the basis of a claim that was later annulled by the royal council, and then continues with an account of Desmond's invasion of the Decies in east Waterford and his subsequent defeat and capture by Ormond: he was sent to England as a prisoner in 1565. The next topics in Book 4 are the rebellion of James Fitzmaurice in 1569 (ended by the siege of Dunloe); the revolt of Thomond in 1570; Fitzmaurice's return at Smerwick (backed by an Italian fleet) in 1579; the revolt of Desmond's brother, John Fitzgerald; his murder of Henry Davells; the reprisals against Desmond by Governor Malby; and the consequent Desmond rebellion. The book ends in 1583 with the despatch to England of Desmond's head by the victorious Ormond. We have sped through more than twenty years of history in this one book. The final book, Book 5, begins with the Ulster rebellion of Sorley Boy MacDonnell, quickly put down by the viceroy and Ormond in 1584. Ormond's elevation to the Order of the Garter (1588) follows. The rest of the book treats of Ormond's involvement in the Ulster rebellion that erupted in 1594, with its subsequent spread into Munster and Leinster. As noted above, the poem closes, abruptly, with Earl Thomas's loss of his sight in 1601. This ended his direct involvement in the Crown's military activities (though, as O'Meara claims, it did not prevent his retention of an important place in the counsels of the realm for some time afterwards).

As interesting as what the poem includes, however, is what it leaves out. Even taking account of the fact that it is a military epic, and so has little or nothing to say about its hero's various political triumphs, its version of Ormond's martial adventures is characterized by some important omissions. One of these is deliberate – the earl's suppression of treason within his immediate family, which he was required to do on no less than three occasions, in 1569, 1580 and 1596. Although his efforts against his errant kinsmen were very effective, leading to hundreds of executions, and as such justified Queen Elizabeth's faith in him and the rest of his bloodline, nonetheless the memory of these events was understandably painful to Ormond.[42] More to the point, in a poem designed to celebrate the loyalty of the Butler dynasty there was little to be gained in dredging up such 'aberrations'. The other main omission, as noted earlier, was probably entirely unintentional – an account of Ormond's confrontations with Tyrone, Owney MacRory O'More and other leading rebels after mid-1598, when the earl was largely responsible for saving English rule in Ireland at the very time it faced its greatest danger. Logically the poem should have gone on from its description of the earl's proceedings in the midlands during the summer of 1598 to include a treatment of his response to Tyrone's victory at the Yellow Ford in August, when he hurried north from Kilkenny into Ulster to block off Tyrone's path to Dublin and the Pale, and then in October had to speed south to put down a dangerous insurrection in Munster and deny the Spanish an easy landing ground there. Likewise, the poem might have dwelt on Ormond's tailing of Tyrone in 1600 when the Ulster lord arrived in Tipperary to try to re-ignite the Munster rising, but had to beat a hasty retreat for fear of being trapped by the Butler forces. Instead of these, however, the poem just stops. In virtually a single bound it jumps from the midlands war – important, yes, but hardly critical – to 1601, when Ormond went blind. Then, after just a few lines, it ends with the earl's death thirteen years later. The sheer alacrity of the ending is astonishing. Having got so far, the poem fails to deliver the climax that its subject most craved – a loud assertion of the central role of Ormond and the Butlers in securing the defeat of the greatest northern rebel of all, Tyrone, and one who, even in 1614, continued to cast a shadow over Irish life. Viewed from this perspective, because it had to be rushed to the printers before it was properly finished, *Ormonius* ended up being something of a failure. From the political viewpoint it represents, in fighting parlance, a series of strong jabs but without a knockout blow. From the literary perspective, it lacks a true climax, such as might have been provided by, for example, a dramatic account of Ormond's part in the strategic discussions on the eve of the vital Battle of Kinsale.

The missing book

It is not just the omission of large amounts of material favourable to Ormond and crucial to the poem's political purpose which suggests that O'Meara's original plan involved a sixth book. Three further considerations also point in this direction. First, the *recusatio* at 5.341–82 for the very first time intimates that there is too much left to tell and hard choices will have to be made about what to include and what to leave out (5.371–82). Even though the implication of 5.375–80 is that there exists a strong possibility that others (viceroys and generals) may have tried to appropriate the glory due to Ormond, only deeds done *by him alone* will now be reported (5.380–1). Contrast the claim to comprehensiveness at 1.1–6. Secondly, although the earlier part of Book 5 works in a leisurely fashion with much poetic and divine apparatus (the Fates contrive to have Cupid fire his arrows at Ursula Bagenal and the earl of Tyrone and the Furies seize their chance to foment rebellion), after the *recusatio* the narrative consists of a hurried series of barely developed vignettes, which do not even constitute the most important of Ormond's achievements. Thirdly, the level of literary embellishment noticeably drops away from this point on: the poet was clearly in a tearing hurry to finish.

Taking this evidence along with the glaring historical omissions mentioned earlier, it may be possible to conjecture what literary shape O'Meara may have put on the rest of his poem, had he been able to complete it and, presumably, do so with the continued ideological guidance of its subject (also, one suspects, missing for the rest of Book 5). Certainly, from the point of view of missing material, his major role in the Nine Years War must have been central to Ormond's own self-image and could not but have been crucial to the narrative. As for the literary shape, however, guesswork is required to fill the gap. Given the importance of Silius Italicus' *Punica* as a model at various points, often to highlight the Scipionic Ormond versus the Hannibalic rebels, it seems possible that O'Meara might have sought a climax such as exists in that epic. It ends with the Battle of Zama and the triumph of Scipio. By 1609, it seems likely enough that the Battle of Kinsale (1601) will have been identified as the crucial turning point of the war. Much emphasis is placed in the coda upon Ormond's continuing role as counsellor even after he went blind. In fact he hosted at Kilkenny the council of war which planned the battle. Contemporary papers record how all the main English commanders who subsequently went on to achieve the great victory – the viceroy, Mountjoy, the Munster president, Sir George Carew, and the marshal of the army, Sir Richard Wingfield – all converged on Kilkenny Castle after news of the Spanish landing near Kinsale had reached them. For eleven days, from September 14th until the 25th, the old earl acted as their host and participated in their discussions. It is entirely possible that Ormond could have claimed that it was his input which produced the success. At any rate, given the care with which the poet was operating until the *recusatio*, it seems at the very least likely that he will have wanted his climax to be just that, and not the damp squib that it turned out to be. It might also be noted that a long section on the Kilkenny council of war would have presented O'Meara with the opportunity for a last great speech by the earl – the most important of his life and the most crucial to the protection of English rule which had been the leitmotif of his life and was the central theme of the *Ormonius*.

Imitating Vergil

The outlines of content in the 'Arguments' focus in Books 2 to 5 upon the series of (mostly military) events in which Ormond played a part. That of Book 1 is notably different. Here O'Meara advertises his introduction of divine machinery. Wyatt's rebellion and its threat to Mary's throne (as represented by O'Meara, at any rate) causes one of the Fates to complain to Jupiter that he is allowing the course of history already laid down as inevitable to be perverted (that Mary will reign for five years, Elizabeth for almost forty-five, and that James will then succeed). Jupiter replies that the Fates remain unmoved and that Wyatt will pay for his behaviour. He then sends Mercury to London, to Ormond, to encourage him to great deeds by displaying all his ancestors, now shining stars in the firmament, and recalling their great deeds for his instruction.

It will escape the attention of no one with the smallest acquaintance with the opening of Vergil's *Aeneid* that O'Meara based this scenario upon the conversation between Venus and Jupiter in Book 1 (223–96), which is followed immediately by the despatch of his messenger Mercury to Carthage to ensure a welcome in the hillsides for Aeneas (297–304). The roll-call of the Butlers, too, has a Vergilian analogue, of course, in the scene from Book 6 where Anchises reveals to Aeneas the *future* heroes of Rome (679–892).

An obvious effect aimed at by O'Meara here is the aggrandizement of his own hero by intertextual assimilation to Vergil's Aeneas. This strategy had been used by the Carolingian poet of *Karolus Magnus et Leo Papa*, but in a slightly different way, in that the comparison was meant to belittle Aeneas, the pagan king who had never founded Rome, as compared with the Christian Charlemagne, who was in the process of rebuilding Rome at Aachen.[43] O'Meara, however, does not, like the Carolingian poet (*pius Karolus* is his way of describing Charlemagne), make any verbal attempt to evoke Aeneas. It is Aeneas' status and his situation that the modern poet calls to mind and the role of the friendly gods in shaping his ends. Ormond is placed immediately on an elevated plane of being, where his actions are monitored and encouraged by the gods themselves. As well as the situation, verbal echoes constantly insist upon the parallelism. Take, for example, the opening of the scene between Clotho (the specific Fate involved, 'she who turns the spindle with her right thumb') and Jupiter (*Ormonius* I.199–206):

> Divûm pater atque hominum rex
> Constitit arce poli summa, terrasque iacentes   200
> Despiciens, quanti quatiant regna Angla tumultus
> Cernit, et ingentes iactantem pectore curas
> De tribus illa soror, dextro quae pollice fusum
> Volvit, adit, lachrymisque oculos suffusa rubentes
> Alloquitur sic. O qui res hominumque Deûmque   205
> Aeternis regere imperijs, atque ordine fixo
> Mandâras

> The father of the gods and king of men
> Stood at the heavens' highest citadel
> And, looking down upon the lands below
> Saw what great tumults shook the English realm.
> Him as he tossed great troubles in his heart
> That sister of the three Fates, whose right thumb
> The spindle turns, approached and, with her eyes
> Red and suffused with tears did thus address:
> 'You who had ordered the affairs of men
> And gods by eternal mandates to be ruled
> And order fixed . . .'

Now compare the model passage in *Aeneid* I. 223–30:

> *Et iam finis erat, cum Iuppiter aethere summo*
> *Dispiciens mare velivolum terrasque iacentis*
> *Litoraque et latos populos, sic vertice caeli*
> *Constitit et Libyae defixit lumina regnis.*
> *Atque illum talis iactantem pectore curas*
> *Tristior et lacrimis oculos suffusa nitentis*
> *Adloquitur Venus: O qui res hominumque deumque*
> *Aeternis Regis imperiis et fulmine terres*

> This episode was already at an end,
> When Jupiter looked down from highest heav'n
> Upon the ship-strewn sea, upon the lands
> Below, the shores and peoples broadly spread,
> And as he stood thus at sky's peak he fixed
> His eyes upon the Libyan realms below.
> Him as he tossed such troubles in his heart,
> Venus, sad, with her eyes suffused with tears,
> Addressed: 'O you who order the affairs
> Of gods and men by everlasting power
> And terrify all with your thunderbolt'

The echoes are very strong (and do not end here: compare also *Aeneid* 10.2f.). A modern reader might say 'too strong'. On the contrary, however, the closeness here seems quite deliberate and serves its purpose in a very efficient manner. It is central to O'Meara's purpose to elevate Ormond's deeds to the level of the greatest classical hero and the echoes simply insist upon the reader's evocation of the famous intertext. Any other explanation leaves O'Meara open to the charge of plagiarism, which would have been ineffably stupid (and not what he appears to have done in the prooemium), especially for an audience which, if it had read no other epic, would certainly have read (and probably learned by heart) the *Aeneid*.

O'Meara performs a similar trick earlier, in his use of a Vergilian arming scene (from *Aeneid* 7.623ff.) to describe the preparations of Wyatt's soldiers for battle in the immediate aftermath of his rousing speech at the walls of Rochester:

> *His furiata cohors imas accensa medullas,*
> *In scelus extemplo conspirant: cuncta furentes*
> *Expediunt quae bella petunt: mordacibus enses*
> *Cotibus exacuunt: nervis melioribus arcus*   145
> *Tendunt: electis pharetras implere Sagittis*
> *Cura erat: aurum splendorem lancea saxi*
> *Accipit; auget eques stimulis calcaria: pingui*

Arvina leves clypeos, et spicula tergent
Pars: pars tela novant: alij thoracas ahenos   150
Et galeas, auri specioso lumine caelant.

His cohort, fired
And maddened to the marrow by these words,
Conspire at once in crime. In furious rage
They ready all that war demands: their swords
With biting stones they sharpen, and their bows   185
They fit with better strings: their quivers to fill
With chosen shafts is now their care: the lance
Receives its shine by rubbing on a rock;
The knight improves his spurs by adding spikes;
Some wipe smooth shields and javelins with rich fat;   190
Some repair weapons; others their bronze cuirass
And helmet chase with the fine light of gold.

Compare the Vergilian passage:

Ardet inexcita Ausonia atque immobilis ante;
Pars pedes ire parat campis, pars arduus altis
Pulverulentus equis furit; omnes arma requirunt.
Pars levis clipeos, et spicula lucida tergent
Arvina pingui subiguntque in cote secures;
Signaque ferre iuvat sonitusque audire tubarum.
Quinque adeo magnae positis incudibus urbes
Tela novant . . .
            alii thoracas aenos
Aut levis ocreas lento ducunt argento.

Ausonia, unroused and unmoved before
Burns; some prepare to march upon the plains
On foot, while others high on lofty steeds
Rage, swathed in dust; all ask for arms. Some wipe
With fat of lambs their smooth shields and bright darts,
And put their axes' edges to the stone;
They joy to bear the standards and to hear
The trumpet's blast. Their arms do now renew
Upon the anvil five cities of size . . .
            Others gild
Bronze breastplates or smooth greaves with silver slow.

As we have already claimed, O'Meara clearly intends his model to be
evoked by the reader – at any rate he would have been mad to believe that
he could get away with staying so close and not bringing to mind the
Vergilian passage. In fact, it will be clear from looking at the two excerpts
above that the modern poet has both retained specific reminiscences so as

to bring the Vergilian passage to mind (*levis clypeos* 'smooth shields'; *alii thoracas aenos* 'others (gild) bronze breastplates') and carefully crafted his piece to reflect modern weaponry. Note that there are no bows in Vergil, but the longbow was still a crucial weapon at this point in the sixteenth century.[44] Wyatt's soldiers sharpen swords, still essential in an age when the personal firearm was in its infancy (and part of the equipment of the *regular* army), while Vergil's sharpen axes. The knights in O'Meara are getting ready what is clearly a contemporary device – a spur with a central boss to which spikes are added when battle, rather than simple display of status, is in question. Wyatt's men are gilding cuirasses and helmets, not silvering cuirasses and greaves, and while the essence of this activity is probably – as in Vergil – idle and wasteful display, the distinction in weaponry is important: Tudor soldiers were armed with cuirasses and helmets – not with greaves. Shields and javelins were both part of the armour of the sixteenth and seventeenth centuries and greasing them part of the normal maintenance procedures. In Vergil, the *lancea* (lance), a crucial feature of the early modern armoury, is significantly missing, and the *spicula* of O'Meara's text would probably bring to mind a quite specific type of short javelin: as schoolboys, his readers would have learned the modern equivalences.

O'Meara's literary purpose goes a step further. When one asks why it is that he takes such care to remodel this specific passage and yet to ensure its outlines are still visible, one receives a clear answer from the intertext. In Vergil, this arming is done by the opponents of Aeneas, at the behest of Allecto: in other words, this is a rebel army. Wyatt's army is also an illegitimate force, called into being by Stygian forces, and this comparison has already been evoked by the question at 56–7 of what Erinys or Furies motivated Wyatt to his crime and also in a long simile borrowed from the action described at *Aeneid* 323ff (Allecto is roused to incite war with Aeneas by Juno) at *Ormonius* 69ff. Here too, then, is probably the reason why Wyatt's men have no firearms – weapons of the legitimate armed forces and not easily available to renegades.

Gaelic games

Yet, as has been mentioned, this intertextuality embraces not only classical and early modern Latin poetry. It also reaches into the Gaelic bardic tradition, for its genre (the *caithréim*) and for at least one literary motif. In Book 1, Ormond has been operating in England. Book 2 sees him return to Ireland. The motivation for this return is given in a dream, which Jupiter sends Morpheus, the shape-shifter, god of dreams, to reveal. However, unlike the undisguised epiphany in Book 1, Morpheus appears here as Hibernia (*Ormonius* II.1–26):

Condignos hic ille diu dum carpit honores,
Tristia cimerias linquit penetralia valles
Morpheus: hoc illi rector superûmque hominumque
Imperat; et nullos strepitus facientibus alis
Per tenebras volitans, intra breve tempus in urbem   5
Londini vehitur, positisque e corpore pennis,
Faemineam adsimulat faciem, tellusque Dynastae
Ormonio apparens Hyberna: his solverat ora:
Nate decus, viresque meae, mea gloria magna,
Tantane te subito cepere oblivia nostri?   10
Tantane Brutiadum telluris gratia? post hac
Ut non nativas digneris, visere sedes.
Usque adeone tuam comes illustrissime mentem
Arbitrer ingratam? te plus debere fatebor,
Quam mihi, Brutigenis. Genetrix est Anglia stirpis   15
Prima tuae; primos at ego, licet omine fausto,
Faelicique, tuos alui compulsa parentes.
Sceptra sed ignoras an nunc Hyberna Britannis
Sic annexa? premant ut qui me cumque Britannos
Quin laedant non posse: et qui me iuverit, Anglos   20
Laedere quod nequeat. Si me non visere nostri
Ergo dignaris, moveat Britannia ad oras
Te properare meas. Placida nunc pace fruuntur
Munere nate tuo Angligenae: civilia deme
Hybernis sic bella, quibus per plurima nunquam   25
Lustra carere, tui nisi cum vetuere parentes.

While Ormond here for long received due praise,
Morpheus relinquished the Cimmerian Vale,
His grim abode (thus had his order come
From the controller of both gods and men).
His wings were silent as he flitted through   5
The darkness and within a little space
Was borne to London city, where he laid
Aside his body's feathers and put on
A female face, appearing as the land
Hibernia to the dynast Ormond. Thus   10
He spoke: 'My honoured son, my glory great,
My strength, has such a great forgetfulness
Of me suddenly taken hold of you?
Is pleasure in the land of Brutus' sons
So great that after this you will not deign   15
To visit more the place where you were born?
Am I to think, most famous Earl, your mind
Is so ungrateful? I'll confess you owe
To Brutus' sons more than to me. Your stock

Had England as its mother first. But I   20
Under compulsion, though with great good luck,
Fostered your first forefathers. Dost not know
That now Hibernia's sceptre is so tied
To Britain's that whoe'er oppresses me
Cannot but harm the Britons, and who helps   25
Cannot do harm to Englishmen? So if
For my own sake thou wilt not visit me,
Let Britain make thee hasten to my shores.
Because of you the English now have peace:
Thus rid the Irish of their civil wars,   30
Which they have never lacked for many years,
Unless it was at your forefathers' will.'

Scholars of Gaelic Irish literary traditions tell us that what we are seeing here is the transference of the idea of the *aisling* ('dream') into Latin hexameter poetry.[45] The *aisling* was always a female dream apparition and, though she has her counterparts in classical literature (in specific females, mortal or immortal, who visit people in their sleep), in the form of Ireland, she is quite specifically borrowed from the vernacular tradition.[46] European readers, of course, could not be expected to see this. But it will send a *frisson* of recognition down the backbone of anyone (obviously a Gaelic-speaking Latin reader) who does. Whether or not it would also have brought delight would have depended heavily on the reader's political views. In the seventeenth century the *aisling* began to represent Éire as a slave, and if O'Meara was picking up this notion, he was also turning it upon its head by having *Hibernia* accept and welcome the rule of the English sovereign – no slave she, but as Anglia says later, a *sister*. Part of the intrinsic interest of the *Ormonius*, then, is that it places itself quite deliberately across the boundaries of a classical, European genre and of a vernacular Gaelic literary tradition.

The significance of the *Ormonius*

What does *Ormonius* tell us? Where does its significance lie? Obviously enough, it is at one level a major Irish political poem of the early seventeenth century, and an outstanding example of the Irish loyalist tradition – a tradition that has as yet been little studied, and has been often misunderstood. Throughout, the various military deeds of the earl of Ormond are constantly celebrated within the context of unwavering loyalty to the English Crown. The fact that such an extended record of his loyalty was deemed necessary, however, indicates the poem's real purpose: to recapture under James I the special status and influence that

Ormond and the Butlers (and, by implication, other Irish loyalists) had previously enjoyed under Elizabeth I, but had since lost.

Accordingly, the central role played by Earl Thomas in the reduction of almost all of the major rebellions to afflict Elizabethan Ireland is recounted in detail, so that the earl and his Butler army – *not* the English army – emerges as the most effective instrument of royal power available to the Crown, a tool that should not, indeed must not, be discarded if the government wishes to secure the country properly. Apart from its sudden ending, in which Earl Thomas's crucial role in thwarting the greatest rebel of all, the earl of Tyrone, is left unfinished, the poem succeeds in portraying Ormond as a great military hero and Crown servant. But whether it succeeded in restoring the Butlers' fortunes is far less certain. Soon after Earl Thomas's death his successor as 11th earl, Walter Butler, was drawn into a long and ultimately doomed struggle with the Jacobean régime about the extent of his inheritance, and all across southern and eastern Ireland the Butler interest was systematically reduced. Though other factors were involved, the principal reason for this was religion, the Butlers and the vast bulk of their supporters being fervent Catholics.

Tellingly, *Ormonius* attempted to ignore religion completely, stressing instead what O'Meara and his patron deemed to be much safer secular virtues, such as bravery and swordsmanship. By 1615 such virtues had become outmoded. While military service was still important for securing political influence, it was now only acceptable if performed by Protestants. Distinguished past service was all very well, but henceforth, and for many years to come, the royal government would view the very idea of Catholic loyalism as a contradiction in terms. As it happens, the Butlers only returned to favour in the person of the *Protestant* 12th earl of Ormond, James, who signed a letter in 1642 accusing Dermot O'Meara of high treason.[47]

On another level, as a work of literature, *Ormonius* was rather more successful. Its language is, by and large, that of classical epic, with Vergil, Ovid, Claudian and Silius Italicus looming large. But in some crucial and interesting ways, it is an Irish poem, for all its classical language and trappings. Significantly, it translates the *caithréim* of the bardic tradition into the language of European culture.

5. 'Making Ireland Spanish':
the political writings of Philip O'Sullivan Beare[1]

HIRAM MORGAN

The forcing-ground for the neo-Latin literature of early modern Ireland was provided by the universities of Counter-Reformation Europe. From the 1570s onwards Irishmen seeking a Catholic education necessarily went abroad and some of them had already established themselves as academics when young noblemen such as Philip O'Sullivan Beare (c.1590–1636) began to arrive in exile. Philip was educated at the University of Santiago de Compostela. 'Ubi ego Patritio Sinoto (Patric oig Sinot) populari meo, grammatico, et rhetorico polito, et limato Latinae linguae . . . sum usus' (Here I studied under my countryman Patrick Sinnott, a polished and finished grammarian and rhetorician of the Latin language).[2] While he also praised the teaching he received there in other disciplines from Spanish professors, it is evident from the correspondence appended to his publications that Philip continued to be mentored by this compatriot who had fostered his literary and astronomical interests and in particular his passion for Irish history. Whereas Sinnott's writings were never published, a substantial part of Philip's work was and it dealt with the major areas of debate then exciting the Irish intelligentsia. The need for extensive research on O'Sullivan has been highlighted by recent ground-breaking articles by Dr Clare Carroll. Her work on O'Sullivan's *Historiae Catholicae Iberniae Compendium* (Lisbon, 1621) has emphasized his debt to Spanish Counter-Reformation historiography and to the natural law theories of Las Casas and Suarez.[3] Over the past 150 years there has been editorial and translation work on O'Sullivan by Matthew Kelly, J.C. O'Callaghan, M.J. Byrne and T. O'Donnell.[4] The present work, however, would not have been possible without the contextual work on the O'Sullivans in Spain by Micheline Kerney Walsh and more recently that undertaken by Ciarán O'Scea.[5]

Philip O'Sullivan was born on Dursey Island off the tip of the Beara Peninsula in County Cork about 1590. After the defeat at Kinsale, and while his father Dermot and his cousin Donal Cam, the leader of the O'Sullivan insurgency, remained fighting a rearguard action, Philip was evacuated to Galicia. At La Coruña he and other refugees were received and assisted by Luis de Carillo, the count of Caracena and governor of Galicia. Philip was subsequently joined by his father, who was granted a pension of 50 crowns a month from the Spanish authorities. Philip himself obtained the degrees of Master of Arts and Bachelor of Canon Laws before being expelled from the Irish College in Santiago – which Donal Cam had established as a residence for Irish nobles – for opposing its takeover by the Jesuits. Instead of proceeding to ordination, Philip emerged in the second half of the 1610s as one of a group of hawkish Irish Catholics headed by Donal Cam O'Sullivan and Fr Florence Conry, the archbishop of Tuam, who were petitioning Philip III for renewed Spanish military intervention in Ireland. It was as a result of Philip's duel with John Bathe in 1618 that Donal Cam, coming upon the encounter, had his throat cut by Bathe. By this time Philip had completed most of the *Compendium* and by the time the book had passed the censors and was eventually published in 1621 he had already served two years in the Spanish navy fighting Moorish pirates. In the late 1620s, following the English attack on the navy's home port of Cadiz, he submitted to government a detailed plan for the conquest of Ireland. About the same time he completed the *Zoilomastix*, a polemic to counter the calumnies of Cambrensis and Stanihurst against Ireland.[6] In 1629 he published his second book, *Patritiana Decas* – a life of St Patrick. In a versified appendix to this, he took the opportunity to attack the Protestant Archbishop James Ussher who had referred to the author of the *Compendium* as 'the most egregious liar of any in Christendom'. This life of Patrick was intended to be the first of a number of saints' lives but only the life of St Mochua, published subsequently by the Bollandists, ever saw the light of day. A further huge work, the *Tenebriomastix*, was prepared by O'Sullivan to defend Ireland's saintly heritage against Scottish aggrandizement, but like the *Zoilomastix*, it remained in manuscript. Philip died without issue in 1636.[7]

Naturally it is O'Sullivan's 1621 *Compendium of the Catholic History* which deserves greatest attention, in that it is the most far-ranging of his works and because as a printed text in Latin it gained wider circulation and a longer-lasting impact. The book's target audience is identified in his preface to the Catholic reader. The central theme is the island's golden age of Christianity being eclipsed as a result of a savage and tyrannical persecution by English heretics. There is a chapter in the section of the book dealing with Tudor conquest where O'Sullivan publishes the verdicts of the doctors of Salamanca and Valladolid on the justice of the recent war. I want to highlight this section because it brings to attention the most important aspects of the *Compendium* – English Protestant tyranny, Irish divisions and Irish reliance on Spain. The doctors' decision in early 1603 came too late to have any influence on the course of the war but O'Sullivan was obviously eager to put it in print because it justified his own arguments.

The university dons and divines had been asked to decide whether O'Neill's war was just and should be supported and whether Irish Catholics, even if their lives or properties were threatened, had any justifiable grounds for assisting Queen Elizabeth's war effort. On the basis of Pope Clement VIII's indulgence of 1600, which declared that the English war against the Catholic religion was unjust and the Irish Catholics opposing it should have the same graces as if they were resisting the Turks, the doctors inferred that

> *At nemini licet iniquo bello favere, aut illi adesse sub poena aeternae damnationis. Peccant ergo gravissime Catholici, qui in castris haereticorum contra praedictum principem pugnant in bello aperte iniquo, et iniusto, et omnes, qui eidem bello favent armis, aut commeatibus, aut quacumque alia ratione, quae per se belli progressum juvent, nec possent rationem inire indifferentis obsequii.*[8]

> No man is justifiable in abetting an unjust war or taking part in it, under pain of eternal damnation. Consequently Catholics sin most grievously who in the camp of the heretics fight against the aforesaid prince in a war palpably iniquitous and unjust; as do all those who aid the same war either with arms or provisions or by any other means whatsoever, which in themselves may help in the progress of the war; nor might they be able to plead the excuse of indifferent loyalty for doing so.

The doctors further stated that the Catholic loyalists in Ireland had no 'surreption' or exemption from the pope. The doctors concluded:

> *Ex quibus omnibus satis manifestum relinquitur, illustrissimum principem Hugonem O'Nellum, et alios Catholicos Iberniae bellum gerentes adversus reginam Haereticam orthodoxam fidem oppugnantem nullo modo rebelles esse, neque debitam obedientiam negare, aut terras reginae injuste usurpare, quin potius illos justissimo bello se, terramque suam ab iniqua, et impia tyrannide vindicare, sacramque orthodoxam fidem (ut Christianos, ac Catholicos decet) pro viribus tueri, atque defendere.*[9]

> From all these circumstances it remains clearly manifest that the most illustrious prince Hugh O'Neill and the other Catholics of Ibernia who wage war against an heretical queen, assailing the orthodox faith, are by no means rebels, nor refuse a due obedience or unjustly usurp the

lands of the queen, but on the contrary that they rather by a most justifiable war defend themselves and their own land from an iniquitous
and impious tyranny and maintain and defend the sacred orthodox
faith to their utmost, as it behooves Christians and Catholics to do.

The doctors' verdict – drawn as it was from the well of Spanish natural
law theory – vindicated, firstly, the rights of the Irish people by pointing
to the iniquities of English heretic rule in Ireland. Secondly, it showed
Irish reliance upon Spain, which in this instance meant the need for
public and authoritative justification because of the pope's failure to
excommunicate Catholics loyal to Elizabeth and by extension his similar
failure to rescind the alleged grant of sovereignty made by his twelfth-
century English predecessor, Adrian IV, under the bull *Laudabiliter*.
Thirdly, by backing the valiant struggle in Ireland for Catholicism and
condemning those loyal to the queen, the Spanish doctors justified
O'Neill's historic demand – and O'Sullivan's current one – for unified militant action against England by Irish Catholics. I now wish to show how
these three points were amplified throughout O'Sullivan's *Compendium*.

The first point is about the political injustices and religious persecution which the Irish suffered as a result of English rule. To strengthen his
contention on these matters, O'Sullivan sought to prove *a priori* that the
English Crown had no right to sovereignty in Ireland. English knights
had originally entered Ireland to support an adulterer, Dermot McMur-
rough, the exiled king of Leinster.[10] More to the point, O'Sullivan claimed
in a chapter entitled 'Do the English hold Ireland justly?' that their title
was a fraud because the papal bull *Laudabiliter* had been obtained by
deception, Henry II having gained the grant by supplying the pope with
false information about the morals of the Irish. He further claimed that
Henry had not been made lord of Ireland but merely the pope's tax collector there and that the Irish kings had received him as such rather than
submit to him as their sovereign. The Irish had accepted the papal bull
and even gave over a revolt under the threat of excommunication from
Legate Vivien because they were faithful servants of the Apostolic See.[11]

> *Hoc vero constituo quod eos omni jure, justitiaque prorsus privat, pontificis
> diploma fuisse falsa relatione surreptum ut aeque sit hoc infirmum et poste-
> riora summorum pontificum rescripta quae hujus robore nituntur invalida
> et nulla. Cujus rei minime leve argumentum est, quod tale quale hoc est,
> nunquam sedes Apostolica scienter concessit. Neque enim credi potest,
> animo pontifici fuisse, Iberniae imperium transferre in externum, qui ad id
> nullo jure vocabatur, superstitibus Ibernis ortis regio sanguine, regulis sin-
> gulorum partium, et Rotherico, qui totius insulae monarcha nonnullis
> colebatur. Hos viros christianissimos, qui ne transversum unguem ab*

*ecclesia unquam discesserunt, num per prudentiam papa haereditate abdi-
caret? Num Pontifex Anglum creaverit Iberniae dominum causa dirimendi
Ibernorum procerum controversias? Non – namque similis rei mentio non
fit in litteris, nec ratio est satis apta, cum ad id Henrici Regis authoritas
minime suffecerit, pontificis autem satis fuerit, cujus nutu motus Ibernorum
in ipsum Henricum, et ejus successores saepe sunt sedati.*[12]

This fact I do indeed establish, which utterly deprives them of all right
and justice, that the papal bull was wrongly obtained on the basis of a
false report, with the result that it is without authority, and later
rescripts of the popes which rely on the strength of this are null and
void. Not the least proof of this matter is that the Apostolic See never
knowingly granted this right, whatever it may be. For neither can it be
believed that it was the pope's intention to transfer the rule of Ireland
to a foreigner who was not called to it by any right, while there survived Irishmen sprung from royal blood, petty kings of individual
parts, and also Ruaidrí, who was regarded by some as monarch of the
whole island. Would the pope in his prudence deny their inheritance
to these most Christian men, who never deviated from the Church
even by a nail's breadth? Surely the pope did not make the king of
England lord of Ireland in order to settle the quarrels of Irish chieftains? No! – for there is no mention of a similar situation in literature,
nor is there any sufficiently fitting explanation, since the authority of
King Henry was not enough for this rule, and yet the authority of the
pope was enough: for at his beck the risings of the Irish against Henry
himself and his successors were often quietened.

Not only had the bull been obtained fraudulently, but the conditions on
which the English king had accepted it had ever since been systematically broken. The English king had agreed to promote morality and
Christian worship among the people and to protect the rights and extend
the possessions of the Church. However, in each instance O'Sullivan
claimed that the English had achieved the exact opposite.[13] O'Sullivan
also recited the letter of Pope John XXII to Edward II in 1318 com-
plaining that the English Crown had transgressed the conditions of the
original grant by oppression of the Irish and insisting that the discrimi-
natory situation should be rectified by reform.[14] The implication here was
that the English treatment of the Irish made a mockery of the idea of a
Christian conquest upheld by *Laudabiliter.*

It is hardly surprising that, since English title to Ireland was, in
O'Sullivan's interpretation, illegitimate, English rule of the country
should likewise be claimed as unjust. Here, in a short and strikingly innovative passage, he made full use of the natural law theories developed by
Spanish Counter-Reformation theologians and jurists. The Irish were
denied rights in their own land being unable to sit in parliament or hold

civic office. They were not citizens, rather they had to become 'denizens' either by grant or application; in effect the Irish had to be naturalized in their own country.

> *Igitur quadam juris Anglici fictione, antiqui Iberni non indigenae sed exteri nasci, et hospites in sua patria esse reputabantur. Quae lex juri gentium et naturali apertissime adversatur, cum contrariam, ut in sua quisque patria civis, in alienis vero finibus hospes habeatur, divina quadam providentia constitutam omnes gentes, etiam Gentiles et barbarae firmam, immutabilemque custodiant.*[15]

Therefore, by a kind of fiction of English law, the ancient Irish were held to be born not native but foreign, and to be guests in their own country. This law most openly contradicts the law of nations and the natural law. The opposite to this law, a law by which each man is held to be a citizen of his native land and a guest in foreign territories, is upheld by all nations, even pagan and barbarian, as fixed and immutable and established by a kind of divine providence.

Furthermore, the Irish lords inaugurated by their customary law were denied the right to sit in parliament:

> *Unde deducitur omnia Parlamenta in Ibernia Britannorum regum authoritate coacta, deincepsque pristino more celebranda, prorsus irrita, infirma, injusta, violenta esse.*[16]

From this it follows that all the parliaments assembled in Ireland by the authority of the British kings, and successively solemnized by ancient custom, were invalid, unsound, unjust and violent.

Later in the book this argument allowed O'Sullivan to assert that Henry VIII's grant of kingship from the Irish parliament – in spite of the presence of two Irish chieftains there – was spurious:

> *illa donatio, in qua fraus inerat, quae metu fuit facta, fuerit invalida, et inutilis, quod illi duo primores Iberni non potuerint etiamsi vellent, regni jus in alium transferre, cum ipsi non plus juris, quam alii multi habuerint: nec etiam magnates possent Iberniae Regem externum creare sine populi consensu, et forsitan summi Pontificis authoritate.*[17]

that concession, which contained a fraud within itself and which was effected by fear, was invalid and useless because those two Irish chieftains could not, even if they wished, have transferred the right of kingship to another, since they themselves had no more right than many others; nor could the chiefs make a foreigner king of Ireland without the consent of the people, and perhaps the authority of the Supreme Pontiff.

The most blatant denial of natural right was that the killing of an Irish non-citizen was not regarded as a homicide under English law but merely a felony. O'Sullivan Beare had found this admitted to in Sir John Davies' *Discovery of the true causes why Ireland was never properly subdued until your Majesties happie reign* (London, 1612) and directed the reader to it.[18] Carroll has noted the telescoping of history as a particular technique of O'Sullivan's argumentation.[19] In this instance O'Sullivan shifts suddenly to contemporary politics, to 'surrender and regrant' and claims that it was a sleight of hand, whereby the Gaelic lords, far from being restored with ownership of the land, were merely granted its usufruct.[20] This interpretation based on information drawn from Davies – who also practised the merging of medieval and modern history – had the effect of turning English justifications from the likes of Davies on their head. The content of O'Sullivan's argument is very close to the ideas of popular sovereignty developed by revolutionary Huguenots and Catholic populists in the course of the French wars of religion.[21] Indeed, though O'Sullivan is plainly trying to uphold the rights of the Gaelic lords in Ireland, there is an obvious implication that their authority, too, ultimately resides in the people. This analysis harks back to the author's discussion of Gaelic inauguration in a section on the customs of the Irish which formed part of his introduction. The inauguration of the lord, whereby he took on sovereign rights and responsibilities, is depicted by O'Sullivan as contractual with judges, churchmen and people in attendance.[22]

Clare Carroll notes the constant refrain of 'heretics' and 'heresy' in this Counter-Reformation polemic.[23] The heretics in O'Sullivan's narrative were the English. They had a history of heresy:

> *Quam sit Angliae regnum religione inconstans, novitatis studiosum, erroribus contaminabile vel eo potest colligi quod Angli postquam in Christianorum album nomen dederunt, per primos quingentos, septuaginta quinque annos septies, vel ex magna parte fuerint Catholicae fidei desertores, ut ex Ecclesiastica Historia Bedae venerabilis, et sancti viri liquido constat.*[24]

> How inconstant is the kingdom of England in the matter of religion, how eager for novelty, how vulnerable to error, can be gathered from the fact that the English, in the first five hundred and seventy-five years after they entered their names into the register of Christians, were, at least in great part, deserters from the Christian faith, as is clearly established by the Ecclesiastical History of Bede, a venerable and holy man.

From the first occasion of Christianity in Britain in AD 156 until its conversion by Irish monks, the inhabitants of England had suffered Arianism and Pelagianism as well as reversions to paganism. After the time of Bede there is again in O'Sullivan's argument a collapsing of the remote past and contemporary developments. Henry II had killed Thomas Beckett; Henry VIII in breaking from Rome had killed Thomas More and the Carthusians and Elizabeth, despite the virtuous efforts of Queen Mary, had returned England 'to its old vomit'.[25] By contrast with the English,

> *Iberni vero quam firmi, stabilesque sint in Religione Catholica . . . cum ab*
> *orthodoxa fide, pontificumque summorum ductu, et imperio nunquam sese*
> *subduxerint; neque subducant, cum persecutio est longe maxime vehemens*
> *et atrox.*[26]

> It is quite clearly established however . . . how firm and stable the Irish are in the Catholic religion, since they never seceded from the orthodox faith and from the leadership of the popes; nor do they secede in the present time, in which the persecution is by far the most severe and savage.

This line not only reversed the historical calumnies of the likes of the twelfth-century ecclesiastic Giraldus Cambrensis;[27] it was also guaranteed to antagonize contemporary Anglicans, the most notable example being Archbishop James Ussher.

The religious situation had been getting steadily worse since Henry VIII broke with Rome and confiscated the lands of the monasteries. The king had ordered the Irish lords to take over these lands and evict the monks.[28] O'Sullivan claimed most of them and their Anglo-Irish equivalents had in fact left the monasteries untouched. Others were on the make, though, and had benefited from the dissolution. Here he cited the case of the Eustaces of Baltinglass who had taken monastic lands. Though pious, indeed zealous, these Catholics had ended up in exile, destitute of property. Evidently they had been punished by God for their greed.[29] Indeed such individual desire for aggrandizement was the reason why the Irish were unable to unite over the previous eighty years against the heretic foreigner.[30] A dynamic new element in the equation had been introduced when Pope Pius V excommunicated Queen Elizabeth and demanded that her subjects remove her.

> *Hinc a multis Ibernis saepe capiuntur arma pro religionis jure: omnia ferro*
> *et flamma devastantur, et corrumpuntur.*[31]

> Because of this many Irishmen often took up arms for the rights of religion: everything was laid to waste with fire and sword, and reduced to ruin.

The English had quickly realized the country's steadfast adherence to Catholicism meant that the cause of religion was a potential source of unity among the Irish. Therefore to destroy them, they had decided to single out the Catholic lords one by one, by accusing them of treason. When a revolt was in progress, the English cleverly reduced the level of persecution in order to prevent a general rising:

> *Partim hac calliditate, partim domesticis bellis quae alii cum aliis gerebant, Catholicorum vires extinguuntur. Clarissimos eorum, qui hac lite vel perierunt, vel contenderunt, eorum aliquas res gestas, ruinamque referemus temporum ordinem sequentes.*[32]

> The strength of the Catholics was destroyed, partly by this cunning and partly by the internal wars which they were waging against one another. Keeping to a chronological order, we shall make reference to the most famous of those who perished under this legal assault and those who contested it, together with some of their achievements and downfalls.

O'Sullivan's account of the Tudor conquest was indeed the usual sequence of the Kildare revolt, war in the midlands, Shane O'Neill's revolt, the Desmond wars and finally the nationwide struggle led by Hugh O'Neill and Red Hugh O'Donnell. What distinguishes the *Compendium*'s version are the stories of heroic Catholic martyrs and the treacherous, sacrilegious and bloody dealings of English heretics. O'Sullivan listed twenty-six bishops and priests who had suffered martyrdom, most famously Primate Richard Creagh, Bishop Dermot O'Hurley and Bishop Cornelius O'Devany.[33] The stoic deaths of such martyrs often result in miraculous cures or conversions. In the wars with the English, the prophecies of ancient Irish saints which hitherto made no sense suddenly gained meaning and potency. For instance, O'Sullivan's attributes the explosion which destroyed the English garrison constructed in the monastery of St Columba at Derry to a miracle foretold in one of prophecies of the saint. Furthermore, Irish allied to the heretics suffered mishaps, like Calvach O'Donnell, who, assisting the Derry garrison, died young in a fall from his horse.[34] The heretics themselves get their comeuppance. The perpetrator of the massacre of Mullaghmast and keeper of the hanging tree at Stradbally, where he hanged children from their mother's hair, is noted among the dead at Glenmalure in 1581 as that 'crudelem *Catholicorum carnificem Franciscum Cosbium Lisiae praefectum*' (cruel butcher of Catholics, Francis Crosby, governor of Leix).[35] The best example is the death of Sir John Norris after his removal from the management of the English war effort in 1597:

> *namque sicuti fertur Moalae (Mallow) cum noctu luderet, quidam, corpore vestibusque Niger, in conclave improviso intrat, quocum Norris, ludo*

relicto, sese in cubiculum abdidit, amotis arbitris praeter unum puerum qui juxta ostium clam consistens colloquium audivit, quod hujusmodo fuisse traditur. Niger, 'Tempus est,' inquit, 'ut rationibus nostris summam manum imponamus.' 'Noli,' inquit Norris, 'id facere, donec Ibernicum bellum confectum relinquamus.' 'Nullo modo,' inquit ille, 'diutius expectabo, quia constituta dies jam cessit.' Mox strepitus ingens sonat, quo moti lusores et domestici, cum cubiculum foribus effractis ingressi fuissent, Nigro, qui quin Diabolus fuerit non dubitatur, nullibi reperto, Norrissem invenerunt genibus flexum, colloque et cervice ita tortum, ut occiput pectori et os dorso immineret, sed adhuc vivum, atque jubentem aeneatores tibicines et tympanistas convocari, ut ipsius mortem cantu celebrarent, quibus canentibus intra dimidiam horam animam profudit. Ejus corpus aromatibus atque fragrantissimis odoribus curatum in Angliam transfertur. Quem ego casum memoria repetens equidem dementia haereticorum obstupefio, cadaver, hominis impii honore magno colentium, sacra vero divorum martyrum inhumata projicientium. Licet etiam colligi quantam Deus optimus maximus O'Nello praelianti operam tulerit, qui non modo Norrissem, peritissimum Anglorum imperatorem, omni pugnandi apparatu superiorem, saepe profligaverit, sed ipsum etiam Diabolum, qui illi ex pacto fuisse opitulatus creditur, vicerit.[36]

It is said that as he was amusing himself by night at Mallow, a person of black visage and garments suddenly entered the room, with whom Norris, leaving his game, retired into his bedroom, whence all witnesses were excluded except one boy, who concealed himself near the door and heard the conversation which is said to have been somewhat as follows: 'It is time,' said the Black one, 'for us to put the finishing touch to our accounts.' 'I do not wish to do it,' said Norris, 'until we have wound up the Irish war.' 'On no account,' said the other, 'will I wait longer than the appointed day which is now come.' Suddenly a great uproar was heard, attracted by which, those at play and servants forced the door and burst into the room, when the Black one, who undoubtedly was the Devil, was nowhere to be found, but Norris was on his knees with his neck and shoulders so twisted that the back of his head was over his chest and his face was over his back. He was, however still living and ordered the trumpeters, pipers and drummers to be called to sound his death-knell, and whilst they were clamouring, he died about midnight. His body was embalmed with aromatic and fragrant perfumes, and sent into England. Apropos of this incident, I am amazed at the folly of the heretics in bestowing this great honour on the corpse of an impious man, while they scatter the relics of saintly martyrs. It may, however, be seen how much the good God helped O'Neill in not only defeating Norris, the most skilled of the English generals and superior in every warlike equipment, but even in conquering the Devil himself, who it is thought agreed to help Norris.

Since Luther had unleashed the Reformation, the Irish had, because of their adherence to Catholicism, been increasingly subject to religious persecution. What had been intermittent because of the wars in Elizabeth's reign had now become systematic under King James.[37] The colonial government issued proclamations from time to time against priests and their protectors but O'Sullivan reveals the prosecution being pursued mainly through a perverted judicial process. This involved explaining to the Catholic reader the workings of the English legal system in Ireland. Lay Catholics could not get justice from English judges, having been falsely accused and refused legal representation. They were placed in a dilemma by demands that they swear the oath of supremacy that the monarch was head of the Church. The juries were coerced and when they refused to convict they were replaced by colonists who had no standing in the community. Lying behind these judicial processes was a drive to find Catholics guilty and thereby confiscate their property. None of this was happening to Catholics in England who had the same legal system.[38] The implication here is that the persecution was compounded by a history of political and racial discrimination. O'Sullivan singled out sheriffs and commissioners as the most rapacious persecutors of Irish Catholics:

> *nervos omnes, et cogitationes intendunt, ut sacerdotes fugent, capiant, occidant et Catholicos omni vi, injuria, clade labefactent. Quod ut facilius consequantur, longa semper habent in suo comitatu, et amicitia sceleratissimorum hominum agmina: et haec nequissimorum atque perditissimorum hominum sentina nihil mali, vel sceleris fingi, aut excogitari potest, quod non in Catholicos concipiat.*[39]

> They stretch every nerve and thought to root out, capture and kill priests, and to ruin Catholics with every manner of violence, wrong and disaster. The more easily to achieve this, they always have in their company and friendship long lines of the most wicked men. And there is no evil, no crime that cannot be invented or thought up against Catholics by this sewer of worthless and dissolute humanity.

The Irish Catholics were able to endure such ferocious persecution because God was giving them the necessary fortitude as a reward for their scrupulous adherence to Catholicism in more peaceful and prosperous times.[40]

O'Sullivan's alternative to English rule in Ireland is to identify Ireland and the Irish with Spain at every possible opportunity. The *Compendium* is dedicated to Philip IV of Spain. He is 'the Catholic king' and Ireland is the only Catholic nation remaining in the north. O'Sullivan hopes, now that Philip from the outset of his reign has determined to take a warlike stand against the Dutch, that Catholic Ireland will also be a beneficiary of his policies.[41] Besides this, O'Sullivan recites the familiar Milesian myth that the Gaelic Irish race is descended from four sons of King Milesius of Spain.[42] This invasion, O'Sullivan reckoned, had taken place in 1342 BC and since then 181 kings of Spanish origin had ruled the whole country. The Irish nobility, like good Spaniards, had preserved their purity.[43] In an echo of the contemporary situation he cites the case of Eoghain Mór, a mythical pagan king of Munster, who is restored with the help of 3,000 Spaniards after he had fled to Spain and married the king's daugther.[44] Some of the Spanish links are stretched to their limit. Thus Ireland is being linked prior to the coming of Patrick with Spain's patron saint: 'Some there are who say that St James the son of Zebedee had come into this island.'[45] Another significant feature was O'Sullivan's rendering into Latin of the long account given by the Catalan Count Ramon of his visit to St Patrick's Purgatory in north-west Ireland and the subterranean tour he had there of Heaven and Hell. This not only served to connect Ireland with sound Counter-Reformation doctrine but also shows the fame of this place of pilgrimage as far away as Perpignan, which remained under Spanish sovereignty until 1659.[46] In 1593 Irish émigrés in Lisbon had tried to exploit interest in the Purgatory in order to promote Spanish support by proposing the establishment of a military order of St Patrick.[47] It seems that O'Sullivan's account provoked wider interest because a few years later Calderón wrote a play on the topic.[48] O'Sullivan stretched other points, noting that Murcia had a big St Patrick's day festival and that Lisbon had the holy relics of St Brigid.[49] Most importantly, to strengthen the identification with Iberia, Ireland throughout the *Compendium* is referred to as Ibernia rather than the more familiar Hibernia.

The Irish connection with Spain was far easier to affirm once O'Sullivan reached the contemporary situation. He mentioned that one of the first foreign missions of the Jesuit order, soon after it was founded by the Spaniard Ignatius Loyola, was to succour the faith in Ireland.[50] Later a familiar roll-call of events during the reigns of Elizabeth of England and Philip of Spain began.[51] The embassies of Fitzmaurice and Stukley to Spain and Rome were recalled, as was the disastrous sequel at Smerwick. The first Irish exiles, both lay and ecclesiastical, begin to seek refuge in Spain. The war in Ireland is not dated from the beginning of Maguire's revolt – the so-called Nine Years War – but instead from the wreck of the Spanish Armada in Ireland and the subsequent English execution of O'Rourke for assisting the survivors, becoming, as a result, the Fifteen Years War. Thus O'Sullivan makes the Spanish connection with Ireland part of the cause of the final conflict; implicitly he also rewrites the historiography of the Armada of 1588 by giving it some sort of result rather than a complete blank.[52] Then comes the embassy of O'Healy to Philip II in 1593–94 which ends in ship-wreck[53] and the intervention of the Spanish agents in the 1596 Anglo-Irish negotiations to establish instead a Spanish–Irish nexus.[54] One image which would have intrigued Spanish readers was O'Sullivan's account of the grisly death of Norris, England's most successful soldier in the war against Spain in the Netherlands.[55] Eventually a Spanish expedition lands at Kinsale but only to see the approaching Irish defeated. The actions of the Spanish commander Don Juan del Águila were not applauded.[56]

More than the historical details themselves, the *Compendium* affirms in several places the strategic importance of Ireland to Spain.[57] In emphasizing this, O'Sullivan barely mentions that Ireland had held a similar strategic importance to France until the 1560s. The only mention of this is a passing reference to O'Brien of Thomond's refusal of military assistance from the Most Christian King, Henry II.[58] At the outset of his book, after describing the position and amenities of Ireland in which he had claimed the country was twice the size it actually was, O'Sullivan asserted that the island was a potential fortress from which heretics might be vanquished:

> . . . *Iberniam, esse orbis terrarum arcem et propugnaculum, aut certe septentrionis, unde gentes aliae Monarchiae et Catholicae Religionis hostes debellari et obtineri, facile possent.*[59]

> Ibernia is the bulwark of the world, or certainly of the Northern portion of it, from whence other nations, foes to monarchy, and the Catholic religion could be easily conquered and held.

Since the days of the Romans, Ireland was a perceived threat to its neighbouring island and English administrators still held to this opinion. Control of the island would enable the Spanish navy to intercept English and Dutch fleets sailing westwards to attack Spanish merchant traffic or the king's treasure fleets or to establish colonies. The country's forests and general fertility promised ample naval stores. The European pirates currently sheltering on the rocky coast of Ireland would be evicted. Possession of Ireland would allow the reduction of first Scotland and then England; finally Holland would be subdued and heresy expunged: '*Ita tota Europa Catholica religione tranquilla et florentissima frueretur*' (Thus all Europe at peace and in the highest state of prosperity might enjoy the Catholic religion).[60] When the Irish delegation of 1593–94 were interviewed by Philip II they had sought to impress similar strategic principles on him.[61] Although O'Sullivan's analysis of 1618 has clear parallels with the memorial which Cerdá addressed to the Spanish state after he visited O'Neill and O'Donnell in 1600,[62] in this case he was obviously taking his cue from Chapter 24 of Tacitus' *Agricola*.[63] It had argued that Ireland could be easily conquered and that, being situated between Britain and Spain and near Gaul, the island would be of immense strategic value, not least in keeping the Britons in check.

Besides the strategic importance of Ireland to Spain, Philip went out of his way to emphasize the loyalty of the O'Sullivans of Beare to the Spanish cause. He began the section of contemporary history with a demonstration of O'Sullivan sea power. An episode in the reign of Henry VIII, unrecorded elsewhere so far as I know, is recounted, where Dermot O'Sullivan, Philip's grandfather, pursued an English fleet and hanged its commander after it had attacked the Spanish merchants and fishermen at the port of Dunboy.[64] Also in the aftermath of the Kildare rebellion, the same Dermot is recorded as having assisted the young Gerald Fitzgerald to escape abroad from the clutches of the English.[65] Philip attempted to assert a specific loyalty to Spain that went back as far as 1579. He asserts that 'Daniel O'Sullevanus adolescens, qui postea Bearrae princeps factus pro Hispanorum salute cum Anglis bellum gessit' (Donal O'Sullivan, a young man who was afterwards made chief of Beare, carried on war against the English for the protection of the Spaniards).[66] The so-called Spaniards here were the mainly Italian mercenaries paid for by the pope which Philip II had permitted to follow Fitzmaurice to Ireland. In the next chapter, Philip's father Dermot makes his appearance in pious mode as a pallbearer at the funeral of Fitzmaurice's religious advisor, the English Jesuit Nicholas Sanders.[67] During most of the Nine Years War the O'Sullivans were quiescent. When Águila arrived at Kinsale, they did not hasten to his side; rather, as Philip admitted, they refused the summons of the Lord Deputy Mountjoy to join him in the siege. They opted for the Spaniards only when Zubiaur arrived at Castlehaven and, under attack, actively requested their assistance.[68] Having saved the day, the O'Sullivans and O'Driscolls then turned over the castles as garrisons for Zubiaur's forces.[69] At the Battle of Kinsale, Philip O'Sullivan portrays Donal Cam O'Sullivan as an advocate of delay, supporting the prudent approach of O'Neill, but then when battle is joined he is portrayed as one of the last to leave the field there, fighting a rearguard action with the redoubtable Captain Richard Tyrrell.[70] Again after the departure of O'Neill and O'Donnell, O'Sullivan is depicted as rallying the Munstermen in an attempt to raise the English siege of Kinsale.

> Aquilae scribens, ne virtutem suam deserat, ne animo deficiat, neu oppidum tradat. Caeterum Aquila cum hoste faedus percusserat ea conditione, ut sibi liceret cum exercitu suo, et rebus omnibus in Hispaniam redire ... Ita Aquila revertitur amissis in ea expeditione quingentis peditibus, et Anglis in Keansaliae tantum obsessione desideratis amplius octo millibus, qui ferro, fame, frigore, pestilentiaque perierunt.[71]

He wrote to Águila not to lose courage or be dispirited, and not to surrender the town, but Águila had struck a bargain with the enemy,

> whereby he and his army and all their effects were at liberty to return
> to Spain . . . And so Águila returned, having lost in this expedition 500
> foot, and the English in the whole siege of Kinsale having lost more
> than 8,000, who perished by the sword, hunger, cold and pestilence.

There is a whole book of the *Compendium* devoted to Donal Cam
O'Sullivan's rearguard action after Kinsale.[72] Philip O'Sullivan's account
of the Munster war makes an interesting historiographical contrast with
the account given by Lord President Carew's natural son, Thomas Stafford
in *Pacata Hibernia* (London, 1633). Philip is very tactful with his Spanish
Catholic audience in not mentioning Águila's questionable surrender of
the O'Sullivan and O'Driscoll strongholds given over to Zubiaur in west
Cork. Instead Donal Cam merely redoubles his effort, strengthening
Munster resistance while sending Dermot O'Driscoll to request further
support from Spain with his eldest son Daniel as a surety of his commitment to Spain. By the time O'Driscoll returned from Spain with money
and munitions, O'Sullivan had already lost Dursey Island and Dunboy
Castle to the English. Soon after O'Sullivan, with the death of Red Hugh
O'Donnell in Spain and the desertion of his followers in Munster, began
his epic mid-winter retreat. In this 300 kilometre flight only 35 of the
1,000 refugees who left Bantry Bay reached Leitrim. Two interventions
apparently saved the O'Sullivans of Beare from oblivion. First there was
the ingenuity of the author's allegedly seventy-year-old father in getting
the party across the Shannon river in improvised horse-hide boats.[73]
Then there was the strange appearance of a white-robed figure to guide
the party to safety when it was lost in woody, mountainous terrain on the
last leg of the trek. This intervention was truly providential – the myste-
rious figure is clearly identified by his dress as one of the angelic
subterranean guardians of St Patrick's Purgatory, mentioned earlier in
Count Ramon's account, which had its entrance on an island in nearby
Lough Derg.[74] The remarkable thing about all this is that Philip III of
Spain eventually recompensed Donal Cam for his endeavours. He
received a large pension and was made count of Berehaven; from being a
relatively rich though decidedly second-rank Munster lord, O'Sullivan
became leader of the exiled Irish nobles in Spain. His son and surviving
heir, Dermot, went on to become a leading courtier to Philip IV.[75] At the
end of the book, Philip is still recording the loyal services of the O'Sullivans to the Spanish Crown – in 1619 the deaths of his brother Daniel and
his kinsman Cornelius O'Driscoll in a naval action against the Moors and
the author's own subsequent service in the Straits of Gibraltar. One irony
here is that the Spanish navy was now fighting alongside Dutch and
English squadrons in an effort to suppress north African piracy but Philip
O'Sullivan evinces considerable anxiety that these heretics are merely

awaiting an opportunity to make an unholy alliance with the Moslems.[76]

Spanish strategic interests in Ireland and the interests of Philip's own family had a subsequent consummation in the *presidio* scheme which Philip O'Sullivan proposed for his patrimony of Dursey Island after the English attack on Cadiz in 1625.[77] This document, written to Philip IV by Philip O'Sullivan, describing himself as Señor de Piñalba[78] in Ireland, is now in the Quai d'Orsay, Paris, among Spanish papers removed there in the Napoleonic era.

> As Your Majesty knows, and as the English themselves are aware of, Ireland offers the easiest means of attacking and destroying the English. I do not dwell on the obvious reasons for this but refer your Majesty to the reports which were submitted to Your Majesty's father (whom may God keep in his glory) and which passed through my hands. I shall only give here a plan for the easiest and safest way of conquering Ireland (leaving the English bound hand and foot) and a detailed account of the equipment and expenses involved.[79]

The plan, originally his father's and approved by the late Donal Cam O'Sullivan and Cornelius O'Driscoll, had been by mulled over by Philip while he was a student and during his time in the army and navy. In fact it shows the influence of the *presidios* by which Spain maintained garrisons in the Mediterranean and north Africa. The small island of Dursey, lying off the tip of the Beara Peninsula, would become a Spanish *presidio* in Ireland. The island, secure from the mainland, had timber, fresh water, arable land and shelter for fleets of up to 300 ships reaching it directly from Spain.

> Given a small garrison, all the navies and artillery in the world could not prevail against it, for there are only two narrow entrances or landing places which could be defended by two hundred men with twenty pieces of artillery. Neither the Rock of Velez, Malta, Rhodes nor Corfu is equal to the island of Dursey in strength of position.[80]

The garrison's presence, O'Sullivan asserted, would facilitate the conquest of Ireland and the eventual collapse of the Stuart monarchy.

Another factor relating to O'Sullivan's history is the question of its accuracy. O'Sullivan used as sources various hagiographies, martyrologies and works of Cambrensis, Camden, Davies, Rothe, Stanihurst and Spenser. O'Sullivan did not know that he had a manuscript by this famous planter-poet – only that he had a political treatise that discussed the extermination of Irish Catholics. He had acquired this manuscript via an Irish gentleman who, having come across the treatise in the house of Sir Robert Cecil, the earl of Salisbury, copied it out and made it available to his fellow countrymen. O'Sullivan was inclined to attribute this treatise, which because of its agenda had been 'industriously concealed' for a length of time, to 'crafty' Cecil himself. However, the bits of evidence he reproduces from it in the *Compendium* are clearly from Spenser's 1596 tract 'A View of the Present State of Ireland'.[81] In spite of the contents of New English writings, it is not against Spenser or Davies that O'Sullivan reacted so vehemently but rather against the work of the Old English Dubliner, Richard Stanihurst.[82] By contrast, the *Analecta Sacra* of David Rothe, the Old English bishop of Ossory, was a major source for O'Sullivan's account of the persecution of Catholics during James' reign.[83] The information derived from these printed and manuscript works was deployed selectively, and with the exception of Stanihurst, often none too critically. Apart from these sources, a good part of the *Compendium*, particularly its account of recent events, is derived from either the reports of participants or mere hearsay. As a result, much of the detail in O'Sullivan's history of Elizabethan and Jacobean Ireland is suspect and should always be corroborated if possible against other sources. O'Sullivan frequently gets the names of English and Scottish participants wrong. More fundamentally he always exaggerates the losses of the English in battle and minimizes those of the Irish. A good example of this is the revolt of Cahir O'Dogherty in 1608, which the *Compendium* expands into a prolonged, major Catholic threat to English security interests in Ulster.[84] Furthermore, the miracles and prodigies which attend the deaths of Catholic martyrs and the divine interventions which wreak God's vengeance on the profane, sacrilegious and tyrannical heretics, though there mainly to entertain, frighten and uplift the Catholic reader, damage the credibility of this Catholic history. Nevertheless the sheer scale of the Protestant assault on Catholicism in Ireland which O'Sullivan relates is hard to gainsay, and ironically his account of the Jacobean persecution contains a number of proclamations and documents no longer extant either in the Short-Title Catalogue or in the Public Record Office.

In fact, Philip O'Sullivan's strength is not details of fact but rather analysis and in this regard he makes an important historiographical contribution to why the Irish lose the war. They lose the war because of internal divisions.[85] It is stated that the Irish are beset by the sins of ambition, vainglory and homicide and that sin is the downfall of nations.

> *Si enim omnes Hiberni in Anglos conspirassent, ullo sine negocio possent haereticorum jugum cervicibus discutere: ut Angli ipsi communi assensione fatentur.*[86]

> If all the Irish had joined together against the English, they would without any trouble have shaken off the yoke of the heretics from their necks; as the English themselves state by common admission.

This idea was part of the analysis proffered as an introduction to the history of the Tudor conquest. The idea was repeated again in far greater depth at the start of the climactic Fifteen Years War.[87] The principal divisions were between the Ancient Irish, descended of Spanish blood, who fought, O'Sullivan claimed, for the Catholic faith; the New Irish of mixed English and Spanish blood who, though Catholic, fought mainly for the queen of England; and also the Catholic Anglo-Irish of the Pale who were wholly pro-English. These pro-English groupings had the most resources and controlled most of the towns in Ireland. On the other hand, O'Sullivan condemned many of the Irish chiefs who stood neutral or never made a concerted effort by all joining the fight at once – though interestingly English commentators had similar opinions about the luke-warmness of their Irish supporters. The big question was why so many pious Catholics not only sided with the English Crown but were willing to fight against their fellow Irish Catholics. O'Sullivan considered that '*Equidem puto fuisse hanc Iberniae paenam a Deo propter crimina Ibernorum inflictam*' (I think this must have been a punishment of God on Ireland for the crimes of Irishmen).[88] Some did not secede from the English because they followed the advice of their priests; some feared the example of retribution dealt out to past rebels; some were waiting for the death of the elderly queen in the expectation of toleration; some thought that since there was no wartime persecution of Catholics, their loyalty to the English Crown might be rewarded by religious toleration; some insisted that neither religion nor the pope's original grant of Ireland to the English Crown under the *Laudabiliter* bull were at stake. When the pope issued a letter encouraging the Catholic cause, they claimed it was a false representation. And by the time the doctors of Salamanca and Valladolid universities issued their 1603 judgement that the Catholics were fighting a just war in Ireland, the war was all but lost.

Not only had the Irish Catholics deluded themselves, but the English launched a number of stratagems to keep them onside. As soon as war broke out they had ceased all persecution of Catholic priests and harassment of Catholic worship. Although O'Sullivan did not know it, there were policy documents by Robert Cecil and Francis Bacon to this effect.[89] The English authorities encouraged the Irish of English descent to think that the Irish coveted their property and had their preachers rehearse the black legend about '*Hispanorum inauditam crudelitatem et leges iniquas*' (the unheard-of cruelty of the Spaniards and the unjustness of their laws).[90] The English were also willing to grant pardons more than once in wartime, whereas in peacetime it was their policy to dredge up false accusations. Besides these political measures, the English also employed a scorched earth policy to induce famine and want, from which everyone suffered; furthermore, they debased the currency in 1601 (the English equivalent of Philip III's *vellón* issue), which damaged all taxpayers, especially the merchant class.[91]

O'Sullivan was certain that the problems facing the Irish Confederates derived from the general division in Irish society might have been overcome . . .

> . . . *nisi alio majori, et intestino morbo confecti penitus delerentur. Quod plerorumque Catholicorum principum, qui se pro Catholica fide tuenda devoverunt, familiae, clientelae, municipes in contrarias factiones abibant, alii alios duces, atque dominos de principatu, et dominationis jure certantes secuti. Quorum minus potentes Anglorum partes amplectebantur spe obtinendi principem locum in familiis suis, si principes dominatione, principatuque deturbarent, spem illam Anglis callide praebentibus . . . Ea enim fuit ars una, qua potuerunt Angli Ibernorum principum vires contundere, quod eorum dignitates, atque vectigalia consanguineis ipsorum, qui clientes, atque socios ab illis subduxerunt, pollicebantur, nec tamen finito bello promissis steterunt.*[92]

> . . . had it not been that they were destroyed from within by another and greater internal disease. For most of the families, clans, and towns of the Catholic chiefs, who took up the defence of the Catholic Faith, were divided into different factions, each having different leaders and following lords who were fighting for estates and chieftaincies. The less powerful of them joined the English party in the hope of gaining the chieftainship of their clans, if the existing chiefs were removed from their position and property, and the English craftily held out that hope to them . . . There was one device by which the English were able to crush the forces of the Irish chiefs, namely, by promising their honours and revenues to such of their own kinsmen as would seduce their followers and allies from them, but when the war was over the English did not keep their promises.

These promises, according to O'Sullivan, had indulged the hopes of Con and Henry O'Neill, the sons of the great Shane, and Art, the son of Turlough Luineach, to fight against O'Neill; had provoked the greed of Niall Garbh O'Donnell to oppose Red Hugh, to the destruction of Tirconnell; and among his own relatives had encouraged the envy of Owen O'Sullivan against his cousin the O'Sullivan Beare. And so on, he might repeat six hundred examples:

> *Certe Iberni mei, quamvis Catholici fidei, religionisque divini cultu, et observantia plerisque gentibus praestent, hujus tamen belli tempore factione, dissidio, ambitione, perfidia Turcis et haereticis plurimi deteriores fuerunt. Idcirco fieri minime potuit, quin tot, tantisque discordiis Ibernia*

penitus devastaretur. Nam, ut Evangelii sacri oraculo proditur, 'Omne
regnum in se divisum desolabitur'.[93]

Assuredly, although my countrymen may stand high among the
nations in the profession of, and devotion to, the Catholic faith and
Divine religion, yet during the war, the majority were far worse than
Turks or heretics in faction, dissension, ambition and perfidiousness.
Wherefore, it could not be otherwise than that by so many and so
great distractions, Ireland should be utterly destroyed, for as the holy
Evangelist has it, 'Every kingdom divided against itself shall be
destroyed'.

Thus the Irish had never been united in their prosecution of the war and,
as it began to go awry, the chiefs leading the unequal struggle were
deserted by their main followers, who joined the English against them.

In his subsequent account of Ireland under King James, O'Sullivan
showed that all those individuals who, like Niall Garbh O'Donnell, had
assisted the English were in turn betrayed by them. Furthermore, the
pro-English Catholics, who had been treated with kid gloves by heretics
in the course of the war, now had to endure full-scale persecution. They
were defenceless, having failed to aid the martial strength of the Irish
nation. For O'Sullivan, they remained spineless and self-interested. He
was incensed that their representatives, having waged a fairly successful
campaign of obstruction at the 1613–15 parliament, should nod through
the illegal confiscation of the lands of the Gaelic lords of Ulster. In particular, he was annoyed at the advice they continued to receive from
some of their clergy.[94] It is probably for this reason that O'Sullivan
returned to the wartime role of the Anglo-Irish clergy in his conclusion to
the *Compendium*:

Cujus mali maxima culpa in aliquot Anglo-Ibernos sacerdotes jure trans-
ferenda est, qui tartareum dogma ab orco in Catholicorum perniciem
emissum non negabant, licere Catholicis contra Catholicos, et suam patriam
pro haereticis gerere arma, et dimicare. Quod si sacerdotes isti sana mente,
et cum caeteris in haereticis oppugnandis unanimes et concordes extitissent,
et Iberni alii aliis non obstitissent, facili negotio potuissent haereticorum
jugum cervicibus discutere, ut ex omni nostra historia fusius, et assertius
constat.[95]

The greatest share of culpability, arising from the occurrence of this
evil, is justly to be attributed to certain Anglo-Ibernian priests, who did
not deny the Tartarean dogma, cast up from hell for the destruction of
Catholics, that it was lawful for Catholics to bear arms and fight for the
heretics against Catholics and their native country. For if those priests
had been of sound mind and unanimous and in accordance with the

others in attacking the heretics, and if the Ibernians had not opposed one another, they could without much difficulty have shaken off the yoke of the heretic from their necks, as our entire history more fully and more clearly demonstrates.

Whether or not the Anglo-Irish priests were to blame, the idea of a nation divided is one that first gains weight in O'Sullivan's analysis of the failure of the Irish in the Nine Years War. This same historiographical point is reiterated by other historians of Ireland to explain similar failures in subsequent wars of putative national liberation.

The Irish abroad were also divided. The Anglo-Irish on the Continent had similarly tried to take a less militant, pro-English approach. This was the reason for O'Sullivan's fierce polemic against the early writings of the Dubliner, Richard Stanihurst. His *De Rebus in Hibernia Gestis* (Leiden, 1584) was seen as an attempt to prejudice continental Catholic opinion against the Ancient Irish and his stance had been made exasperatingly plain by his intervention during the embassy of Archbishop O'Healy to the Escorial in 1593–94.[96] The same sort of tripartite division observed among the Irish in O'Sullivan's *Compendium* is also found in the Irish College of Salamanca in a document called '*Breve Relación de Yrlanda y de tres diferencias de Yrlandeses que hay en ella*'.[97] There is a good likelihood that this document was written by O'Sullivan. Besides the tripartite division, much of the analysis and detail is similar to that of the *Compendium*; O'Sullivan himself said in his post-1625 reconquest plan that many of the Irish memoranda passed to the council in Madrid had gone through his hands. Furthermore, the English translation of this document held by TCD under the title 'A Brief Relation of Ireland and the diversity of the Irish in the same' is annotated 'presented to the councell of Spayne in Anno 1618 by Florence the pretended archbishop of Tuam and thought to be written by Philip O'Sullivan Beare'.[98] Indeed the interesting thing about the 'Brief Relation' is its profile of the Irish abroad. It claims that the same ethnic divisions which beset the Irish at home are also apparent among the Irish abroad – 'These three sortes of Irish haue their aboue inclynations soe deeply rooted in them, that in what state so euer they liue, they keep them still.'[99] It is distrustful of Anglo-Irish manoeuvring. They were now making overtures to Spain, having realized belatedly how they had foolishly over-committed themselves to the English in the late war, 'but if they were shutt of their persecucion and troubles, their naturall inclynations carrieth them more towards the English king and nation'.[100]

Most crucially the divisions in the Irish camp in Spain were the cause of the assassination of Donal Cam O'Sullivan Beare near the Royal Palace in Madrid on 16 July 1618. We know that at this time, coinciding with the renewal of hostilities in Europe, Donal Cam was actively exploring the possibilities of a rising in Munster followed by an O'Sullivan-led invasion.[101] Philip O'Sullivan's *Compendium*, which was then nearing completion, would have supported and justified the whole project with its interpretation of Irish history. Meanwhile, the Anglo-Irish were beginning to explore an alternative possibility of Catholic toleration in the event of a Spanish match between Prince Charles and the Infanta being achieved. Furthermore, the murderer, the Palesman John Bathe, brother of the former head of the Irish College of Salamanca and something of an intellectual himself, was probably aware that the history being written was not favourable towards the Irish of English descent. This would have been the general political context. According to the *Compendium*, John Bathe, having borrowed money from Donal Cam, insulted the honour of the O'Sullivans in comparing them in status to his own family. Philip O'Sullivan wounded John Bathe in the subsequent duel with a gash in the face. However, the latter ended up killing Donal Cam who came upon the aftermath of the encounter, first stabbing the war veteran in the arm and then in the throat.[102] Writing from his prison cell, Bathe gave a different account. His letter seems to imply an ambush in the street by his Gaelic compatriots rather than a pre-planned duel that Donal Cam was trying to break up. He claimed that he had neither defensive nor offensive weapons with him but only a demi-sword and a dagger which he did not have an opportunity to draw. There is, though, an overlap with what Philip wrote in his history. This exculpatory letter, incidentally signed 'Don Juan Batheo y Finglas', states that the O'Sullivans considered him 'a base man of humble lineage'.[103]

However, we should also return to the bigger picture. The Gaelic Irish émigrés believed that Bathe was an English agent. Earlier in 1618 Archbishop Florence Conry had warned the Spanish state about him. He asserted that Bathe, whom he dismissed as a courtier rather than servitor, had become an informer during a recent visit to Dublin and that instead of trusting him they should send him away to fight in the navy.[104] Interestingly the English ambassador, Lord Cottington, was anxious to assist Bathe out of his predicament. He claimed that the master of Berehaven, lately honoured with the title 'conde', had been killed 'upon a private quarrel'. As the Irish stood howling over the corpse of their dead leader, they sighted Philip III's coach and ran alongside it, shouting 'Justice, Justice' and alleging that he, the English ambassador, had had O'Sullivan slain, until his majesty ordered his cavalcade to halt. The king on the spot ordered Bathe's removal from the nearby church in which he had taken sanctuary and a full investigation of the incident. The ambassador, writing ten days later, cleared himself of any alleged involvement in the murder and was endeavouring to have Bathe removed from the gaol back to the sanctuary of the church 'whence he will easily make an escape'. The ambassador's letter to the secretary of state in London does not indicate any prior involvement in the murder of O'Sullivan or any acquaintance with Bathe – but he is obviously glad of O'Sullivan's demise and attempting to take advantage of it by winning over his murderer.[105] Meanwhile, and somewhat ironically in the light of Conry's plans for Bathe, Philip O'Sullivan, the other major participant in the events of 16 July, having taken refuge in the French embassy, left for Cadiz to take up a commission in the navy.

Neither of the two Irish factions involved in the O'Sullivan killing succeeded in developing their political projects, though both had their opportunities. The Old English exiles had an opportunity to pursue a historic compromise with Prince Charles's wooing of the Spanish Infanta in 1623, but the Spanish match proved a failure and with it the prospects of religious toleration underpinned by an international treaty disappeared.[106] During the time that the Prince of Wales was in Madrid, O'Sullivan's book was frowned upon and he himself was warned to stay away from court.[107] When war broke out with England in 1624, the Gaelic Irish made a comeback with plans from O'Sullivan and others for Spanish intervention in Ireland again being favourably considered. However, Spain had far too many foreign commitments to devote dwindling resources to Ireland and so the plans stayed on the drawing board. Meanwhile John Bathe had returned to Ireland, having been knighted by James I after he arrived in England, probably in the entourage of the duke of Gondomar. It was he who first suggested 'the Graces' and who had a substantial part in negotiating these concessions from the state.[108] When he died in October 1630, the concessions promised when England was at war with Spain had not received parliamentary confirmation.[109] The Treaty of Madrid, signed the month following Bathe's death, not only ended Anglo-Spanish hostilities but also made the Graces a remote possibility. The same peace treaty likewise put paid to the dreams of the Gaelic Irish exiles because it undermined their political usefulness to the Spanish state. Philip O'Sullivan died six years after Bathe; also politically unfulfilled. However, his analysis of Ireland's dilemma remained a valid one and unsurprisingly the fatal divisions which his writings so powerfully exposed were again all too obvious in the failed national struggle of the 1640s and in its historiographical replay in the 1650s.

6. The Scotic debate:
Philip O'Sullivan Beare and
his *Tenebriomastix*

DAVID CAULFIELD

The Irish historian, Philip O'Sullivan Beare (*c.* 1590–*c.* 1637), is best known for his *Compendium of the Catholic History of Ireland*,[1] a work invaluable to historians for being the only extensive contemporary Catholic account of the Elizabethan wars in Ireland. In writing his *History*, he had much material and first-hand knowledge to draw upon, for these events had dramatically affected the fortunes of his own family and those of the O'Sullivan Beare clan generally. His father had been active in the Munster wars between 1569 and 1585, while his first cousin Donal 'Cam' O'Sullivan, head of the Beara branch of the family, played a significant role in events during the Battle of Kinsale: it was he who led the celebrated retreat of the O'Sullivans from Beara to Leitrim following the destruction of Dunboy Castle and the forfeiture of the family lands. This epic march and the O'Sullivans' subsequent exile in Spain were duly recorded in the *Compendium*. Philip himself, while still a boy, was sent by ship to La Coruña in February 1602, never again to return home.

On arriving in Europe, many Irishmen like O'Sullivan were faced for the first time with having to deal with the detrimental effects of the adverse image of Ireland and its inhabitants, which had long been prom-ulgated by Giraldus Cambrensis[2] and, more recently, by Richard Stanihurst,[3] and which had by this time become ingrained in the minds of educated people in Europe.[4] The Irish, of both Gaelic- and Anglo-Irish descent, from their different perspectives, gradually came to realize the importance of refuting Giraldus and Stanihurst in works of their own. Some of these works, composed for the most part by ecclesiastics of Anglo-Irish stock, began to appear in the course of the second and third decades of the seventeenth century; others, although circulated in manuscript form, remained unpublished at that time.[5] O'Sullivan, who had greater reason than most to set the record straight, contributed to this effort with the *Compendium* and his first polemical work, the

109

Zoilomastix of *circa* 1626,[6] in which he refuted both Cambrensis and Stanihurst.

Another field of literature, that of hagiography, became the forum in which a further matter of growing concern to the Irish had also to be addressed. A controversy arose between Irish and Scottish exiles on the Continent regarding the true 'ownership' of the name *Scotia*, (the ancient name for Ireland along with *Hibernia*) and of those eminent medieval saints, churchmen and scholars, who had been styled *Scoti*. The question was: to what land, and at what time could the name *Scotia* be properly ascribed? The controversy that began in the sixteenth century, gave rise to a 'paper war',[7] which became particularly acrimonious in the early years of the seventeenth century, and whose reverberations could still be felt in the eighteenth century (in the affair of the Macpherson forgeries).[8] O'Sullivan was deeply interested in early Irish saints and martyrs,[9] and had published his own work on the life of St Patrick, the *Patritiana Decas*, and sought to have some *Lives* included in church martyrologies then being compiled.[10] Seeing it as his literary mission[11] to defend this aspect of his heritage, Philip entered the lists around 1636 with his *Tenebriomastix* – 'a scourge for the trickster'[12] – the work that I will consider presently.

The question as to the term *Scotia* has long been resolved[13] (although there may be lingering doubts regarding the identity of some *Scoti*),[14] and historians are generally agreed that Ireland, while it was also known by its more ancient name, *Hibernia* (and called by its inhabitants 'Ériu'), had had exclusive ownership of the name *Scotia*[15] until the beginning of the eleventh century.[16] Until this time also, the region now known as Scotland (while it had also been known to the Romans by the name *Caledonia*)[17] was included in the general name *Britannia*, which applied to the entire island of Britain.[18] At the beginning of the sixth century, a branch of an Irish (Scotic) tribe from the north-eastern region of Ireland established a colony and subsequently an independent kingdom (known as *Dalriada*) in a region of Argyll on the western coast of Scotland. In the course of the ninth and tenth centuries, having conquered or somehow absorbed the indigenous people of neighbouring Pictland, the *Scoti* became the dominant power in the northern region of Britain. That region, known to its Gaelic-speaking inhabitants (as also to the indigenous Picts)[19] as 'Alba' (or 'Alban') began to be described by Latin writers as *Scotia Minor*[20] in distinction from Ireland itself, *Scotia Maior* (also *Hibernia*). In the eleventh century the term *Scotia*, having been gradually superimposed on the native 'Alban', and used in tandem with it until the thirteenth century, came to denote the region north of the Forth and Clyde; and it was not until the beginning of the fifteenth century that the name *Scotia* came to be generally applied to present-day Scotland alone.[21] Thereafter, Ireland became designated by the term *Hibernia*,[22] and increasingly 'Ireland', a term which occurs from as early as the tenth century.[23]

However, the ambiguity enveloping the terms *Scotia* and *Scoti*, since these came to designate different entities at different times, had the inevitable result of leaving many people, especially continental Europeans, confused as to who, or what country, was being referred to in any piece of writing containing these terms; because it meant that one had not only to identify the person or place being referred to, but also to establish the nationality of the writer, if he should refer to himself as *Scotus*, so as to establish *his* frame of reference.[24] For both Scottish and Irish in the sixteenth and seventeenth centuries, this ambiguity also gave rise to questions of national identity, and served to engender a growing animosity between them in the matter of which of the two had rightful title to being called by the name *Scoti*, and what land, *Scotia*.

The question had important implications for both Scottish and Irish Catholic exiles in Europe at that time: both contended for prestige and patronage at foreign courts. By establishing their credentials in regard to their unbroken loyalty to the Catholic religion from early Christian times, and by claiming for their respective countries those medieval churchmen and scholars who had been so prominent in revitalizing and maintaining the Christian faith and learning in Europe, they could strengthen their case when it came to seeking aid in the education of young men needed as missionaries to continue the Catholic struggle in their respective homelands.[25] The very recounting of this glorious past would, in itself, serve as an inspiration for their missionary effort.[26] The Irish, having already been dispossessed of their homeland, felt that they were now being robbed of their cultural heritage, and thus, their very identity. The Gaelic Irish, for their part, must have felt beleaguered on all sides: as *Hiberni*, they had been branded as uncivilized, and generally calumniated by the likes of Giraldus and Stanihurst; now their glorious heritage as *Scoti* was being systematically plundered by the Scots. Already in the late sixteenth century, Scottish churchmen had sued for and succeeded in getting possession of some of the Irish monasteries in Germany – the *Schottenklöster* – on the basis of their claim to the name *Scoti*.[27] It therefore became increasingly important for the Irish, both for practical purposes and for their own self-respect, to establish the true ownership of this past, and to make a convincing argument for their case. This simmering animosity culminated in open dispute between representatives of the Irish and Scottish Colleges in Paris in 1620, following the publication of an address given by the newly appointed bishop of Ossory, David Rothe, in praise of St Brigit to the students of the Irish College there.[28] Rothe had attached to this a warning to the Scottish academic, Thomas Dempster, currently championing the Scottish cause with his so-called *Nomenclatura* or 'list' of celebrated '*Scoti*', to refrain from any further attempts to claim Irish saints for Scotland.[29] There followed a series of publications of mutual refutation – and vilification – the tenor of which became such as to cause the Catholic authorities some alarm.[30] It is probably for this reason that works by both Dempster and Rothe were almost immediately placed on the Roman Index of Prohibited Books.[31] But while this marked the end of the immediate flare-up, the controversy continued to smoulder for some time yet; and this is where O'Sullivan became involved.

In 1631 a follower of Dempster, a certain David Chambers, sometime rector of the Scottish College in Paris, published a work, *On the Courage, Piety, and Learning of the Scots.*[32] This work, which drew heavily upon Dempster's highly imaginative *Catholic History of the Scottish People*,[33] consisted mainly in a 'Menology' or calendar of Scottish saints, and three short dissertations recounting the courage of the Scots and their learning and piety, at home and abroad, from the earliest times.

In his introduction, Chambers presented the usual fabulous scheme of history – his *Scoti* coming from Ireland to the Hebrides in 695 BC, settling in mainland Britain before 600 BC, and establishing a kingdom there around 330 BC. For the rest, Chambers simply took any literary reference to *Scotia* and the *Scoti* – regardless of its date – and in the course of the remainder of the book, creatively applied it to Scotland and the Scots, as proof of their fortitude, piety and so on. In the 'Menology', Chambers made extensive use of Dempster's *History,* and so reproduced many of the errors and sleights of hand which littered that work, and appropriating in the process many well-known medieval Irish saints such as Brigit, Kilian and Columba. The work also contained a *Dissertation against the Irish* (*Hiberni Hirlandici*) – including a refutation of Richard Stanihurst and David Rothe (in the matter of *Scotia*).[34] In the course of this, however, Chambers went so far as to claim that Scotland was once called Ireland![35] – altering a passage (on the subject of islands) from St Isidore's *Etymologies* to support this notion.[36]

Finally, having cited in his support much the same authors as those adduced by the Irish, he offers the following general explanation to anyone still in doubt as to who and what were intended by the terms *Scoti* and *Scotia*:

> *Quaeres si Hibernia Irlandica nunquam fuit appellata Scotia, unde factum sit ut tot viri docti hoc existimarint? Respondeo ex eo factum esse quod cum apud authores viderent Scotiam aliquando confundi cum Hibernia existimarint Hiberniam aliquando Scotiam appellatam cum tamen, ut ex dictis constat, potius colligere debuissent Scotiam nempe nostram*

appellatam Hiberniam, et certe (ut rem totam concludamus) si Hibernia olim Scotia appellata fuit, mirum est non ita ne semel quidem a Caesare, Solino, et aliis ita appellari.[37]

You will ask: if Irlandic Hibernia had never been called Scotia, how has it come about that so many learned men should have supposed this? My response is that this is due to the fact that when they saw that in authors' works [the name] 'Scotia' was sometimes used in combination with Hibernia, they may have supposed that Hibernia was at some time called 'Scotia' – when, however, they ought to have judged (as is plain from what these actually said) that it was clearly our own Scotland that was once called 'Hibernia'. And indeed (so that I may put the matter to rest) if Hibernia [Ireland] had at one time been called 'Scotia', it is a wonder that not even once was it so named by [Julius] Caesar, Solinus and the others.

The tenor of Chambers's argument is at all times moderate, and nowhere in his *Dissertation* is there an acrimonious word. In his brief *Letter to the Irish*, he presents himself as a model of goodwill and reasonableness, urging Irishmen to:

Quidquid a nobis dictum est, pro defensione veritatis aequi bonique consulite, candidè et sine ulla amaritudine quantum licuit egimus: nec fuit unquam consilium nostrum ex aliena depressione laudem quaerere. Hoc unum à vobis peto ne ad convitia, siquid contra dicendum vobis videbitur, veniatis. Quod à pluribus vestrum minus modestè in viros ornatissimos factitatum est hactenus . . . Quoniam autem, ut diximus, sine felle agimus, si quid dicendum adversum nos habetis, pari modestià et candore proponite, ne dum de Sanctis agimus, minus sanctè agere videamur.[38]

Take in good part anything right and proper that I have said in the defence of Truth – it being plain how much I have made my case candidly and without bitterness. And it has never been my intention to acquire esteem through belittling the views of others. This one thing I ask of you: if you should think it necessary to say anything to the contrary, do not resort to insults – something many of you have, before now, repeatedly and too intemperately levelled against the most distinguished men . . . Since, as I have said, I have conducted my case without acrimony, if you have anything to say in refutation of my argument, present it with a like moderation and candour – lest while we are treating of the Saints we should appear to conduct ourselves in a less than saintly manner.

However, for all its plausibility, this appeal did little to mollify O'Sullivan – coming as it did from a 'trickster'[39] and a saint-stealer. The *Tenebriomastix*, at almost 700 pages, is a refutation of Chambers, and represents O'Sullivan's main contribution to the Scotic debate.

The work itself comprises a short Prologue, six 'books', and a short Epilogue. Each of the books is divided into chapters called *retaliationes* ('tit-for-tats', wherein O'Sullivan takes controversial items from his opponent's work as general themes for counter-attack) and sub-headings called *certamina* ('engagements', wherein particular items of contention within these larger headings are taken up for debate and responded to). A transcription of a late recension of Henry Fitzsimon's *Martyrology*, identical with that included in the *Zoilomastix*, has been inserted towards the end of the MS.[40] The work is without any form of dedication. The scheme of the *Tenebriomastix* (accompanied by the relevant manuscript pagination) is as follows:

Bk 1. Prologue	1–6
Description of Ireland and its names	7–137
(according to the evidence of ancient and contemporary authorities)	
Bk 2. Refutation of Chambers's *Introduction*	138–224
Bk 3. Refutation of Chambers's Bk 1 (*de Fortitudine*)	225–278
Bk 4. Refutation of Chambers's Bk 2 (*de Doctrina*)	279–333
Bk 5. Refutation of Chambers's Bk 3 (*de Pietate*)	334–374
(and the *Menology*)	375–409
Bk 6. Refutation of Chambers's *Dissertation against the Irish*	410–621
(Henry Fitzsimon's *Martyrology*	622–653
and further material to be inserted in text)	654–658
Refutation of Chambers's *Letter to the Irish*	659–668
The religious fidelity of the Irish	669–676
Epilogue	676
Index	677–688
(further material for insertion in text)	689–691

Here, as in the *Zoilomastix*, O'Sullivan combines a scholastic method of arrangement with the style of a Ciceronian *actio*, or judicial case, in order to respond to Chambers – taking each chapter of the latter's work and refuting it, point by point, under the headings and sub-headings described.[41] Judging from examples in both the *Zoilomastix* and *Tenebriomastix*, it is clear that O'Sullivan owed his rhetorical skills, such as they are, to Cicero; and he also appears to have made extensive use of the *Rhetorica ad Herennium*,[42] a textbook for aspiring rhetoricians, many of the rules and exemplars in which he followed quite closely. The degree to which he succeeded in this may be seen from some of the extracts from the work that follow.

O'Sullivan's Prologue represents, as it were, a persuasive opening address, in which he sets out his case and intentions, following all the classical rhetorical guidelines. What is primarily under attack (he says) is not Ireland, but the truth; and this, in O'Sullivan's eyes, is tantamount to heresy:

> *Cum in istud anile Camerarij fabulamentum inciderem, reprimerem, necne eius exultantem furorem? mox retuli (Catholice lector) ad amicos. Alij eum dimittendum censebant, quod apertis mendacijs quilibet historiae septentrionis peritus sine ulla opera nostra facillime fidem deroget: iam optimi historici monuerint a Caledonijs scriptoribus multa fingi vaneque iactari: et ea tandem veritatis vis sit, ut saepenumero contra ingenia calliditatem, solertiam hominum sese ipsa defendat: neque vel obteri calumniae magnitudine, vel diuturnitate temporis obrui, vel ullo violentiae impetu opprimi possit, sed quo gravius et inimicitius vexatur et ad calamitatem depellitur, eo firmior (velut palma pondere pressa) ipsa se erigat, et (ut aurum igne probatum) suae potentiae, maiestatisque splendorem omnium oculis illustriorem ostendat.*[43]

When I happened upon that book of old wives' tales of Chambers, presently, my dear Catholic reader, I had recourse to friends in considering whether or not I should check his hopping madness. Some judged that he ought to be dismissed, since anyone conversant with the history of the north of Europe would, without any exertion on my part, easily undermine belief in his blatant fictions: historians of the highest calibre have already shown that many things have been fabricated and groundlessly boasted of by Caledonian writers; and, in the end, the power of truth is of such a kind that, time and again, it defends itself against the inventions, cunning and sleight of mortal men; and the truth cannot be either trampled on by the great bulk of calumny or obscured by the passage of time or overwhelmed by any violent attack; but the more gravely and hostilely it is abused, and thrust down toward harm, so much the more firmly does it raise itself up again (like a palm branch when it has been pressed down by a weight) and (like gold that has been tested by fire) displays, even more brightly, the splendour of its own power and majesty before the eyes of all.

In deciding to take on Chambers, he declares his intention:

> *Hoc opere toto praestigiosi fabulatoris portentosa figmenta refutare, nefarijsque conatibus obviam ire: gentium, quarum honorem oppugnat, causam defendere: de Britannicarum insularum moribus veteribus, atque recentibus, religione, divis, rebus gestis quaedam scitu digna referre: praecipue Caledonios historiam suam docere: ubique turpia mendacia refellere, sacram veritatem tutari, studiosis historiae viris consulere conor.*[44]

> Throughout the whole of this work, I attempt to refute the monstrous fabrications of this conjuring tale-spinner, and to make a stand against his nefarious undertakings; to defend the cause of the nations whose honour he assails; to recount certain matters worthy of note, concerning the ancient and more recent traditions of the British Isles, their religion, their saints, their history; I attempt especially to instruct the Caledonians in their own history; to disprove loathsome untruths at every turn, and to safeguard holy truth; and to consult the interests of men who are studious of history.

O'Sullivan would seem to have felt it necessary to establish from the beginning (and, perhaps, once and for all) the validity of Ireland's claim to the name *Scotia*, and devoted Book 1 entirely to this. Thus, beginning with the earliest references to Ireland as *Hibernia, Iuverna, Scotia*, etc., in the works of writers such as Tacitus, Caesar, Ptolemy, Solinus, Festus Avienus and Ammianus, he continues with a lengthy trawl of medieval authors such as Orosius, Ethicus, Isidore, Adomnán, Bede, Einhard and, later, Vincent of Beauvais, Jacobus de Voragine, Trithemius and, nearer his own times, Laurence Surius, Conrad Gesner, Ortelius and William Camden. In doing so, however, he was merely retailing evidence already adduced by both Peter Lombard and David Rothe in their works, and in much the same order. But whereas Lombard and Rothe were content to extract an essential phrase from a passage to establish their case, O'Sullivan often felt obliged to quote the entire piece. The passages cited from Orosius and Ethicus (almost identical) are an example of this: whereas Rothe merely takes the phrase, 'It [*Hibernia*] is inhabited by the nations of the *Scoti*', O'Sullivan quotes not only the entire passage of Orosius but also that of Ethicus. Thus, by the end of Book 1, one is ruefully aware that 'Ireland is an island . . .' (many descriptions of Ireland begin with this phrase).

In Book 2, which deals with Chambers's dedicatory letter (to Charles I) and introduction, O'Sullivan begins with an *argumentum ad hominem* or, rather, an *argumentum ad nomen* – an attack on his opponent's name:

> *[Camerarius] principio mox operis David regium nomen nobis praetendit: quippe tenebrionum rex. Camerarij vero vocabulum quid sibi in Calvinidonia vult? In ista regione haeretica nullam nobilem (si quam nobilitatem haeresis ignominia reliquam facit) nullam etiam ignobilem familiam nomine Camerarium adhuc novi. Quin Camerarius a Camera deducatur, quis dubitat? Camera vero Latinis aedificiorum curvatus arcus alio nomine fornix appellatur, sed vulgo Latrinam significat. Utraque significatio Camerario libro, qui tum Curvus distentus, atque falsus, tum olidus, et coenosus est, sedet. Fornicis autem significatio, qua meretricum Lupanaria notantur, meretriciae Calvinidoniae, quae Christi Dei Ecclesiae*

Catholicae sacratissimae sponsi Divinam Religionem Lutheri, Calvini, et impurissimorum puritanorum nefarijs complexibus, posthabet, convenit.[45]

[Chambers], directly at the beginning of his work, offers us the royal name of David – obviously the king of tricksters![46] And what does the word 'Chambers' mean in Calvinidonia? I know no family of that name in that heretical region, either noble – if the disgrace of heresy has left anything noble there – or ignoble. Who doubts but that Camerarius comes from camera. But camera (to Latin speakers, the curved arch of buildings) is also called by another name, 'fornix' – or in common parlance, a latrine! Each of these meanings applies to Chambers's book, which is curved, distended and bent, as well as stinking and bemired. However, the sign of the arch, by which houses of prostitutes are identified, befits the prostitute Calvinidonia, which holds the divine religion of Christ our God, bridegroom of the most holy Catholic Church in less esteem than the abominable embraces of Luther, Calvin and the impurest Puritans.

On the supposed antiquity of Scotland as a kingdom, O'Sullivan again relies on Rothe and Lombard, and like Stephen White and James Ware,[47] he says of the Scottish historians, Boece, Buchanan and their ilk that because of their utter ignorance of the Irish language, they were unable to read the Irish annals.

Isti vero magistellus Hector Boethius, TurneroLeslaeus, Buchananus transfuga, Thomsonus, Dempsterus, Camerarius, similesque, tenebriones sunt Picti Iberniae, sive Scotiae, linguae prorsus ignari: qui non ex Ibernicis monumentis veras historias: sed ex suorum capitum vertigine futiles fabulas deprompserunt.[48]

But these men, young master Hector Boece, Turner-Lesley, the fugitive Buchanan, Thomson, Dempster, Chambers and their ilk, are Pictish tricksters, entirely ignorant of the Irish (or Scotic) language, who did not draw authentic accounts from Irish annals, but worthless tales out of the whirling of their own heads.

O'Sullivan's general argument about the courage,[49] learning and piety of the Scots (Books 3, 4 and 5) is that already rehearsed by Rothe, which was that Scotland did not begin to share the name *Scotia* with Ireland until at least the middle of the ninth century.[50] Thus, it was the Irish who harassed the Romans, established the university at Paris[51] and the monasteries in Europe – not the Scots – and it is a case of Chambers (whom he now calls the 'porridge-maker' (*Lablalyarius*)[52] putting a contrary construction on the text in each case. As to Scottish piety, O'Sullivan does little to conceal his contempt for such a notion, and throughout the work prefers to stress the current ('heretical') state of affairs in Scotland:

> *Eo . . . isti Caledonii Picti vana iactatione ducuntur, ut quoniam quidem*
> *sanctissimam vitam divinamque doctrinam fugiunt, exspuunt, execrantur,*
> *extinguere parant, eorum tamen nomina sibi vendicent, atque adeo cum*
> *domi inglorii haeretici vivunt, peregre Catholici gloriosissimi velint haberi.*[53]

To such a degree . . . are these inglorious Caledonian Picts susceptible to empty boasting that, whereas they flee, spit out, curse and make to destroy the most holy life and doctrine, yet they wish to claim for themselves the renown of those [saints]. And so it is that Scots, although they live as heretics at home, wish to be regarded as the most honoured Catholics abroad.

Their sovereign, Charles I, to whom Chambers had dedicated his work, would seem at that time (*c.* 1636) to have held out little hope for the Irish abroad, for O'Sullivan also brands him with the mark of a heretic whose 'faith is false, whose hope is empty, whose charity is non-existent and whose life also will rightly be judged ill-fated and wretched':

> *Iuxta haec cum Carolus Stuartus haereticus rex Diabolum imitatus a*
> *pietate defecerit, multo maioris terrae voluptatum blandimenta, quam*
> *aeternam beatitudinem habeat: Catholicos a vero a Dei cultu avertere*
> *suique sceleris, et impietatis consortes facere conetur[:] quandoquidem*
> *Diabolus miserrimus est, ipse quoque tam infoelicis archetypi imitator*
> *potius infaustus, quam beatus dici debet.*[54]

Morever, since Charles Stuart, the heretic king, following the pattern of the Devil, revolted against piety, holds the allurements of earthly pleasures in much greater esteem than eternal happiness, attempts to turn away Catholics from the truth, from the worship of God, and make them the partners of his own crime; and seeing that the Devil is the most wretched creature, he [Charles] also is so much the imitator of his accursed archetype that he should rather be adjudged ill-fated than fortunate.

O'Sullivan even perceived Scotland itself as synonymous with heresy, as he now and again indulges his fondness for invective, name-calling and (usually disparaging) neologisms:

> *Nihilominus qualis sit? rimari scriptorum auxilio conabar. oque variis*
> *nominibus Alba, Albana, Albia, Albion, Albium, Albiana, Caledonia, Pictia,*
> *Pictlandia, Scotia, Scotlandia, Calvinidonia, CalvinoPictia, LutheroPictia,*
> *HaereticoScotlandia dicta.*[55]

I tried, with the help of the Authors to discover what sort of place Scotland was. That place was also called by various names: Alba, Albana, Albia, Albion, Albium, Albiana, Caledonia, Pictia, Pictlandia, Scotia, Scotlandia, Calvinodonia, CalvinoPictia, LutheroPictia, HaereticoScotlandia.

Answering the Scots' claim to Irish saints, O'Sullivan says:

> *Equidem si nostros viros illustres Pictos historici nominassent, non mirarer eos Pictiae attribui. Cum vero annos circiter quingentos quos potissimum nostri Divi in terris vixerunt, steterit in Caledonia Pictorum Regnum, & Plebs adhuc extet, magnum mirum esset, tam innumerabilem sanctissimorum hominum vim ibi genitam esse, & tamen nullos (quod ego observaverim) a scriptoribus Pictos vocari. Quod minime levi argumento est, illos neque Pictos fuisse, neque in Caledonia natos.*[56]

> If historians had named our illustrious saints Picti, I would not wonder at their being attributed to Pictia. But since, during the period of almost five hundred years[57] in which our saints were most prominent in the world, there was established in Caledonia the Kingdom of the Picts (and its people still exists), it would be a great wonder that such a countless number of the most saintly men should have been born in that place, and yet (so far as I have noticed) that none should be described by the authors as Picti. This represents substantial proof that these saints were neither Picts, nor born in Caledonia.

On the supposed conversion in AD 203, O'Sullivan cites Cesare Baroneo (for the year AD 429):

> *Scimus tamen recentiores scriptores, qui hoc nostro saeculo res Scotorum sunt prosecuti longe antiquiorum vendicare sibi Scotorum Christianitatem nempe a tempore Victoris Papae et Martyris, qui legatione interpellatus Donaldi primi huius nominis Scotorum Regis in Scotiam miserat Roma clericos, qui eos docuerint Evangelium. Sed miramur tanta haec antiquiorem Scotorum Chronographum Marianum prorsus ignorasse: et Bedam illis propinquum penitus latuisse. et nescivisse ista Hieronymum, qui ad Oceanum scribens, de Scotis adhuc gentilibus ista habet.*[58]

> I am aware that writers in our own times, who have written the history of the Scots, claim a much earlier Christianity, indeed from the time of Victor, Pope and Martyr, who upon being importuned by Donald, the first Scottish king of that name, sent priests from Rome in order to teach them the Gospel. But I am surprised that the ancient historian of the Scoti, Marianus [Scotus], especially, should have been ignorant of such important matter as this, and that it should have been completely hidden from Bede, a neighbour to them, and that St Jerome, who, writing to Oceanus treats of these things in respect of the Scoti, who were still pagan, was unaware of these matters.

Chambers had prefaced his bizarre claim that Scotland was once called 'Hibernia' by saying that nobody denied that Scotland had been once called 'Caledonia' and 'Albion' and the like, but that some people, such as John Capgrave,[59] Cambrensis, and more recently the Irish, Stanihurst,

Fitzsimon and Rothe, denied that it was once called 'Scotia': 'He would
show that, even from the time of Christ, Scotia (Scotland) was also called
"Hibernia".'[60] In mentioning Capgrave, Chambers, for some strange
reason, states that he lived in the third century, 'or a little thereafter',[61] and
goes on to cite a passage from Capgrave's *Life of St Columba*. This error
affords O'Sullivan ample opportunity to, as it were, play to the gallery:

> *Heus Camerari, dormisne? Haec quomodo cohaerent? Capgranius a saeculo
> tertio ad sextumque usque annos trecentos vixit, an fuit a morte revocatus?
> Hoc miraculum qua via factum est? Divinaene omnipotentiae, an Picticae
> mentiendi licentiae? Hoccine Caledonii ingenii acumen est? Ex quo
> gymnasio hoc argumentum producit? Ex Zenonis stoa, ex Platonis
> Academia? ex Aristotelis Lycaeo an ex haeretica Aberdonia? Mihi crede
> Tenebrio haec tua placita, non quae Pater Fitzsimon, et Donatus Orruarkus
> adstruunt, sunt repugnantia.*[62]

> Hey there, Chambers, are you asleep? How can these two things be
> consistent? Did Capgrave manage to live for 300 years, from the third
> to the sixth century, or is it that he was restored from the dead? How
> did this miracle come about? Was it through Divine omnipotence – or
> the Pictish predilection for lying? Is this the incisiveness of the
> Caledonian mind? From what school of thought does it draw this line
> of reasoning? Zeno's Stoa? Plato's Academy? Aristotle's Lyceum? Or is it
> from the heretical one at Aberdeen? Trust me you trickster: it is your
> opinions that are contradictory, not those advanced by Father
> Fitzsimon and Donatus O'Rourke [i.e. David Rothe]!

O'Sullivan proceeds to deal with Chambers's claim to Hibernia. In order
to achieve this feat, Chambers had changed the word *Iberia* to *Hybernia*
when citing a passage in Vincent of Beauvais' *Speculum Historiale* (this
passage being originally from Isidore's *Etymologiae* [14, 6]). The correct
passage is as follows:

> *Scotia eadem et Hibernia proxima Britanniae insula spatio terrarum
> angustior, sed situ foecundior. Haec ab Africa in Boream porrigitur, cuius
> partes priores in Iberiam et Cantabricum Oceanum intendunt. Unde et
> Hibernia dicta est.*[63]

> Scotia the same as Hibernia, the island next to Britain, is narrower in
> the extent of its lands, but more fertile in its location. It extends from
> the south-west to the north, its nearest parts tending towards Iberia
> and the Cantabrian Ocean. Whence it is also called Hibernia.

Chambers claimed that Vincent had changed the word Iberia to Hibernia
'for the sake of clarity',[64] and that he had then properly construed
Hibernia as meaning Scotland, whose nearest parts (the Hebridean

Islands) face towards Ireland and the Bay of Biscay (Cantabricum Oceanum)! Having cited the original passage from Isidore, and the 1624 edition of the *Speculum Historiale*, as well as an almost identical passage in the *Speculum Naturale*, O'Sullivan replies as follows:

> Hanc indubitatam Divi Isidori, Vencentiique sententiam Camerarius ut pervertat, in tenebris erroris, inscitiaeque densissimis versatur: seseque in Labyrinthicos anfractus coniectum minime expedit. Eam enim cum Calvinidoniae suae non posset aptare, Hebridibus Insulis videtur accommodare. Ad id, Iberiae nomine non Hispaniam (ut debuerat) sed Insulam nostram Iberniam intelligi vult: Hancque a parte altera , et ab altera Cantabriam Hispaniae Regionem ex Hebridibus respici asseverat . . . Futilis commentatio Pictici ingenii vano fuco digna est. Etenim eam descriptionem non prius Hebridibus accommodabit quam Heraclis cothurnos infanti aptet. Principio iam, quod ipse promiserat, non est assecutus: hîc Calvinidonicam suam Iberniae Scotiaeque vocabulo significari: quoniam iis nominibus hîc ea Insula nuncupatur, quae ad Iberiam, Cantabricumque Oceanum versus protenditur: Quo si Hebrides vergere hîc dicuntur, eas etiam Iberniae, Scotiaeque nominibus, non Calvinidoniam hîc appellari, necesse est.[65]

Chambers, in order to pervert the indisputable opinion of St Isidore and of Vincent, has landed himself in the densest darkness of error and ignorance and, having been thrust into these labyrinthine turnings, can in no way extricate himself. For since he was unable to adapt this meaning to his own Calvinidonia, he appears to apply it to the Hebridean Islands. Moreover, he wants the name Iberia to be construed not as Spain (as it should have been) but as our island of Ireland; and he asserts that this is to be seen on one side, and the Cantabrian region of Spain on the other from the Hebrides . . . His worthless treatise of Pictish 'ingenuity' well befits a dissimulating charlatan. For he will no sooner apply this description to the Hebrides than fit the buskins of Heracles on a baby. Already, at the outset, he has not achieved what he intended to establish: that in this passage it is his Calvinidonia that is denoted by the terms Ibernia and Scotia. For in this passage, it is 'that *island* [singular] which extends towards Iberia and the Cantabrian Ocean' that is called by these names. But if in this passage it is the Hebrides which are said to face towards that place [Spain] then these also must necessarily be called here by the names Ibernia and Scotia, and not by the name Calvinidonia!

For the remainder of the work, O'Sullivan replies to Chambers's claim that the term 'Scotia' referred to Scotland from the first, and his rejection of arguments by Stanihurst,[66] Rothe, Hugh MacCaghwell and others that it meant Ireland. In doing so, he points out the disinterestedness of foreign witnesses and also makes unwonted alliance with Stanihurst, of whom he had some harsh things to say otherwise.[67] Having cited a variety of authors of international repute, he continues:

> *Talium testium rectissimo Iudicio, qua fronte Camerarius homo semissis*
> *suas Caledonias naenias anteponit. Quam miserum est impudentiae, quod*
> *libet licere? Richardo Stanihursto, a me in praesentia tantum authoritatis*
> *tribui, quantum eius argumenta merentur, satis superque est: Quoniam si*
> *non nebulonum trutina, sed Doctorum statera examinentur, sola Camerarii*
> *Apollogum refutant.*[68]

> With what audacity does Chambers place worthless Caledonian nonsensical babble before the most accurate judgement of witnesses of such a calibre! How lamentable it is to cede anything to impudence! For the present, it is more than enough that I afford to Richard Stanihurst as much authority as his proofs merit – inasmuch as if these are weighed, not in the street-monger scales of scoundrels but tested in the goldsmith-balance of learned men, on their own they refute Chambers's narrative.

In dismissing Stanihurst's evidence (a hymn for matins, cited both in the *De Vita Sancti Patricii* and the *De Rebus Gestis*)[69] that St Patrick had been sent to Ireland to 'remove the darkness of Idolatry of the Scotic people', Chambers had suggested that St Patrick, *sacerdos Scoticae gentis* ('a priest of the Scottish race'), had eradicated heresy from Scotland – his *Scotia* in this case referring to the Orkney Islands (*insulae Scotiae*), which Patrick (according to him) had converted somewhat later than the rest of Scotland by proxy, as it were, through St Sernanus, and that it was quite in order that Patrick should be credited with this, being in overall charge as the Apostle of Scotia (Scotland). As an alternative explanation, he suggests that the Scoti converted in this case were returnees from Ireland, Denmark and elsewhere who, during the short period of their expulsion from Scotland (an episode invented by an earlier Scottish historian, John of Fordun), had embraced idolatry.[70] Such claims inevitably elicited a predictable response from O'Sullivan:

> *Quod etiam nihil aliud est, nisi futile figmentum. Isti Scotlandi, si Christiani*
> *ex Scotlandia profugissent, cur exules non retinuissent fidem? Cur etiam*
> *Christiani suos liberos saluberrimis, fidei documentis non instituissent?*
> *Fueruntne ea ingenii pravitate, qua hodierni haeretici Caledonii, qui in*
> *Hispaniam, Italiam, Belgium, profecti inter Catholicos quidem sese quoque*
> *simulant Catholicos esse; in patriam vero suam reversi pristinas Caledonias*
> *haereses profitentur.*[71]

> This too was nothing if not a worthless fiction. These Scotlanders, if they had fled from Scotland as Christians, why did they not retain

their faith while in exile? Why, being Christians, had they not instructed their sons in the most wholesome teachings of the faith? Did not these [exiles] possess the same depraved mentality as the heretical Caledonians maintain today, whereby, on their arrival among Catholics in Spain, Belgium and Italy, they pretend to be Catholics also,[72] yet are no sooner returned to Scotland than they profess their former Caledonian heresies?

Rhetorical questions, needless to say.

Again, in quoting a passage from Surius' *Life* of St Kilian (which Stanihurst 'took most faithfully from Surius' as proof of that saint's Irish origin), Chambers provided another example of his creative ability, when he entirely changed the meaning of the passage by placing the full stop in a more convenient place. Where the correct text reads:

> *Beatus Kilianus Scotorum genere nobilibus ortus parentibus divinae tamen gratiae factus est nobilitate clarissimus. Scotia quae et Hibernia dicitur, insula est maris Oceani foecundus quidem glebis, sed sanctissimis clarior viris.*

> Blessed Kilian was born to noble parents of the nation of the Scoti, but became most illustrious through the nobility bestowed by Divine Grace. Scotia, which is also called Hibernia, is an island of the sea of Ocean.

Chambers had written:

> *Beatus Kilianus Scotorum genere nobilibus ortus parentibus divinae tamen gratiae factus est nobilitate clarissimus, Scoti quae et Hibernia dicta est.*

> Blessed Kilian was born to noble parents of the nation of the Scoti, but became most illustrious through the nobility bestowed by Divine Grace, in Scotia, which was also called Hibernia.

O'Sullivan duly dealt with this subterfuge at length.[73]

By way of a final sortie against Chambers, O'Sullivan began his reply to the latter's mellifluous *Letter to the Irlandic-Hiberni*[74] (to distinguish these from the 'original' *Hiberni* – the Scottish variety, naturally) by saying that Chambers's attempts at subtle distortion of authentic ancient writings (which to O'Sullivan amounted to a form of heresy) was wholly in keeping with the practices of his heretical fellow Scotsmen; and that this was a problem to which St Jerome was no stranger when struggling with the Pelagian heresy in his own time. Jerome in his preface to the third book of his *Commentaries on Jeremiah* had written that he would have liked to imitate Homer's Ulysses, who 'is said to have closed his ears to the Sirens' song' in order to 'turn aside the rage of heretics', but had been harassed by the Devil:

sed ita agit diebus, et noctibus, et aperte, et per insidias, veris falsa miscendo, imo inversa mendacia subdolo melle circumliniens, ut qui audit verborum dulcedinem, venena pectoris non formidet.[75]

But he so strives day and night, both openly and with stratagems, and by combining falsehoods with truths – or rather by smearing over his ambiguous falsehoods with deceiving honey – that anyone who hears the sweetness of his words will not fear the poison of his heart.

But, according to O'Sullivan, Jerome had the measure of the likes of Chambers's compatriots, who were:

. . . *homuncionibus vanissimis, atque futilissimis, qui in id operam impendunt, ut veritatis tuendae specie, veritatem exagitent et opprimant.*[76]

. . . deceptive and worthless little men, who, on the pretext of defending the truth, strive to disturb and suppress it.

O'Sullivan, with a zeal worthy of Jerome, continues:

Ridiculos vero tenebriones, qui veritatis defendendae fuco veritati excidium affere machinantur, de veritate, quam pessime mereri quis ignoret? Quis etiam risum teneat, cum tenebrio candide, sineque felle se dicat egisse: qui tot mendaciorum commentis insulae catholicae ornamenta nonnulla in Hebrides, et Orcades rupes abdere, plura in suam Haereticam Calvinidoniam transferre, pleraque extenuare conatus, nostros etiam maiores, qui divi Ethbini tempore et florentissima Religione fulgebant, et ampliore principatu erant potiti, barbaros appellavit. Et cum timidus roget ne nos in se vehementius invehamur, id accidit, quod homini nimiae arrogantiae solet contingere, ut postquam peccavit, supplicium deprecetur. Alii Iberni, qui ante me de hoc argumento scripserunt, quam modestos gesserint se, id fidem facit, quod Caledonios Pictos Catholicae veritatis desertores ne haereticos quidem nominarint. Eo vero nomine a me, qui et si non licentiam, tamen libertatem loquendi proprietatemque sermonis amo, eos vocari, aequo animo fera[n]t.[77]

Who would not be aware that those ridiculous tricksters (who upon the pretext of defending the truth in fact conspire to destroy it) are not in the least deserving of trust so far as the truth itself is concerned? And who could refrain from laughter when the trickster says that he has acted openly and without animosity – when, having attempted, using the fabricated accounts of so many liars, to spirit away many of the glories of our Holy Isle to the Hebrides and the Orkney rocks, and to transfer many more to his own heretical Calvinidonia, and to belittle most of our claims, he has even described as 'barbarous' our ancestors, who in the time of St Ethbin were not only illustrious in the most vigorous religious life but also ruled over a greater dominion? And since he meekly pleads that we should not attack him too vehemently, it happens (as it usually does to a man who is too arrogant) that having committed a sin, he seeks to avoid the punishment. It is a measure of how moderately other Irishmen, who have written about this question before me, conducted themselves that they did not even call the Caledonian Picts, deserters of the Catholic truth, 'heretics'. But let my countrymen patiently allow *me* (who am if not wholly in favour of unbridled verbal abuse, yet disposed to speaking candidly, and to attaching the proper signification to language) to call those [Caledonians] by that name ['heretics'].

This then is something of the content and tenor of the *Tenebriomastix*. For his unflagging devotion to his native land, and unstinting effort in the defence of Gaelic Ireland and its cultural and religious traditions – at a time when these most needed defending – Philip O'Sullivan is owed a debt of gratitude by all who value the survival of that culture, and rightly holds an honoured place in our literary history; and his *Compendium* is acknowledged, not only as an invaluable historical document but also for having provided a much-needed alternative voice in the recounting of events in which he was himself intimately involved. Were it not for O'Sullivan's *Compendium*, the published accounts of Irish history of that period would have been almost entirely those of the victors. His polemical works, as contributions to Gaelic Ireland's struggle for cultural survival (a struggle which succeeded to a great extent), while they are to my mind no less valuable as a constituent of Ireland's overall literary heritage, for the insight they provide into many religious and political concerns of the Irish in Europe during that period, must nonetheless be regarded as being of less importance in the impact they made, if only for the fact that neither the *Zoilomastix* nor the *Tenebriomastix* was published, and had a limited circulation in manuscript form – MS 259 being one such copy (and the only extant text) of the *Tenebriomastix*.[78]

7. A case study in rhetorical composition:
Stephen White's two *Apologiae* for Ireland

JASON HARRIS

In 1584 the precociously talented Dubliner Richard Stanihurst published his *De Rebus in Hibernia Gestis* (see Chapter 2, this volume). This text offered to a European-wide audience what purported to be an introduction to the culture and history of Ireland. Published in Antwerp at the prestigious workshop of the scholar-printer Christopher Plantin, the work was in fact an elegant Ciceronian rewriting and updating of the medieval author Giraldus Cambrensis. Giraldus had been a contemporary apologist for the Norman invasion of Ireland, and his propagandistic descriptions of the country contained a great many obfuscations, misinterpretations and libels about Gaelic Irish culture. Although Giraldus was largely ignored by his contemporaries, the rediscovery of his manuscripts in the late sixteenth century resulted in a series of publications that presented him as the leading medieval authority on Ireland.[1] To Irish historians of the seventeenth century, anxious to defend their country's reputation for sanctity and learning, Giraldus became something of a *bête noire*, whom they attempted to discredit as prejudiced, unsophisticated, even incoherent – in short, the antithesis of the cultivated humanist scholar. It was therefore all the more embarrassing and troubling that the Irishman Stanihurst had propagated many of Giraldus' misrepresentations, repackaged in the eloquent prose of an accomplished humanist stylist.[2] Several Irish authors in the first half of the seventeenth century wrote refutations of Giraldus and Stanihurst, but it was not until 1662 that a definitive rebuttal made it into print, the *Cambrensis Eversus* of John Lynch. The earlier works survive in manuscript, and two of them written by the Irish Jesuit Stephen White are the subject of the following analysis.

Stephen White was born in Clonmel in 1574. Nothing certain is known about his early education, but by the mid-1590s he had joined the community of young Irish Catholic exiles in Spain, and on 13 October 1596 he became the first student of the Irish College in

Salamanca to become a Jesuit, being then a Bachelor of Arts. While pursuing studies for a doctorate in theology, he taught arts and metaphysics at Salamanca until 1605, when he travelled to Ingolstadt to take up a lectureship in scholastic theology. He continued in this post until 1609, when he swapped places with Sebastianus Heiss, taking the latter's position as professor of theology at Dillingen, where he lectured on scriptural exegesis and scholastic theology until 1622. From 1623 to 1627 he was in the province of Champagne, and confessor of the Germans at Pont-à-Mousson; and from 1627 to 1629 he was confessor of the Germans and spiritual father at the college of Metz. Then he returned to Ireland in 1630, spending most of his time in Waterford and Clonmel. He seems to have travelled to Dublin on several occasions, making use of the library of Archbishop Ussher, among others. The last years of his life were spent in Galway, where he died at some time in the late 1640s.[3]

Apart from his teaching, White's earliest known contribution to intellectual life was the assistance he provided William Bathe, the spiritual director of the Irish College in Salamanca, to write his widely renowned *Janua Linguarum*, though precisely what White's contribution was remains unclear. White was also the praeses for numerous theological theses that were published during his years in Germany, and he himself wrote two compendious theological treatises on matters of Catholic controversy, though these were never published.

The works under consideration in this article belong to a second group of writings that White left in manuscript. He was among the first Irish authors who attempted to vindicate the honour of his country against Scottish historians who attributed to Scotland rather than Ireland the saints and scholars of ancient Scotia (see further Chapter 6, this volume). Throughout his years in Germany and France, White transcribed manuscripts and compiled lists of Irish saints; in later years he sent transcripts to Hugh Ward, James Ussher, Peter Fleming and John Colgan, and his catalogue of Irish saints occupied a substantial place in early Irish hagiographical scholarship. Such studies may have contributed to his broader interest in Irish historiography, but his earliest surviving writings were almost certainly inspired by the Englishman William Camden's publication of Giraldus Cambrensis' *Expugnatio Hibernica* and *Topographia Hibernica*. White responded by composing an *Apologia pro Ibernia*, which, although begun in 1611, was still in preparation after 1613, as it refers to Rosweyde's *Old Roman Martyrology*, published in that year. This *Apologia* is a systematic rebuttal of Giraldus Cambrensis; however, it remained unpublished twenty years later when White again took up his pen to write an *Apologia*, this time rebutting Stanihurst's *De Rebus in Hibernia Gestis* (1584). As such, it might seem an obvious target for Stephen White, yet his rebuttal was composed fifty years subsequent to the publication of *De Rebus*. The occasion for White's renewed efforts may have been his return to Ireland, where he would have found a receptive audience stirred up by the increasingly ill-tempered Scotic debate. After his return, White composed several historical studies pertaining to the country's history, though they were never published. Lack of money is normally adduced as the reason for this, but political sensitivities about the simmering Scotic controversy may have quelled enthusiasm for perpetuating the debate in print. After White's death, the task of deciding whether his manuscripts were worth publishing was left to the Irish antiquarian scholar John Lynch; yet the works still did not appear, perhaps because Lynch, judging by his subsequent publications, disagreed with many of the arguments presented in them.

In what follows, I examine White's two *Apologiae* for Ireland (rebutting Giraldus and Stanihurst), and I consider in particular the rhetorical dimension of these texts. In the earlier of the two works White already noted his displeasure with the way in which Stanihurst had written '*stylo longe limatiore quam lex historiae praecipiat aut permittat*' ('in a style far more refined than the rule of history enjoins or permits').[4] In the later *Apologia* he elaborated on his concerns:

> *et quamquam nemo sapiens lectorue peritus Richardi librorum quatuor, non potest eosdem damnare tanquam infectos memoratis malis ac vitijs tam moralibus quam historicae imperitiae rerum Patriae et Peregrinarum plurimum: non desunt tamen etiamnunc multi exterarum Gentium, vti saepe sum expertus, qui valde ignari rerum, Regionis, Nationis Ibernorum, et delectati latina Richardi elegantia, eloquentia, acumine, facilem ex animi leuitate fidem illi accomodant narranti plurima fabulosa, iniuriosaque nationi suae.[5]*

> And although no wise man or reader acquainted with Richard's four books could fail to condemn them as infected with the evils already mentioned, and with faults both in morals and in historical ignorance of domestic and foreign affairs; nevertheless even now there are many from foreign races, as I have often found, who know nothing of the Irish, what they do, where they live or who they are, and, entertained by Richard's Latin elegance, eloquence and acumen, out of levity of mind they grant to him ready credence as he relates many things fictitious and insulting to his own people.

In this passage, White revives a criticism that faced the early humanist reformers of Latinity: the charge that their works valued the medium over the message, form over content. Humanist attempts to recover classical eloquence were dogged by the suggestion that they corrupted the rhetorical category of *inventio* (which deals with the selection of material for a discourse) by substituting in the place of logic mere *copia*, that is, a charming abundance of witty and apposite phrasing. According to White, 'levity of mind' caused many to be deceived by the shallow polish of Stanihurst's text, despite its poor command of history and its faulty morality. Implicit in White's phrasing is a concept that had by the mid-seventeenth century come to offer an alternative ideal to the early Renaissance valorization of eloquence: *gravitas*, that is, weightiness, profundity, sagacity.

Later in the same text, White cites Plutarch's criticism of Herodotus as an apt reflection of Stanihurst's failures as a historian: rather than concentrating on historical accuracy, he revels in '*ostentatione facundiae suae laminae*' (showing off the cutting edge of his eloquence)[6] and, while doing so, he says that Stanihurst is able to create a polished veneer that hides his injudicious selection and rejection of evidence. Thus, Stanihurst's fluent and bewitching style of writing gives a '*velo honesto*' (veil of respectability)[7] to false and partisan argument. This is not simply because Stanihurst can write well, or can make what sounds like a convincing argument; it is because in the Renaissance good writing style required a command of classical literature that could only be attained by the learned, and, then as now, learning was easily equated with intelligence or wisdom. It is therefore important to assess White's own style and use of rhetoric in the text he composed to refute Giraldus, and more particularly in his refutation of Stanihurst, whose use of rhetoric he criticized.

The two texts under consideration, then, are Stephen White's *Apologia pro Ibernia*, a refutation of Giraldus Cambrensis written around 1615; and the same author's *Apologia pro innocentibus Ibernis*, a refutation of Richard Stanihurst written around twenty years later in the late 1630s. Both these works, therefore, present judicial cases, as White himself makes clear in his address to the reader at the beginning of his refutation of Giraldus:

> *Tu vero, humanissime lector, si vis et vacat haec nostra legere, rogatum volo, ut neque mihi dicenti, neque Gyraldo contradicenti assensum accommodes; sed si placet, meis probationibus (quando videris esse plenas ac probas) et vestris oculis fidem habeas.*[8]

> Truly, most cultivated reader, if you wish and have leisure to read these our writings, I wish to ask you to give your assent neither to me pronouncing nor Giraldus contradicting; rather, if you please, place your trust in my proofs (when you find them full and sound) and in the evidence of your own eyes.

Both *Apologiae* employ a common argumentative strategy and writing manner, in accordance with the genre and the author's own style; they also contain many cognate passages and similar turns of phrase owing to the close relationship between their subjects, the writings of Giraldus and those of Stanihurst. For judicial cases such as these, early modern authors could follow classical precedent as represented by the rhetorical handbook most commonly used in the seventeenth century, the *Rhetorica ad Herennium*. The *Rhetorica* outlines a six-part structure for a judicial case: an introduction, statement of agreed facts, enumeration of points to be considered, presentation of one's own case, refutation of one's opponent, and finally a conclusion. Yet the text also admits of circumstances in which it may be appropriate to adapt the arrangement of an argument to the needs of the occasion (*ad casum temporis*).[9]

In both his *Apologiae*, White initially seems to follow the schema outlined in the *Rhetorica*, but departs from the oratorical format owing to the length and complexity of his material. Instead of outlining his own arguments, followed by refuting those of his opponents, he adapts his argument to the form of a systematic commentary that shadows the contours of the texts he is analysing. These commentaries gradually give way to increasingly extended discussions which can seem somewhat like digressions. While the earlier text, the *Apologia pro Ibernia*, ultimately winds up in a conclusion of sorts, the *Apologia pro innocentibus Ibernis* merely ends, without summation, by commenting on the last sentences of Stanihurst's *De Rebus*. On the one hand, this rhetorical arrangement is less balanced and cohesive than the schema presented in the *Rhetorica*; yet, on the other hand, it is not ill-considered and combines systematic analysis with flexibility as regards the space granted to commentaries on matters of greater or lesser importance. Nevertheless, given the length and complexity of White's argument accumulating critical notes on Giraldus and Stanihurst, it is striking that the *Apologia pro innocentibus Ibernis* ends without a concluding section or passage. In the *Apologia pro Ibernia* he had devoted the large part of a chapter to summarizing his argument and restating his main criticisms of Giraldus; yet he then took the unusual step of providing one more quotation which shows his opponent contradicting himself. Thus the final sentences of the work are given over to quotation, perhaps a gesture towards White's claim (quoted above) that he wishes the reader to judge the evidence rather than merely being swayed by claim and counter-claim.[10] By contrast, his rebuttal of Stanihurst seems to run out of steam, and it suffers greatly from the lack of a closing peroration.

An explanation for the differences in structure between the two works may be deduced from the state of the surviving manuscripts. The *Apologia pro Ibernia* survives in two copies (one imperfect) that offer few variant readings. Written much earlier in White's life, it shows all the characteristics of being a finished work that has undergone authorial revision. By contrast, only one manuscript of the *Apologia pro innocentibus*

Ibernis is known to survive, and it is an imperfect scribal copy apparently commissioned after the author's death when White's compatriot John Lynch arranged for a transcript of the work to be made so that he might assess its worth for publication.

The copy that Lynch received, which appears to have outlived its exemplar, was extensively corrupted during the process of transmission. Some of the scribes employed on the task appear to have had only limited command of Latin, wandering attention, and difficulties with spelling that appear to have been compounded by local variations in pronunciation. Numerous passages in the text have been rendered incoherent, and while the sense of some of these can be reconstructed, others remain thus far impenetrable. It is also quite noticeable that the scribes have struggled to fit the text on to the 200 sheets of paper that were provided for the task – the number and length of lines on each page increases dramatically towards the end. Yet the original composition has not been entirely occluded. Idiosyncrasies of style remain evident, orthographic peculiarities can be systematically analysed to eliminate scribal error and identify authorial design, and some solecisms can be attributed to authorial rather than scribal error. What is most important is that the manuscript contains evidence of incomplete composition. While it is impossible to be sure how much haste or deliberation lay behind each sentence and passage, it is clear that the author had not yet taken the time to fill in all the gaps, never mind to polish the whole work.

There are thus two reasons to focus more on the Latinity of the *Apologia pro innocentibus Ibernis* than on its better-crafted predecessor. Not only does its refutation of Stanihurst more explicitly raise discussion of the value of rhetoric itself, but also the text provides an opportunity for assessment of the fluency of the author's Latin and the fluidity of his rhetorical process of invention. Yet both texts must be read together – there will be no risk of attributing to hasty composition solecisms which also occur in the more polished work, while those that do not can be identified and scrutinized with an eye to the unfinished character of the text.

Let us first examine White's attitudes towards historical style, a matter discussed at the beginning of the *Apologia pro Ibernia* in the address to the reader. As we have seen, White insists that he does not want the reader to be persuaded by the claims and counter-claims either of Giraldus or of White himself, rather he wishes the reader to attend to the evidence presented in the text. He suggests that he will make his case not through assertion but through evincing examples of places where Giraldus contradicts himself.

*illud maxime curavi, ut in illo facilius, majore cum auctoritate et fide
refutando, vix meis utar verbis aut amplificationibus, vel coloribus argu-
mentorum longe petitorum, sed ipsius Gyraldi verbis contra Gyraldum
aperte testantibus, partim manifestam prae se absurditatem, piarumque
aurium offensionem ferentibus; vel verbis utar S Bernardi, et aliorum.*[11]

Above all I have taken care that, for refuting more easily and with
greater authority and assurance, I shall scarcely use my own words or
elaborations, or styles of argument sought from far and wide, but
rather the words of Giraldus himself clearly testifying against
Giraldus, and in part carrying before them their manifest absurdity
and their offensiveness to pious ears; or else I shall use the words of St
Bernard and others.

This declaration betrays reserve about the truth value of rhetoric or, better,
about the type of rhetoric that is appropriate to a historical treatise. Not
only did Giraldus fail to distinguish probable historical fact from legend
and rumour, nor did he merely distort his evidence to suit his patrons or
relatives, but also he wrote scathing criticisms of all those who met with
his disapproval. White felt that contemporary readers should clearly have
been able to discern how unreliable Giraldus was because his style was
too corrosive and he favoured pure rhetoric instead of solid reasoning:

*. . . quem nimis mordacem esse et intolerandum non minus heretico quam
Catholico lectori insinuavi superius, ubi videtur quaerere colores magis
quam reddere rationes veras.*[12]

. . . which [style] I suggested above was too mordant and intolerable,
not less for a heretical than for a Catholic reader, when he seems to
seek rhetorical colours rather than to provide reliable arguments.

White suggests here that the savage aggression of Giraldus' Latin and the
emptiness of his rhetorical assertions are in themselves irreligious.
Throughout the subsequent commentary White argues that the clergy,
saints and pious laymen of Ireland are maliciously misrepresented by
Giraldus, and he seems to feel that there is an organic connection
between Giraldus' loose morals, writing style and accuracy as a historian:

*Nemo est modestioris mentis, et animi Catholici, qui vel mediocri judicio
pollet, qui paulo attentius illa legens, non statim videat et passim observet
plurima quae non parum detrahant honori Dei.*[13]

There is no one of balanced mind and Catholic sensibility – having
even a modicum of judgment – who on reading those things a little
more attentively would not immediately see and observe throughout
many things which greatly detract from the glory of God.

This assessment of Giraldus' writings as sacrilegious affects his method of arguing; he attempts not only to demonstrate the falsity of Giraldus' rhetorical veneer, but also the irreligious motivation behind it. His text is littered with exclamations and insinuations about the sacrilegious impulse concealed within Giraldus' putative historical account.

Rhetoric, then, is clearly, in White's eyes, a dangerous tool in the hands of a fool or malicious critic; yet he certainly does not himself eschew eloquence or rhetoric. The best examples of this are, naturally, to be found in his more polished work, the *Apologia pro Ibernia*. The text itself is carefully wrought to bolster the analysis with well-crafted arguments and elegant sentences. At the beginning and end of the work it is particularly evident that the author has aimed for literary felicity to cultivate and confirm the appeal of his arguments. The opening sentence is an attractively constructed period which foregrounds the substance of what is to be refuted before identifying the author:

> *In contumeliam multorum cum sanctorum ecclesiae triumphantis et militantis, tum diversarum Europae provinciarum, personarum, ac potissimum totius Ibernorum nationis, olim ante 400 circiter annos, plures suos libros sparsit, quidam apud multos nostrae aetatis homines immerito in pretio habitus Silvester Giraldus.*[14]

> Formerly, about 400 years ago, a certain man called Silvester Giraldus, unjustly well-regarded by many men in our time, spread far and wide his many books in slander of many holy men of the church triumphant and militant, and particularly of the diverse provinces of Europe, of individuals, and above all of the entire race of the Irish.

The sequence of conjunctions '*cum . . . tum . . . ac potissimum*' creates a harmonious sense of crescendo as the period reaches its mid-point, which is then followed by a concrete temporal referent, and the main clause, before the period rolls out into a final sequence in apposition to the subject of the main verb, Giraldus. The rhythm of the period is carefully controlled so that the short central clauses are sandwiched between the more flowing beginning and ending. In terms of metrics, the sentence opens: $-/-$ v $-$ v $-/-$ $-$ $-$, which is sonorous, but perhaps not specific enough an arrangement for us to be sure that it is deliberate. The final words of the sentence, however, suggest that White was conscious of the rhythm with which he closed the period. He refers to Giraldus, slightly unusually, by his full name, Silvester Giraldus, rather than the more common Giraldus Cambrensis. This provides a combination of a molossus and cretic ($-$ $-$ $-$ /v $-$ v) that grants impressive closure and underlines the pun – Silvester means 'wild man'.

The ending of the prefatory letter to the reader is not less elegant, confidently rolling together flattery and modesty in a formulation that is characteristic of humanist stylistics, and ending with a sequence of verbs in classical Ciceronian fashion:

> *Confido conatum industriamque meam qualemcumque a sincera mentis et professione pietatis in sanctos, in religionem Catholicam et in patriam profectam, apud tuam humanitatem et candorem, si non laudem, quam nequeo ambio neque aveo, saltem excusationem exoraturam, si minus tibi satisfecero quam optarim aut promiserim.*[15]

> My effort and labour, of whatever quality, begun with pure mind and profession of piety towards the saints, the Catholic religion, and my country, will obtain from your cultivation and illustriousness, if not praise (which I am neither seeking nor desiring) at least forgiveness if I turn out to have been less pleasing to you than I have wished or promised.

This concern with the rhetoric of culmination or closure is also evident at the end of the book. White opens his final chapter with a peroration that provides a forceful recapitulation of the book's arguments:

> *Audisti, lector, Cambrensem cum laude recensentem nomina, resque gestas Ibernorum sanctorum . . . Vidisti quoties, quam severe, citoque vindex Deus a temeratoribus sanctorum, vel violatoribus locorum, quae illis sacrata erant, poenas exegerit. Quotquot autem temerarii a Gyraldo recensiti fuerunt, constat omnes fuisse ipsius vel cognatos, vel cognatorum famulos, vel populares suos Brittanos, nam, ipso teste, fuerunt sagittarii, hoc est, milites qui acu et sagitta utebantur in turmis Brittannorum, qui Iberniam invaserunt. Vide vero ut Gyraldus confestim vela convertat, et occasione vindictae sumptae de suis popularibus temeratoribus sanctorum Iberniae locorum, obloqui videatur.*[16]

> You have heard, reader, Cambrensis recounting with praise the names and deeds of Irish saints . . . You have seen how many times, how harshly and swiftly the vengeful God exacted satisfaction for wrongs from the ravishers of saints, the violators of places which were sacred to them. But however many of these rash men were recounted by Giraldus, it is clear that all were known to him, or were his relatives, or his fellow Britons, for, by his own testimony, they were archers, that is, soldiers who used the arrow or dart within the squadrons of the Britons who invaded Ireland. See, in truth, that Giraldus quickly turns his sails and seems to speak ill of them on the occasion when revenge is taken on his countrymen who were ravishers of the holy places of Ireland.

The repetition of syntax and rhythm in each sentence creates a cumulative cadence that culminates in the change of tense and mood to the imperative '*vide*'. This direct address to the reader induces a sense of closure and circularity, and the allusion to the opening of the book is reinforced by the resumption of a metaphor used earlier (*vela convertat*). An impressive sense of finality is conveyed by the use of formal periods that conclude with orotund final phrases (*poenas exegerit, Iberniam invaserunt*, and *obloqui videatur*). White thus closes his book with a certain stylistic felicity, demonstrating his ability to compose elegantly balanced sentences. Although it appears that he has not studiously shaped the rhythm of each sentence, he seems to have written with an ear well attuned to cadence.

Nevertheless, the majority of the *Apologia pro Ibernia* is written in a less sophisticated style that largely eschews periodic form, intricate wordplay, and elaborate metaphor or syntax. The few passages in which he does employ metaphors or more vivid prose stand out all the more because of their exceptional character, such as the following description of his own text as a remedy against poison. He says that he has written:

> . . . in gratiam Catholici lectoris, aut alterius cujus, bonae mentis, avidae veritatis et cupidae scorpiaci sive alexipharmaci adversus gravissime noxios de rebus variis errores plurimos, et non pauciores morsus venenatos famosarum chartarum.[17]

> . . . for the sake of the Catholic reader, or anyone else of good mind which, avid for the truth and eager for an antidote or remedy against the very numerous mortally poisonous errors on various matters, and not fewer envenomed bites from scandalous writings.

While medical metaphors are standard fare in polemic, White's choice of words is exotic: '*scorpiacum*' is a remedy against a scorpion's sting, used of argument by Tertullian in his attack on the Gnostics; and '*alexipharmacon*' is a Graecism meaning antidote, found transliterated in Pliny's *Natural History*, but normally rendered in Latin by '*remedium*'.[18] White thus extends the standard poison metaphor beyond commonplace expression. This is all the more striking because of the paucity of such metaphorical ingenuity elsewhere in the text. Although the book is scattered with exhortations and ejaculations addressed to his long-deceased interlocutor, the *Apologia pro Ibernia* is, in comparison to other texts of the time, a remarkably even-tempered polemic. Disinclined to respond in kind to the insidious and impious vigour of Giraldus' rhetoric, White opted for a milder (though not less insistent) argumentative strategy. This style chimes well with his, admittedly rhetorical, self-presentation as an author who eschews rhetoric in favour of analysis. Thus, he explains that his approach is intended:

> *Ut vero videar (ut revera sum) non male animatus in Gyraldum, sed in mala ejusdem scripta, vanitatem, immodestiam et maledicentiam in sanctos Dei, et patriam gentemque meam.*[19]

> So that I might seem (as in fact I am) to be not ill-intentioned towards Giraldus, but towards his evil writings, his vanity, his lack of restraint, and his slander against the devout followers of God and against my country and people.

A rhetorical pose in itself, this stated goal is White's own *Apologia* for his style of writing and arguing. The idea is to appear modest and balanced, and to seem to let Giraldus' manifest errors speak for themselves. Hence the bathos of the book's last words: '*Haec et his plura Gyraldus Cambrensis.*' (These things and more than these did Giraldus Cambrensis [write]).

In summary, White's view of Giraldus is that he was an inaccurate historian whose biases led him to impiety and superstitions which he then set forth in a heap of rhetoric designed to distract attention from the tenuous evidence for the arguments he promulgated. Yet White is faced with the difficulty of accounting for the fact that his adversary is '*apud multos nostrae aetatis homines immerito in pretio habitus*' (unjustly well-regarded by many men in our time).[20] He was not satisfied, therefore, merely to expose these historical inaccuracies, but also wished to discredit Giraldus and his writings altogether, to ensure that sacrilege and superstition were thoroughly expunged from Irish historiography. To achieve this, he had to tackle the rhetorical elaboration of Giraldus' texts, a problem that was compounded by Stanihurst's sophisticated recasting of them.

What already exercised White's anxieties in the 1610s was that all the devices of neo-Latin humanist scholarship and craft had been employed to revive Giraldus' intolerable misrepresentations. It was bad enough that the English antiquarian William Camden had popularized Giraldus' ideas in the English vernacular, and that he had been the source for Abraham Ortelius' quotation of Giraldus in his best-selling atlas, the *Theatrum Orbis Terrarum*. Thanks to the efforts of these men, a European-wide audience was at risk of being duped by this putative medieval authority on Ireland.[21] Yet it was worse still that a contemporary Irish author had supported many of Giraldus' absurdities. The flamboyant Irish Latinist Richard Stanihurst had reinforced the rhetorical impact of the text by recasting it in polished humanist Latin in his popular history of Ireland *De Rebus in Hibernia Gestis* (1584). It was to rebut Stanihurst's work (and, indirectly, Giraldus) point by point that White decided to compose his *Apologia pro innocentibus Ibernis*. Although Giraldus had been well able to use rhetoric to shape his argument and obviate objections, his writing contained many of the medievalisms that humanists were so keen to expunge from Latinity. To write sophisticated and elegant Latin in the pure style of the ancients, as Stanihurst did, required considerable learning and thus conferred added authority upon the author and his text. Thus rhetoric would be even more important to White's rebuttal of Stanihurst than it had been to his refutation of Giraldus.

Already in the *Apologia pro Ibernia* White was conscious of the importance of Stanihurst in transmitting the ideas of Giraldus:

> *Quae omnia, ut et alia a me postmodum de Gyraldo proferenda, si occurrissent oculis aut memoriae duorum inter alios virorum, vere, nisi vehementer fallor, et piorum et eruditorum Joannis Picardi et Richardi Stanihursti, non redegisset iste, ut fecit, in compendium et stylo longe limatiore quam lex historiae praecipiat aut permittat, Vaticinalem Cambrensis Historiam, passim fabulosam.*[22]

> All of which, along with other things which I will later present from Giraldus, if they had occurred to the eyes or memory of two men (among others), the pious and learned Joannes Picardus and Richard Stanihurst, truly, unless I am totally mistaken, the latter would not then have, as he did, redacted the Visionary (and everywhere fictitious) History of Cambrensis into a compendium in a much more refined style than the law of history demands or permits.

Stanihurst should have seen through Giraldus' rhetoric, but instead (White felt) he compounded the errors of his precursor by elaborating them without regard for truth or historical rigour. This would become a recurrent focus of his criticisms in the *Apologia pro innocentibus Ibernis*:

> *Vt supra monui moris est Stanihursto in hyperbolicis tam laudibus adulatorijs Britannorum qui Iberniam Iure Turcico inuaserant, quam vituperijs Ibernorum, qui sese inuasoribus opposuerant, vsurpare Maximas et Minimas superlatiui generis phrases, dicendo saepe, Maximas Ibernorum copias a minima Britannorum manu fusas, fugatas, caesas, interdum etiam et ab vno, vel duobus aut tribus tantum armatis Britannis erectos triumphos de numerosa illorum multitudine.*[23]

> As I noted earlier, it is Stanihurst's custom in exaggerating, both with sycophantic praises of those Britons who invaded Ireland in Turkish style, and his vituperations against those Irish who had opposed themselves to the invaders, to use both the greatest and smallest expressions of the superlative kind, often saying that the greatest multitudes of Irishmen were overthrown, put to flight, and cut down by the tiniest band of Britons, and sometimes that triumphs over a numberless multitude of these were won even by one, two or three armed Britons.

Again, the problem of reception preoccupied White. Stanihurst's glittering Latin prose ensured him a wider audience than his material deserved, and the success of his misrepresentations was further guaranteed because his entertaining style brought his work to the attention of the casual reader who had neither the prior knowledge nor sagacity to see through the shimmering web of empty rhetoric:

> *Et quamquam nemo sapiens . . . non potest eosdem damnare . . . non desunt tamen etiamnunc multi exterarum Gentium . . . qui . . . delectati latina Richardi elegantia, eloquentia, acumine, facilem ex animi leuitate fidem illi accomodant.*[24]

> And although there is no wise man . . . unable to condemn [those books]. nevertheless there are not lacking even now many from foreign races . . . who . . . entertained by Richard's Latin elegance, eloquence and sharpness, easily lend credence to him out of levity of mind.

To object to the slippery evasions covered by Stanihurst's eloquence and inventive fictions was one thing; to dismiss the value of rhetoric itself would have been entirely another. Instead, White merely opts for a different kind of rhetoric, supposedly more restrained by piety, patriotism and veracity. On closer examination, his practice appears less lofty than his stated aims.

White begins his refutation of Stanihurst with a standard technique of judicial rhetoric – the indirect opening, in which the opponent's character is questioned. In this instance there is a twist: because Stanihurst had in later life become a priest and a favourite of Philip II (the aggressively religious monarch of Catholic Spain), White has to make a clear distinction between the young and old Stanihurst. To do otherwise would have been to question the character of a Catholic clergyman, a fault which he had criticizzed in Giraldus and would also criticize in Stanihurst. The first words of the introduction thus begin by making this distinction:

> *Praecipitis ingenij, arrogantisque ignorantiae Iuuenem Ricardum Stani-hursthum eo refutatum, non Richardum senem, sapientem, sacerdotem, sacellanum Serenissimorum Archi-ducum Austriae et Belgij, Alberti et Isabellae, Paenitentem, atque inter caetera delicta iuuentutis et ignorantias lugendas numerantem famosa sua scripta in Patriam, quae sub ementito titulo Historiae de rebus gestis in Ibernia, absque praeuio examine, Appro-batione, et Censurâ publicâ Catholici Magistratus aut Censoris, anno Christi 1584: Antuerpiae curauit mandari typis Christofori Plantini, quo tempore tam iste, quam Ciues Antuerpienses fuere Rebelles aduersus suum legitimum dominum, et Catholicum Regem Hispanorum stetereque a Part-ibus Hereticorum.*[25]

I am going to refute the young Richard Stanihurst, of precocious mind and arrogant ignorance; not the old Richard, the wise man, priest and chaplain to the Most Serene Archdukes of Austria and Belgium, Albert and Isabella, the old man who was penitent and numbered among other errors and lamentable ignorances of his youth his notorious text about his homeland, which went by the false title of a history of the past events in Ireland, and which, without previous examination, approval or public censure by the Catholic magistrate and censor, in the year of Christ 1584, he sent to the press of Christopher Plantin, at which time both Plantin and the citizens of Antwerp were rebels against their legitimate lord and the Catholic king of Spain and stood on the side of the heretics.

The syntax forcefully emphasizes the parallel between the young Stanihurst (of rash mind) and the old Stanihurst (bearing the subsequently listed qualities); indeed it is a kind of extended chiasmus. The apposition of a sequence of participles moves the sense forward rather than merely bracketing extra information: '*sapientem . . . paenitentem . . . numerantem*'. The rest of the sentence spirals down into two subordinate clauses governed by the relative pronouns '*quae*' and '*quo tempore*', the first governed by the construction '*curauit mandari typis*' (a standard neo-Latin phrase meaning to send to the press, i.e. to publish) and the second switching to the historical and poetic forms '*fuere*' and '*stetere*' (for *fuerunt* and *steterunt*). There is no periodic structure, and the sentence dwindles away into relative clauses which insinuate a logical connection that is not explicit. Nevertheless, the message is effectively delivered in a lengthy sentence whose complexity is mastered by the elegant supine construction '*eo refutatum*'. Nor is this the end of White's opening salvo. He moves fluidly into the next sentence with a relative pronoun:

> . . . *quae sua praecipiti scripta ingenio Iuuenili, iudicio imaturo, ac plena falsitatis et iniuriarum, publicata, senex Richardus non verbo tantum, palamque multis in Hispania et Belgio, vti saepe fecit, sed etiam calamo, chartisque praelo mandatis parabat retractare, quo tempore coeptis, ne perficerentur, mors obstitit, quam ille plenam christianae Pietatis obiuit Bruxellis in Belgio, anno christi 1618, 18 Octobris.*[26]

> . . . which things of his, written with the rash mind and immature judgement of youth, and published full of inaccuracies and insults, the old Richard was in the process of retracting, not only orally in the presence of many people in Spain and Belgium, as he often did, but also in writing, in pages sent to the press; but at this time he was prevented from the completion of what he had begun by the fully Christian death, which he met at Brussels in Belgium on 18 October 1618.

Thus the contrast between the young and old Stanihurst is fleshed out while the illusion of concrete fact is cultivated by merging the (unprovable) claim that Stanihurst was preparing a public recantation with a statement of the precise date of his death. Again, the sentence lacks periodic structure to co-ordinate the sinews of its argument, but the form is not loose or sloppy. The opening section '*quae . . . publicata*' is a temporal construction with the passive participle, meaning 'when these had been published . . .'; the main clause is sandwiched in the middle '*senex . . . retractare*'. This part of the sentence is balanced by a '*non tantum . . . sed etiam*' construction. The second half of the sentence is introduced by '*quo tempore*', and it tails off with the relative clause '*quam . . . obiuit . . . Octobris*'.

White proceeds to explain the reason for his bothering to refute the worthless writings of the young Stanihurst, claiming (as quoted above) that many foreign readers have been fooled by the elegance of Stanihurst's Latin into believing the substance of his text. Further, the excesses to which Stanihurst's style led him (especially his criticisms of the Gaelic Irish) provided ammunition for the 'irreverent' Scottish antiquarian Thomas Dempster, who pillaged *De Rebus* in order to bolster his claim that the renowned ancient nation of 'Scotia' was not Ireland, as Stanihurst had asserted, but Scotland (see further Chapter 6, this volume). White's *Apologia* is therefore presented as a defence of the innocent who have been greatly wronged. Indeed, the sense of injustice that permeates White's writing leads him into error. He asserts that Stanihurst endured eternal exile from Ireland on account of the offence he had caused by his slanderous writings; in fact, the cause was Stanihurst's Catholicism and association with the martyr Edmund Campion.[27] White, himself a Catholic exile, blithely exploits Stanihurst's predicament with a clever twist of the knife, calling him a stranger to his own country even before he left:

> *Peregrinum autem in patria non vane voco iuniorem Richardum (ausum nihilominus scribere historias Patriae) qui tam etsi Patria genteque fuerit Ibernus, prorsus tamen ignorabat, et loqui et scribere, et intelligere idioma patrium ac genuinum, id est Ibernicum.*[28]

> However, not without reason do I call the young Richard a stranger in his homeland (who nevertheless dared to write its history), since, even though he may have been Irish by fatherland and family, could neither speak, write nor understand a single word in the inborn local idiom, that is, Irish.

Once again, the lack of periodic structure is made up for by the skilful balance of sense and syntax. The slick alliterative rhythm of the opening words oils the blade, and the closing gloss places the key word '*Ibernicum*' at the end of the sentence (in structural contrast to the opening word '*peregrinum*').[29]

White continues in this vein, devoting his first chapter to a potted biography of Stanihurst which emphasizes the contrast between the ambitious young tiro and the pious priest he would later become. Then, having set the scene for combat, he undertakes in the second chapter a systematic commentary on Stanihurst's text, chapter by chapter. The level of argument is at first disappointing. Lengthy quotations are interspersed with outbursts of indignation, or sarcastic interjections addressed to the deceased adversary, such as: '*Repete altius mendacia tua improbabilia et perge*' (Repeat louder your improbable lies and continue).[30] These occasionally are drawn out into strings of invective:

> *Numera si nosti quales hic describis ex quam minime paucis illis, vel tres quatuorue ab annis retro ducentis, et me mendacem infamemque nomina, O Mendax Iuuenis, Patriae tuae Infamator, atque sacri ordinis Ecclesiae praelatorum summorum o laice irreuerens.*[31]

> Number them if you know whom you are describing out of those very very few, perhaps three or four, two hundred years ago, or call me a liar and infamous, O lying young man, slanderer of your country and of the greatest prelates of the holy order of the Church, O irreverent layman.

White was particularly incensed because Stanihurst had used the generic Roman satiric figure of 'Cornelius' as the focus for his characterization of unlearned Irish bishops. He complains that:

> *Quales depingis Cornelios esse mere Platonicos Pontifices nusquam visos nisi in tuo phantasmate perturbato percitoque stimulis malarum irarum in Patriae tuae cuius honori is pessime consultum, episcopos.*[32]

> The types of Cornelius you depict are purely Platonic priests nowhere seen except in your disturbed imagination, which is over-excited by the stimuli of evil fits of rage against the bishops of your country, the honour of which you are going to serve in the worst possible way.

This level of debate can hardly be called rebuttal. The author's anger is conveyed by the alliterative plosives and rolling liquids (*stimulis malarum irarum*) of the first part of the sentence which wind up in the distended syntax caused by the exasperated interjection of the '*cuius*' sub-clause. However, not all of White's splenetic outbursts lack substance:

> *quaeso quo idiomate tunc iste Cornelius qui totam aetatem contriuit in numerandis domi, in Ibernia ouis gallinae, alloquatur remotarum Nationum obuios viatores Anglos, Belgas, Francos, Germanos, Italos; nam latiné penitus ignarum Cornelium negas hic et expressius postea. Dic aliquem saltem, dic o Stanihurste, colorem.*[33]

> Please tell me, in what language then did this Cornelius of yours (who
> spent all his life in counting hen's eggs at home in Ireland) speak to
> the travellers that he encountered from remote nations, English,
> Belgian, French, German, Italian; for here you deny that he was thor-
> oughly ignorant of Latin, as you do later more explicitly. Utter at least
> some – speak O Stanihurst – rhetorical colour!

Here at least White has found a contradiction in Stanihurst's portrait of
the stereotypical Irish bishop – if he knows no Latin on leaving the island,
how can he communicate with the various foreigners he meets abroad on
his search to become a cardinal? White's triumph leads him to the sarcastic
invitation to Stanihurst to '*Dic aliquem saltem . . . colorem*', where colour is
used in the sense it has in the medieval rhetorical handbooks.

In these early stages of his argument, White seems eager to quote
extensively, intervening at length only to provide lists of names and
instances that disprove Stanihurst's wilder claims. For example, he enu-
merates dozens of Irish saints and martyrs to counter Stanihurst's
depiction of the land as having been inadequately Christian in the Middle
Ages, and he cites numerous instances of inter-ethnic marriages to refute
the claim that the native Irish and 'Anglo-Irish' are socially, culturally and
racially distinct. Through the combination of incredulous expostulation
and detailed citation of evidence, White endeavours to convey the pre-
posterous character of his opponent's claims.

As his argument proceeds and he has dispensed with the early literary
flourishes in Stanihurst's text, White inclines to a more discursive, ana-
lytical approach. Thus, in his lengthy discussion of the controversial bull
Laudabiliter, which was purported to give a papal grant of dominion over
Ireland to the English monarch, White produces a multi-faceted critique
of the document as a historical source. He questions its authenticity by
arguing the lack of contemporary evidence for its existence, by claiming
to identify several instances of manuscript corruption, by pointing out
manifest errors in the chronology of Stanihurst's account, by outlining a
series of historical records that present a contradictory impression of
papal policy, and by denying that the bull is consistent with canon law,
natural law or human law. Throughout, he exploits the rhetorical device
of *commoratio*, dwelling on the point that the bull's author was a fabri-
cator, that Giraldus (in whose text it is recorded) was an idle flatterer of
whatever monarch reigned in England, and that the motives of the
English in Ireland were far from religious, a fact clearly evident to the
papacy, which had long been in conflict with Henry II over the privileges
of the Church in England. That White was manifestly wrong about the
authenticity of *Laudabiliter* does not detract from the fact that he mar-
shals his arguments impressively to expose the weaknesses and

inconsistencies in the evidence provided by Giraldus and Stanihurst.

White's ability to construct and clearly present a sophisticated, multi-layered argument is evident in the second half of his book. He frequently links his arguments to what has been mentioned before and what is yet to come in the text, though he never gives precise references. The overall structure of the book continues to follow the contours of Stanihurst's text in the form of a commentary, but there is a kind of thematic unity to the work that appears as he accumulates points relating to consistent topoi – the pious history of the Irish, the impious goals of the English conquerors, and the incoherent chronology in Stanihurst's account. He quotes extensively from writers such as Bede, Gildas, Bernard of Clairvaux, Henry of Huntingdon, William of Newburgh and Roger Hoveden to reinforce his critique of Giraldus and Stanihurst. By contrast, he quotes selectively from Stanihurst to present a simplified version of his argument. Indeed, he is not often sensitive to nuances in Stanihurst's text, consistently adopting the most damning interpretation, and it is clear that he has a larger purpose in mind than faithful commentary. Woven throughout are sarcastic expressions of the author's disdain for the historical skills of his opponent, and scandalized outbursts against the sacrilegious import of Stanihurst's Giraldine attack on the religious and cultural character of the Irish people.

Despite the consistency of attitude and the recurrence of key themes, there is no sense of co-ordinated movement in the overall work. White does not systematically develop various stages of a unified argument. The commentary format may be partly to blame, and certainly the book becomes more compelling once this structure is loosened towards the end of the work. Yet it is at the very end that the lack of structure is most apparent. The book closes without any peroration, and there seems to be no reason for the work to finish except that the commentary has reached the end of Stanihurst's book. The commentary format thus dictates the point of closure. There is no concluding paragraph, not even at the beginning of the chapter (as was the case in the *Apologia pro Ibernia*). Instead, a damning quotation from Roger of Hoveden is offered as a final consummation of the inaccuracies of Stanihurst's account, which had concealed the true atrocity of the English invasion of Ireland:

> *sed fallitur fabellator. teste Rog: qui ad an. 1197 ait praelia magna et caedes multas in Ibernia factas inter Ioannem Curceum Anglum comitem Vltoniae et Regulos Ibernos, et eodem anno ab Henrici proceribus Anglis in Ibernia factas iniurias ingentes archiepiscopo Dublin: Ioanni Cummin, et millenis et millenis ecclesiasticis alijs et Archiepiscopum exulasse &a.*[34]

> But the tale-teller has tripped up, according to the account of Roger of Hoveden who, for the year 1197, says that 'Great battles and many murders were carried out in Ireland between the English Earl of Ulster

> John de Courcy and the Irish chiefs, and in the same year great
> injuries were done in Ireland by Henry's English commanders to the
> archbishop of Dublin, John Cummin, and thousands and thousands
> of other churchmen, and the archbishop was exiled', etcetera.

The closing word 'etcetera' may be the key to understanding the flaccid
rhetorical structure of the text – what survives is an unfinished draft. This
is confirmed by the fact that at several points in the text a note indicates
that the author cannot remember a name, or an 'etcetera' suggests that
more detail may be added. The search for evidence of incompletion is,
however, greatly hampered by the fact that the multitude of scribal errors
in the manuscript obscures the degree to which the composition was polished. With regard to the end of the text, comparison with the earlier
Apologia pro Ibernia is instructive. In that work White had included
towards the end a recension of his main arguments, but his final paragraph was (as outlined above) only marginally less abrupt than the
ending of the *Apologia pro innocentibus Ibernis*. It seems that White
favoured closure through the words of others – a striking final statement
that the facts may speak for themselves.

If the overall structure of the work exhibits some rationale but lacks
finality, more polish might be expected of smaller-scale units such as
chapters and sentences. The chapters are, indeed, generally quite simply
structured: an opening heading introduces the subject, perhaps followed
by a brief introduction or link to the previous section; then follows a
quotation from Stanihurst or Giraldus which is to be contested; these are
either interrupted with commentary (in the earlier chapters) or subsequently analysed through ratiocination or quotation from relevant
authorities; and finally each chapter closes with a peroration that either
sums up the argument or reflects on the folly of Stanihurst/Giraldus. This
pattern is sometimes rendered more complex (increasingly towards the
end of the work) through the subdivision of the chapter into sections.
Nonetheless, the basic principle of introduction, quotation, and commentary, is followed quite consistently in these sub-sections, and
coherence of theme holds each chapter together.

White's construction of sentences is of course more varied. As in the
earlier *Apologia pro Ibernia*, most of his sentences reveal little effort to cultivate periodic form; instead, they seem to follow the flow of the author's
thought, with some concessions to Latinity and a few to stylistic effect.
The following is a telling example:

> *Vix diem vidit Richardi historia infaelix quando communi voce Gentis Iber-*
> *norum fuit clamatum, temere illum, iniurioseque famam Patriae prodidisse*
> *et perdidisse apud exteras nationes (quas ille caelare priusquam reuelare*

debebat dedecora suae gentis, etiamsi falsa non fuissent vt vere falsa fuere pleraque).[35]

Richard's ill-favoured history had hardly seen the light of day, when there was a clamour from the common voice of the people of Ireland that he had rashly and harmfully betrayed and destroyed the reputation of the country among foreign peoples (from whom he ought to have hidden the disgraces of his people rather than revealing them, even if they had not been false, as indeed the majority were false).

The flow of the sentence is clear. The tenses are formed in appropriate sequence, though again White uses the form *'fuere'* for *'fuerunt'* – a device that is common in neo-Latin prose. The syntax of the first half of the sentence is quite stylish, with two idiomatic verbal phrases (*diem vidit* and *fuit clamatum*) balancing each other at either end of the temporal construction, followed by a transition into *oratio obliqua* with the subject in the accusative bracketed by adverbs that receive particular emphasis so early in the clause. The unusual position of *'apud exteras nationes'* (which would normally come before the verb) may be explained by the wish to emphasize it syntactically as the antecedent of the subsequent pronoun *'quas'* – though such an arrangement is not necessary for the sake of clarity. The remainder of the sentence is an after-thought, but it is dealt with quite stylishly. The placement of the verbs prior to their object allows *dedecora* to dominate the remainder of the sentence, and the oddly emphatic placement of *'pleraque'* after *'fuere'* brings out the oxymoron *vere falsa*. Overall, the sentence seems spontaneous but measured; distended by the occurrence of additional thoughts, but not altogether lacking art.

This curious hybrid between eloquent Latin and rolling, uncrafted syntax is typical of the work as a whole. Hasty composition may be the principal explanation, but, if so, then White's success (for the most part) in avoiding solecisms is all the more remarkable. That is to say, given that the text in places appears to have been composed quite quickly and without revision, the author's control over the grammar and coherence of long sentences is impressive. Of course, the length of time devoted to different passages may have varied greatly. Immediately subsequent to the passage just discussed comes the following:

Tum vero Richardus ad se redijt, sua scripta reprehendit, quae commune odium sibi Gentis Patriaeque suae, pepererunt: in qua deinceps viuere nec iucundum fortasse nec tutum (quod inimicitias graues multorum in se Incolarum Patriae excitarit) arbitrabatur, ratusque non se iam saniore consilio posse vti, quam si vna cum vxore, et liberis, voluntario, vel necessario exilio aeterno sese damnaret.[36]

Then indeed Richard returned to his senses and censured his own writings, which had generated the widespread hatred of his people and country for him. He immediately judged it to be neither pleasant nor even perhaps safe to live in this land (because he felt he had aroused against himself the serious hostility of many of the inhabitants of his country), and considered that he could now use no safer plan than together with his wife and children to condemn himself to eternal exile, whether voluntary or necessary.

In this instance, the periodic form is not only properly employed but chimes in with the sense of the passage by conveying the swelling and ultimate culmination of causes in the final decision of Stanihurst to choose exile.

The most typical sentence structure employed by White is, however, not modelled on the classical period, nor is it an inelegant hybrid between vernacular and Latin rhetorical forms. It is the baroque sentence: a lengthy, versatile and highly wrought edifice that is characterized by vigorous language, hyperbole, lists of various kinds and synonymy (of nouns, adjectives and verbs). Since several of the sentences quoted earlier fit this pattern, I will give only one further example:

> *Stultum praeterea dictu fuit, et incredibile per se et contra consuetudinem mansuetudinis, caritatis, sapientiae, sedis Apostolicae, et iniuriosum famae Adriani Papae quod ipse quamuis Anglus et propensus in suam gentem eiusque regem, credatur adeo exorbitasse contra commune lumen rationis, contra ius gentium, contra legem Iustitiae, et humanitatis vt ad Henrici regis Angli accusationem petitionem, informationem relationem, malam de Ibernis, legationem solemnem aut canculariam inauditis, non examinatis Ibernis concederet illi eosdem et eorum Patriam omnem, in hostilem (vt vterque Matthaeus mendax et maledicus loquitur) praedam, in captiui-tatem, in vincula suorum Regum, et in aeternum libertatis auitae amissionem; praesertim vero gentem Ibernorum illam, quae in oculis eiusdem Adriani ante biennium fuerat tam gloriose exaltata, laudata, mag-nificata, inuentaque valde catholica, reformataque ab Apostolicae sedis Papa Eugenio 3 et eius oculato teste legato Cardinali.*[37]

Moreover, it was stupid, and unbelievable in itself, and contrary to the customary gentleness, charity, and wisdom of the Apostolic See, and insulting to the reputation of Pope Adrian, to say that this pope, even though he was English and favourable towards his own people and their king, may in fact be believed to have deviated from the common light of reason, the law of peoples, and the divine law of justice and humanity, that in response to the English King Henry's accusation, petition, document, ill report about the Irish, and solemn or secret legation, without hearing or examining the Irish, he should have conceded to the king those people and all their country, as the enemy's spoils (as both deceitful and ill-speaking Matthews[38] say), into captivity, into the fetters of their kings, and the loss forever of their ancestral liberty – and especially, indeed, that Irish people which before the eyes of this same Adrian two years previously had been so gloriously exalted, praised, extolled, and found to be extremely Catholic and reformed by Pope Eugene III of the Apostolic See, and his eyewitness, the cardinal-legate.

This lengthy, rolling sentence bears only a remote resemblance to the oratorically based period of antiquity; rather, it is a literary fulmination swollen by *parataxis* and *epanaphora* (co-ordinate constructions and repetition of the initial words of phrases). Wordplay, unusual syntax or learned allusion would easily cause confusion in such long sentences; hence repetition and synonymy foster clarity as well as rhetorical exuberance. Careful cultivation of prose rhythms or balanced sentence construction (*concinnitas*) would have added lustre without causing confusion, but, as can be seen from the above quotations, White seems not to have been particularly concerned with such devices. It may be that his death did not permit him to put the finishing touches to his work, yet sentences like the one just quoted are so typical of seventeenth-century baroque style that one can probably safely assume that White would not have altered them substantially.

The *Apologia pro innocentibus Ibernis* was clearly not intended to be a masterpiece of pithy expression, yet the text does not altogether lack the jewellery of rhetorical detail. Although it is not loaded down with the wealth of classical allusions found in many humanist works, there are several instances where the author offers maxims and echoes of the ancients. Most of these are merely commonplaces, such as the following:

> *Verum, vt, Aristotele authore, et Seneca descriptore, nullum magnum ingenium fuit sine mixtura dementiae.*[39]

> Truly, as argued by Aristotle, and quoted by Seneca, there is no great mind without some mixture of madness.

As well as quotations, there are quite a few citations, instantly recognizable to the early modern reader. For example, Stanihurst is taken to task for not paying heed to Plutarch's criticism of the excessive harshness and credulity in the writings of Herodotus.[40] Elsewhere, White counters Stanihurst's characterization of Henry II by the acid remark, '*Credat Iudaeus Apella, non ego qui Regem Henricum noui in cute et intus*' (Iudaeus Apella might believe it, but not I who know King Henry inside out).[41] This alludes to Persius' *Satires*, 3, 30: '*ego te intus et in cute novi*' (literally,

I know you within and under the skin); and also to Horace, *Satires*, Book 1, 5, 100: '*credat Iudaeus Apella*'. Likewise, Diarmuid MacMurrough is several times referred to as a second Sardanapalus (that is, a weak king devoted to luxuries).[42]

Alongside these commonplace allusions can be found several references to more recent figures, notably Machiavelli and Thomas More – the former used as an epithet for tyranny, the latter associated with utopian ideas.[43] Biblical reference also adds to the texture of White's prose. Thus, for example, Gerald of Wales's description of his own countryman Raymond Giraldus is mockingly described as follows:

> *Crederes, Reymundum hunc (quem suus Rex Henricus cum socijs praedones appellauit etcetera) alterum Iosue per medios alueos Iordanis pede sicco cum exercitu traijcientem.*[44]

> You might have thought this Raymond (whose own king called him and his associates robbers, and so forth) was another Joshua crossing dry-footed with his army through the middle of the Jordan's river bed.

Such citations, sparse as they are, reveal the echoes that would naturally occur to an author educated through memorization of the classics and biblical material; they do not suggest profundity of erudition or exceptional imagination.

White's stock of literary allusions and rhetorical devices is almost always used to enliven his habitually ironic or sarcastic tone. Along with adjectival lists, sarcasm is perhaps the most characteristic feature of his style in the *Apologia pro innocentibus Ibernis*; doubtless, this is in part owing to his writing within the genre of rebuttal, yet the extent of his reliance on sarcasm is distinctive. This can be seen in his frequent use of the prefix '*pseudo-*', the adverb '*scilicet*' and the rhetorical device of *paralipsis* frequently invoked through phrases such as '*ut omittam dicere*'.[45] Often he repeats terms and phrases of Stanihurst or Giraldus several times, gradually making them seem more and more foolish; sometimes he merely cites them once, prefaced by a phrase such as '*inepte/ridicule ab illo dictus*' (foolishly said/laughably phrased by him). This technique is related to White's concerns about his opponent's use of rhetoric, in which is embedded his innovative use of terms to describe distinctive characteristics of Ireland. A good example of this is his extended and recurrent attack on Stanihurst's coinage of the term '*Anglo-Ibernus*' (Anglo-Irish), which is frequently dismissed as ill-informed, inept and inappropriate. Likewise, White objects to Stanihurst's description of *De Rebus* as a '*dentata charta*', which is an echo of a passage from Cicero's letters. While Cicero thereby indicated the quality of the paper on which he was writing, Stanihurst used the phrase to refer to his own literary style.[46]

White, perhaps deliberately, misreads the word '*dentata*' as meaning 'biting' rather than 'polished' (it is not clear which meaning Stanihurst intended, though the meaning of Cicero's original is clear). This technique of abstracting and disputing the terms employed by one's opponent is, of course, discussed in the *Rhetorica ad Herennium*; yet, White employs the technique in support of his claim to expose the deceptive, unhistorical style of Giraldus and Stanihurst.[47] The summary of these arguments is characteristically expressed through sarcasm, often enhanced by the repetition of the words that have been disputed, as in the following instance:

> *Scilicet Stanihurste, tuus ille Syluester erat pereruditus, acerrimusque vetustatis Ibernicae contemplator.*[48]

> Yes, Stanihurst, of course this Sylvester of yours was 'extremely erudite' and 'a very discerning judge of the history of Ireland'.

To underline the irony in this pretended concurrence, White turns to *frequentatio*, giving a summary of the errors of Giraldus that have just been exposed. As a writer, White was not inclined to brevity; sarcasm took its place. Only occasionally and in passing does White's style approach the level of aggression found in the polemics of his bombastic Irish contemporary Philip O'Sullivan Beare (see further Chapter 6, this volume). Normally, he recounts his arguments, as in the following case:

> *Bone Deus! quis Ibernicorum est Richarde tutus a tuis telis? a tuis (contra fidem datam) aculeis, convitijs, ironijs, sarcasmis, contumelijs? non Ecclesiasticus, non Episcopus, non Dynasta, non Nobilis, non Iudex, non Poeta, non Miles, non Medicus, non Musicus, vnus.*[49]

> Good God! Is there any Irishman safe from your weapons, Richard? From your (contrary to the promise you gave) stings, insults, ironies, taunts and slanders? Not a churchman, not a bishop, not a chieftain, not a nobleman, not a judge, not a poet, not a soldier, not a doctor, not even a single musician.

The structure of this list is particularly felicitous because it follows the sequence of subjects that have been discussed by White, ending with the matter of the chapter he is then embarking upon (music). Yet it is in his discussion of the legal rights of the Norman conquest that White employs both the best of his arguments and the most choice rhetorical devices:

> *Quonam porro Iure alio quam donationis constantini imaginariae Adrianus si concessit, concesserit Henrico Dominium Iberniae? an Iure diuino fuerit Papa vllus Dominus temporalis vllius Terrarum Regni, Insulae Iberniae aut*

> *alterius? Ride. An iure humano politico vel Ecclesiastico? Ride. nam huius*
> *Iuris nullum fuit visum auditumve vestigium? An iure naturali? Ride.*[50]

> Moreover, is there any other right, setting aside the imaginary Dona-
> tion of Constantine, by which Adrian, if he had made such a
> concession, could have conceded dominion of Ireland to Henry? By
> divine law, could any pope have been temporal lord of any kingdom
> on earth, the island of Ireland or any other? Laughable. By human law,
> political or ecclesiastical? Laughable, for there is neither sight, sound
> nor vestige of such a right. By natural law? Laughable.

The combination of ratiocination and one-word response, as well as concise
enumeration of the various options, is simple and striking, though perhaps
somewhat less studied than a similar passage in Stanihurst's *De Rebus*, where
the answer is subtly varied to avoid mechanical repetitiveness.[51] Yet White
does not seem concerned with demonstrating fecundity of invention; force-
fulness of expression is his goal. He follows the textbook devices of
commoratio and *expolitio* (dwelling on a point and returning to it from
various angles and with different approaches) to expand and elaborate upon
his refutation of the legitimacy of the Norman conquest, but the sum of his
argument is effectively conveyed by his repeated use of the phrase 'ius tur-
cicum' – the law of the Turk, i.e. rule of force or tyranny. The phrase was not
coined by White, but its use in this context is remarkable. It is a culmination
of the accusations made early in the text that Giraldus and the young Stanihurst were irreverent in their sacrilegious criticisms of the clergy; but it also
taps into the anxieties and paranoia of seventeenth-century Christians that
the Ottoman Empire was about to sweep across Europe as a scourge for
divided, post-Reformation Christendom. On to this kindling White throws
the incendiary statement that quasi-legal justifications for the Norman conquest were invented and promulgated:

> *ab animo plusquam Turcico et Antichristiano, et humaniter hostili, et atro-*
> *cissime calumnioso, et imaniter infamante vniuersam Nationem eius*
> *temporis Ibernorum.*[52]

> by a worse than Turkish and anti-Christian mind, both exceedingly
> hostile and most atrociously slanderous, and monstrously defaming
> the entire Irish race of that period.

Nothing could better encapsulate White's argument that Stanihurst's
defence of the Norman conquest was both slanderous to his own nation
and hurtful to the pious. The pairing of 'Turkish' and 'anti-Christian'
echoed with the millenarian anxieties of the 1630s and 1640s – the reign
of the anti-Christ was looming.[53] White further exploits the idea several
pages later, summing up his arguments as follows:

> *quo quaeso iure? rapinae, iureque Turcarum violento, et Macchiauelli.*[54]

> By what right, I pray? The law of plunder, and the violent law of the
> Turks and Machiavelli.

Again, White's sensitivity to contemporary issues is revealed –
Machiavelli had recently passed from being the unthinkable, immoral
pragmatist to providing the subtext for English projects for reforming
Ireland. White insists on the abominable nature of such legitimation,
projecting backwards into the twelfth century a provocative web of
connotations from the mid-seventeenth century. Shortly afterwards, he
narrows his focus to one word which sums up the whole argument:

> *sed quid iuris habuit Henricus in Waterfordiam, Desmoniam, Mediam
> etcetera, quas extorsit a raptore Richardo priusquam ille ab Iberniae mag-
> natibus illum sibi postularet pugione ad illorum pectora stricto vel minante?
> Turcicum.*[55]

> But what right did Henry have over Waterford, Desmond, Meath,
> etcetera, which he took forcibly from the plunderer Richard before he
> summoned him to himself away from Ireland's magnates while his
> dagger was unsheathed or threatening at their chests? A Turkish way of
> operating.

Thus, even when Henry reprimanded his own agents in Ireland for their
excessive cruelty and self-aggrandizement, White sharply observes that
he did so to his own benefit, without returning to the Irish the ill-gotten
gains of the English, in this instance Richard de Clare, alias Strongbow.
Yet it is the sharpness of White's style when dealing with this topic that is
most important here. Although he is normally prolix, his revulsion and
sarcasm combine in this instance to prompt condensed and pungent
expression. Towards the end of his text, this ability to express himself
with biting concision appears several times; thus: '*ilicet, hoc verum est si
fas est credere falsis*' (Done! This is truth if falsehoods may be believed) –
which scans as a hexameter.[56] The schoolroom Latinity of '*ilicet*' (meaning
'it is permitted to go', a phrase used at the end of a class) is transposed
out of context here with intense irony, compounded by the hexameter
ending '*si fas est credere falsis*' – the lesson is over, truth has been replaced
by falsehoods. Such clipped and forceful quips lend a freshness and
vigour to White's prose towards the end of his work, which had been
lacking in earlier passages where ironic interjections took the place of
argument rather than pithily condensing them.

By contrast, the few examples of extended metaphors are found early in
the work, and they relate to Stanihurst's style rather than to the development
of an argument. The following two examples almost exhaust the supply:

> *sic Richardi adhuc Iuuenculi, vixque discipuli nomen et sedem deferentis,*
> *ingenium cum literaturae quali quali copia parum digesta suas alebat,*
> *despumabatque vt mustum faeces seu potius euaporabat fumos vanitatis,*
> *ambiebatque famam quasi perfecti Philosophi, idoneique doctoris ignoran-*
> *tium, et scriptoris logices.*[57]

> Thus the mind of Richard, at this point still a young man and scarcely
> bearing the name and position of a student, with some kind or other
> of abundance of literature poorly digested, was nourishing his dregs
> and spewing them out like fresh wine, or rather was emitting fumes of
> vanity, and seeking a reputation as of an accomplished philosopher, of
> a suitable teacher of the ignorant, and of a writer of a work of logic.

This passage plays on the commonplace metaphor that compares the
knowledge of ancient texts to fine wine – grapes were one of the most
common elements in humanist emblems and impresa. The following
metaphor depends on the fact that '*vela*' can mean 'pages' as well as 'sails':

> *vela late expandis, implesque, et inflas ventosa verborum hyperbolicorum,*
> *assentatione, laudibusque adulatorijs Tyrannicorum illorum, qui quondam*
> *inuaserant Iberniam.*[58]

> You copiously expand, fill up and inflate sails/pages with the puffed-
> up flattery of exaggerated words, and with adulatory praises of those
> tyrants who once invaded Ireland.

These passages show an ability to develop metaphors wittily and effectively, but White does not favour this style of writing. Normally his
metaphors are verbal, or are condensed into brief parenthetical similes,
or are found in the lists of adjectives and nouns that he heaps upon his
opponents. His restraint in this respect is perhaps related to his more
general reservations about elaborate style, its potential for misuse in historical writing, and its effect on the reader. Thus, in response to a fine
piece of rhetorical inveiglement by Stanihurst, he comments:

> *Vbinam Ricardus in re conferat tot, tantaque sua verba, raro aut nuncquam*
> *inuenio: sed saepissime inuenio contra vacua verba, etiam et aduersa.*[59]

> I rarely or never find where Richard has relevantly gathered his so
> many great words, but most often on the contrary I find his words
> empty and also negative.

It is impossible to be sure whether White's comments on the misleading
effects of Stanihurst's eloquence are sprung merely from the jealousy of a
less competent writer or whether they express substantive concerns about
the truth value of rhetoric. It is clear that White's refutation of Stanihurst

is inconsistent in the degree of care that seems to have been given to its rhetorical composition. Its overall structure is unbalanced, unpolished and ineffective; its sentences are inflated with venom and bombast, but frequently bathetic; and much of the text is devoid of flair or felicitous expression. Nevertheless, White's arguments become more sophisticated as the work progresses, developing from the puerile interjections of his opening chapters into lengthy, sophisticated and profoundly learned deployment of evidence towards the end. Although his sarcasm initially seems to have more bark than bite, later on his use of irony is often pithy and incisive. Despite his criticisms of Stanihurst's rhetoric, he uses a broad range of rhetorical devices himself in an attempt to ridicule as much as to disprove his opponent's arguments. While Stanihurst's rhetoric may be more noticeable because it is more impressively skilful, White's is equally embedded in the very structure of his work.

In conclusion, the text of the *Apologia pro innocentibus Ibernis* appears to have been in need of a final revision, and as such it lacks the lustre that careful polishing might have brought. Scribal corruption obscures the author's Latinity, though it is clear from comparison with the earlier *Apologia pro Ibernia* that many of the deficiencies of the work are attributable to the author, not the scribe. Genuine solecisms that can be identified as authorial are few; non-classical usage is more common but explicable because of the nature of the subject matter. Yet both texts, roughshod as they are, contain sufficient evidence to argue that the author could be eloquent, albeit that he lacked the highest literary talent. If the evidence of hasty composition in the *Apologia pro innocentibus Ibernis* is reliable, then White's command of Latin and of the literature of both antiquity and the Middle Ages is all the more impressive for being so fluent and so ready-to-hand. Nevertheless, possessed of an antiquarian's dislike for circuitous rhetoric and a theologian's suspicion of ornamentation, White is unlikely to have intended a revision that would have recast his text into glittering eloquence to rival Stanihurst. His prose is baroque in its serpentine distension, Tridentine in its polemic zeal and its suspicion of classicism or aestheticism, and yet distinctively inclined towards irony and sarcasm, which enlivens a style that can otherwise be limpid and diffuse. While it is not especially inspiring as literature, it is deeply revealing of the Latinity and intellectual fibre of early and mid-seventeenth-century Europe.

8. Latin invective verse
in the
Commentarius Rinuccinianus[1]

GRÁINNE McLAUGHLIN

> 'S ón lá fuair Cromuil an chonair 'na slaodaibh,   259
> 'nar sgaoil fá chumas an brusgar so an Bhéarla . . .
> Ní fhoidhnid teagasg ar Laidin ná ar Ghaelge   279
> ná d'aon bheith gasda 'sna healadhnaibh saora.[2]

> From the day when Cromwell gained control of the land
> And from when he powerfully released this English-speaking rabble . . .
> They do not tolerate the teaching of either Latin or Irish
> Or for anyone to be skilful in the noble arts.

Sometime between 1654 and 1657 the Cork poet Dáibhí Condún wrote these words in the course of his angry lament on the state of the country since the arrival of Cromwell and his English 'scum' (*Scum na Sagsan*: 35).[3] He contrasts the tradition of native learning, both in Irish and in Latin, which appears side-by-side in the above quotation, with what the invaders brought to replace it. His presentation of his own learning contrasts with the crudity of Cromwell's men. Although O'Rahilly, the poem's editor, appears to have found this section of the poem rather pedantic, classicists will note the poet's respect for the original literary trinity of Greek, Latin and Hebrew (154–62):

> Do léas leabhair seannda na nGréagach,   154
> is gach stair dár ceapadh i dteanga na n-Éabhrach
> is gach ar sgríobhadh ar Phuímp is ar Caesar . . .
> 's ar sgríobh Cicero i gcoinne na méirleach.[4]   160

> I have read the ancient books of the Greeks,
> And every history ever written in Hebrew
> And every word written on Pompey and Caesar . . .
> And that Cicero wrote against the looters.

The poet lists his key authors as Plutarch (157), Homer (158), Vergil (159), Hector Boetius (161) and Marcus Aurelius (162). Throughout the poem he details all the misfortunes befalling Ireland, and even uses English phrases, a significant switch in the context of the theme of the poem, in order to encapsulate the Cromwellian contribution to the cultural milieu of his day: '*Transplantátion*' [to the West Indies] (223); '*phrécept*' [of Calvin] (228); 'Yes, by Gad, I'd swag my béaver' (303); 'To kick my arse' (305); and 'To break my chaps' (306). The English language is used here as a political weapon against its own nation: civilized people speak Latin and Irish.

However, the poet has no simplistic, xenophobic view of the reason for his country's misfortunes. He attributes them to the Irish nation's mistreatment of the nuncio, because they have occurred '*ó tugadh masla do theachtaire an phréamhfhlaith*' (245) (since the nuncio of the supreme pontiff was insulted).

The extraordinary nuncio in question is John Baptist Rinuccini, sent to Ireland by Pope Innocent X in 1645 with a view to uniting the Catholic Confederate forces against their heretical enemies. The nuncio entered into a political situation which was complex even by papal standards, and his mission cannot be said to have been a success. After his return to Italy, the Capuchin Fr Richard O'Ferrall was asked by the nuncio to write an account which would present the nuncio's version of events. Although O'Ferrall died in 1663 before he could complete the task, this request resulted in the production of one of the most important Counter-Reformation historical sources for Ireland in the seventeenth century, a source which is particularly important because it is Irish, Catholic, virulently anti-Ormond and anti-Cromwell. As such, given the rarity of sources of this type, it is a very significant counterpoint to Carte and other apologists for Ormond and Cromwell. The Latin text runs to over 3,000 printed pages and is currently being translated by an international team of translators.[5] In addition to the wealth of documents and correspondence, which is of great interest to historians, the work is a treasure trove that reveals its main author's love for classical Latin.[6] In this article I highlight Fr Robert O'Connell's virulently mischievous use of classical Latin poetry for a broadly invective purpose.[7] I show that his discourse with these ancient texts is exuberant, heartfelt, sophisticated and provocative. O'Connell's passionate engagement with classical Latin can be seen from his apposite use not just of direct quotation but of oblique references, as the following attack upon Inchiquin demonstrates:

> *majoribus nedum parentibus ter Catholicis natus ad haereticorum synagogam*
> *parvulus obtorto collo raptatus ita illa animarum peste se demum infecit, ut*
> *in popularibus, imo etiam plurimis sibi necessitudine conjunctis fame,*
> *flamma, ferro, frigore necandis omnem humanitatem exuisse videatur, illique*
> *haud injuria ei applicari possit illud Virgilianum (Aeneid 4[366–7]):*
> > *duris genuit te cautibus horrens*
> > *Caucasus, Hircanaeque admorunt ubera Tygres*

Et illud Ovidianum [Heroides 7.37–8]:
Te lapis et montes, innataque rupibus altis
Robora, te saevae progenuere ferae.[8]

Though born into a family that had been Catholic for at least three generations, when no more than a little boy he had been abducted against
his will and forced to keep the company of heretics. In the end he
became so infected with this soul-destroying disease that he seems to
have divested himself of his own humanity. That is how it appears at
any rate from the way he killed by starvation, burning, the sword and
the cold not only members of the public at large but even many individuals with whom he had a personal connection. It does not, therefore,
seem unfair to use the following words of Vergil to describe him:

It was the ice-cold Caucasus with their rough rocks that gave birth to
      you:
And Hircanian tigresses let you drink their milk.

And Inchiquin also brings the following words of Ovid to mind:

It was rocky mountains with their native oaks on high summits
And wild beasts that gave birth to you.

A good example of O'Connell's manipulation of elements from Latin epic
and elegy can be seen in this depiction of the cruel turncoat Inchiquin.[9]
In order to hammer home his indictment of him, O'Connell first depicts
him as the Ganymede or catamite of the upper echelons of heretic
English society, for Inchiquin was a ward of court and educated by
Protestants. This is seen in his use of the phrase 'abducted . . . and
forced', a situation familiar from Ovid's *Metamorphoses*, and Pindar's
Odes.[10] Moreover, O'Connell's engagement with Roman culture is
unlikely to have been limited to knowledge of classical Latin texts. He
was the prime author of the *Commentarius*, which was written in Florence
during 1661–66. This was after he had finished his training and had been
ordained in Paris in 1651; and he had also spent a period studying rhetoric at the Jesuit college in Bordeaux in 1640.[11] Therefore, in addition to
classical written sources for abduction and rape, he probably was familiar
with classical sculptural images such as those of Zeus abducting
Ganymede, or various other depictions of rape from classical myths.[12]

   There is no sympathy shown for Inchiquin as the victim of what we
would regard as child sexual abuse, for O'Connell makes him take full
responsibility for the choices he made: the reflexive phrasing of Inchiquin's
corruption (*se . . . infecit*) implies that he *allowed himself* to remain infected.
The register of the diction employed by O'Connell will be examined below.
It is sufficient for our purpose here to note that it is par for the course as far

as contemporary English political discourse was concerned, as McElligott has shown: after all, the English republican member of parliament Henry Marten is revealed in *Mercurius Dogmaticus* as a catamite who, in ever increasing circles of depravity, has in turn his own catamite.[13] There is also the fact that O'Connell would have been aware of at least two relatively recent capital trials concerned with homosexual activity. The first trial concerned Mervin Touchet,[14] the father of the 3rd earl of Castlehaven, who features in Volumes I, II, IV and V of the *Commentarius*.[15] Mervin Touchet was convicted of rape and sodomy and hanged on 14 May 1631. His hanging is referred to in the contemporary Irish manuscript written in English and entitled *An Aphorismical Discovery of Treasonable Faction* (which, as its editor John Gilbert noted, was probably written between 1652 and 1660[16]) in the context of what is in effect a pejorative pen-portrait of Ormond's 'refractorie Peeres', in which the emphasis is on their treacherous and disloyal natures.[17] The second case concerned the English-educated Church of Ireland bishop of Waterford and Lismore, John Atherton, who was hanged for buggery on 27 November 1640.[18] Atherton was personally known to Inchiquin and his case was so notorious that it was a topic for discussion as far away as Massachusetts.[19]

Having established Inchiquin as a paragon of villainy, O'Connell uses quotations from two distinct classical Latin genres, epic and elegy, to emphasize the cruelty of the man. The appropriateness of the equivalence of Inchiquin to Aeneas at his most inhuman and heartless when he is about to abandon Dido is obvious. Inchiquin used, abused and betrayed Hibernia (Ireland), just as Aeneas used, abused and abandoned Dido; both can therefore be viewed as operating out of merciless self-interest. What is more compelling and complex is the equivalence of Dido and the personification of Ireland. Like Dido at the point in the epic narrative from which the quotation is taken, Hibernia, a stalwart and strong Catholic kingdom, is being betrayed by a weak man – and not only by Inchiquin but by the ultimate target of the author's wrath, the duke of Ormond, who, like Inchiquin, was another ward or catamite of the English in his youth. Hibernia is, as was Dido when pursued by the African princes who wished to possess her and her kingdom, surrounded by barbaric vultures, some of whom are indigenous species, such as Inchiquin and Ormond. Both females are suffering because of disloyal males. Another point of similarity in the analogy is that Dido remained a faithful widow to Sychaeus, just as Hibernia has always been a faithful witness to the Catholic faith: this is a crucial point given the fact that the *Annales Ecclesiastici* of Caesar Baronius, an important source for the opening of the *Commentarius* and O'Connell's other work, the *Historia Missionis Hiberniae Minorum Capucinorum* (discussed below), describe

Ireland as *insula tenacissima catholicae fidei*, the most faithful of witnesses to the Catholic faith.[20]

The repetition of these sentiments in the quotation from the more elegiac Ovid is arguably not necessary, but for our purposes it shows the author's enjoyment of rhetorical *exempla* and his delight in his knowledge of classical Latin poetry. This passage as a whole shows a confident assimilation of the classical Latin corpus which transcends narrow considerations of genre, since O'Connell essentially uses epic and elegiac poetry for the purpose of invective prose. Moreover, the verbal cues in the diction of the text leading up to the quotation arguably show a creative connection with the classical sources beyond mere apposite quotation. This can also be said of the next section of the *Commentarius* I would like to discuss, which takes us further along the invective pathway, for O'Connell uses Latin verse panegyric as a form of invective verse, when he disapproves of a poet's patron, the poet himself and his unacceptable verse.

> *Quid autem nocebit hic subnectere carmina, quae tunc Kilkenniae typis mandata inter multa alia phreneticae laetitiae a partibus Ormonicis palam testatae specimina impius Richardus Blakus, Eques auratus, et pseudo-Comitiorum prolocutor, Ormonio cecinit, vernilis adulator:*
> *'Soteria de Iberniae pace anno 1649 mense Januario inita'*
> *Quis fuit ille dies . . .*[21]

Moreover, what harm will it do at this point to insert verses which were then published in Kilkenny, being as they are representative of the many blatantly hysterical acts of celebration perpetrated by the Ormondists. Richard Blake, a profane man, decorated [gilded?] Knight, Speaker for the pseudo-Assembly, and a bottom-feeding lick-spittle, composed the following for Ormond:
'*A Congratulatory Poem on the Peace which Saved Ireland in January 1649*'
What a day it was when . . .

The use of the introductory question '*Quid autem nocebit . . .?*' clearly illustrates O'Connell's familiarity with rhetorical techniques. Less obvious for the translator is how to communicate the classical Latin nuances in the phrase *vernilis adulator*. The original servile associations in *vernilis* within the context of the Roman *familia* and *patria potestas* must be replaced by reference to a power matrix of greater relevance to the modern Latinless reader; and the translator must avoid the unduly positive modern English associations potentially present in expressions such as 'won the adulation of the crowd'. A strongly negative rendition is required, because it is through these words in the original Latin that O'Connell converts Blake's encomium to Ormond into an invective against him. It is easy to see why O'Connell felt obliged to foam at the mouth. The duke of Ormond, who, seen as a traitor to his own people in matters of both faith and politics, for O'Connell was as near to the anti-Christ as it is possible to have on this earth, is described in line 55 as '*Ille tibi Ormonius longo promissus ab aevo*' (That man Ormond, promised to you from time immemorial).

The messianic echoes of Vergil and Ovid were bound to annoy.[22] So was the earlier description in line 15 of England, not Ireland, as '*Sanctorum mater pia dicta virorum*' (Acknowledged devout mother of Holy men). However, I believe O'Connell's literary sensibilites may also have been offended.[23] In line 16, immediately after the insulting description of England, not Ireland, as the 'Land of Saints and Scholars', Ormond is described as '*deliciaeque soli, deliciaeque poli*' (darling of heaven and earth). The adoption of *deliciae* '[illicit] pleasure', a well-known euphemism in Latin sexual vocabulary, is hardly accidental and arguably crass: the ghost of the dead sparrow, bewailed by Lesbia in Catullus, may have loomed too close for comfort.[24]

And yet the question must be asked: is the elegy against the peace which immediately follows this panegyric really any better? Close analysis of the diction of the two poems reveals familiarity with the same classical authors. As classicists work their way through Blake's poem, they will detect extensive use of the Roman epic tradition (Vergil, Lucan, Valerius Flaccus, Statius, Silius Italicus), love poetry (Catullus, Ovid) and epigram (Martial); other influences include the poetry of Horace and Lucretius, Cicero's speeches, philosophical works and letters, Seneca's moral essays, and the historical works of Livy and Tacitus. When they move on to the opposing poem by Edmund O'Meara[25] they will similarly recognize the diction of Catullus, Cicero, Ovid, Martial, Vergil, Tacitus, Lucretius, Horace, Tibullus, Propertius and Lucan.[26] In this respect both poets are in tune with the anonymous author of the *Aphorismical Discovery*. The *Commentarius* was written between 1661 and 1666 but many of the documents date from 1600 (Volume I: Part III) to 1666 (Volume V), and the poems discussed above are from 1648. The *Aphorismical Discovery* is therefore an indispensable source for anyone interested in the Latin reading habits of Irish people in the years of the seventeenth century to which most of the *Commentarius* is devoted. Gilbert characterizes the Irish royalist author's English and linguistic pedigree as follows:

> The language of the narrative is the English spoken in Ireland in the first half of the seventeenth century, with a mixture of Gaelic, Spanish, and military terms . . . The work supplies abundant evidence of the author's learning and familiarity with Latin, Spanish, Italian, French and Gaelic; it is, however, noteworthy that in his numerous quotations and references he does not cite the writers of England.[27]

This highlights the European perspective also noteworthy in the *Commentarius*, at a time when Latin could still be said to be the *lingua franca* of the educated. That the author was not atypical for his time can be seen from biographical information that O'Connell gives in the *Historia Missionis Hiberniae Minorum Capucinorum* (f. 475): we learn of the Capuchin Fr George, who died in Dublin in 1640, but who spoke Irish, English, Scottish Gaelic, Flemish, German and Latin. With regard to why the author of the *Aphorismical Discovery* chose to write in English but not to use English sources himself, it may be that he did not wish to give any credit to the culture from which he saw his political and religious opponents as emanating. Whatever the reason, the numerous marginalia citing classical Latin sources, together with the quotations of Latin poetry embedded in the text, testify to the very real connection the author felt with so-called golden and silver age Latin and Greek literature. The density of the referencing can be seen in the following representative sample taken from a fraction of the text, and citing individual authors at their first occurrence only: Livy, Ovid (p. 13), Thucydides (p. 29), Pliny, Tacitus, Lucan (p. 36), Plautus, Lucian (p. 53), Valerius Flaccus, Cicero, Seneca (p. 55), Vergil (p. 70), Polybius, Plato (p. 81), Xenophon (p. 90), Silius Italicus (p. 91), Aristotle (p. 92), Plutarch (p. 104), Horace, Curtius Rufus (p. 123), Persius (p. 128), Hesiod, Justinian (p. 136), Suetonius (p. 140), Euripides (p. 142), Juvenal (p. 147), Claudian (p. 171), Caesar (p. 178), Gellius (p. 179), Sallust (p. 180) (Vol. I: Part I); Petronius (p. 188: Vol. III: Part I: 1880).

This is the literary context in which the two opposing poems at issue must be located. O'Meara may indeed be the more accomplished poet of the two, but his imagery is also undeniably more acceptable to O'Connell on a political and religious level. In line 87 he says of Ormond, '*Herba latet anguis in ista*' (There is a snake hiding in that grass). O'Connell could not resist writing a note about O'Meara in the margin: '*Ormonium intelligit*' (he knows Ormond for what he is).

The critical conundrums posed by the above use of panegyric as invective, as opposed to panegyric as panegyric, are absent in the next sample of verse, which has its feet firmly placed in the footsteps of not just classical writers of satire such as Juvenal, but also Ciceronian forensic oratory at its most offensive best:

> *Pseudo-pater vidique tuum, legique libellum,*
> *Qui dignus genio est, ingenioque tuo:*
> *Ille tuo dignus genio, quia continet omne*
> *Quod ructare potest mens scelerata scelus.*
> *Ille tuo ingenio dignus, quia mortua moles.*
> *Estque carens omni pondere pondus iners.*
> *Sed quid? magna nimis tibi crevit fama libello:*
> *Magna nimis (fateor) sed nimis illa mala:*
> *Imo malam famam tibi subtrahit iste libellus.*

Cur? dicam. Facta est pessima, fama mala.[28]

Begetter-of-Bastards,[29] I have seen your book and read it:
It is just what I would expect from you and your ilk.
It is so quintessentially you, since it is full of the vomit
Only a diseased mind such as yours can produce.
It is the very image of your intellect: a morbid mass.
And it is a deadweight of course – for it is content-free.
So what? Aren't you very famous because of it?
Well, let me tell you: very infamous is what you are.
That book comes complete with notoriety attached.
Why? I'll tell you: a bad deed brings its own bad press.[30]

This anonymous invective against John O'Callaghan (also known as Callaghan, Mac Ceallachán, etc.), whose pseudonym was Philopater Irenaeus,[31] was occasioned by the publication in Paris in 1650 of his work *Vindiciarum Catholicorum Hiberniae*.[32] O'Connell hated O'Callaghan, as is clear from his references to him elsewhere in the *Commentarius*. Perusal of the entry for him in the Index to the *Commentarius* (Vol. VI, p. 220) shows that he is mentioned in every volume, always in the context of his having been a malign influence on the Irish nation at home and at an international level. However, in addition to political and religious differences (for O'Callaghan was an Ormondist as well as a Jansenist and attacked the nuncio in the first book of the *Vindiciae*) there was probably a more personal element to the hatred. As Corish has noted, O'Callaghan's patrons were the MacCarthys of Muskerry, who took the premier title from the McCarthy Mór in 1658.[33] It was to the old McCarthy Mór branch that both O'Ferrall and O'Connell, the two authors of the *Commentarius*, were loyal. Given that the *Historia Missionis Hiberniae Minorum Capucinorum* contains Latin verse composed by O'Connell (e.g. ff. 573–4), it would not surprise me if it emerged that O'Connell was in fact the author of the poem. There is an undeniable verbal echo between the incipit of the poem, 'Pseudo-pater vidique [my emphasis] *tuum, legique libellum*' (Begetter-of-Bastards, I have seen your book and read it) and O'Connell's lead-up to his introduction (ff. 2,142): '*Etenim P. Joanni Poncio in vicis Parisiensibus obvius: Hodie (inquam) Ceallachani libellum venditioni expositum* vidi [my emphasis]' (As a matter of fact, I met Fr John Ponce in the street in Paris and I said to him: 'I have seen Callaghan's book on sale today').

The poet begins by spitting twice at O'Callaghan in a double plosive quadrisyllabic Greek pseudo-pseudonym which pokes fun at the pretentious irony of Callaghan's 'real' pseudonym: in O'Connell's opinion O'Callaghan specialized in flaming the fires of war, and, contrary to the original Greek meaning of *Irenaeus*, brought 'peace' to no one (he hisses at him again in *scelerata scelus* and *iste libellus*). The epithet *pseudo* is particularly meaningful for O'Connell, given the tradition of celebrating Ireland as the most faithful witness to the Catholic faith, as noted above in relation to Baronius.[34] The use of *pater* likewise counterpoints, to negative effect, O'Callaghan as the opposite of Hibernia: she is the positive personification of Irish motherhood, who gives forth true Catholics, not illegitimate liars like O'Callaghan has produced in the form of this book and his other works; nor do good parents betray their progeny and set them against each other as O'Callaghan has done by the publication of the *Vindiciae*. Moreover, he is a *pseudo-pater* because a real parent or priest would not abuse his position of authority, whereas O'Callaghan has abused his position of authority among the Irish community abroad, in addition to misrepresenting his nation as a whole. Nor is the author finished with this Greek coinage: he will return to it in an oblique form later in the poem.

Just as the author's love of wordplay is seen in the first word of the first line, it is also apparent in his use of the word *libellus* at the end of the line. This diminutive form of the word for 'book' is often a synonym for *liber* in late Latin. Here, however, the author is punning on the literal meaning of the word, for the book sits comfortably in the palm of the hand.[35] But there is more to it than that, for in the author's opinion O'Callaghan is guilty of libel in the modern, legal sense of the word, which was of course current in the English of this period.

The diction is obviously classical, as can be demonstrated from a sample of the classical models I have been able to identify: terminal *libellus* Ovid *Tristia* 3.14.51, Martial *Epigrams* 2.6.10, 8.1.3 and cf. Cicero, *Pro Archia Poeta* 25; *scelerata scelus* cf. Ovid *Heroides* 2.29–30 and note the preference for *figura etymologica* in *pondere pondus*; *pondus iners* Ovid *Ars* 3.215, *Metamorphoses* 1.1.5; *fama libello* Martial *Epigrams* 7.88.1; *mala . . . malam famam . . . fama mala* Ovid *Epistulae ex Ponto* 2.3.83, Livy 27.8.5, Tacitus *Annales* 2.28.3. The oxymoronic *mortua moles* and *pondus iners* may indirectly recall Horace *Carmina* 3, 4, 65: *vis consili expers mole ruit sua* and such an echo from the pagan poet would certainly be a further insult for the cleric O'Callaghan, who had studied philosophy and was a doctor of theology at the Sorbonne.[36]

Yet it is the last sentence with its repetitions of key words from the preceding lines which make an indelible stain on O'Callaghan: his writing of the *Vindiciarum* can bring him only the worst sort of *fama*. There is another use by O'Connell of *fama* earlier in the *Commentarius* which also demonstrates this. The text deals with the impending surrender of New Ross by Governor Taaffe upon completion of the agreement of terms. In the course of the rather one-sided negotiations Cromwell wrote to Taaffe in English on 19 October 1649 and concluded his letter, 'If you accept of this offer, I engage my honour for a punctual performance thereof.' In the *Commentarius*, O'Connell's translation of this preamble to the surrender of New Ross into Latin is sodden with reproach – yet he does so without altering the meaning of the original English: no small feat:

> *His legibus si deditionem subeas, ego eas exacte observandas obsidem esse iubeo famam meam.*[37]

Given the reader's prior knowledge of the treacherous slaughter at the end of the siege of Drogheda, which is called to mind by O'Connell's use of the word *obsidem*,[38] precisely how much was Cromwell's 'honour' worth? A clue is provided by O'Connell's use of the word *fama*. We have already seen from his quotation of *Aeneid* 4, also familiar to the writer of the *Aphorismical Discovery*, that the negative side of *fama* in the modern sense of 'infamy' will have been fully appreciated by readers of the time, given their fondness for Vergil's epic. And so here there is no doubt for the anonymous author that for Philopater, as for Cromwell, it is a poisonous form of fame which beckons.

It is O'Callaghan's intellectual depravity which is the focus of the poem. This is forcefully communicated with an admirable degree of humour and classical insensitivity. The physical manifestation of his incontinence is signalled by *ructare*. I would argue that another quadrisyllabic double-plosive Greek name is evoked here: that of the monstrous Polyphemus in the *Odyssey*, who is graphically depicted spewing up the remains of the men he has eaten in wine-soaked vomit: the scene is repeated in Latin in the *Aeneid*, complete with wine-soaked regurgitated remains.[39]

The strongest connection between this poem and the classical tradition on which the author was drawing lies in the tone of Ciceronian invective which pervades his depiction of O'Callaghan, thereby assimilating him to two infamously incontinent Romans: Piso and Mark Anthony. In his *Speech against L. Calpurnius Piso*, Cicero addresses the man as a *belua* (1: savage beast) and *immanissimum ac foedissimum monstrum* (31 [14]: most frightful and filthy monster), thereby putting him into the same category as Polyphemus. He then does not hold back in depicting his victim's brutish and uncontrolled behaviour (13 [6]):

> *Meministine, caenum, cum ad te quinta fere hora cum C. Pisone venissem, nescio quo e gurgustio te prodire, involuto capite soleatum, et, cum isto ore foetido taeterrimam nobis popinam inhallasses, excusatione te uti valetudinis, quod diceres vimulentis te quibusdam medicaminibus solere curari? Quam nos causam cum accepimus – quid enim facere poteramus? – paulisper stetimus in illo ganearum tuarum nidore atque fumo; unde tu nos cum improbissime respondendo, tum turpissime ructando eiecisti.*

You piece of shit, do you remember when I came to you at about eleven in the morning with Gaius Piso? How you were wearing nancy-boy sandals and a fancy head-dress when you were coming out of some drinking den? How you gave the excuse that you were in the habit of curing an ailment you had by drinking for certain medicinal purposes, when you breathed on us with your rancid breath and turned our stomachs with the stench of what you had been eating? How, when we had accepted your excuse – for what else could we do – we stood for a little while in the stinking fumes of your greasy-spoon? This was when you let fly not only with a completely inappropriate response, but also with the most toxic belch when you turfed us out.

At least Piso did not actually vomit. The same cannot be said for Mark Anthony, who, in modern parlance, 'followed through':[40]

Tu istis faucibus, istis lateribus, ista gladiatoria totius corporis firmitate tantum vini in Hippiae nuptiis exhauseras, ut tibi necesse esset in populi Romani conspectu vomere postridie. O rem non modo visu foedam, sed etiam auditu! Si inter cenam in ipsis tuis immanibus illis poculis hoc tibi accidisset, quis non turpe duceret? In coetu vero populi Romani negotium publicum gerens, magister equitum, cui ructare turpe esset, is vomens frustis esculentis vinum redolentibus gremium suum et totum tribunal inplevit!

You drank so much wine at Hippias' wedding, you, with your mouth wide to the world, your gaping gut, and your big, bulked-up body, that the next day you had to vomit in front of the Roman people. This wasn't just horrible to look at – it was horrible to listen to! If it had happened to you at dinner when you were getting completely wrecked, wouldn't everybody have been disgusted? But the chief of the cavalry, in the course of performing his public duty at an assembly of the Roman people, a person for whom it would be unacceptable behaviour to belch, threw up in his own lap and filled it and his magistrate's seat with lumpy vomit, good enough to eat and marinaded in wine!

It is no wonder O'Connell says that O'Callaghan did not appreciate the joke of being inserted into such a tradition of writing. Be that as it may, the poem is clearly in the tradition of classical satire, even if the concept of *decorum* at issue as the impetus for the poem's composition is a seventeenth-century Irish version with a profoundly theologico-political emphasis. And, of course, there is another connection between O'Callaghan and his classical analogues; for Piso and Mark Anthony, like O'Callaghan, were traitors of sorts.

Like the previous example, the anti-elegy on Cromwell, printed here as an appendix, is also anonymous; and, also like the previous example, on balance its composer is likely to have been Irish. Two elements in other

verse quoted in this discussion certainly feature in it: in lines 39–40 the
wordplay on *Angli* (the English) and *Angeli* (angels), familiar from Bede,[41]
also occurs in the poem by Blake, to which O'Connell took such exception,
just before the reference to England not Ireland as the Land of Saints and
Scholars; and O'Meara's biblical image of the enemy as a snake (whether
Ormond or the devil, if there was any perceived difference) is used here of
Cromwell (47). We can only speculate, however, given that Ó hÓgáin has
shown that standard English royalist motifs of abuse in connection with
Cromwell crossed easily and quickly over the Irish sea and were assimilated
into an Irish context.[42]

The curse on the dead Cromwell in Latin, as preserved in the *Commentarius*, reveals a blend of classical and appropriated English motifs in
a seventeenth-century Irish context. These include the reference to
Cromwell's humble origins, and his connection with the devil (40–1),
which is particularly strong in the Irish tradition.[43] Another example of
appropriation may be the way Cromwell is portrayed not as a man but as a
man-monster, bad enough to have as his mythological *exemplum* Cerberus
from Aeneas' journey to the Underworld in Book 6.[44] Indeed, it is the degree
of hyperbole that may support the contention that this is an Irish production, as Smith has noted that it is most often in the Irish tradition that
Cromwell is encountered as a myth, not a man.[45] The classical allusion to
the katabasis in the *Aeneid* will not have been lost on readers: Aeneas goes to
the Underworld and finds monsters there, whereas Cromwell has gone there
to find himself – because the man was a monster (*Homo Bellua*: 30; cf.
chimera 22), and a three-headed one at that (16–17).[46]

The final sample of invective verse from the *Commentarius* that I would
like to discuss is a potent synthesis of Irish and classical elements: Irish verse
satire combined with Latin verse and prose. The following is the Irish
source-text:

> *Med do thoile d'fhearan cille*
> *Bhera gan iarmhuirt do bhaile*
> *Racha do shliocht uait uile*
> *Mar chith duille do druim aille.*

A literal English translation of the Irish is as follows:

> The greatness of your desire for the land of a church
> Will cause your house to be without offspring
> All your descendants will go away from you
> Like a shower of leaves from off a cliff.

O'Connell translated the Irish verses into Latin elegiac couplets:

> *Sacrati Christo fundi tua tanta cupido*

Efficiet viduam posteritate domum.
Succus ut in praeces [sic = *praeceps*] *frondis dilabitur imber*
Sic tibi citra spem tota propago ruit.[47]

I translate the Latin as:

Your great desire for the land consecrated to Christ
Will make a widow with no future of your household.
As the sap of the leaf slips headlong away like a shower,
That is how all your seed rushes to its irrevocable ruin.

O'Connell's treatment of his source material here is very powerful. The curse in Irish is uttered in a vision, in a sort of an anti-*aisling*, by an individual who is '*minitantem et prophetizantem hoc carmine Ibernico*' (threatening and prophesying in this Irish curse). The use of the word *carmen* and its Irish equivalent here is particularly laden, for, in both the Latin and Irish, it can mean 'spell' as well as 'verse'. The curse is against the grandfather of James Eustace, Viscount Baltinglass. The grandfather in question was Thomas Eustace, baron of Kilcullen, who had come into possession of land formerly owned by the Cistercian monastery at Baltinglass. Almost immediately after citation of the curse, O'Connell uses a passage from Peter Lombard which contains a shocking and gruesome image of impending infertility, a sign in the Irish tradition of a bad ruler.[48] This image is part of a description of the acts of savagery perpetrated against the local people by land-grabbing, marauding English in the time of Elizabeth and thereafter. The passage tells how (334):

matribus in crucibus levatis, parvuli qui lactantes sive vagientes, in earum reperti ulnis, earundem capillis strangulati, hac nova laquei forma simul etiam suspenderentur.

Mothers were hung from crosses. Their baby boys, who were feeding at the breast or crying, were found dead in their mothers' arms: they had been strangled by their own mothers' hair and hung, like their mothers, in this new form of noose.

Neither dead mothers nor their dead children – particularly, dead sons – can secure the continuance of a family line. The juxtaposition of the curse or *aoir* of extinction in Irish, with respect to the target's family, with the description of the horrors inflicted by his kind on the local population magnifies his guilt and validates the *aoir*: for a curse to work, it must be deserved.[49] There is an added edge, in that the extinction of the locals ultimately is another form of sterility or infertility, for the indigenous population was, in a sense, a crop which a good ruler would harvest and cultivate, not destroy.

On one level, the curse is the text in the Irish. But in his demonstration through reference to Lombard's text of the validity of the *aoir*, and in his incantatory repetition of the words of the curse in Latin, O'Connell performs his own *aoir*, no less powerful than the original, for he too is a poet and prophet.[50] And not only was he aware of his own, Irish, traditions, but he was also aware from his knowledge of classics of the incantatory power of repetitive language, since this can be traced back to Theocritus *Idyll* 2 and beyond.[51] Likewise, the equation of a good ruler with fertility will have been familiar from, for example, Horace: '*tua, Caesar, aetas / fruges et agris rettulit uberes*' (Your reign, Caesar, brought back rich fruits to the fields).[52] Of course, the topos can be traced further back, as it appears in ancient Greek poetry, particularly in the odes composed by Horace's hero Pindar, for Syracusan tyrants.[53] In summary, the Irish lines are not merely quoted and then translated into Latin by O'Connell in a superficial or passive way. He is familiar enough with both the Irish and the classical traditions to assume the *persona* of *poeta* or *vates* and sing his own Hiberno-Latin *carmen*. He is not just acknowledging his ancient sources from the two traditions: he is an instantiation of their continuation.

I will conclude by discussing the following bardic fragment quoted in the *Historia Missionis Hiberniae Minorum Capucinorum*, and Robert O'Connell's translations of it:

> *Gaoidil dar gcur a gcleith ghall*
> *is Goill dar bhfogradh dar bhfearann*
> *don croinne ce beug ar gcuid*
> *mar ubhall tuinne a tamuid.*[54]

These Irish lines, quoted by O'Connell in the course of comments on the critical political situation in 1648, can be translated thus:

> The Irish put us to the cudgel of the English
> And the English excluded us from our land.
> How small is our share of the total land available
> We are like an apple on a wave.

O'Connell translated these lines into Latin as:

> *Anglorum numero ascribit nos priscus Hibernus,*
> *Et nostros Angli depopulantur agros.*
> *Scilicet in terris quamvis sit portio nostra*
> *Parva; sumus pomo, quod fugat unda, pares.*

I translate his Latin as follows:

> It is our Irish forefathers who put us under the rule of the English,
> And it is the English who destroy our land.
> Needless to say, all they have left us is a paltry portion:
> We are like an apple at the mercy of the waves.

Robert O'Connell, the chief author of the *Commentarius*, wrote the *Historia* in France between 1652 and 1656, ostensibly as a history of the Capuchin mission to Ireland but actually a work much more panoramic in its vision than the title would suggest. Its many marginalia cite sources for passages without attribution in the *Commentarius* (such as Baronius for the opening page of the *Commentarius*) and O'Connell quotes the *Historia* in the *Commentarius*.[55] With respect to the verses from the *Historia* quoted above, the Capuchin transcript in the Capuchin Archives, Church Street, Dublin, of the original French manuscript has been used to provide the Irish and Latin text and English translation of the Irish original.[56] However, copyright clearance has now been obtained from Troyes and the Capuchin Order to produce an edited text and translation of the *Historia Missionis Hiberniae Minorum Capucinorum*, after the current translation project on the *Commentarius* has been completed. The two texts are inextricably linked.

According to a preliminary examination of extant manuscript sources, the four lines of poetry above appear in the *Historia* a century earlier than their preservation elsewhere. The *Historia* is dated 1653 but the earliest version of the verses identified so far can be dated from the eighteenth century, as internal evidence in the form of scribal dates cover the period 1723–29.[57] As regards O'Connell's knowledge of these Irish verses on f. 562 of the *Historia*, another eighteenth-century version of them may give us a clue as to how he came to know them. The manuscript in question is RIA 23 O 35 (55), written between 1772 and 1778. According to the catalogue, the scribe of this manuscript is Brían Ó Fearraghail from County Longford, in all likelihood a kinsman of the second author of the *Commentarius*, Fr Richard O'Ferrall, who was himself from Annaly, County Longford.[58] The verses may therefore have been passed down in the family and preserved by Richard O'Ferrall via his friend and colleague Robert O'Connell in the *Historia* in 1653, and then subsequently in a later generation by Brian O'Ferrall.

Some time after the *Historia* was originally written, it was felt necessary to translate the Irish into English in the margin as follows:

> The Irish put us to English hands
> The English driv'd us from our lands.
> Betwixt them both we have no ease,
> Like an aple toss'd between two seas.

There is a marginal note beside the English translation which states that it was 'Englished thus by L. D.' From an examination of a ledger in the Capuchin Archives, I believe I have identified 'L. D.' as the Capuchin Laurence Dowdall, who was at Aube as '*Concionator et Vice Custos Hib.*' in 1702.

Although many Irish were abroad for considerable periods of their lives, in the context of an examination of the relationship in the seventeenth century between the Irish-speaking population of Ireland and the Latin language, and the latter's specifically classical literary legacy, L. D.'s Englishing of the Irish and Latin verse is both telling and poignant. This chapter began with a quotation from an Irish poem which, among other things, applauded the marriage of Irish and classical Latin learning. Within half a century, this marriage can be seen to have become a linguistic *ménage à trois*, one which may yet prove fatal for two out of the three parties involved. The above image of an apple floating at the mercy of the waves is therefore both a potent and a particularly appropriate image with which to end this chapter, for the apple in bardic poetry was an encomiastic symbol, often used of the *laudandus* to whom the praise poem was dedicated.[39] The apple represented something which was portrayed in the poetry of the culture as important and valuable to the society as a whole. When the apple was cut off from the structure which nourished it and was discarded as excess baggage to float with common or garden flotsam and jetsam, what was a symbol of fertility, desirability and power was transformed into an image of impotent despair and irreparable desolation: there can be no more salutory metaphor for the current perilous state of both Latin and early modern Irish.

Liber 1⁰

RIA MS 23 O 35 (55)

Appendix 1

ANNOTATED SCHEDULE OF POETRY
IN THE *COMMENTARIUS*

Volume I:

Part I: S8: f. 15	positive analogy from Latin epic: the English 'go native' (*Aeneid* 2.574: Queen Dido)
Part II: S49: f. 273	ominous prophecy from Latin epic: Elizabeth's race will regret her words: cf. S98 below
Part II: S98: f. 313–313v:	invective prophecy of Irish verse satire (*aoir*) combined with prose of Peter Lombard

Volume III:

S1096: f. 1599v:	classical Latin epic verse used against Inchiquin and Ormond

Volume IV:

Part I: S38: ff. 1758–59v:	Soteria ('Congratulatory Poem') for Ormond by Richard Blake
Ormond as the Messiah	
Part I: S39: ff. 1759v–1761v	Panegyric for Nuncio by O'Meara: Ormond as the anti-Christ
Part I: S40: ff. 1761v–1762	Thanks to O'Meara from the Nuncio
Part I: S41: f. 1762v:	Panegyric for Nuncio by O'Meara
Part I: S611: ff. 1981v–82:	The Catamite Inchiquin
Part I: S674: ff.2016v–	2017: Elegy for Eoghan Ó Néill [Owen O'Neill]
Part I: S675: ff. 2017–	2017v: Anagram on Eoghan Ó Néill
Part I: S676: f. 2017v	Elegy on Eoghan Ó Néill
Part II: S281: ff. 2142v–43:	Invective against Philopater Irenaeus

Volume V:

Part I: S189: ff. 2318v–2320	Epitaph for Patrick Comerford
Part II: S183: f. 2400v:	Epitaph for Nuncio
Part III: S18: f. 2416:	The Treacherous Surrender of Galway
Part III: S92: f. 2462:	Epitaph for Thomas Walsh
Part IV: S165: f. 2549v–51:	Anti-elegy on the Death of Oliver Cromwell

Appendix 2

ANTI-ELEGY ON
OLIVER CROMWELL

'*Oliveri Cromwelli Britanniae Protectoris, Tyranni novissime fato perempti
Elegiacum Epitaphium*'

Quorsum praeceps, viator, novo hoc declinas a tumulo?
Num forte inclusos exhorres cineres?
Et quem vivum Tyrannum nosti, vel extinctum formidas   5
                    Ne dubita.
Mortis compedibus vincta larva Brittanica
Nulli amplius, sibi soli terribilis spirat.
Quique vinculis tot dedit cives,
Carcerem sibi adinvenit, vi, dolove non reserandum.   10
Moras ergo parumper sustine,
Ut nigro inscriptos lapillo hos lustres characteres.
                    Lege.
Claudit fatalis haec urna
Trium Regnorum Angliae, Scotiae, Iberniae,   15
Tyrannumne dixerim an Tricerberum?
Utrumque Tricerberum Tyrannum, Cromwellum
Suo satis nomine clarum et obscurum.
Hunc natura parvum genuit, magnum fortuna regeneravit.   20
Ut obstuperet Anglia natam sibi extemplo chimaeram
Regio sanguine conceptam non semine.
Sui tamen illam erroris paenituit.
Dum repente quem extulit ex improviso dejecit
                    E solio ad solum   25
Triplici pro Regno tres illi terrae palmos indulgens.
Quam certum violenti nihil durabile?
Obiit aetate sexagenarius circiter, malitia millenarius.
Ultimo, quo vixit, decennio Princeps non Princeps,
Homo Bellua Tyrannum egit et monstrum.   30
Brittanicum Diadema humi dejectum pavit assumere

Ne securim, quae Regium Caroli cruorem gustaret,
Suum alliceret in caput.
Sceptrum nihilominus strinxit: ut regeret an verberaret?   35
Calvini propugnator, Calvino compar,
Christum Brittania novo edicto exulem fecit
Et Anglos, quondam Angelos, ex toto deformavit in Daemones.   40
Ipso scelestiori velut Lucifero, suadente non modo sed et impellente.
           Calidus genio, callidus ingenio,
           Seditionem fovit; Religionem confodit.
           Ausus plura, adeptus plurima.   45
           Omnia dum ambit, omnia deperdit.
Faedus Coluber cum Gallo faederatus, Aquilam lacessivit in praelium
Pro qua dimicans Libitina, brevi faedus vertit in funus.   50
Quaeris quam vixerit vitam? Ventosam, ambitione scilicet faetam.
Scire cupis qua morte decesserit? Crepuit medius.
           Emeritus utris inflati exitus:
           Ni potius Judae aemulum velis asserere   55
           Et proditione et supplicio.
Filia paucos ante dies fato absumptu viam
Patefecit ad inferos.
           Lusit cum eo fortuna, dum vixit
           Cum mortuo nunc ludit Pluto   60
           Cui aeternum mancipatus
Indignae Tyrannidis dignas exolvit paenas.
Funestum cinerem execrare viator ac perge.

'The Funeral Epitaph of Oliver Cromwell, recently deceased
Tyrant-Protector of Britain'

Hey, you! Traveller! Why are you running away from this new tomb?
Don't tell me you're actually afraid of the ashes inside it?
Or that you're scared of him now – when he's dead?   5
Sure you knew him when he was a real, live, tyrant!
Don't be in any doubt about it: he really is dead!
The Public Face of Britain has been bound by the shackles of Death:
He frightens nobody now – except himself.
The man who put so many citizens behind bars
Has got himself his very own prison.
And nothing will get him out of it – not brute force,   10
not trickery.
So take it easy for a minute:
Read these outstanding letters carved on the black stone – read them!

This funerary urn contains the 'Tyrant of the Three
Kingdoms of England, Scotland, and Ireland' –   15

Or should that be the 'Three-Headed Monster of
England, Scotland, and Ireland'?
It doesn't matter whether you call him 'Triple-
Headed Monster' or 'Tyrant', it's all the same:
The urn still has Cromwell's name on it, Famous or not.
He was born small but Fortune made him great.   20
England was gob-smacked suddenly to have borne
A chimera sired not by Royal semen but by the blood of a King.
England, however, regretted her error,
When she demoted him just as quickly as she had promoted
    him unexpectedly:
from the throne to the dirt in an instant,   25
granting him three spans of land instead of Three Kingdoms.
But what lasting legacy can a violent man have?
Into his life he fitted about sixty years' worth of age –
but a millennium's worth of evil.
For the last ten years of his life he was, and yet was not,
    Emperor.
The Man-Monster was a Tyrant and an Ill-Omen.   30
He was afraid to take up the Crown of Britain,
which had been thrown on the ground,
in case he brought down on his own head the axe
which had tasted the gore of King Charles.
Nevertheless, he took up the royal staff: but did he
mean to rule with it or to beat his people? – that is the question. 35
He was Calvin's champion and comparable to Calvin.
In a new edict he sent Christ out of Britain into exile
and completely corrupted the English, who were
formerly 'Angels', turning them into Devils   40
as though Lucifer himself were not just persuading
an even greater criminal, but urging him on.
Hot-headed but congenitally calculating,
He fostered ferment and stabbed Religion through the heart.
He chanced his arm often but filled his arms even more often.   45
In trying to acquire everything, he lost it all.
The vile Snake allied itself with the Cock and called the Eagle to battle.
The funeral goddess, Libitina, took the side of the
Eagle, and soon turned their alliance into an autopsy.   50
What sort of life did he have – is that what you want to know?
His was a life of arrogance, pregnant with ambition.

Do you want to know how he died? He shook from the inside out –
a spent force – and busted like a blown-up bladder.
In terms of his treachery and the punishment it deserves
you might think his only equal is Judas.   55
His daughter, who died a few days before him,

cleared a path to Hell for him.
While he lived, Fortune had her fun with him.
Now that he's dead, Pluto plays with him.   60
Cromwell will be his debtor for all eternity while he pays the
    penalty
he deserves for his despicable despotism.
Damn his deadly ashes to Hell, traveller,
And then be on your way.

9. Ussher and the collection of manuscripts in early modern Europe

ELIZABETHANNE BORAN

Narcissus Marsh, provost of Trinity College Dublin (TCD) from 1679 to 1683, has a sorry tale to tell concerning Ussher's manuscript collection. Writing to Thomas Smith in October 1680, he explained his reluctance to issue a printed catalogue of the Greek manuscript library of TCD, on the grounds that he

> would not have it divulg'd, that Primate Usher's Library (both MSS and printed books) comes very short of its and its owner's fame; it might have been thought a good library for another man, but not for that learned Prelate unless you value it by number, not weight, or that the best Books are dispers'd'.[1]

This assessment is in marked contrast to the reputation of Ussher's library following his death in March 1656. On that occasion, kings and cardinals, colleges and learned academics across Europe spoke of it as, in the words of Frederick Spanheim, 'the Library of the learned world'.[2] It is clear from Ussher's correspondence that the fame of his library had spread across Europe: John Buxtorf II and Constantine L'Empereur, professors of Hebrew in the University of Leiden, writing to him in 1633, acknowledged his renown as a collector of '*antiquis et raris manuscriptis*' (old and rare manuscripts) whose '*instructissima bibliotheca*' (most well-furnished library) was public knowledge.[3] In this paper I would like to examine Ussher's collection in the context of British and European manuscript collecting in the early modern period. It is only by viewing Ussher in this broader context that we can truly appreciate the nature of Ussher as a collector of manuscripts.

Marsh's comment on Ussher's collection is mirrored in tone by Humphrey Wanley's similar conclusion concerning the collecting habits of Sir Simonds D'Ewes, a correspondent and fellow collector of Ussher's. Wanley, writing in 1703 to his patron Robert Harley, the eventual purchaser of the D'Ewes collection, stated rather huffily that among the oriental manuscripts were many which D'Ewes had paid dearly for, but which were of little moment.[4] Perhaps in both cases we are simply dealing with changing tastes – and it must be remembered that attitudes to manuscripts varied profoundly from our twenty-first century preoccupations.[5] Indeed, Simonds D'Ewes admitted on one occasion that manuscripts he had once 'highly prized' were, on later viewing, of little regard.[6] But lest we are too dismissive of Marsh we must acknowledge that there were concrete reasons why he might have been disappointed with the collection before him in 1680. The gap between the expectation of Ussher the man and the expectation of what that meant in bibliographical terms was, given Ussher's repute, bound to be a broad one. More pertinently, the collection before Marsh's eyes was not the collection Ussher would have been used to himself.

Ussher's biographers give us various accounts of the vicissitudes which his library endured throughout the turbulent period of the 1640s and 1650s. It had miraculously escaped the flames of Drogheda in 1641 – only to be sequestered by parliament at Chester in 1643.[7] The peripatetic lifestyle of Ussher in the 1640s was not conducive to manuscript preservation. According to Parr, 'many others of his loose Papers and Manuscripts . . . were either lost in his often forced removals, or fell into the hands of the Men of those spoiling times, who had no regard to things of that Nature'.[8] Rebel forces were likewise responsible for the 1645 Welsh incident when Ussher and his party were waylaid while on their way to St Donat's Castle in Glamorgan. This was even more harrowing for Ussher because he was present at the time and we are told by Bernard that 'it did much grieve him'.[9] The brigands stole his books and papers and threw them to the four winds. Ussher was lucky enough to get back most of the material but we know that 'he lost two *Manuscripts* of the *History of the Waldenses*, which he never got again'.[10] Finally, the hiatus between the purchase of Ussher's library for the University of Dublin and its eventual entry into the library of TCD in 1661 meant that from July 1657 to 1661 the manuscripts were left in Dublin Castle. Though many of the manuscripts stolen during this period were later returned, it is not clear how many were lost.[11]

We are hampered in understanding the growth of Ussher's library by a lack of library catalogues devoted to his manuscript collection and by the apparent idiosyncrasies of those which survive.[12] A number of catalogues, each diverging slightly, exist for the period following his death, and they are later supplemented by TCD catalogues from 1670 onwards, but there is little correlation between the two sets.[13] Correlating the entries in Trinity College Cambridge MS 1319, which appears to be a recension of the 'Ur' text of Ussher's collection, drawn up by Ware after his death, with our present records, is by no means an easy task, given the partial nature of the former catalogue and its blithe method of cataloguing.[14] Other facts serve to complicate the issue yet further – over time Ussher would have rebound different manuscripts together and even if he did not follow this common practice (Sir Robert Cotton was quite notorious for it) subsequent librarians such as John Lyons's have not been so bashful.[15] Lyons' 1742 TCD catalogue provides ample evidence of the effects of this rebinding programme – to give but one example, a manuscript which has one of the 'original' Ussher call marks BBB.8 (dealing with Irish material) is now divided between TCD MSS 363, 545, 582 and 591.[16] The location and identification of Ussher manuscripts were substantially aided by the researches of William O'Sullivan, the former keeper of manuscripts in Trinity College Dublin, but much work remains to be done in this area and it must be remembered that not every Ussher manuscript ended up in the college.[17]

In a sense though, it is easy to become enmeshed in the issue of the correlation of catalogues and thereby lose sight of the significance of Ussher's collecting policies. What I would like to argue is that instead of trying to view Ussher's collection in a static form we should think of it as an essentially fluid entity. His manuscript collection was constantly subject to growth and diminution – he was always adding to it and, at the same time, giving items away. It is this aspect which captures the nature of Ussher as a collector – or more broadly – as a facilitator of manuscript collection in early modern Ireland, Britain and Europe.

Ussher was not working in a vacuum. He was part of a group of scholars across Europe who were assiduously collecting material for a host of different projects, usually involving the preparation for publication of national histories. The sixteenth and seventeenth centuries witnessed an explosion in the market for manuscript collecting, not only in the British Isles (especially England) with the dissolution of the monasteries and the subsequent dissemination of their manuscript hoards, but also on the European mainland where war-torn countries offered opportunities to the wily collector. Ussher's habit of hanging on to manuscripts which did not belong to him was by no means unusual – and to give him credit, when he thought he was dying at St Donat's in the mid-1640s he was anxious enough about it to ask that any books he had which belonged to others be returned to them.[18] Others were not quite so conscientious: Robert Cotton's method of acquiring some of his twenty-six manuscripts from Thomas Allen's collection, following the death of the old man, raised eyebrows, and even the great Jacques-Auguste de Thou, the French collector par excellence, had gotten up to some very havey-cavey dealings with the understandably bitter monks of Corbey Abbey.[19]

The market was simultaneously both competitive and collaborative. Ussher's friendship network included some of the most famous collectors of the day and each node in the network passed on information concerning what was on offer and what might be coming onto the market. The deaths columns were hot topics, as they gave an indication of what collections might be up for grabs.[20] Since, as Bernard Meehan reminds us, Ussher's collection was primarily a purchased one, it was vital to know where manuscripts were and which were available for sale – hence the insistence on getting up-to-date catalogues of manuscripts.[21] William O'Sullivan has outlined the principal sources of Ussher's collection, and these include a large bank of manuscripts bought following the death of Thomas Allen, Henry Savile of Banke, others bought once John Dee's library was released to the market, and, of course, the headline-grabbing purchase of the Samaritan Pentateuch and other Syriac manuscripts in the 1620s.[22]

Purchase was ultimately dependent on income and Ussher was lucky to have at his disposal the revenues of first the bishopric of Meath and, following his elevation in 1625, those of the archbishopric of Armagh. Parr places considerable emphasis on the revenues of the latter: 'After his being Arch-Bishop he laid out a great deal of money in Books, laying aside every year a considerable Sum for that end, and especially for the procuring of Manuscripts, as well from foreign Parts, as near at hand.'[23] However, the chronology of the purchase of the jewel in the crown, the Samaritan Pentateuch, suggests that Ussher was already on its track *before* his elevation – the first letter we have about it from Thomas Davies is dated Aleppo 29 August 1624.[24] A list of the highlights of Ussher's collection, drawn up in 1660, included the following items which 'were procured and bought at a great rate':

> The Samaritan Pentateuch; The Arabico-Samaritan Pentateuch; The Syriack: whol Old Testament and Apocryphall Books; The Syriack Pentateuch at the End whereof is the chronographia Eusebii.; The Psalms of David. Syriack.[25]

The price for the Samaritan Pentateuch alone was, we are told, '600 sicles of Silver which by the Jewish account would rise to £125 English'.[26] Given the difficulties which both Ussher and his agent Thomas Davies encountered in collecting these manuscripts, it is unsurprising to hear that Ussher valued them 'as Jewels'.[27] They were, however, the tip of the iceberg. Ussher continued to extend his purchased collection in the 1630s by buying a number of Waldensian manuscripts in 1635–6, for which he paid £22, and in the 1640s he acquired items from the library of the Dutch theologian Francis Gomar, the celebrated opponent of Arminius.[28]

It should be remembered, however, that Ussher and his fellow collectors spent even more time borrowing manuscripts and organizing transcripts to be made of others than they did poring over book-sellers' catalogues. It is in their borrowing patterns and the making of transcripts that we see the collaborative nature of manuscript collection in the early modern period. Borrowing raised certain difficulties – manuscripts were by their nature precious to their owners and few were sanguine about sending their favoured volumes across the seas. L'Empereur was not alone in his comment to Ussher in November 1633 when he said that '*neque committendum censeo ut liber adeo rarus cum discrimine et amittendi periculo in incertum mittatur*' (I did not think it right that so rare a book should be sent into any situation of uncertainty, given the serious danger of its being lost).[29] Merchant and diplomatic networks certainly oiled the wheels of manuscript borrowing by giving scholars the opportunity to send manuscripts via reputable connections such as William Boswell,[30] but one always ran two risks: first, that the work might be lost, as happened to Ussher's Egyptian breviary *en route* to the Netherlands;[31] secondly, and more commonly, that the recipient might not return it. The collaborative nature of the exercise might, however, offset the latter disadvantage. As Samuel Ward, master of Sidney Sussex College, Cambridge, explained to Ussher in 1625:

> I notwithstanding brought with me the Manuscripts of Bede's Ecclesiastical Story which I have of Sir R. Cotton's, and have sent it unto you by this bearer Walter Mark. I will expect the Book from you, when you have done with it, for that I would keep it till Sir Robert restore a Book of mine, which he had of Mr Patrick Young.[32]

Here we see not only the possibility of holding a book to ransom in order to restore a prized item, but also the complex chain of borrowing that was the norm in the early modern period.

Not all were happy about borrowing manuscripts and already some of the main collections were becoming reference rather than lending libraries. Given that Ussher was based in Ireland and so could not habitually frequent the college libraries of Oxford and Cambridge, it was inevitable that he, as every other early modern collector before him, became dependent on the use of transcripts. Transcripts make up a large proportion of Ussher's collection – be they in his own hand or in the hand of others whom he evidently had commissioned on his behalf. Transcripts are at the heart of such working libraries as those of Ussher, Cotton, Selden and De thou – they provided material which could not be bought, borrowed or easily accessed. Access to libraries such as the Bodleian might not provide many difficulties, but for someone like Ussher, who had a limited amount of time at his disposal, the sometimes arcane entry rules might prove too cumbersome.[33] Much time might also be wasted in attempting to locate manuscripts – contemporary catalogues were often faulty and the information on which Ussher was basing his search might, at times, prove equally so (though this is relatively rare in his case).[34]

Manuscript transcription could either be done by Ussher himself, by one of his network of friends, or by an employed transcriber. Among the Ussher manuscripts in TCD are a host of transcriptions in Ussher's own hand. This reflects not only necessity but also an acceptance of Trithemius' well-known adage: 'For those things that we copy we impress more deeply in the mind.'[35] However, as a busy prelate of the Church of Ireland, Ussher had increasingly to rely on friends and employees. Manuscript transcription was, in this instance, as Ussher himself puts it, a process of 'negotiation'.[36] One either had to ask a friend to transcribe the piece, as Ussher asked Camden in June 1618, or one had to arrange for a transcriber to undertake the work.[37] And here negotiations of a monetary kind were paramount. Professional transcribers were not always easy to come by and there was much demand for men such as the 'Feathery scribe'.[38] Joseph Mede, writing to Ussher in 1630, opined: 'Could I have gotten an orthographical Scribe, I would have sent your Lordship all ere this, both Specimina and the larger Expositions upon the first half. But I had no such of mine own, and those who have are not so kind as to lend them for any hire.'[39] It was important to employ a professional because otherwise the value of the transcription as an authentic text would be jeopardized.

Much depended on the skill of the transcriber: writing to Sir Robert Cotton in May 1625 Ussher was overwhelmed by the need to complete his researches, prior to returning to his new archepiscopal appointment in Ireland. He needed a transcriber who had sufficient experience and asked for Cotton's help in finding someone 'that hath already been tryed in transcribing of manuscripts, and will sitt close to worke'.[40] Transcription demanded both patience and a knowledge of languages. Lydiat, writing to Ussher in 1619, stated that he had 'alreadie written . . . over a quire of paper: but so enterlined and faille, as I thinke it will bee a quarter of a year's worke for mee to copye it out'.[41] Some texts were more difficult than others and, since transcription was such an arduous task, it could prove costly. Arnold Boate, Ussher's chief agent in Paris, makes this point very clear in his letter to Ussher dated 6 September 1651:

> I sent you . . . an Extract of the *Obelisci* and *Asterisci* [Membranarum Sardoianarum]; the which being a Work of much more Time and Pains, than I was able in my present condition to bestow upon it, I

was fain to hire Mr *Coque*, your Professor of the Greek tongue, for to do it; who would have done it for five Franks (and not under) if I would have been content with the bare transcription of the Obelisks and Asterisks out of the Membranes.[42]

When Boate remonstrated that he needed the entire text for collation purposes, Coque demanded twenty francs,

protesting, when he had done, that if it were to do again, he would not do it for double the Monies, as having been a whole sevennight busied with it, and found it incomparably more toilsome than he had imagined it. And although he be a very able Grecian, and wonderful diligent and faithful in what-ever he undertakes, yet I would not rely solely upon him, but compared every Obelisk and Asterisk of his transcription.[43]

Boate's insistence on checking the transcript is a frequent theme throughout the Ussher correspondence – transcripts were only useful if they were accurate renditions of the text, since they were primarily, though not exclusively, being used for collation purposes.

When transcriptions were needed from works further afield Ussher could use not only diplomatic connections but also far-flung merchant networks. A note on TCD MS 454 records one such mercantile network:

Mr John Collier a merchant at Marklane (borne about Tralye in ye County of Kerry) and Mr Henry Reily at Grayes Inne, to sent unto Mr Edward Fulham (with Mr Robert Santhill, ye Kings agent at Legorme) for transcribing of Greek books out of Florence, Venice, or ye Vatican (by Sr Kelham Digbyes means).[44]

In a letter dated 12 November 1639 to Christian Rave, who was based in Constantinople, Ussher gives some indication of how the system could work:

Hos libros omnes sollicite vestiges velim quaqua transibis, et si quos reperias, diligenter in adversariis notes locos ubi extant, et nomina eorum in quorum manibus sunt, itidemque pretium quo eos divendere velint, ut et nomina nostratium mercatorum in iisdem locis commorantium, ut sic postea, quando ad nos reversus fueris, accersere eos, si pretium placuerit, possimus. Quod si et alii probi authores Graeci aut Syriaci, praeter supradictos, in manus tuas inciderint, qui apud nos desiderantur, poteris et circa illos eadem uti diligentia.[45]

I would like you to search carefully for all these books, wherever you pass by, and if you find any of them, take precise notes of the places where they are extant, the names of the people in whose hands they are, the price at which they might be willing to sell them, and also the names of our merchants residing in the same places: so that afterwards, when you return to us, we can send for them, if the price is acceptable. And if other reliable Greek or Syriac authors, besides those mentioned above, which we lack, should fall into your hands, you can use the same careful procedure about them too.

It is clear that Ussher's collection of originals and transcripts had its roots not only in the monastic, academic and urban libraries of Ireland and Britain but, owing to transcripts, was linked to libraries right across Europe. Parr gives us the following information about the sources of Ussher's manuscript collection:

> I may here likewise take notice of those many Volumes of his Collections, and several of them, all of his own hand, on particular subjects, both Theological, Philological, and Historical, most of them extracted out of several Manuscripts in the Libraries of the Universities, Cathedrals, and private men's Studies, there being scarce a choice Book, or Manuscript in any of them but was known to him, nor was he conversant in the Libraries of our own Nation alone, but also knew most of the choice pieces in the Vatican, Escurial, and Imperial Library at Vienna, as likewise in that of the King of France, of Thuanus at Paris, and Erpenius in Holland, as still appears by the Catalogues he had procured of them, divers of which I have now in my Custody: out of which Libraries he at his great cost procured divers Copies for his own use, which made the most considerable Ornament of his Study.[46]

If this transcription network was dependent on sufficient finance it was equally, if not more so, dependent on goodwill. The network of scholarship in the Republic of Letters was the overarching framework for such negotiations. Ussher's friendship network in mainland Europe was predominantly with Calvinist bastions but he could and did develop mutually beneficial contacts with Roman Catholic scholars.[47] Collaboration across religious lines was possible, and in Ussher's case we have much evidence for interaction with Franciscans such as Thomas Strange and Luke Wadding, the latter conveniently placed in Rome – convenient for Ussher, perhaps less so for Wadding, who rather plaintively points to the distance between the Vatican library and the Irish College.[48] However, lest we paint too rosy a picture of inter-denominational scholarly collaboration in the search for texts, we would do well to remember that religious fault lines could all too easily emerge. Ward, writing to Ussher after the fall of Heidelberg, expressed deep concern about the fate of the Heidelberg manuscript collection, hoping that it had been sent to the duchy of Württemberg rather than fall into the hands of those 'who are so faithless in setting them out'.[49] Claude Sarrau echoes this assessment in a letter to Ussher of 9 November 1648, when he bemoans the intransigence of the Vatican which, he says, had the copy of Cardinal Rochefoucauld's treatise on the prophets which Ussher wanted, but refused to allow it to be transcribed.[50] Petrus Scavenius, writing to Ussher from Rome two years later, highlights the reasons for this growing intransigence:

> *In bibliothecae Vaticana maximus certe est thesaurus librorum MS. nec ubivis obviorum, quos saltem per transennam inspicere nobis licet. Pessime nostris rebus consuluere ii, qui antehac quaedam descripsere, ac postea Romanis invitis et innominatis publicarunt. Nec desunt, qui inde tela quaesivere, quibus ipsos confodere, ac ita proprio ense ipsos necare studuerunt. Hoc modo Itali male remunerati, cautiores ac difficiliores in communicando exteris sua mysteria evasere.*[51]

> In the Vatican library, certainly, is the greatest treasury of manuscript books, such as not to be met with anywhere else, which we can inspect, at least through a grille. They have acted very unhelpfully, from our point of view, who have previously described some things, and later published them, when the Romans were unwilling or ill-disposed. There is no lack of people who have sought weapons there, with which to strike them themselves, and thus have made efforts to kill them with their own swords. In this way the Italians have been repaid, and have become more cautious and difficult in communicating their mysteries to outsiders.

The language used in this letter is striking – here manuscripts are weapons, the library an arsenal which must be guarded lest its contents be used against itself. Implicit also is the acceptance that there are rules which must not be infringed – that transcripts given in good faith should be used similarly.

The importance of Ussher's friendship network in the location and transcription of texts cannot be exaggerated. By using his scholarly connections, Ussher was able to make contact with scholars whom he had never met but who had access to relevant documents. He used his contacts with men such as Sir Henry Spelman and Patrick Young, the librarian of the Royal Library, to extend the web of his communication network into continental Europe. He himself had direct contacts with Dutch scholars based in Leiden and Utrecht, but men like Spelman and Young had links to some of the most famous European collections of their day. Spelman was a correspondent of Nicolas Claude Fabri de Peiresc, one of the most famous scholars of early modern Europe.[52] Peiresc collected everything – nothing was too humble for his antiquarian regard. Ussher ultimately had no direct contact with Peiresc, but the latter was always on the fringes of Ussher's immediate network. In April 1628 Ussher had asked Spelman to contact Peiresc for a book.[53] Six years later Ussher was still trying to make contact with Peiresc via Spelman, sending the latter a wish list from Peiresc's library.[54] For Ussher, Peiresc's chief importance lay in his connection to Joseph Scaliger, the foremost biblical chronologer of late sixteenth-century Europe. Any texts that Peiresc might have on that subject were vital for Ussher's biblical chronology project. It seems likely that Spelman was not the only chain linking Ussher to Peiresc: Peiresc's closest English contact was William Camden, who in turn was another node in the network, joining Ussher at one remove with the most substantial private collection of the day: that of Jacques-Auguste de Thou.

Ussher had far greater success in getting transcripts from the famous library of De Thou (1553–1617).[55] Working through contacts with Pierre and Jacques Dupuy, the librarians of the phenomenal De Thou collection, Ussher received a number of important transcripts which are now in the following manuscripts in TCD: MSS 197, 225, 236, and 239.[56] Most of the transcripts in these manuscripts deal with the thorny topic of predestination and were transcribed for Ussher in the 1630s. MS 197 and MS 225 evidently date from 1637, since some of the material in them is mentioned in a letter of Battiere to Ussher, dated August of that year.[57] Though some sources such as the Penitential of Theodore, a seventh-century archbishop of Canterbury, were clearly needed for his 1639 work the *Britannicarum Ecclesiarum Antiquitates*, most of the transcripts from De Thou's collection dealt with the topic of predestination.[58] MS 197 includes a number of transcripts on different aspects of the semi-pelagian views of Faustus of Riez, a fifth-century theologian, and this trend is continued in MS 239, where works by Hincmar, archbishop of Reims, the ninth-century opponent of Ussher's hero, Gottschalk of Orbais, are collected alongside works by Rabanus Maurus, Gottschalk's abbot at Fulda, and works by supporters of Gottschalk's position on the issue of double predestination: Ratramnus of Corbey and Galindo Prudentius, the bishop of Troyes, who had argued for the Augustinianism of Gottschalk's position.[59] We know from Ussher's correspondence that he had been trying to access material on these writers, especially Ratramnus, since at least December 1630 – probably much earlier – given their relevance to his book on Gottschalk, which was published in 1631.[60] In 1635 another important conduit of information, James Frey, gave him news about Sirmond's intentions on publishing material on Hincmar – and the latter's consequent unwillingness to part with any material.[61]

De Thou and Ussher had in a sense remarkably similar trajectories. Both were educated under a Ramist system; both were influenced by ecclesiastical uncles, Ussher by Henry Ussher, archbishop of Dublin, De Thou by Nicholas de Thou, bishop of Chartres; both were intended for the law – Ussher rebelling in favour of an ecclesiastical career; both travelled to libraries in neighbouring countries to locate manuscripts; both used their official positions to augment their overall libraries; and, finally, both eventually utilized their collections in a series of massive historical works.[62] The fame of De Thou's collection, coupled with the success of his outstanding *Historia sui Temporis*, ensured that he was a household name among collectors. He had been a close contact of Camden and Cotton and in a sense provided a model for collectors across Europe. De Thou's method of listing manuscripts used in each of the 138 books of his *Historia sui Temporis* was a practice which Ussher adopted. Access to the De Thou collection was vital for Ussher's plans in the 1630s and 1640s. By 1617, De Thou's manuscript collection alone held 830 manuscripts – a figure which would rise to *c.* 1,000 by 1643. It was, like Ussher's, a collection built upon co-operation. De Thou's friends Pierre Pithou and Nicolas Le Fevre located manuscripts for him before leaving him their own collections, in much the same way as men like John Bainbridge had done for Ussher.

At the heart of the manuscript collecting network was the economy of exchange. Collectors were constantly either sending gifts of manuscripts and transcripts or exchanging them with other collectors. There were at least three possible motives for doing so. Sir Robert Cotton was no doubt attempting to curry favour with a possible political patron, the earl of Arundel, when he gave him the earl of Northampton's book of prayers. Since Northampton had been Cotton's previous patron the gift acted as both a generous and ingenious declaration of loyalty.[63] Likewise, Cotton himself was often the recipient of grateful and possibly bibliographically motivated donations: Simonds D'Ewes spent £2.10s.0d. on a manuscript from Peterborough Abbey which he gave to Cotton – again, hoping no doubt to build bibliographical bridges with the best known English collector of his day.[64]

Ussher too seems to have employed manuscripts as politically charged gifts to potential patrons. His gift of a number of Dee manuscripts to Laud for the Bodleian in 1630 was two-pronged: they would augment the store of one of Ussher's most loved libraries, but the honour for the donation would rest with Laud. It was a very generous gift by all accounts. Ussher lists the works as follows:

> I have sent with here sixteen Manuscripts (of such as I had here at hand) to add unto to the store which your Lordship is providing for the Universitye of Oxford . . . There is also among them an Hebrew Logick; and an Arabick Psalter . . . There is likewise an exceeding

> good copye of Bedes Ecclesiasticall Historye, etc. If the Samaritan
> Bible, which was more perfect, had not bene absolutelye promised by
> me unto Sir Robert Cotton at my last being in England: I should have
> counted none so worthye of it, as your Lordship.[65]

This gift had strings attached. Ussher immediately follows this passage
with a plea to Laud to overlook whatever offence might be taken from his
book on Gottschalk. The implication is clear: Ussher knew that writing
on Gottschalk of Orbais was a politically charged action, since it involved
discussing the now forbidden subject of predestination. He hoped that
Laud might decide to ignore this aspect of the work and by giving him
manuscripts sought to placate him.

Manuscript gifts might be used to influence potential patrons in this
way but more generally they were utilized to ensure mutual co-operation
between scholars. Clearly not all gifts were one-sided affairs: exchange of
manuscripts played an important role in the development of collections
such as those of Simonds D'Ewes and Cotton.[66] Ussher too engaged in this
practice. This aspect was even more important when the links of the
friendship network were far flung. Ussher had alluded to the '*quid pro quo*'
nature of manuscript gifts when he had originally asked Spelman to
contact Peiresc. The latter and any other scholar were to be assured that
any assistance given would be reciprocated: 'you may promise for some
recompense unto the learned men with whome you deale, a transcript of
an other monument in the same kinde, which I have, and they (I suppose)
do want'.[67] Reciprocity was essential and it was hoped that the giving of
manuscripts as gifts would not only facilitate the growth of the collection
of the recipient but would, in the longer term, be an investment which
would ensure both goodwill and further transcripts.

But manuscripts and transcripts were not the only commodity which
interested Ussher. In July 1650 he sent copies of his Annals of the Old
Testament to Arnold Boate, Sarrau, the Dupuis brothers, Sirmond, Petau
and Bignon, primarily as a gracious acknowledgement, not only of their
help in arranging transcripts but also, and just as vitally, because they had
proved useful in another way: they had provided news of what was available and who could locate it.[68] This third motivation for sending
manuscripts as gifts was thus to build up relationships with those 'in the
know'. Giving manuscripts in exchange for information was, if anything,
more important than using them for political influence. Knowledge of
what was on the market and what could be accessed via other means was
crucial for a scholar like Ussher. In 1639 Ussher asked Patrick Young to
contact Sirmond to enquire of him 'what other Churches and Monasteries
there are in France, where such books may be had: for I know none that
can better inform you thereof, than hee'.[69] The Jesuit Sirmond might not

always play ball (on at least one occasion he was not forthcoming with relevant information) but in the main Ussher was able to find out what he needed to know concerning the whereabouts of manuscripts in early modern Europe.[70] This was vital if he was to develop his collection and pursue his projects.

But with Ussher we must also consider a fourth motivation for both collecting and giving manuscripts – his desire to act as a facilitator of other scholars' projects. For Ussher was not solely concerned with the growth of his own collection – he was also constantly keeping an eye on other collections which might be of benefit to the Republic of Letters. If he himself could not buy them (or if they did not chime with his own interests) he was nonetheless anxious to make sure that collections found worthy academic homes. When the manuscript collection of Thomas Erpenius, the renowned Dutch scholar, came on the market in 1625, Ussher had suggested to Sir Robert Cotton that if he wanted to get the famed collection of oriental works, he would have to act fast – otherwise the Jesuits of Antwerp would make a deal before him.[71] On the death of the duke of Buckingham, who had purchased the collection, Ussher was again active, suggesting to William Herbert, the 3rd earl of Pembroke, that he advise Charles I that the Erpenius collection would be a fitting component for the royal library. At the same time, January 1629, Ussher was also anxious that the library of Giacomo Barocci find a good institutional home in England. He had been alerted to its availability on the market by the book-seller Henry Fetherston and passed on the news, with heavy hints, to Pembroke:[72]

> That famous Library of *Giacomo Barocci*, a Gentleman of *Venice*, consisting of 242 Greek Manuscript Volumes, is now brought into *England* by Mr *Fetherstone* the stationer. Great pity it were, that such a Treasure should be dissipated, and the Books dispersed into private hands. If by your Lordship's mediation, the King's Majesty might be induced to take them into his own hand; and add thereunto that rare Collection of Arabic Manuscripts, which my Lord Duke of *Buckingham* purchased from the Heirs of *Erpenius*, it would make that of his Majesty's a Royal Library indeed, and make some recompence of that incomparable loss which we have sustain'd in the Library of *Heidelberg*.[73]

Equally, when the manuscript collection of George Carew came on the market in 1629, Ussher had high hopes of obtaining the collection, not for himself but for his *alma mater*, Trinity College Dublin.[74] Archibald Hamilton, one of his agents in London, had to break the bad news that Sir Thomas Stafford had got there before them.[75] This was fairly quick for Sir Thomas since Carew was only dead ten days and was not yet buried, but since Stafford was reputed to be Carew's son it might be said that he had the inside track.

Ussher's correspondence with his Dutch counterparts in Leiden is especially important for understanding his motivations as a collector. It is clear from his very first letter to Louis de Dieu that while Ussher might have thought of his Samaritan Pentateuch and related texts 'as Jewels', they were only precious because of their utility. Far from wishing to hoard manuscripts for his own benefit, Ussher was actively trying to bring them to a wider audience. His assurance to de Dieu of 1 October 1629 that he wished '*thesauros ex oriente advectos primo quoque tempore communicare*' (to communicate treasures brought from the east for the first time) was no idle boast, since Ussher included a copy of the Samaritan Pentateuch for de Dieu.[76] He did so because he needed the expertise of the Leiden philologists – he wanted them to publish his Samaritan Pentateuch, so that it would be accessible to all scholars. The Leiden contingent still had the Samaritan type, left by Erpenius, so Ussher could see no possible problem – it should, in his view, be '*proximis vernalibus nundinis opus absolutum publice edi possit, ac passim divendi*' (finished and distributed everywhere by the next spring fair).[77]

The Samaritan Pentateuch was not the only text he entrusted to the Dutch – in June 1632 he sent de Dieu the Syriac Pentateuch through James Frey, and proceeded to outline the contours of his oriental collection, listing a host of texts which he was more than willing to make available for publication.[78] For Ussher, his Samaritan and Syriac manuscripts were not just for his own benefit – they were to be used by all. Indeed, his search for manuscripts in the east was meant to be collaborative in every meaning of the word. Given the cost of obtaining manuscripts, he was anxious to avoid duplication and asked De Dieu in 1636 for a list of which Ephraim manuscripts were held at Leiden '*ne operam ludamus ac impensam emendo illa quae jam possidemus*' (lest in that matter we waste effort and expense in buying things which we already possess).[79] The use of the first person plural here is important. Ussher did not think in terms of 'me and mine' but rather 'we and ours'.

Ussher in turn expected assistance. His letter of 7 July 1637 outlined a new project he was involved in – an edition of the Syriac Old Testament, which he hoped to publish in England, and for which he needed De Dieu's assistance in obtaining transcripts and collations of parts of the Syriac Bible in Leiden.[80] It is clear, though, that in this commerce of exchange Ussher was the principal donor. He was at all times willing to assist whatever request his Dutch colleagues might have. He immediately responded to De Dieu's 1636 request of Irish material for his colleague Johann Elichman, who was involved in a comparative linguistic study of the languages of German, Latin, Greek, Arabic and Persian in an attempt to '*experiri, quid nobis Europaeis cum remotis illis Asiaticis affine sit*' (explore what affinities there are between us Europeans and those remote Asiatics).[81] Apologizing that he could not send exactly what Elichman desired, an Irish dictionary, since there was none available, he sent instead an Irish alphabet and the Irish New Testament. When called on to assist in Christophe Justel's projected ecclesiastical history, Ussher did not hesitate, sending whatever was needed to Isaac Basire in 1648.[82] Given that an original codex was involved rather than a transcript, this was very generous indeed.

Ussher also acted as a facilitator of manuscript collecting by other scholars by locating sources for them – certainly by the end of his life he was famous in this regard. Isaac Gruter, writing from The Hague in February 1650, asked Ussher's advice on the whereabouts of the papers of Sir Henry Savile: '*non aliunde quam ex te melius constare mihi posse videatur*' (indeed it seems to me that I can enquire nowhere else better than from yourself).[83] Henri de Valois had a similar request for Ussher in December 1654, asking his advice on the manuscript codices he had examined for his study of the ecclesiastical historian Eusebius – and asking for any pointers on material he might have missed and for help in organizing someone to collate the sources in England.[84] Ussher wrote back immediately, giving him his own collation of the relevant texts.[85]

His advice was constantly sought by other scholars thinking of publishing editions of their manuscripts who knew of Ussher's commitment to this area of manuscript collection. After all, he had himself published some very rare pieces from his Irish manuscripts in the 1632 source book, *Veteres Epistolae Hibernicae*.[86] This aspect of his interaction with manuscripts had been evident from his early career. For example, Thomas Gataker had written to him as early as March 1617 to ask his advice on the publication of manuscripts in his possession which 'might not be unworthy to see the light'.[87] John Hanmer, bishop of St Asaph, wrote to Ussher ten years later to request his assistance with the projected edition of his father's history of Ireland.[88] Meric Casaubon asked for his help in 1650 in the disposal of the papers of his father Isaac Casaubon, whom Ussher would have known himself.[89] Many times Ussher would not only comment on the specific text but also suggest alternative texts with which to collate it – or indeed, go to the trouble of buying texts which might be of use to his fellow scholars. Thus Ussher was known not only as a collector but as a facilitator of the collection and publication of manuscripts.

He likewise played an important role in actively encouraging other scholars' projects. John Greaves, writing to him in 1644, acknowledged the encouragement Ussher had given him in his Arabic studies:

> According to your Grace's advice, I have made a Persian Lexicon out of such words as I met with in the Evangelists, and in the Psalms, and in two or three Arabian and Persian Nomenclators. So that I have now a stock of above 6,000 words in that Language, I think as many as *Raphelengius* hath in his Arabick Dictionary. Wherefore I have a greater mind than ever to go to *Leyden*, and peruse their Oriental Manuscripts, which were procured by the expence of the States, a thing which long since your Grace would have had me to have done.[90]

John Bainbridge could confidently ask for Ussher's help in tracking down necessary Arabic manuscripts. Writing to Ussher in October 1626, Bainbridge asked Ussher to use his contacts in the Levant 'to take in all Arabick Books of the Mathematics and Chronology, and amongst the rest a good Arabick Copy of the Alkoran, the only Book whereby that Language is attained'.[91] It is notable that this request could be made despite Ussher's rather minimal interest in Arabic.[92] A subject he was noticeably more enthusiastic about, Anglo-Saxon, received quite a lot of attention, and his concern for the preservation of Anglo-Saxon texts received public acknowledgement after his death by the University of Oxford. Two scholars in particular received not only encouragement but practical help. Abraham Wheelock, Parr tells us,

> in an Epistle before the Saxon Translation of Bede's History, acknowledgeth the solemn direction and encouragement he received in Cambridge from the Lord Primate of Ireland, in order to the prosecuting of his publick Saxon Lectures in that place: And in his Notes upon the Persian Gospels, the same Author shews what information he received from that Reverend Person, concerning the Doxology in the Lord's Prayer, which is found in the very Ancient Translation of the Gospels into Gothick.[93]

Francis Junius was no less grateful for Ussher's help, and it seems likely that the strong contingent of Anglo-Saxon texts among Ussher's collection may be connected to the needs of these two scholars and that this common shared interest in Anglo-Saxon may have been one of the things connecting Ussher to Simonds D'Ewes.[94]

Ussher was so generous that at times he was willing to give away not only manuscripts but whole projects of his own. Gerard John Vossius, writing to Ussher in January 1633, had much to thank him for.[95] Although Ussher had himself been working on Marianus Scotus, once he heard that Vossius intended to prepare an edition, he immediately sent over his manuscript of Marianus Scotus and suggested that Vossius use whatever was useful. In his letter to Vossius of the previous June, Ussher had not only categorically stated his desire '*ut, sicut tua opera, ita etiam sub tuo nomine, integer prodiret Marianus*' (that the whole Marianus should come out – as it is doing so by your efforts – so also under your name) – before giving a detailed and highly useful analysis of the various manuscripts involved.[96] From the latter it is clear just how much work Ussher had already expended on the project: he had collated three other copies with the Cottonian version: one written by '*Wigornensis quidam monachus regis Stephani temporibus*' (a monk of Worcester, in the time of King Stephen); '*Duo alia apud Oxonienses vidi, in Bodleiana unum, in collegii Corporis Christi bibliotheca alterum*' (I saw two others at Oxford, one in the Bodleian library, the other in the library of Corpus Christi College). On top of this he also decided to send Vossius a copy of Florence of Worcester and an '*epitomen a Roberto Lotharingo, Herefordensi episcopo, eodem quo Marianus mortem obiit anno concinnatam*' (epitome put together by Robert Lotharingus, bishop of Hereford, in the same year as Marianus died).[97] As if this was not enough, he also promised '*alia quoque de Mariani patria et variis editionibus collectanea missurus similiter si ad editionis tuae ornatum aliquid inde accessurum a te intellexero*' (I will send other collections on Marianus' fatherland and various editions, if I learn from you that they would add any value to your edition).[98]

Perhaps the best litmus test of Ussher's extreme generosity with manuscripts was his decision to give the best copy of his Samaritan Pentateuch to Sir Robert Cotton. The only time Ussher is ever effusive about a manuscript is when he discusses his Samaritan and Syriac texts, but that did not stop him from giving them to his colleague. In July 1625, Ussher had already involved Cotton by asking him to arrange for the binding of his new acquisition.[99] Almost four years later he sent Cotton the

> ancient copye of the Samaritan Pentateuch, which I have long since destinated unto that librarye of yours, to which I have beene beholden for so many good things no where else to be found. I shall (God willing) ere long finish my collation of it with the Hebrew text: and then hang it up, ut votivam Tabulam, at that sacrarium of yours.[100]

It is significant that of Ussher's six copies of the Samaritan Pentateuch four are now in the Bodleian, Cotton's copy is in the British Library, and the final copy, the one given to Louis de Dieu, is now lost. In that sense Marsh's conjecture that 'the best volumes are dispers'd' was not so far from the mark.

For Ussher, though, this would not have been a problem. He was a facilitator, rather than an acquisitive collector, of manuscripts. Of course he took pleasure in uncovering rarities but his motivation for collecting manuscripts was based on something deeper than personal acquisition. It is clear that his profile as a collector fits neatly into that of Camden,

Cotton, Peiresc and De Thou. All these collectors collected not just for themselves but for the public good, a phrase which Ussher himself employs to describe his collecting policy. But for Ussher what mattered was 'bono publico Ecclesiae ac literarum' (the public good of the Church and of letters).[101] This religious motivation for collecting manuscripts was deep-seated and is elaborated in a long-running correspondence with Thomas James, the librarian of the Bodleian, who held similar views. As early as 1608, James and Ussher began devising a project – one might call it Ussher's Project – for manuscript collection. Ussher sets out the criteria very clearly:

> of Manuscripts you are in a manner that only man among us that make search for the furthering of Gods cause . . . If in all other Manuscripts which you read, you would observe the same course 1. to publish full treatises which shall make for the truth, and against the abuses of the Church of Rome. 2. To collect out of all others (of whatsoever profession) whatsoever may be found scatteringlie to that purpose, and digest them common place wise according unto the heads of the Controversies (as you have done in your *Apologie for J. Wickleffe:*) how much should all the professours of the truth be indebted unto you?[102]

Ten years later, Thomas Morton, the bishop of Chester, spoke in similar terms of the motivation of Ussher's collection: 'for so I interprett your diligent search of Antiquities Ecclesiasticall, for the tryall of such poynts as are controverted betweene us and the Romanists'.[103] It seems as if Ussher had taken the words of William Eyre to heart: 'paper will kill Antichrist'.[104]

This religious motivation for collecting was intimately connected to Ussher's historical interests and his historical method. It is clear in all his works that his favoured method was to present the sources in their original state. This was first elaborated in his magnum opus of 1613, the *Gravissimae Quaestiones*. This, I would like to suggest, is a seminal work for understanding Ussher's whole output and his motivation for collecting. We see in this, his first published work, the genesis of his historical method – namely to allow the manuscript texts to speak for themselves. Ussher was urged to employ this method by George Abbot, the archbishop of Canterbury, who argued that a strict rendition of the original text could not be confuted by Roman Catholic opponents.[105] Ussher might have expressed misgivings as to the literary style but he succumbed to the method and continued to employ it as a rhetorical tool throughout his later works.

Ussher's emphasis on the 'public good' of the Church also ensured that he did not view his collection in strictly national terms. His Irish and

British collections might account for a large section of his manuscript library, but it is clear that Ussher viewed his collection from a European perspective. He was well aware that his interests transcended the sometimes regionalist obsessions of his contemporaries in the British Isles. Writing to John Selden in 1627 about his Samaritan Pentateuch, he made the telling observation that the Pentateuch was 'a worke which would very greedilye be sought for by the learned abroad; howsoever such things are not much regarded by ours at home'.[106] Ussher was thus not solely collecting with the Irish and English markets in mind, but was anxious that he might be of service to the public good of the Church and letters throughout Europe.[107]

Parr suggests that as a collector Ussher was like an architect: '. . . who collected all sorts of materials for his building, before he begins his work, but . . . who knew Artificially how to frame and put together the materials before Collected, till they became one strong, entire, and uniform Structure'.[108] What we need to recognize is that for contemporaries, Ussher's utility lay not in the fact that he had an extensive and available library but that he could also further their studies by directing them to other manuscripts in collections elsewhere. The eulogies on his death proclaiming him to be a 'breathing library', a 'walking library', are thus more than mere rhetoric.[109] They remind us that however substantial the remains of his collections might be today, they are in no way comparable to the man himself.

Notes and references

INTRODUCTION

1 Forthcoming as *The Cambridge Handbook of Irish Neo-Latin* from Cambridge University Press.

2 To be published as volumes in the new series *Officina Neolatina: Selected Writings from the Neo-Latin World* from Brepols Publishers, Turnhout. *Ormonius* is scheduled to appear in summer 2009. Other proposed Irish additions to the series are Stephen White's *Apologia pro innocentibus Hibernis* (Jason Harris) and works by Philip O'Sullivan Beare (David Caulfield).

3 Statistics from F. Waquet, *Latin or the Empire of a Sign* (London: 2001), p. 102f.

4 Quoted by J. Ijsewijn, *Companion to Neo-Latin Studies, Part I: History and Diffusion of Neo-Latin Literature* (Leuven: 1990), p. 246.

5 H. Helander, *Neo-Latin Literature in Sweden in the Period 1620–1720: Stylistics, Vocabulary and Characteristic Ideas* (Uppsala: 2004), p. 13.

6 J.W. Binns, *Intellectual Culture in Elizabethan and Jacobean England* (Leeds: 1990), p. 253f.

7 For the unpublished poems of Francis Molloy (*c.* 1606–*c.* 1677), preserved in MS. Bibliotheca Apostolica Vaticana Chigi D.III.40, see Dirk Sacré, 'Ab oblivio vindicentur . . . Francisci Molloy . . . poetae ex Hibernis oriundi, epigrammata inedita', *Melissa*, vol. 128, 2005, pp. 9–11. We are grateful to Professor Dirk Sacré for this information and a copy of his paper. Francis Molloy's Latin-Irish Grammar (*Grammatica Latino-Hibernica*) was published in Rome in 1677 and his *Lucerna Fidelium* in Rome in 1676.

8 See further Jean-Michel Picard, 'The Latin Language in Early Medieval Ireland', in Michael Cronin and Cormac Ó Cuilleanáin (eds), *The Languages of Ireland* (Dublin and Portland, Oregon: 2003), pp. 44–57. The period from around 1100 to 1500 is not well researched, but see Richard Sharpe, 'A Handlist of the Latin Writers of Great Britain and Ireland before 1540', *Publications of the Journal of Medieval Latin*, vol. 1 (Turnhout: 1997).

9 For analysis of the breakdown of consensus government, see Ciaran Brady, *The Chief Governors: The Rise and Fall of Reform Government in Tudor Ireland 1536–1588* (Cambridge: 1995). For assessment of the impact of Gerald of Wales's writings within England and Ireland, see Hiram Morgan, 'Giraldus Cambrensis and the Tudor Conquest of Ireland', in idem, ed., *Political Ideology in Ireland, 1541–1641* (Dublin: 1999), pp. 22–44.

10 The best survey of sixteenth-century Ireland is provided by Colm Lennon,

Sixteenth Century Ireland: The Incomplete Conquest (Dublin: 1994).

11 The definitive study of the escalation of violence in the sixteenth century is David Edwards, 'The Escalation of Violence in Sixteenth-Century Ireland', in David Edwards, Padraig Lenihan and Clodagh Tait (eds), *Age of Atrocity: Violence and Political Conflict in Early Modern Ireland* (Dublin: 2007), pp. 34–78.

12 'Orders of the general assembly . . . 24 Oct. 1642' (BL Add MSS 4,781ff 4–11; J.T. Gilbert (ed.), *History of the Irish Confederation and the War in Ireland,* 7 vols. (Dublin: 1882–91), vol. 2, p. 85.

13 Micheal Ó Siochrú, *Confederate Ireland, 1642–1649: A Constitutional and Political Analysis* (Dublin: 1999).

14 Thomas Herron and Michael Potterton (eds), *Ireland in the Renaissance, c.1540–1660* (Dublin: 2007).

15 Nicholas Canny, *Making Ireland British 1580–1650* (Oxford: 2001).

16 Thomas O'Connor, *Irish Jansenists, 1600–70* (Dublin: 2008).

1. SOME REFLEXES OF LATIN LEARNING . . . C. 1450–C. 1600

1 W. Keith Percival, *Studies in Renaissance Grammar* (Aldershot and Burlington, Vermont: 2004), [collected reprints] I, p. 231.

2 Compare, for example, Manfred Fuhrmann, *Latein und Europa: Geschichte des Gelehrten Unterrichts in Deutschland von Karl dem Grossen bis Wilhelm II* (Cologne: 2001), pp. 65–6. For the Renaissance and Ireland generally, see e.g. F.X. Martin, 'Ireland, the Renaissance and the Counter-Reformation', *Topic,* vol. 13, 1967, pp. 23–33; John J. Silke, 'Irish Scholarship and the Renaissance, 1580–1673', *Studies in the Renaissance,* vol. 20, 1973, pp. 169–206; Mícheál Mac Craith, 'Ireland and the Renaissance', in Glanmor Williams and Robert Owen Jones (eds), *The Celts and the Renaissance: Tradition and Innovation* (Cardiff: 1990), pp. 57–90.

3 See, for example, R.H. Robins, *A Short History of Linguistics*, 3rd edn (London: 1990), pp. 106–26.

4 Norman French and English came with the Normans at the end of the twelfth century. It appears that Norman French was never very widely spoken in Ireland, though its use for legal purposes in the common law areas continued into the fifteenth century: Jean-Michel Picard, 'The French Language in Medieval Ireland', in Michael Cronin and Cormac Ó Cuilleanáin (eds), *The Languages of Ireland* (Dublin and Portland, Oregon: 2003), pp. 57–77. By the sixteeth century the English language had retreated to the Pale around Dublin, Forth and Bargy, in south Wexford, and pockets, mainly in towns: see, for example Jeremiah J. Hogan, *The English Language in Ireland* (Dublin: 1927).

5 See, for example, Brian Ó Cuív (ed.), *Seven Centuries of Irish Learning*, 2nd edn (Cork: 1971). For translations see J.E.C. Williams and M. Ní Mhuiríosa, *Traidisiún Liteartha na nGael* (Dublin: 1979), pp. 112–14, 119ff; Nessa Ní Shéaghdha, *Translations and Adaptations into Irish* (Dublin: 1984); William B. Stanford, *Ireland and the Classical Tradition* (Dublin: 1976), pp. 73–89; Máirtín Mac Conmara (ed.), *An Léann Eaglasta in Éirinn 1200–1900* (Dublin: 1988), pp. 113–38. The translations inculded some philosophical texts.

6 Brendan Bradshaw, 'Manus "The Magnificent" O'Donnell as Renaissance Prince', in Art Cosgrove and Donal McCartney (eds), *Studies in Irish History presented to R. Dudley Edwards* (Dublin: 1979), pp. 15–36, at p. 15.

7 ibid., p. 23ff.

8 A. O'Kelleher and G. Schoepperle, *Betha Colaim Chille: Life of Columcille* (1918; reprinted Dublin: 1994), pp. 6–7, xlvi–xlvii: Only a shorter recension of Adamnán's life of Columcille was available to Ó Domhnaill at the time: Richard

Sharpe, *Medieval Irish Saints' Lives* (Oxford: 1991), p. 37. It was a hundred years later that the manuscript now known as Schaffhausen Generalia I, which had been preserved at Reichenau, at Lake Constance, containing Adamnán's full text, was rediscovered when it came to the notice of Stephen White S.J. See Dagmar Ó Riain-Raedel, 'The Travels of Irish Manuscripts: From the Continent to Ireland', in Toby Barnard, Dáibhí Ó Cróinín and Katharine Simms (eds), *A Miracle of Learning* (Aldershot and Brookfield, Vermont: 1998), pp. 52–67, at p. 54.

9   Timothy O'Neill, *The Irish Hand* (Mountrath: 1984), pp. 84–5. See also Brian Ó Cuív, *Catalogue of Irish Language Manuscripts in the Bodleian Library at Oxford and Oxford College Libraries*, 2 vols (Dublin: 2001), vol. 1, pp. 261–74.

10   Bradshaw, 'Manus "The Magnificent"', pp. 25–6.

11   ibid., p. 23.

12   E.G. Bowen, *Britain and the Western Seaways* (London: 1972); Timothy O'Neill, *Merchants and Mariners in Medieval Ireland* (Dublin: 1987).

13   O'Neill, *Merchants and Mariners*, p. 30. See also Ada K. Longfield, *Anglo-Irish Trade in the Sixteenth* Century (London: 1929), pp. 41–5.

14   O'Neill, *Merchants and Mariners*, p. 36. Cf Colin Breen, *The Gaelic Lordship of O'Sullivan Beare* (Dublin and Portland, Oregon: 2005), pp. 113–21, 212–14; Michael M. Barkham, 'The Spanish Basque Irish Fishery and Trade in the Sixteenth Century', *History Ireland*, vol. 9, no. 3, Autumn, 2001, pp. 12–15.

15   Declan M. Downey, 'The Irish Contribution to Counter-Reformation Theology in Continental Europe', in Brendan Bradshaw and Dáire Keogh (eds), *Christianity in Ireland: Revisiting the Story* (Dublin: 2002), pp. 96–108, at p. 97.

16   Ciaran O Scea, 'The Significance and Legacy of Spanish Intervention in West Munster during the Battle of Kinsale', in Thomas O'Connor and Mary Ann Lyons (eds), *Irish Migrants in Europe after Kinsale, 1602–1820* (Dublin and Portland, Oregon: 2003), pp. 32–63, at p. 36, n. 11. For a similar report from Ulster *c.* 1600 see Patricia Palmer, *Language and Conquest in Early Modern Ireland* (Cambridge: 2001), p. 44.

17   Colmán Ó Clabaigh, *The Franciscans in Ireland, 1400–1534* (Dublin and Portland, Oregon: 2002), p. 49; F.X. Martin, 'The Irish Augustinian Reform Movement in the Fifteenth Century', in J.A. Watt, J.B. Morrall and F.X. Martin (eds), *Medieval Studies Presented to Aubrey Gwynn S.J.* (Dublin: 1961), pp. 230–64, esp. pp. 239–41.

18   Downey, 'The Irish Contribution', p. 97.

19   Katherine Walsh, 'The Clerical Estate in Later Medieval Ireland', in John Bradley (ed.), *Settlement and Society in Medieval Ireland* (Kilkenny: 1988), pp. 361–78, at p. 367.

20   Ó Clabaigh, *The Franciscans*, p. 75. The Youghal friary had become observant before that: compare Ó Clabaigh, p. 33.

21   Regina Whelan Richardson, 'The Salamanca Archives', in Agnes Neligan (ed.), *Maynooth Library Treasures* (Dublin: 1995), pp. 112–47, at p. 118; Ó Clabaigh, *The Franciscans*, p. 128. The Irish colleges proper do not emerge as formal establishments until the end of the sixteenth century. Irish students are found attending continental universities in much greater numbers after the start of the Reformation. So, for example, Irish students begin to be found increasingly in the University of Louvain from 1548 onwards: Brendan Jennings, 'Irish Students in the University of Louvain', in Sylvester Ó Brien (ed.), *Measgra i gCuimhne Mhichíl Uí Chléirigh* (Dublin: 1944), pp. 74–97.

22   See, for example, Jean-Michel Picard, 'The Latin Language in Early Medieval Ireland', in Michael Cronin and Cormac Ó Cuilleanáin (eds), *The Languages of Ireland* (Dublin and Portland, Oregon: 2003), pp. 44–57, at p. 56; Thomas O'Loughlin, 'The Latin Sources of Medieval Irish Culture', in Kim McCone and

Katharine Simms (eds), *Progress in Medieval Irish Studies* (Maynooth: 1996), pp. 91–106. See also A.B. Scott, 'Latin Learning and Literature in Ireland, 1169–1500', in Dáibhí Ó Cróinín (ed), *A New History of Ireland*, vol. I (Oxford, 2005), pp. 934–993; Benignus Millet, 'Irish Literature in Latin, 1550–1700', in T.W. Moody, F.X. Martin and F.J. Byrne (eds), *A New History of Ireland*, vol. III (Oxford: 1976), pp. 561–86.

23 See, for example, Henry A. Jefferies, 'Erenaghs and Termonlands in Late Medieval Ireland', *Archivium Hibernicum*, vol. LIII, 1999, pp. 16–19.

24 See, for example, Robin Flower, *The Irish Tradition* (Oxford: 1947), pp. 67–106; Proinsias Mac Cana, 'The Rise of the Later Schools of *Filidheacht*', *Ériu*, vol. 25, 1974, pp. 126–46; Katharine Simms, 'Literacy and the Irish Bards', in Huw Pryce (ed.), *Literacy in Medieval Celtic Societies* (Cambridge: 1998), pp. 238–58.

25 For example, Palmer, *Language and Conquest*, pp. 187–8, 191, 193, 198; Douglas Hyde, *A Literary History of Ireland*, 2nd edn (London: 1967), pp. 529–30. According to Dónal Cam O'Sullivan Beare (†1618), the O'Sullivan heirs were always taught to speak English and Latin (Palmer, p. 145). On another occasion, he emphasized that the Irish college which he founded at Santiago de Compostela for the young Irish nobility (and where Don Philip the historian was educated) always taught Latin: Gareth A. Davies, 'The Irish College at Santiago de Compostela: Two Documents about its Early Days', in Margaret A. Rees (ed.), *Catholic Tastes and Times: Essays in Honour of Michael E. Williams* (Leeds: 1987), pp. 81–126, at pp. 94–5.

26 Lucien Febvre and Henri-Jean Martin, *The Coming of the Book: The Impact of Printing, 1450–1800*, translated by David Gerard (London: 1986), pp. 329–32.

27 Cecile O'Rahilly, *Tóruigheacht Gruaidhe Griansholus: The Pursuit of Gruaidh Ghriansholus*, vol. XXIV [1922] (London: Irish Texts Society, 1924), pp. 68–9.

28 E.S. Bates, *Touring in 1600: A Study in the Development of Travel as a Means of Education*, 2nd edn, introduction by George Bull (London: Century, 1987), p. 119.

29 Kevin McGrath, 'The Bruodins in Bohemia', *Irish Ecclesiastical Record*, vol. 77, May, 1952, pp. 333–43 at p. 334, n.2. Walter Butler was made famous (or infamous) by Friedrich Schiller in his *Wallenstein*, see Hubert Butler, 'Walter Butler', *Journal of the Butler Society*, vol. I, no. 3 (1970–1), pp. 191–5; no. 7 (1977), pp. 551–5; Florian Krobb, 'A Wild Goose in Wallenstein: Walter Butler in Schiller's Trilogy, *Irish-German Studies*, vol. 1, 2001/2002, pp. 111–21. The O'Meara family, of Toomevara, in Tipperary, may have been, before the Reformation, one of the families controlling Church offices requiring Latin mentioned above: Patrick Logan, 'Dermot and Edmund O'Meara, Father and Son', *Journal of the Irish Medical Association*, vol. XLIII, 1958, pp. 312–17, esp. p. 312.

30 A. Martin Freeman, *Annála Connacht: The Annals of Connacht* (Dublin: 1944), pp. 600–1. Compare John O'Donovan (ed.), *The Annals of the Kingdom of Ireland by the Four Masters*, 3rd edn, 6 vols (Dublin: 1990), vol. IV, pp. 1224–5: '*Féichsamh coitcheann daonnachta ⁊ einigh iarthair mumhan saoi eccnaidhe i llaidin ⁊ i mberla …*' (general supporter of the humanity [*daonnacht*], and hospitality of west Munster, a wise man, learned in Latin and in English).

31 Diarmuid Ó Murchadha, *Family Names of County Cork* (Cork: 1996), p. 233.

32 Breen, *The Gaelic Lordship of the O'Sullivan Beare*, pp. 85, 114–21, 213–14.

33 Ó Murchadha, *Family Names of County Cork*, p. 233.

34 Breandán Ó Conchúir, *Scríobhaithe Chorcaí 1700–1850* (Dublin: 1982), p. 316, n. 40; Robin Flower, *Catalogue of Irish Manuscripts in the British Museum*, vol 2 (London: 1926), p. 540.

35 Ó Murchadha, *Family Names of County Cork*, p. 233.

36 Winifred Wulff and Kathleen Mulchrone, *Catalogue of Irish Manuscripts in the Royal*

Irish Academy, vol X (Dublin: n.d.), pp. 1,180–1. It appears from the catalogue that this, like many of the Irish medical manuscripts, may have significant Latin content.

37 Ó Murchadha, *Family Names of County Cork*, p. 233. The title 'psalter' does not necessarily indicate that this manuscript contained a copy of the psalms. The title was regularly applied to Irish manuscripts.

38 Whitley Stokes, 'The Gaelic Maundeville', *Zeitschrift für Celtische Philologie*, vol. 2, 1899, pp. 1–63, 225–312. It has been said that the history of this work's transmission 'demonstrates the links between the European courts . . . Over the following centuries, Isabella of Castile and many lesser nobles across Europe owned manuscripts [of it]', Rosemary Tzanaki, *Mandeville's Medieval Audiences* (Aldershot: 2003), pp. 12–13. This text is almost certainly the 'Mandavile' ['Maundvile' in French in earlier list] found in the Kildare library: see below.

39 This is perhaps the only manuscript which can now be identified as having been written in the fine scriptorium which can still be identified in the ruined friary of Kilcrea, near Cork city. Another copy of Finghín's translation is found in B. Lib. Eg. 1781: Flower, *Catalogue of Irish Manuscripts in the British Museum*, vol. 2, p. 540.

40 Stokes, 'The Gaelic Maundeville', p. 2.

41 Ó Murchadha, *Family Names of County Cork*, p. 233; Séamus Ó hInnse, *Miscellaneous Irish Annals* (Dublin: 1947), p. ix. Ó Ficheallaigh's MS is lost. Ware stated that he saw it in the hands of a later noble scholar and patron, Finghín (Florence) MacCarthy, in London in 1626, where MacCarthy was detained for many years before his death: James Ware, *De Scriptoribus Hiberniae* (Dublin, 1639), p. 78; Ó Murchadha, ibid., pp. 54–5.

42 Donnchadh Ó Corráin, 'Corcu Loígde: Land and Families', in Patrick O'Flanagan and Neil Buttimer (eds), *Cork History and Society* (Dublin: 1993), pp. 63–82, at p. 74, quoting Mr Kenneth Nicholls. For others who appear to have been of this family see, for example, Cataldus Giblin, 'Vatican Library: MSS Barberini Latini', *Arch Hib*, vol. XVIII, 1955, pp. 67–144 at pp. 77, 80, 81; compare Paul Walsh, *Irish Leaders and Learning Through the Ages*, edited by Nollaig Ó Muraíle (Dublin: 2003), p. 448.

43 Ó Corráin, 'Corcu Loígde', p. 74.

44 Tony Sweeney, *Ireland and the Printed Word* (Dublin: 1997), p. 233; Mac Conmara (ed.), *An Léann Eaglasta in Éirinn 1200–1900*, pp. 65–72. 'It was not unusual to see humanists of all ranks and every level of renown take service under the entrepreneurs of the book trade and work as correctors in a printing workshop for a few months, or a few years . . .' Robert Mandrou, *From Humanism to Science 1480–1700*, translated by B. Pearce (Middlesex: 1978), p. 29.

45 See Ware, *De Scriptoribus Hiberniae*, p. 79.

46 See, for example, Anthony M. McCormack, *The Earldom of Desmond 1463–1583* (Dublin and Portland, Oregon: 2005), pp. 58–61.

47 Edmund Curtis, *A History of Medieval Ireland from 1086 to 1513*, 2nd edn (London: 1938), p. 330. For the Fitzgeralds generally see, for example, Bryan Fitzgerald, *The Geraldines* (New York: 1951).

48 Séamus Pender (ed.), 'O Clery Genealogies', *Analecta Hibernica*, vol. 18, 1951, p. 174.

49 John O'Donovan (ed.), 'The Annals of Ireland, from the Year 1443 to 1468 . . .', *Miscellany of the Irish Archaeological Society*, vol. 1, 1846, pp. 198–302, at p. 263. These annals are lost. Only a fragment of a translation remains. Nollaig Ó Muraíle, *The Celebrated Antiquary: Dubhaltach Mac Fhirbhishigh c. 1600–1671* (Maynooth: 1996), pp. 271–2.

50 A.J. Otway-Ruthven, *History of Medieval Ireland*, 2nd edn (New York: 1980),

pp. 389–92. For further sources, see Brian Ó Cuív, 'A Fragment of Irish Annals', *Celtica*, vol. 14, 1981, pp. 83–104.

51 George Butler, 'The Battle of Piltown, 1462', *Irish Sword*, vol. VI, 1964, pp. 197–212. The exact identification of the second MS today is problematic. 'An Charraig' is almost certainly Carrick-on-Suir, County Tipperary. Brian Ó Cuív, *Catalogue of Irish Language Manuscripts*, 2 vols (Dublin: 2003), vol. 1, pp. 67, 75; Flower, *Catalogue of Irish Manuscripts in the British Museum*, vol. 2, pp. 470–1; I thank G. De Buitléir for this information.

52 Curtis, *A History of Medieval Ireland*, pp. 329–30.

53 The text and translation are taken from Henry F. Berry (ed.), *Statute Rolls of the Parliament of Ireland, 1–12, Edward IV* (Dublin: 1914), pp. 368–9.

54 '*Study generale*': this is a rendering of 'studium generale': see for example, William Boyd and Edmund J. King, *The History of Western Education*, 11th edn (London: 1975), pp. 128–9.

55 See, for example, ibid., pp. 129, 153, 183–4.

56 Fergus McGrath, *Education in Ancient and Medieval Ireland* (Dublin: 1979), pp. 220–1; Curtis, *A History of Medieval Ireland*, pp. 329–33.

57 Gearóid Mac Niocaill, 'Duanaire Ghearóid Iarla', *Studia Hibernica*, vol. 3, 1963, pp. 7–59. Mícheál Mac Craith, *Lorg na hIasachta ar na Dánta Grá* (Dublin: 1989), pp. 42–60; Seán Ó Tuama, 'Gearóid Iarla – the First Recorded Practitioner', in Seosamh Watson (ed.), *Féilscríbhinn Thomáis de Bhaldraithe* (Dublin:1986), pp. 78–85; Jean-Michel Picard, 'The French Language in Early Medieval Ireland', pp. 57–77, at p. 69. Dr Jason Harris, to whom I am grateful for very helpful comments, has observed that these vernacular initiatives reflect developments in vernacular poetry across Europe as part of the Renaissance.

58 Ó Clabaigh, *The Franciscans*, pp. 155–80. For example, the Augustinian friary at Callan, County Kilkenny, which became the headquarters of the Augustinian observant reform in Ireland, is stated to have had a good library: William Carrigan, *The History and Antiquities of the Diocese of Ossory*, 4 vols (Dublin: 1905), vol. III, p. 312. This house was affiliated in 1472 directly with the friary of Santa Maria del Popolo in Rome, which remains to this day a showpiece of the art and architecture of the early Italian Renaissance: see F.X. Martin, 'The Irish Agustinian Reform Movement in the Fifteenth Century', in J.A. Watt, J.B. Morall and F.X. Martin (eds), *Medieval Studies Presented to Aubrey Gwynn S.J.* (Dublin: 1951), pp. 230–64, at pp. 246–8. No medieval collection has survived *in situ* in Ireland, comparable, say, to the material of Irish interest in the library of St Gallen, Switzerland: for which see, for example, Michael Richter, 'St Gallen and the Irish in the early Middle Ages', in Michael Richter and Jean-Michel Picard (eds), *Ogma* (Dublin and Portland, Oregon: 2002), pp. 65–75. The topic is bedevilled by the loss of material. See, for example, Donnchadh Ó Corráin, 'Cad d'imigh ar Lámhscríbhinní na hÉireann?', in Ruairí Ó hUiginn (ed.), *Oidhreacht na Lámhscríbhinní*, Léachtaí Cholm Cille, vol. 34 (2004), pp. 7–27.

59 Rossbrin and over 1,000 acres were taken from the O'Mahonys by agents of the English Crown in 1584 because of their support for the Desmond rebellion and they never recoverd them again. Ó Murchadha, *Family Names of County Cork*, p. 234. The Desmond papers did not survive the destruction of the Desmonds in the 1580s: McCormack, *The Earldom of Desmond*, p. 41.

60 See also Vincent Carey, '"Neither Good English nor Good Irish": Bilingualism and Identity Formation in Sixteenth-Century Ireland', in Hiram Morgan (ed.), *Poltical Ideology in Ireland 1541–1641* (Dublin and Portland, Oregon: 1999), pp. 45–61.

61 *Hec sunt nomina librorum existencium in libraria Geraldi comitis Kildarie.* Gearóid Mac Niocaill, *Crown Surveys of Lands 1540–41* (Dublin: 1992), pp. 355–7; Mac Craith, *Lorg na hIasachta*, pp. 228–32.

62 'Bokes remayning in the lyberary of a Geralde fitzGeralde erle of Kyldare the 5 day of Februarii anno Henrici VIII 17o [1526]': Mac Niocaill, *Crown Surveys*, pp. 312–14.

63 According to Standish Hayes O'Grady, *Catalogue of Irish Manuscripts in the British Museum*, vol. I (London: 1926), p. 154, immediately after the list of English books in the 1526 list there is a blank page headed 'Irsh Bokys'. This perhaps suggests that the compiler of the later list awaited the assistance of someone else to deal with the Irish books but that this had not been done when other events intervened. A 1518 list of the contents of a manuscript in the earl's library refers to a list of Latin books, a list of French Books and English books, and a list of Irish books: Mac Niocaill, *Crown Surveys*, p. 237. The list of Irish MSS which survives does not contain an Irish MS purchased by Gearóid Mór in 1500, a translation from Latin of Bernard of Gordon's famous medical work (*c.* 1305), *Lilium Medicinae*, now British Library MS Egerton 89: O'Grady, ibid., pp. 220–1. For continued Fitzgerald ownership of Irish MSS in the mid-sixteenth century, see, for example, William O'Sullivan, 'The Manuscript Collection of Dubhaltach Mac Fhirbhisigh', in Alfred Smyth (ed.), *Seanchas* (Dublin and Portland, Oregon: 2000), pp. 439–47, at pp. 443–4.

64 Taken as references to the same work.

65 Taken as references to the same work.

66 Taken as references to the same work.

67 The editor notes this item as a cancellation: Mac Niocaill, *Crown Surveys*, p. 355.

68 Mac Niocaill, *Crown Surveys*, p. 314.

69 ibid., pp. 313–14.

70 This is almost certainly the text noted above as having been translated by Ó Mathúna.

71 Among the English books, 'The sege [siedge] of Thebes' may be the first-century AD *Thebaid* of Statius. In relation to 'The distruccion of Troy', in the same list, it has been stated that there were five versions of the Troy story in English at the end of the fifteenth century: *Éigse*, vol. III, 1941–2, pp. 70–1. Versions of both of these (and of the *Aeneid*) were also in circulation in Irish: see Stanford, *Ireland and the Classical Tradition*, pp. 80–9, and, for example, Uáitéar Mac Gearailt, 'Togail Troí: an Example of Translating and Editing in Medieval Ireland', *Studia Hibernica*, vol. 31, 2000–01, pp. 71–85. It has been suggested that 'Ercules' in the French list could be (part of) Raol Lefevre, *Recueil des Histoires de Troyes* completed about 1464 and first printed in 1478: *Éigse*, vol. III, 1941–2, pp. 70–1; Gordon Quin (ed.), *Stair Ercuil ocus a Bás: The Life and Death of Hercules*, Irish Texts Society, vol. 38 (Dublin: 1939), p. xiv.

72 For Boethius and Gregory the Great see L. Marthaler et al (eds), *New Catholic Encyclopedia*, 2nd edn (Washington: 2003), vol. II, pp. 454–7, and vol. VI, pp. 478–84. 'Le graunte Boece' in the French list is surely to be identified as a translation or edition of Boethius also. The *Dialogues* of Gregory the Great and works by Boethius appear in the Youghal Franciscan library also: Ó Clabaigh, *The Franciscans*, pp. 170, 173, 179.

73 Simon Hornblower and Anthony Spawforth, *The Oxford Classical Dictionary*, rev. edn (Oxford: 2003), p. 1584. I thank John Barry for this suggested identification.

74 Mac Niocaill, *Crown Surveys*, pp. 314, 356. See e.g. John J. O'Meara, *The History and Topography of Ireland: Gerald of Wales* (Harmondsworth: 1982) and see William O'Sullivan, 'The Manuscript Collecton of Dubhaltach Mac Firbhisigh', as in n. 63 above.

75 Ó Clabaigh, *The Franciscans*, pp. 158–80.

76 ibid., pp. 102, 151–2, 173, 178. There were two copies of this in the Youghal library and the Franciscan Third Order at Slane in County Meath also had a copy.

Ó Clabaigh says (p. 151) that this book was one of the three burned publicly by Luther at Wittenberg in 1520!

77 Ó Clabaigh, *The Franciscans*, pp. 149–50, 174. There was a copy in the Youghal library also. Ó Clabaigh, pp. 150–5, has shown that there are strong similarities between a section of this text and an Irish text found in a number of fifteenth- and early sixteenth-century manuscripts, including B. Lib. Eg. 1781, a manuscript which appears to contain a number of texts also found in the Maynooth library.

78 See Ó Clabaigh, *The Franciscans*, pp. 123, 163, 165, 167, 168. *Tabula utilissima super Liram* [*Tabula utilissima super Lyram*] appears to be another work on this writer.

79 See Penelope Woods, 'Books Rich, Rare and Curious', in Agnes Neligan (ed.), *Maynooth Library Treasures from the Collections of Saint Patrick's College* (Dublin: 1995), pp. 29–63, at pp. 35–6; compare Ó Clabaigh, *The Franciscans*, p. 149.

80 See Woods, 'Books Rich, Rare and Curious', pp. 36–7

81 Nicholas Orme, 'Schools and Schoolbooks', in Lotte Hellinga and J.B. Trappe (eds), *The Cambridge History of the Book in Britain*, vol. 3, rev. edn, pp. 449–69, at pp. 452, 464.

82 Orme, 'Schools and Schoolbooks', pp. 453, 460; A.W. Pollard and C.R. Redgrave, *A Short-Title Catalogue of Books Printed in England, Scotland and Ireland and of English Books Printed Abroad 1475–1640*, 3 vols, rev. edn (London: 1986), vol. I, p. 601, § 13,829.

83 Orme, 'Schools and Schoolbooks', pp. 453, 460–4. Also, Manfred Fuhrmann, *Latein und Europa* (Cologne: 2001), p. 25ff.

84 Rudolf Pfeiffer, *History of Classical Scholarship from 1300 to 1850* (Oxford: 1976), pp. 35–41; Percival, *Studies in Renaissance Grammar*, pp. 254–6; chapter XVII, pp. 133–52.

85 At least sixty-seven Renaissance manuscripts of it have survived and there were fifty-nine printed editions between 1471 and 1536: John Monfasani, *Greeks and Latins in Renaissance Italy* (Aldershot and Burlington, Vermont: 2004), [reprinted essays] chapter XI, pp. 1, 13; Fuhrmann, *Latein und Europa*, p. 31.

86 Fuhrmann, *Latein und Europa*, pp. 66, 72.

87 Émile Legouis and Louis Cazamian, *A History of English Literature*, rev. edn translated by Helen Douglas Irvine (London: 1971), p. 203. The 1526 list of English books contains what appears to be another work by More, 'Sir Thyomas Moore his booke [[of]]{agayni}s the new opinions that hold agayns pilgremages'. Mac Niocaill, *Crown Surveys*, p. 314.

88 Mac Craith, *Lorg na hIasachta*, p. 228.

89 Pfeiffer, *History of Classical Scholarship from 1300 to 1850*, p. 107; Percival, *Studies in Renaissance Grammar*, p. 22.

90 Sweeney, *Ireland and the Printed Word* p. 537. I am grateful to Mr Éamonn de Búrca for sending me a photograph of an extract from a copy of this work in his hands. For patronage, see, for example, Lucien Febvre and Henri-Jean Martin, *The Coming of the Book* (London, 1976), pp. 160–1.

91 Ó Clabaigh, *The Franciscans*, p. 69.

92 Mary Ann Lyons, *Gearóid Óg Fitzgerald*, Historical Association of Ireland: Life and Times Series, No. 12 (Dublin: 1998), p. 22: Mac Craith, *Lorg na hIasachta*, p. 22.

93 I thank John Barry for this observation and for his other most helpful suggestions.

94 The library also reflects the wider Irish culture of the time. For example, a MS in Irish, written in the midlands in the 1480s, now B. Lib. MS Egerton 1781, contains (1) a copy of *Togail na Tebe*, an Irish version of the work of the *Thebaid* of Statius tentatively identified in the English list (n. 71 above); (2) a copy of Ó Mathúna's translation of Mandeville, a work found in the French list as mentioned above; (3)

the text *Leigheas Coise Chein*, which is 'The Leeching of Kene is Legg', found in the Irish list (not reprinted in this article) and (4) a text for confessors, apparently based on a section of the *Confessionale* of St Antoninus of Florence, which, as suggested above, n. 77, may have been one of the works in the Latin lists above: Mac Niocaill, *Crown Surveys*, pp. 354–7, 312–14; Flower, *Catalogue of Irish Manuscripts in the British Museum*, vol. 2, pp. 526–45, esp. p. 532; Ó Clabaigh, *The Franciscans*, pp. 152–3, 174.

95   Robin Flower, 'Manuscripts of Irish Interest in the British Museum', *Analecta Hibernica*, vol 2 (1931), pp. 292–340, at p. 325.

96   Gearóid Mac Niocaill (ed.), *The Red Book of the Earls of Kildare* (Dublin: 1964); Flower, 'Manuscripts of Irish Interest in the British Musuem', pp. 325–9. K.W. Nicholls, 'Philip Flattisbury' (*fl.* 1503–1526), *Oxford Dictionary of National Biography*, edited by. H.C.G. Matthew and Brian Harrison (Oxford 2004), vol. 20, p. 1.

97   Colm Lennon, *Sixteenth-Century Ireland*, rev. edn (Dublin: 2005), p. 84.

98   For the Great Earl see Donough Bryan, *The Great Earl of Kildare* (Dublin and Belfast: n.d.). See also Mary Ann Lyons, *Church and Society in County Kildare, c. 1470–1547* (Dublin and Portland, Oregon: 2000).

99   Lyons, *Gearóid Óg Fitzgerald*, pp. 21–2.

100 I thank John Barry for this observation.

101 Lyons, *Gearóid Óg Fitzgerald*, p. 23.

102 ibid.; Marquis of Kildare, *The Earls of Kildare and Their Ancestors*, 3rd edn (Dublin: 1858), pp. 120–1.

103 Lyons, *Gearóid Óg Fitzgerald*, p. 26. The foundation had been initiated by Gearóid Mór before his death in 1513: ibid. See also Lyons, *Church and Society*, pp. 87–96.

104 Lyons, *Gearóid Óg Fitzgerald*, pp. 26–7. Unfortunately, this institution was suppressed in the 1530s as a result of the Reformation. It may have been intended to provide education for lay students also as, it appears, some similar institutions in England did.

105 Lyons, *Gearóid Óg Fitzgerald*, pp. 20, 22. Christopher Nugent, in the Latin/English introduction to the Irish language which he presented to Queen Elizabeth of England in the early 1560s, described how this Elizabeth Zouche, his great-grandmother, had, 'in short tyme . . . learned to reade, write and perfectlye speake' Irish, according to a particular method of language teaching then in use among the Kildare Fitzgeralds. This method was used by Fr William Bathe S.J., another great-grandson of Gearóid Óg and Elizabeth Zouche, as the basis of his *Janua linguarum* (Salamanca, 1611), written as a textbook for the teaching of Latin at the Irish College, Salamanca. This book became a seminal work in the history of the teaching of Latin and other languages in Europe through its influence on Comenius (Jan Amos Komenský, 1592–1670): Seán Ó Mathúna, *An tAthair William Bathe C.Í, 1564–1614* (Dublin: 1980), pp. 90–1, 168–9, 87, 89, and *passim*.

106 McGrath, *Education in Ancient and Medieval Ireland*, p. 190.

107 Jean-Michel Picard, 'The Italian Pilgrims', in Michael Haren and Yolande de Pontfarcy (eds), *The Medieval Pilgrimage to St Patrick's Purgatory* (Enniskillen: 1988), pp. 169–89, at p. 158ff.

108 See, for example, O'Neill, *Merchants and Mariners*, pp. 66–7; A.F. O'Brien, 'Commercial Relations between Aquitaine and Ireland *c.* 1000 to *c.* 1550', in Jean-Michel Picard (ed.), *Aquitaine and Ireland in the Middle Ages* (Dublin and Portland, Oregon: 1995), pp. 31–80, at p. 38, n. 50.

109 O'Neill, *Merchants and Mariners*, pp. 78–9

110 Picard, 'The Italian Pilgrims', p. 170.

111 T.D. Kendrick, *British Antiquity* (London: 1950), pp 57–8. See below in relation to export of Irish horses to Italy at this time.

112 Marquis of Kildare, *The Earls of Kildare and Their Ancestors*, pp. 1–5; Bryan Fitzgerald, *The Geraldines* pp. 13–18.

113 Dominic de Rosario O 'Daly, *Initium, incrementa, et exitus familiae Geraldinorum Desmoniae Comitum, Palatinorum Kyerriae in Hybernia* . . . (Lisbon: 1655), pp. 1, 2; C.P. Meehan, *The Rise, Increase, and Exit of the Geraldines, Earls of Desmond* . . . *transalted from the Latin of Dominic O'Daly O.P., with Memoir and Notes*, 2nd edn (Dublin and London: 1878), pp. 33, 34. O'Daly was a highly regarded diplomat. He was founder of the Irish Dominican College and the Irish Dominican Convent in Lisbon. His ancestors, the O'Dalys of Kilsarkan, near Castleisland, County Kerry, had been hereditary poets to the Fitzgeralds of Desmond for generations. Benvenuta Curtin, 'Dominic O'Daly: An Irish Diplomat', *Studia Hibernica*, vol. 5, 1965 pp. 98–112; Marc Caball, 'An Elizabethan Kerry Bardic Family', *Ériu*, vol. 43, 1992, pp. 177–92, at pp. 179–80. I thank Prof. Keith Sidwell and the Centre for Neo-Latin Studies at UCC for making this work of O'Daly and other early texts available to me.

114 O'Daly, *Initium* [Dedication, pp. 11–12], see Meehan, *The Rise, Increase, and Exit*, p. 4. For the Barberini, see, for example, Anthony Majanlahti, *The Families who Made Rome* (London: 2005), pp. 216–28.

115 See especially Eugenio Gamurrini, *Istoria genealogica delle famiglie nobili toscane et umbre*, 4 vols (Florence: 1668–73), vol II, pp. 111–38. As this work is not easily accessible, references are also given here to an English translation of the relevant section: A. Fitzgibbon, 'Appendix to the Unpublished Geraldine Documents – The Gherardini of Tuscany', *Journal of the Royal Society of Antiquaries of Ireland* (hereafter *JRSAI*), vol. 4, 4th series (1877), pp. 246–64: See also Meehan, *The Rise, Increase, and Exit,*' pp. 241–51. I thank Prof. Bruno Busetti, Director, and Mr Naoise Mac Fheorais of the Istituto Italiano di Cultura, Dublin, for kind help in locating and obtaining access to a copy of Gamurrini.

116 Gamurrini, *Istoria*, p. 111; Fitzgibbon, 'Appendix', *JRSAI*, vol. 4, 4th series (1877), p. 247. Meehan, *The Rise, Increase, and Exit* p. 247. Mannini also visited St Patrick's Purgatory and left an account of it: Picard, 'The Italian Pilgrims' p. 180.

117 Gamurrini, *Istoria*, p. 11; Fitzgibbon, 'Appendix', *JRSAI*, vol. 4, 4th series (1877), p. 247; Meehan, *The Increase, Rise, and Exit*, pp. 246–7. See Picard, 'The Italian Pilgrims', p. 187. The Fitzmaurices were a branch of the Fitzgeralds who controlled the Ardfert district at this time; being a member of that family 'was one of the most potent qualifications at that time for preferment to any of the higher offices associated with the cathedral'. J. O'Connell, 'The Church in Ireland in the Fifteenth Century: I. Diocesan Organisation: Kerry', *Proceedings of the Irish Catholic Historical Committee* (Dublin: 1956), pp. 1–4, at p. 2.

118 Meehan, *The Rise, Increase, and Exit*, pp. 243–4.

119 Pfeiffer, *History of Classical Scholarship*, pp. 27–30, at p. 27.

120 Columbus, of course, at this time had not yet sailed for America, so Ireland was the edge of the known world.

121 Latin text and translation (slightly adapted and corrected) from Meehan, *The Rise, Increase, and Exit*, pp. 243–45.

122 Curtis, *A History of Medieval Ireland*, p. 307.

123 Colm J. Donnelly, 'Tower Houses and Late Medieval Secular Settlement in County Limerick', in Patrick J. Duffy, David Edwards and Elizabeth Fitzpatrick (eds), *Gaelic Ireland c. 1250–1650*, 2nd edn (Dublin and Portland, Oregon: 2004), pp. 315–28, at p. 327.

124 T.W. Moody, F.X.Martin and F.J. Byrne (eds), *New History of Ireland*, vol. IX (Oxford: 1984), p. 168.

125 This letter was almost certainly written in Latin but I do not know if a copy of the

Latin text survives. Gamurrini gives an Italian version, stating that this is a faithful rendering: *Istoria*, p. 112; Fitzgibbon, 'Appendix', *JRSAI*, vol. 4, 4th series (1877), p. 248–9; also, Meehan, *The Rise, Increase, and Exit*, pp. 113, 248–9.

126   Walter Harris (ed.), *The Whole Works of Sir James Ware Vol. 2: The Antiquities of Ireland* (Dublin: 1745), pp. 166–7; O'Neill, *Merchants and Mariners*, pp. 102–6; Eric Haywood, '"La Divisa dal Mondo Ultima Irlanda" Ossia la Riscoperta Umanistica dell'Irlanda', *Giornale Storico della Letteratura Italiana*, vol. CLXXVI – Fascicle 575 (1999), pp. 363–387 (380–1; 384–5). The Curragh of Kildare was probably even more famous for horses in pre-industrial times before the horse was displaced by technology in so many areas. For some references to the Kildare Fitzgeralds' horses about this time, see Mac Niocaill, *Crown Surveys*, pp. 319–50. I thank Éamonn Ó Ciosáin for material by Eric Haywood.

127   Cristoforo Landino, *Commento Sopra la Comedia*, 2 vols (edited by Paolo Procaccioli) (Rome: 2001), vol. 1, p. 245: see also Fitzgibbon, 'Appendix', *JRSAI*, vol. 4, 4th series (1877), p. 263. For Landino see, for example, *Dizionario Biografico degli Italiani*, vol. 63 (Rome: 2004), pp. 428–33.

128   Ludovico Ariosto, *Orlando Furioso* (edited by Italo Calvino and Lanfranco Caretti), 2 vols (Turin: 1992), pp. 1, 250–1; see also Eric G. Haywood, 'Is Ireland Worth Bothering About? Classical Perceptions of Ireland Revisited in Renaissance Italy', *International Journal of the Classical Tradition*, vol. 2, no. 4, Spring, 1996, pp. 467–86. Ernst Robert Curtius described *Orlando Furioso* as that which in the poetry of the Italian Renaissance compared best to the great achievements of the *cinquecento* in the visual arts: Ernst Robert Curtius, *Europäische Literatur und Lateinisches Mittelalter*, 8th edn (Munich and Bern: 1973), p. 248.

129   Gamurrini, *Istoria*, p. 113; Fitzgibbon, 'Appendix', *JRSAI*, vol. 4, 4th series (1877), p. 249; Meehan, *The Rise, Increase, and Exit*, p. 251. For Verino see, for example, *Enciclopedia Italiana*, vol. 35 (Rome: 1937–45), p. 164.

130   Vincent Carey, *Surviving the Tudors* (Dublin and Portland, Oregon: 2002), pp. 46–53. The escape was masterminded by his aunt, Eleanor, sister to Gearóid Óg, a widow, who in the process married Maghnas Ó Domhnaill and made use of his continental connections: Fitzgerald, *The Geraldines*, pp. 229–36. The diplomacy of the entire exercise has been analysed in Renaissance terms by Fr Bradshaw, 'Manus "The Magnificent"', pp. 22, 30–33.

131   Fitzgerald, *The Geraldines*, pp. 236–45. See most recently Mary Ann Lyons, *Franco-Irish Relations, 1500–1600: Politics, Migration and Trade* (Suffolk, England, and Rochester, NY 2003), esp. pp. 37–44.

132   In Raphael Holinshed, *Chronicles* (London: 1577), p. 104. A report from Florentine merchants in London, who had long had dealings with the English court, also recalls the visit of the young heir to Florence: Gamurrini, *Istoria*, p. 113; Fitzgibbon, 'Appendix', *JRSAI*, vol. 4, 4th series (1877), p. 249; Meehan, *The Rise, Increase, and Exit*, pp. 249–51.

133   Compare Robert Oresko, 'The Sabaudian Court 1563–c.1750', in John Adamson (ed.), *The Princely Courts of Europe* (London: 1999), pp. 231–54, at p. 243, and note 126 above.

134   Stanihurst, author of *De Rebus in Hibernia Gestis* (Antwerp: 1584) and other works, remained in that position, in Ireland, and later in London, until about 1580: Colm Lennon, *Richard Stanihurst the Dubliner, 1547–1618* (Dublin: 1981), pp. 35–40.

135   William Bathe, *A Briefe Introduction to the Skill of Song*, edited by Kevin C. Karnes (Aldershot and Burlington, Vermont: 2005), pp. 3, 112, note 'd'.

136   P.N.N. Synott, *Kilkea Castle: A History* (Kilkea: 1973), pp. 16–17.

137   Dáithí Ó hÓgáin, 'An Stair agus an Seanchas Béil', *Léachtaí Cholm Cille*, vol. 14, 1983, pp. 173–96, at pp. 184–9, 194–5); *Myth, Legend & Romance: An*

Encyclopaedia of the Irish Folk Tradition (London: 1990), pp. 227–30, 263; Carey, *Surviving the Tudors*, p. 12.

138 Synott, *Kilkea Castle*, p. 16. Richard Stanihurst, mentioned above, later displayed an interest in alchemy.

139 Carey, *Surviving the Tudors*, pp. 11–12.

140 Gamurrini, *Istoria*, p. 113; Fitzgibbon, 'Appendix', *JRSAI*, vol. 4, 4th series (1877), p. 249; Meehan, *The Rise, Increase, and Exit*, pp. 250–1. For Irish wolfhounds as presents, see above.

141 Carey, *Surviving the Tudors*, p. 104.

142 In fact, a curious legend soon developed around this poem, 'that Lord Surrey, at a tournament at Florence, defied all the world to produce such beauty as hers, and was victorious. He is also said to have visited, at that time, Cornelius Agrippa, the celebrated alchymist, who revealed to him, in a magic mirror, the form of the fair Geraldine lying on a couch, reading one of his sonnets by the light of a taper . . .' Marquis of Kildare, *The Earls of Kildare and Their Ancestors*, p. 127; James Graves, 'Notes on an Autograph of the Fair Geraldine', *JRSAI*, vol. 4, part II, 1873, pp. 561–70; Legouis and Cazamian, *History of English Literature*, pp. 223–6.

143 Edmund Campion, *A Historie of Ireland*, facsimile with introduction by Rudolf B. Gottfried (New York: 1940), p. 5; Raphael Holinshed, *Holinshed's Irish Chronicle* (Dublin: 1979), p. 19v.

144 Holinshed, *Holinshed's Irish Chronicle* , p. 25.

145 Nicholas Williams, *Dánta Mhuiris Mhic Dháibhí Dhuibh Mhic Gearailt* (Dublin: 1979), pp. 7–8. Compare: 'The courtier must be at home in all noble sports . . . a good dancer . . . an accomplished rider. He must be master of several languages; at all events of Latin and Italian . . . he must be familiar with literature and have some knowledge of the fine arts . . . In music a certain practical skill was expected of him . . .', Jacob Burckhardt, *The Civilization of the Renaissance in Italy*, translated by S.G.C. Middlemore (Vienna and London, n.d.), pp. 200–1; Baldassare Castiglione, *The Book of the Courtier*, edited by Virginia Cox (London and Rutland, Vermont: 1994).

146 Williams, *Dánta Mhuiris Mhic Dháibhí Dhuibh*, pp. 7–8.

147 Katharine Simms, 'Literacy and the Irish Bards,' , p. 251.

148 See, for example, Pádraig Ó Riain, *Feastdays of the Saints: A History of Irish Martyrologies* (Brussels: 2006), pp. 267, 275–6, 279.

2. Derricke and Stanihurst

1 This article was first presented as a paper at the conference of the Renaissance Society of America which was held in Cambridge in 2005.

2 Richard Stanihurst, *Harmonia, sive Catena dialectica in Porphyrianas Institutiones* (London: 1570).

3 Edmund Campion, *Two Bokes of the Histories of Ireland*, edited by A.F. Vossen (Assen: 1963); L. Miller and E. Power (eds), *Holinshed's Irish Chronicle* (Dublin: 1979).

4 Richard Stanihurst, *De Rebus in Hibernia Gestis* (Antwerp: 1584); J.J. O'Meara, *Gerald of Wales: The History and Topography of Ireland* (Harmondsworth: 1982); A.B. Scott and F.X. Martin, *Giraldus Cambrensis: Expugnatio Hibernica* (Dublin: 1978).

5 The edition used for this paper is D.B. Quinn (ed.), *The Image of Irelande by John Derricke 1581* (Belfast: 1985).

6 From the dedicatory epistle addressed to Baron Burghley at the beginning of Holinshed's *Chronicles of Englande, Scotlande and Irelande* (London: 1577). For an account of the genesis of the *Chronicles*, see Miller and Power, *Holinshed's Irish Chronicle*, Introduction, pp. viii–x.

7   Holinshed's dedicatory letter to Sir Henry Sidney, in Miller and Power (eds), *Holinshed's Irish Chronicle* (Atlantic Highlands, New Jersey: 1979), p. 4.

8   Stanihurst, 'Description of Ireland' in *Holinshed's Chronicles*, p. 113.

9   Stanihurst, *De Rebus*, p. 4. The translations from *De Rebus* are my own, unless otherwise stated. They are the product of a lively seminar on Stanihurst held under the auspices of the Centre for Neo-Latin Studies, University College Cork. Any errors are, of course, mine.

10 D.B. Quinn, in his commentary on this picture ,says 'to the left . . . is a kern . . . in his right hand he is holding a long-handled halberd-like weapon, apparently intended to represent the galloglass axe'. I am indebted to Mr K. Nicholls of UCC for the observation that a kern may also be a gallowglass. However, Stanihurst makes a clear distinction between kern and gallowglass (*De Rebus*, pp. 41–2), and to my knowledge Derricke makes no mention of gallowglass. Quinn's hesitation in identifying the weapon may be justified.

11 Stanihurst, 'Description', p. 114.

12 Stanihurst, *De Rebus*, p. 42.

13 ibid., p. 32.

14 ibid., p. 41.

15 ibid., p. 40.

16 ibid., p. 41.

17 ibid., p. 42.

18 Stanihurst, 'Description', p. 114.

19 Stanihurst, *De Rebus*, p. 44.

20 Stanihurst, 'Description', p. 115.

21 Stanihurst, *De Rebus*, p. 34 – translation by Dr Colm Lennon in his excellent biography, *Richard Stanihurst the Dubliner* (Dublin: 1981), p. 147.

22 Stanihurst, *De Rebus*, p. 39.

23 For example, p. 49: 'Priests are held in great honour among them . . . In any raid they consider it an impious deed to touch even a farthing of the priest's property.'

24 Stanihurst, 'Description', p. 115. It may be that, with the mention of the 'fryer' (Smellfeast), Derricke is sniping at Stanihurst ('they honour fryers').

25 Stanihurst, *De Rebus*, p. 6.

26 ibid., p. 8–9.

27 ibid., p. 4. This could be a reference to Derricke.

28 On the other hand, he has the highest praise for grammar school education within the Pale. His own schoolmaster, Peter White of Kilkenny, is fulsomely praised in 'Description', pp. 59 and 111, and in *De Rebus*, p. 25.

29 Stanihurst, 'Description', p. 114.

30 O'Moore says '*ve mihi misero*' (literally translated, 'Woe to wretched me'), and one of the wolves says '*ve atque dolor*' ('Woe and grief'). For discussion of O'Moore's depiction, see Vincent Carey, 'John Derricke's *Image of Irelande*, Sir Henry Sidney, and the Massacre at Mullaghmast, 1578', *Irish Historical Studies*, vol. XXXI, 1999, pp. 305–27.

31 A good account of this relationship is to be found in C. Lennon, *Richard Stanihurst*, pp. 29–32.

32 Stanihurst, *De Rebus*, p. 22.

33 Cf. D.B. Quinn (ed.), *Image of Irelande*, preface, p. x.

34 Sir Walter Scott, cited from John Small (ed.), *The Image of Irelande by John Derricke* (Edinburgh: 1883).

35 For the connection to Spenser see A. Hadfield, 'Rory Oge O'Moore, The Massacre at Mullaghmast, John Derricke's *The Image of Ireland* (1581), and Spenser's Malengin', *Notes and Queries*, vol. 47, no. 4 (Dec. 2000), p. 423.

36 At least temporarily: in 1571 Sidney warned Campion that he was in danger of arrest by the authorities. See C. Lennon, *Richard Stanihurst*, pp. 30–1.

3. THE RICHARD STANIHURST–JUSTUS LIPSIUS FRIENDSHIP

1 The exchange of letters between Stanihurst and Lipsius in 1592 is published in Jeanine De Landtsheer and J. Klyskers (eds), *Iusti Lipsi Epistolae* (Brussels: 1991), vol. V, pp. 92–5, 160–2.

2 For a synopsis of his career down to the early 1590s, see Colm Lennon, *Richard Stanihurst the Dubliner* (Dublin: 1981), pp. 13–46. Stanihurst's works published before 1586 were: *Harmonia seu Catena Dialectica in Porphyrianos Institutiones* (London: 1570); 'A Plain and Perfect Description of Ireland' and 'A History of the Reign of Henry VIII', in Raphael Holinshed (ed.), *Chronicles of Englande, Scotlande and Irelande*, 3 vols (London: 1577); *The First Four Books of Vergil's Aeneis Translated into English Heroical Verse* (Leiden: 1582); *De Rebus in Hibernia Gestis Libri Quattuor* (Antwerp: 1584); and *De Vita Sancti Patricii Libri Duo* (Antwerp: 1587).

3 There is no full-length, modern biography of Justus Lipsius, but see J.L. Saunders, *Justus Lipsius: The Philosophy of Renaissance Stoicism* (New York: 1955); Mark Morford, *Stoics and Neo-Stoicism: Rubens and the Circle of Justus Lipsius* (Princeton: 1991); and Marc Laureys (ed.), *The World of Justus Lipsius: A Contribution towards His Intellectual Biography* (Rome: 1998).

4 *De Constantia* was published in 1584 at Leiden, the *Politicorum . . . Libri Sex* in 1589, also at Leiden, and his first great edition of Tacitus appeared in print in 1575.

5 As did Erasmus, Justus Lipsius composed a treatise on letter-writing and literary friendships, entitled *Epistolica Institutio*, published at Antwerp in 1601.

6 See Edward Peacock (ed.), *Index to English-Speaking Students who were Graduates at Leyden University* (London: 1883), p. 93.

7 De Landtsheer and Klyskers (eds), *Iusti Lipsi Epistolae*, vol. V, p. 161.

8 ibid., p. 93.

9 The extant correspondence of Justus Lipsius comprises about 4,300 items, less than three-quarters of which have been published: Morford, *Stoics and Neo-Stoicism*, p. 67; it has been pointed out that the disciples of Lipsius compared their following of him to the cult of Erasmus in the earlier sixteenth century: Simone Zurawski, 'Reflections on the Pitti Friendship Portrait of Rubens: In Praise of Lipsius and in Remembrance of Erasmus', *Sixteenth Century Journal*, vol. 23, 1992, pp. 727–53.

10 For an overview of this discourse, see Brian Copenhaver and Charles Schmitt (eds), *A History of Western Philosophy: 3: Renaissance Philosophy* (Oxford: 1992), pp. 239–60.

11 De Landtsheer and Klyskers (eds), *Iusti Lipsi Epistolae*, vol. V, p. 94.

12 ibid.

13 ibid.

14 Archivio General de Simancas, Seccion de Estado, legajo 593, f. 65.

15 It was entitled, 'Breve tractado intitulado toque de alquimia', 1593 (Biblioteca Nacional, Madrid, MS G-139-2.058); for Stanihurst's own comments on his scientific experiments, see A.J. Loomie, 'Richard Stanihurst in Spain: Two Unknown Letters of August 1593', *Huntington Library Quarterly*, vol. 28, 1969, p. 151.

16 De Landtsheer and Klyskers (eds), *Iusti Lipsi Epistolae*, vol. V, p. 95.

17 ibid.

18 For his use of the phrase, see Loomie, 'Richard Stanihurst in Spain', p. 154.

19 For a discussion of this aspect of Stanihurst's career, see Colm Lennon, 'Richard Stanihurst's "Spanish Catholicism": Ideology and Diplomacy in Brussels and Madrid, 1586–1601', in Enrique García Hernán et al. (eds), *Irlanda y la Monarcquía*

Hispánica: Kinsale 1601–2001. Guerra, Política, Exilio y Religion (Madrid: 2002), pp. 75–88.

20 De Landtsheer and Klyskers (eds), *Iusti Lipsi Epistolae*, vol. V, p. 161.

21 ibid., p. 162.

22 ibid., p. 94. For a brief account of the career of von Mespelbrunn, see *Catholic Encyclopedia* (New York: 1909), vol. V, p. 271.

23 De Landtsheer and Klyskers (eds), *Iusti Lipsi Epistolae*, vol. V, p. 94. Lipsius wrote about 'reasons of state' in Book 5 of *Politicorum sive Civilis Doctrinae Libri Sex*; for a modern commentary on Lipsius' political thought in this area, see Robert Bireley, *The Counter-Reformation Prince: Anti-Machiavellianism in Catholic Statecraft in Early Modern Europe* (Chapel Hill: 1989), pp. 72–100, and see also Gerhard Oestreich, *Neo-Stoicism and the Early Modern State* (Cambridge: 1982), pp. 1–75.

24 De Landtsheer and Klyskers (eds), *Iusti Lipsi Epistolae*, vol. V, p. 93.

25 ibid., p. 161.

26 ibid.

27 ibid.

28 See Justus Lipsius, *Diva Virgo Hallensis* (Antwerp: 1605), p. 1; for an account of the success of the Confraternity of the Blessed Virgin in Counter-Reformation Europe, see Louis Châtellier, *The Europe of the Devout: The Catholic Reformation and the Formation of a New Society* (Cambridge: 1987).

29 De Landtsheer and Klyskers (eds), *Iusti Lipsi Epistolae*, vol. V, p. 161.

30 ibid., pp. 374–5.

31 For a near-contemporary critique, see William Crashaw, *The Iesuites Gospell: Written by Themselves* (London: 1621), pp. 1–3, 15–33. The defence of Lipsius' writings by the Belgian Jesuit Charles Scribanius in his *Amphitheatrum Honoris* (1605) compounded the impression of his being under the influence of the Society of Jesus. For the analysis of modern writers, see J.L. Saunders, *Justus Lipsius*, pp. 44–5; Morford, *Stoics and Neo-Stoicism*, pp. 118–22.

32 See Alastair Hamilton, *The Family of Love* (Cambridge: 1981), p. 98.

33 These works were, respectively, Albert van Oosterwijck, *I.Lipsii Heylige Maghet van Halle* (1605); Peter Denaise, *Dissertatio de Idolo Hallensi* (1606); George Thomson, *Vindex Veritatis. Adversus Iustum Lipsium Libri Duo* (1606); and William Crashaw, *The Iesuites Gospell: Written by Themselves* (1621).

34 See Saunders, *Justus Lipsius*, pp. 44–5; Morford, *Stoics and Neo-Stoicism*, pp. 118–22; Jean-Pierre Massaut, 'Avec Juste Lipse, à la Recherche du Temps Perdu', in Marc Laureys (ed.), *The World of Justus Lipsius* (Rome: 1998), pp. 12–13; Rudolf de Smet, 'Les Etudes Lipsiennes 1987–1997: Etat de la Question', ibid., pp. 24–7, 41–2.

35 Morford, *Stoics and Neo-Stoicism*, pp. 96–118; Gerrit Voogt, 'Primacy of Individual Conscience or Primacy of the State? The Clash between Dirck Volckertsz. Coornhert and Justus Lipsius', *Sixteenth Century Journal*, vol. 28, 1997, pp. 1231–50.

36 For an account of the culture of the archdukes' court, see Hugh R. Trevor-Roper, *Princes and Artists: Patronage and Ideology at Four Habsburg Courts, 1517–1633* (London: 1976); see also *Catalogue of Exhibition, Albert and Isabella, 1598–1621*, Koninklijke Musea voor Kunst en Geschiedenis, Brussels, 17 September 1998–17 January 1999.

37 Crashaw, *The Iesuites Gospell*, p. 3.

38 Justus Lipsius, *De Cruce Libri Tres* (Antwerp, 1593), p. 97.

39 Justus Lipsius, *Diva Virgo Hallensis* (Antwerp, 1604), p. 1.

40 Justus Lipsius, *Diva Sichemiensis sive Aspricollis*, preface (Louvain, 1605).

41 Lipsius, *Diva Virgo Hallensis*, p. 1.

42 ibid., pp. 1, 70–2.

43 In Chapters 2–4 of Book 4, Lipsius discourses on the question of the prince's

position vis-à-vis religion: Justus Lipisus, *Six Bookes of Politickes or Civil Doctrine*, translated by William Jones (London: 1594).

44   See Voogt, 'Primacy of Individual Conscience or Primacy of the State?', pp. 1236, 1248.

45   ibid., pp. 1240–1, 1245.

46   For a synopsis of the career of Plantin and an overview of his influence as a printer, see F. De Neve and L. Voet (eds), *The Plantin-Moretus Museum, Antwerp* (Antwerp: 1995).

47   See Hamilton, *The Family of Love*.

48   Voogt, 'Primacy of Individual Conscience or Primacy of the State?', p. 1,249.

49   Zurawski, 'Reflections on the Pitti Friendship Portrait of Rubens', pp. 731–52.

50   For a synopsis of the last years of Stanihurst's career, see Lennon, *Richard Stanihurst the Dubliner*, pp. 51–6; see also Harry R. Hoppe, 'The Period of Richard Stanihurst's Chaplaincy to the Archduke Albert', *Biographical Studies, 1534–1839*, vol. 3, 1955, pp. 115–17.

51   'Breve tractado intitulado toque de alquimia', 1593: Biblioteca Nacional, Madrid, MS G-139-2.058, siglo xvi, tomo 5, f. 249v.

52   Brussels (Bibliothèque Royale) MS 3816; Richard's son, William, who also became a Jesuit, was director of the Sodality: J. Andriessen, *De Jezuiten en het Samen-horigheidsbesef Der Nederlanden, 1585–1648* (Antwerp: 1957), pp. 171, 180.

4. 'THE TIPPERARY HERO'

1   The following article is designed to serve as a brief introduction to *Ormonius* and to advertise the authors' forthcoming edition of the poem, with full Latin text, translation, literary and historical commentary, and an overview of its problems and themes. It will be the first of a new series from Brepols Publishers, Turnhout, entitled *Officina Neolatina: Selected Writings from the Neolatin World*. By and large KS has been responsible for philological work and DE for historical, though this division underplays the level of discussion and collaboration which has characterized the enterprise. Our understanding of various aspects of the poem has been materially enhanced by the contributions of members of the Neo-Latin seminar run by the Centre for Neo-Latin Studies at University College Cork, to whom abundant thanks are due.

2   Dermot O'Meara, *Ormonius*, title page (the original is in the ablative: *Hyberno et . . . alumno*). For full details of O'Meara's life, see John Barry, 'Dermot O'Meara, physician and author', *Oxford Dictionary of National Biography*, vol. 41 (Oxford 2004), pp. 801–8 [hereafter *Oxford DNB*]. The prefatory letter to Walter Butler makes it clear that the poem was at the press when Earl Thomas died. See below.

3   ibid., A2.

4   Two surviving copies (Bodleian 8 F 42 (2) and that held by Trinity College Dublin[TCD]) contain different versions of an *errata* page, and the additional poems were reprinted with corrections to the *Epicedion* and *Acrostic* in British Library 1213.g.14, Bodleian Wood 82 (3) and the TCD copy, and to the *Chronological Poem* in the TCD copy.

5   This work contains a *Relatio Geraldinorum*. See 118f. for a response to *Ormonius*, quoting O'Meara's text in several places. For a nineteenth-century translated edition see C.P. Meehan, *The Rise, Increase, and Exit of the Geraldines, earls of Desmond, and Persection after their Fall* (Dublin: 1878), pp. 109–17.

6   John Lynch, *Alithinologia, sive veridica responsio ad invectam mendaciis, falaciis calumniis et imposturis foetam in plurimos antistites, proceres et omnis ordinis Hibernos a R.P. R.F.C.* (St Malo: 1664), p. 19, citing *Omearius in ormonio* (O'Meara in his *Ormonius*) for the fact that Gilbert Becket was the founder of the Butler clan (this

information is to be found in Book 1. 320f.). Walter Harris, *The Works of Sir James Ware Concerning Ireland Revised and Improved*, vol. II (Dublin: 1739–46), p. 108. Harris also mentions an English verse translation (now lost?) by William Roberts, Ulster king at arms. A copy from the library of John Fergus and his son was sold at auction in Abbey Street on 3 February 1766 (item 502, *A Catalogue of the Libraries of John Fergus and his son, both deceased*, Dublin, 1766). And in the same year William Nicholson gives a brief account of the work in his *The English, Scotch and Irish Historical Libraries. Giving a short view and character of most of our historians, either in print or manuscript . . .* A new edition, corrected (London: 1776), p. 46.

7   There was a revival of scholarly interest in Latin writing of the seventeenth century during the nineteenth century, witness the texts of O'Sullivan Beare's *Compendium* (Dublin: 1850) and Peter Lombard's *Commentarius* (Dublin: 1868). But Stanihurst's clear intention in re-presenting Giraldus Cambrensis' account of the Norman conquest in an elegant Ciceronian Latin was to provide a humanistic support for England's territorial claim to Ireland, and this must have had something to do with the fact that the work received no edition between its publication in 1584 and its appearance on the website of the Centre for Neo-Latin Studies at UCC: http://www.ucc.ie/acad/classics/CNLS/ (click on link to Documents of Ireland).

8   James Carney (ed.), *Poems on the Butlers* (Dublin: 1945), Appendix, pp. 173–6.

9   David Edwards, 'Thomas Butler, tenth earl of Ormond and third earl of Ossory (1531–1614)', in *Oxford DNB*, vol. 9 (Oxford: 2004), pp. 220–5, provides a basic outline of his life and times. For more detailed discussion of his role as a provincial ruler see idem, *The Ormond Lordship in County Kilkenny, 1515–1642: The Rise and Fall of Butler Feudal Power* (Dublin: 2003). Other treatments of his career are Cyril Falls, 'Black Tom of Ormonde', *Irish Sword*, vol. 5, 1961–2, pp. 10–22 and Ciaran Brady, 'Thomas Butler, earl of Ormond (1531–1614), and Reform in Tudor Ireland', in C. Brady (ed.), *Worsted in the Game: Losers in Irish History* (Dublin: 1989), pp. 49–59.

10   *Letters & Papers, Foreign and Domestic, Henry VIII*, vol. xix/1, no. 473.

11   For the importance of the liberty see David Edwards and Adrian Empey, 'Tipperary Liberty Ordinances of the Black Earl of Ormond', in D. Edwards (ed.), *Regions and Rulers in Ireland, 1100–1650: Essays for Kenneth Nicholls* (Dublin: 2004), pp. 122–31.

12   C.A. Empey and Katharine Simms, 'The Ordinances of the White Earl and the Problem of Coign in the Middle Ages', *Proceedings of the Royal Irish Academy*, 75 C, 1975; Edwards, *The Ormond Lordship*, pp. 17–19, 22–3, 30, 59–63, 65–8.

13   Information against Ormond, n.d., 1584 (PRO, SP 63/107/107).

14   *Acts of the Privy Council, 1547–1550*, edited by J.R. Dasent (London: 1890), p. 220.

15   Cathuldus Giblin (ed.), 'Catalogue of Irish Material in the Nunziatura di Fiandra', *Collectanea Hibernica*, vol. 1, 1958, p. 46.

16   Diarmaid MacCulloch (ed.), 'The Vita Mariae Angliae Reginae of Robert Wingfield of Brantham', *Camden Miscellany*, vol. 28, 1984, p. 284.

17   His performance against Tyrone will be analysed in David Edwards's forthcoming paper, 'The General in his Labyrinth: The Black Earl of Ormond and the Nine Years War'.

18   Thomas Churchyard, *A Scourge for Rebels . . . as farre as the painfull and dutiful service of the Earle of Ormond . . . is known* (London: 1584). Churchyard was a hack that wrote frequently about the Irish wars, usually from the perspective of Ormond's enemies among the English officers. *A Scourge for Rebels* is notable mainly for the eyewitness accounts it contains of Desmond's capture and killing by Ormond's Irish troops.

19   J.T. Gilbert (ed.), *Facsimiles of the National Manuscripts of Ireland*, 4 vols (Dublin: 1874–8), vol. 4, part 1, plate 19.

20 *Calendar of State Papers, Ireland, 1586–8*, pp. 52–3.

21 *Calendar of State Papers, Ireland, 1601–3*, 73, pp. 84–6.

22 For an introduction to this English victory literature see Hiram Morgan, 'The victor's Version', 'Birchensha's Discourse', and 'England's Joy', in H. Morgan (ed.), *The Battle of Kinsale* (Bray: 2004), pp. 379–90, 391–407, 408–14.

23 Edwards, *The Ormond Lordship*, pp. 106–8, 266–74.

24 Anthony à Wood, *Athenae Oxoniensis: An exact history of all the writers and bishops who have had their education in the University of Oxford*, 4 vols. (London: 1813–20), vol. II, p. 275 for Dermitius meara or de Meara.

25 TCD, MS. 842, ff 137–61.

26 The main events of these northern campaigns are outlined in J. Michael Hill, *Fire and Sword: Sorley Boy MacDonnell and the Rise of Clan Ian Mor, 1538–90* (London: 1993), pp. 44–50, 188–209.

27 Jane Ohlmeyer, '"Civilizinge of those rude partes": The Colonization of Ireland and Scotland, 1580s–1640s', in Nicholas Canny (ed.), *Origins of Empire: The Oxford History of the British Empire*, vol. I (Oxford: 1998).

28 Michael Lynch, 'James VI and "the Highland problem"', in Julian Goodare and Michael Lynch (eds), *The Reign of James VI* (East Linton: 2000), pp. 206–27.

29 Though written first, this actually appears as the second dedicatory letter, following a dedication to Walter Butler, Earl Thomas's successor.

30 Representative Church Body Library, Rathfarnham, Dublin: Graves Papers, MS 11.2.

31 Excerpts from this can be found in Peter Godman, *Poetry of the Carolingian Renaissance* (London: 1985), pp. 196–206.

32 See further J. Ijsewijn and D. Sacré, *Companion to Neo-Latin Studies* Part II (*Supplementa Humanistica Lovaniensia* XIV) (Leuven: 1998), pp. 27–8.

33 Ijsewijn and Sacré, II, pp. 39–40. This genre was a humanist continuation of the medieval *Speculum historiale* (Mirror of history).

34 Of the four epics on Gustavus Adolphus treated by Hans Helander in *Neo-Latin Literature in Sweden, 1620–1720: Stylistics, Vocabulary and Characteristic Ideas*, Uppsala: 2004), p. 379, the *Gustavis* of Venceslaus Clemens (1632) has nine books, that of Narssius three plus one (1632, 1634), while the works of Jollyvet (1636) and Garissole (1649) each have twelve.

35 Hans Helander , '*SO* debate: Neo-Latin Studies: Significance and Prospects', *Symbolae Osloenses*, vol. 76, 2001, p. 24.

36 See, for example, Carney, *Poems*; Michelle Ó Riordan, *The Gaelic Mind and the Collapse of the Gaelic World* (Cork: 1990), pp. 81–9, 141–51.

37 For example, the punitive depredation of Rathlin is dwelt on in *Ormonius*, Book 3, pp. 621–759, and is otherwise reported only in *Taghaim Tomás* lines 1779–80: *Tug óRachluinn a ccrích Alban/ le ró spairne spréchreacha* (He brought from Rathlin in the land of Scotland/ by fierce battles great preys): Carney, *Poems*, p. 75 (reference and translation are owed to Gearóidín Butléir).

38 Nikolaus Thurn, in a paper given to the conference The Role of Latin in Early Modern Europe: Texts and Contexts III, in Lauterbad, 26 May 2005, entitled 'Vernacular Songs in Neo-Latin Poetry: Cristoforo Landino, Juan de Vilches, Christian Schesaeus' suggested that imitation of vernacular themes and genres presages the rise of nationalism.

39 Both Vergerio's *De ingenuis moribus et liberalibus adulescentiae studiis* and Guarino's *De ordine docendi et studendi* can be found in the volume *Humanist Educational Treatises* edited by Craig Kallendorf in the I Tatti series (Cambridge, Massachusetts: 2002).

40 In the third line he writes *Urgentur, ignoti longa* instead of *Urgentur, ignotique longa.*

41 For allegorical understanding of the gods, see, for example, the Prooemium to Alberti's *Momus*, paragraph 6 (now available in the I Tatti edition (Cambridge, Massachusetts: 2003), edited by Sarah Knight and Virginia Brown). For a recent study of Vergil in the Renaissance, see Craig Kallendorf's *Vergil and the Myth of Venice: Books and Readers in the Italian Renaissance* (Oxford: 1999).

42 For these events see especially Edwards, *The Ormond Lordship*, Chapter 4.

43 See Godman, *Poetry of the Carolingian Renaissance*, pp. 196–207 for excerpts.

44 Cf. the number of longbows found in store on the *Mary Rose*, which sank in the early 1540s.

45 In fact the motif goes back very early. Often the *aisling* appears as an old hag to a group which includes the future king of Ireland. His companions turn away, but the chosen one kisses her and she turns into the beauteous Éire ('Ireland'). In later poetry, the woman in the dream is young and lovely. When asked by the dreaming poet who she is, she says she is Éire, once a queen, but now a slave. For a treatment of the motif in the seventeenth and eighteenth centuries, see Breandán Ó Buachalla, *Aisling Ghéar: Na Síobhartaigh agus an tAos Léinn 1603–1788* (Dublin: 1996), and especially Chapter 11.

46 For example, Athene appears to Nausikaa in *Odyssey* 6.20f. as the daughter of Dymas, famed for his ships.

47 Barry 'Dermot O'Meara', p. 808 (n. 1 above).

5. 'MAKING IRELAND SPANISH'

1 This essay corrects and extends an earlier version which appeared under the title 'Un pueblo unido . . . the politics of Philip O'Sullivan Beare', in Enrique García Hernán, Miguel Ángel de Bunes, Óscar Recio Morales and Bernardo J. García García (eds), *Irlanda y la Monarquía Hispánica, Kinsale 1601–2001. Guerra, Política, Exilio y Religión* (Madrid: 2002), pp. 265–82. The author wishes to thank Jason Harris and John Barry, UCC, Professor Clare Carroll, Queen's College, City University of New York, Dr Glyn Redworth, University of Manchester, K.W. Nicholls, Department of History, UCC and Ciarán O'Scea of the European University Institute. A special thanks goes to Cronán Ó Doibhlin, formerly the librarian of the Cardinal Tomás Ó Fiaich Library and Archive, Armagh, and now Special Collections Librarian at UCC. The author gratefully acknowledges the financial assistance of the Arts Faculty Research Fund at UCC.

2 Philip O'Sullivan Beare, *Historiae Catholicae Compendium*, Tom. III, Lib.VII, cap.I; Fragmenta. Except when otherwise stated, the translations of the *Compendium* given in this article are taken from the MS translation of the *Compendium* in the National Library of Ireland (NLI), sometimes with minor emendations. In certain instances, where noted, I have used translations by John Barry of the Classics Department in UCC, or by Byrne in his *Ireland under Elizabeth, chapters towards a history of Ireland in the reign of Elizabeth being a portion of the history of Catholic Ireland by Philip O'Sullivan Beare* (Dublin: 1903).

3 Clare Carroll, 'Irish and Spanish Cultural Relations in the Work of O'Sullivan Beare', in Hiram Morgan (ed.), *Political Ideology in Ireland, 1541–1641* (Dublin: 1999), pp. 229–53, and 'Custom and Law in the Philosophy of Suárez and in the Histories of O'Sullivan Beare, Céintinn and Ó Cléirigh', in Thomas O'Connor (ed.), *The Irish in Europe, 1580–1815* (Dublin: 2001), pp. 65–78.

4 Matthew Kelly (ed.), *Historiae Catholicae Iberniae Compendium* (Dublin: 1850); J.C. O'Callaghan's unpublished translation of O'Sullivan's Catholic history, NLI MS 988, mid–late nineteenth century; M.J. Byrne (translator and editor), *Ireland under Elizabeth, chapters towards a history of Ireland in the reign of Elizabeth being a portion of the history of Catholic Ireland by Philip O'Sullivan Beare* (Dublin: 1903);

Thomas J. O'Donnell (ed.), *Selections from the Zoilomastix of Philip O'Sullivan* (Dublin: 1960).

5   Micheline Kerney Walsh, 'O'Sullivan Beare in Spain: Some Unpublished Documents', *Archivium Hibernicum*, vol. XLV, 1990, pp. 46–63. More generally see her *Spanish Knights of Irish Origin – Documents from the Continental Archives*, 4 vols (Dublin: 1960–78). Ciarán O'Scea 'The Devotional World of the Irish Catholic Exile in Early-Modern Galicia, 1598–1666', in O'Connor (ed.), *Irish in Europe*, pp. 27–48 and 'The Significance and Legacy of Spanish Intervention in West Munster during the Battle of Kinsale', in T. O'Conner and M. Lyons (eds), *Irish Migrants and Migration after Kinsale* (Dublin: 2003), Chapter 2.

6   Appended to the manuscript of the *Zoilomastix* (Uppsala: Universitet Bibliotek, MS H.248) is a surviving fragment of Philip O'Sullivan's lost work on astronomy.

7   This short sketch of Philip O'Sullivan's life, based on the introduction to T.J. O'Donnell, *Selections*, viii–xv, is supplemented by information from Ciarán O'Scea. For discussion of the *Tenebriomastix*, the location of which was unknown to O'Donnell, see further Chapter 6 that volume.

8   *Compendium*, Tom. III, Lib. VIII, Cap.VII (O'Callaghan's translation, emended, p. 340). *Indifferens obsequium*, or 'indifferent assent', refers to something which is morally preferable but a matter of choice rather than obligation.

9   *Compendium*, Tom III, Lib.VIII, Cap.VII (O'Callaghan's translation, p. 341).

10 For an examination of the Anglo-Norman conquest of Ireland, see Marie-Thérèse Flanagan, *Irish Society, Anglo-Norman Settlers, Angevin Kingship: Interactions in Ireland in the Late Twelfth Century* (Oxford: 1989).

11 *Compendium*, Tom. II, Lib. I, Cap. III–VII.

12 *Compendium*, Tom. II, Lib. I, Cap.VII (Barry translation).

13 *Compendium*, Tom. II, Lib. I, Cap.VII.

14 *Compendium*, Tom. II, Lib. I, Cap. VIII.

15 *Compendium*, Tom. II, Lib. I, Cap.VIII (Barry translation).

16 ibid.

17 *Compendium*, Tom. II, Lib. II, Cap. III (Barry translation).

18 O'Sullivan failed to mention that one of Davies' arguments was that the Irish and English now enjoyed – at least theoretically – equal legal rights as a result of the full establishment of the common law in Ireland under James I.

19 Carroll, 'Irish and Spanish Cultural Relations', p. 235.

20 *Compendium*, Tom. II, Lib. I, Cap.VIII.

21 Quentin Skinner, *The Foundations of Modern Political Thought*, 2 vols (Cambridge: 1978), vol. 2, Chapters VIII and IX.

22 *Compendium*, Tom. I, Lib. III, Cap. IV.

23 Carroll, 'Irish and Spanish Cultural Relations', pp. 232–3.

24 *Compendium*, Tom. II, Lib. II, Cap. I (Barry translation).

25 ibid.

26 ibid.

27 For a discussion of Giraldus Cambrensis, see Hiram Morgan, 'Giraldus Cambrensis and the Tudor Conquest of Ireland', in Morgan (ed.), *Political Ideology*, pp. 22–44.

28 The best history of this subject is Brendan Bradshaw, *The Dissolution of the Religious Orders in Ireland* (Cambridge: 1974).

29 *Compendium*, Tom. II, Lib. III Cap. I.

30 *Compendium*, Tom. II, Lib. II, Cap. VI.

31 *Compendium*, Tom. II, Lib. II, Cap. IV.

32 *Compendium*, Tom. II, Lib. III, Cap. III (Barry translation).

33 *Compendium*, Tom. II, Lib. II, Cap. IV; Lib. IV, Cap X; Cap. XIX; Tom. IV, Lib I, Cap. XVIII.

34   *Compendium*, Tom. II, Lib. IV, Cap. III.

35   *Compendium*, Tom. II, Lib IV, Cap. VI and XIII (Byrne translation, *Ireland under Elizabeth*, p. 19).

36   *Compendium*, Tom. III, Lib. III, Cap X (Byrne translation, *Ireland under Elizabeth*, pp. 97–8 – slightly emended).

37   For the religious situation in the reign of James I, see Colm Lennon, *The Lords of Dublin in the Age of the Reformation* (Dublin: 1989), esp. Chapter 6; John McCavitt, *Sir Arthur Chichester: Lord Deputy of Ireland, 1605–16* (Belfast: 1998), *passim*.

38   *Compendium*, Tom. II, Lib. II, Cap V.

39   *Compendium*, Tom. II, Lib. II, Cap V (Barry translation).

40   *Compendium*, Tom. II, Lib. II, Cap VI.

41   *Compendium*, Epistola Dedicatoria.

42   On the Milesians see John Carey, 'Did the Irish Come from Spain?: The Legend of the Milesians', *History Ireland*, Spanish issue, vol. IX, no. 3, Autumn 2001.

43   *Compendium*, Tom. I, Lib. II, Cap. I.

44   *Compendium*, Tom. II, Lib. I, Cap. I.

45   *Compendium*, Tom. I, Lib. IV, Cap. V.

46   *Compendium*, Tom. I, Lib. II. Shane Leslie (ed.), *St Patrick's Purgatory: A Record from History and Literature* (London: 1932); and Michael Haren and Yolande de Pontfarcy (eds), *The Medieval Pilgrimage to St Patrick's Purgatory, Lough Derg and the European Tradition* (Enniskillen: 1988).

47   Micheline Kerney Walsh, 'The Military Order of St Patrick, 1593', *Seanchas Ard Mhacha*, vol. IX, 1979, pp. 274–85.

48   Anita Howard, 'Reforming the Savage: The Ireland and England of Pedro Calderon de la Barca', in Ruth Connolly and Anne Coughlan (eds), *New Voices in Irish Criticism*, V (Dublin: 2005), pp. 241–54. For a modern edition of the play see J.M. Ruano de la Haza (ed.), *El Purgatorio de San Patricio* (Liverpool: 1988).

49   *Compendium*, Tom. I, Lib. IV, Cap. X.

50   *Compendium*, Tom. II, Lib. III, Cap. VIII.

51   For account of relations between Spain and Ireland see J.J. Silke, *Ireland and Europe, 1559–1607* (Dundalk: 1966) and Enrique García Hernán, *Irlanda y el rey prudente* (Madrid: 2000).

52   The third tome of the *Compendium* is entitled 'De Bello Quindecim Annorum'. For a history of a beginning of the conflict see Hiram Morgan, *Tyrone's Rebellion: The Outbreak of the Nine Years War in Tudor Ireland* (Woodbridge: 1993).

53   Kerney Walsh, 'The military Order of St Patrick'.

54   See Morgan, *Tyrone's Rebellion*, Chapter 7.

55   John S. Nolan, *Sir John Norreys and the Elizabethan Military World* (Exeter: 1997).

56   The modern account of Del Águila's expedition is J.J. Silke, *Kinsale: The Spanish Intervention in Ireland at the End of the Elizabethan War* (Liverpool: 1970). For a review of the Kinsale campaign see Hiram Morgan's 400th anniversary commemorative volume, *The Battle of Kinsale* (Bray: 2004).

57   On grand strategy post-Reformation, see Hiram Morgan, 'British Policies before the British State', in Brendan Bradshaw and John Morrill, *The British Problem, 1534–1707* (London: 1996).

58   *Compendium*, Tom. II, Lib. III, Cap. IX. For grand strategy in the early sixteenth century see James Hogan, *Ireland in the European System* (London: 1920): for the French angle see David Potter, 'French Intrigue in Ireland during the Reign of Henri II, 1547–1559, *International History Review*, vol. V, no. 2, May, 1993, pp. 159–316.

59   *Compendium*, Tom. I, Lib. I, Cap. VII (O'Callaghan translation, p. 20).

60   *Compendium*, Tom. I, Lib. I, Cap. VI (O'Callaghan translation, p. 22).

61 *Compendium*, Tom. III, Lib. II, Cap VIII.

62 Silke, *Kinsale*, pp. 77–8.

63 I owe this reference to my colleague, Dr Diarmuid Scully, in the Department of History UCC.

64 *Compendium*, Tom. II, Lib. III, Cap. IV.

65 *Compendium*, Tom. II, Lib. III, Cap. V.

66 *Compendium*, Tom. II, Lib. IV, Cap. XV (Byrne translation, *Ireland under Elizabeth*, p. 26).

67 *Compendium*, Tom. II, Lib. IV, Cap. XVI.

68 *Compendium*, Tom. III, Lib. VI, Cap. VII.

69 *Compendium*, Tom. III, Lib. VI, Cap. VIII.

70 *Compendium*, Tom. III, Lib. VI, Cap. IX.

71 *Compendium*, Tom. III, Lib. VI, Cap. X (Byrne translation, *Ireland under Elizabeth*, p. 148 – slightly emended).

72 *Compendium*, Tom III, Lib VII.

73 This claim is incidentally countered in an earlier source emanating from Donal Cam himself: Kerney Walsh, 'O Sullivan Beare in Spain', p. 52.

74 *Compendium*, Tom. I, Lib. III, Cap II.

75 Denis J. Doherty, 'Domnal O'Sullivan Beare and His Family in Spain', *Studies*, vol. XIX, March, 1930, pp. 211–26.

76 *Compendium*, Fragmenta.

77 I have drawn this concept from Ferdnand Braudel, *The Mediterranean and the Mediterranean World in the Age of Philip II*, 2 vols (London: 1972), vol. 2, pp. 854–865. Bear Island, later used by the British as a naval base, might have made more sense than Dursey for a garrison.

78 Señor de Piñalba, Lord of White Rock: a place we can identify as Cloghfune in Kilnamanagh parish on the way to Dursey.

79 Bibliothèque Nationale de France Affaires Étrangères, Espagne, vol 264, no.142, ff. 228–33 entitled 'Proposicion de la conquista de Irlanda'. I have used a translation among the papers of Micheline Kerney Walsh in the Ó Fiaich Library, Armagh.

80 ibid.

81 *Compendium*, Tom. I, Lib. I, Cap V; Cap. VII; Lib. III, Cap. VII. Most obviously, the figures for the ploughlands in each province in Edmund Spenser, *A View of the Present State of Ireland* (edited by Andrew Hadfield and William Maley) (Oxford: 1997), pp. 121–32, are replicated in chapter 5 of Tome I, Book I. There is no evidence elsewhere for Cecil having written such a large manuscript about Ireland but there is every likelihood that he would have acquired a copy of Spenser's treatise which was not printed until 1633.

82 Anti-Stanihurst remarks in *Compendium*, Tom. I, Lib. IV, Cap. I; Tom. III, Lib. II, Cap. VIII; Tom. IV, Lib. III, Cap.V.

83 David Rothe, *Analecta Sacra*, 3 parts (Paris and Cologne: 1616–19).

84 *Compendium*, Tom. IV, Lib. I, Cap. V. For a modern account see McCavitt, *Chichester*, pp. 140–8.

85 For internal divisions during the war see Hiram Morgan, 'Hugh O'Neill and the Nine Years War in Tudor Ireland', *Historical Journal*, vol. 36, 1993, pp. 21–37;'Faith and Fatherland in Sixteenth-Century Ireland', *History Ireland*, vol. 3 no. 2, Summer 1995, pp. 13–20; and 'Faith and Fatherland or Queen and Country? An Unpublished Exchange between O'Neill and the State at the Height of the Nine Years War', *Dúiche Néill: Journal of the O'Neill Country Historical Society*, vol. IX, 1994, pp. 6–65.

86 *Compendium*, Tom. II, Lib. II, Cap. VI (Barry Translation); For the perceived effects of sin see Marc Caball, 'Providence and Exile in Early Seventeenth-Century Ireland', *Irish Historical Studies*, vol. 29, 1994, pp. 174–88.

87 *Compendium*, Tom. III, Lib. I.

88 *Compendium*, Tom. III, Lib. I, Cap. III (Byrne translation, *Ireland under Elizabeth*, p. 54).

89 Richard Bagwell, *Ireland under the Tudors*, 3 vols (London: 1885–90), vol. 3, pp. 474–6; Morgan, 'Faith and fatherland or Queen and Country?'

90 *Compendium*, Tom. III, Lib. I, Cap. IV (Byrne's translation, *Ireland under Elizabeth*, p. 56).

91 For the 1601 currency changes in Ireland see Joseph McLoughlin, 'What Base Coin Wrought: The Effects of Elizabethan Debasement in Ireland', in Morgan (ed.), *The Battle of Kinsale*, Chapter 10.

92 *Compendium*, Tom. III, Lib. I, Cap. V (Byrne translation, *Ireland under Elizabeth*, pp. 57–8).

93 *Compendium*, Tom. III, Lib. I, Cap. VI (Byrne translation, *Ireland under Elizabeth*, p. 58 – slightly emended).

94 *Compendium*, Tom. IV, Lib. II.

95 *Compendium*, Tom. IV, Lib. III, Cap. V (O'Callaghan translation, p. 440).

96 *Compendium*, Tom. III, Lib. II, Cap. VIII.

97 Now Maynooth MS Salamanca 52 6 17 ff. 14r–24v.

98 TCD MS 580, ff. 95–8; 'A Brief Relation of Ireland and the diversity of the Irish in the same'.

99 ibid., f. 95v.

100 ibid., f. 96r.

101 Micheline Kerney Walsh, *Destruction by Peace: Hugh O'Neill after Kinsale* (Armagh: 1986) pp. 107–13.

102 *Compendium*, Tom. IV, Lib. III, Cap. IV.

103 Madrid, Palacio Real, Gondomar MS II/2165, doc 57.

104 Plainly the English were able to acquire information from within the Irish circle of exiles in Madrid, as indicated by TCD MS 580. In this way a translation of a document of the Breve Relación which the Irish in Spain were presenting to the state there came into the hands of Archbishop James Ussher among whose manuscripts it is now found.

105 UK, National Archives, SP94/23, ff. 53–5.

106 For the situation towards the end of the Spanish match negotiations see Glyn Redworth, 'Beyond Faith and Fatherland: "The Appeal of the Catholics of Ireland", *c.*1623', *Archivium Hibernicum*, vol. LII, 1998, pp. 3–23. See also Glyn Redworth's *The Prince and the Infanta: The Cultural Politics of the Spanish Match* (Yale: 2004) and 'Perfidious Hispania: Ireland and the Spanish Match, 1603–23', in Morgan (ed.), *The Battle of Kinsale*, Chapter 15.

107 Bibliothèque Nationale de France, Affaires Étrangères, Espagne, vol. 264, no.142, ff. 232v–233r.

108 *Calendar of State Papers, Ireland, 1625–32*, pp. 67–8, 100–1, 308–12.

109 Aidan Clarke, 'Bath, Sir John' (1569/70–1630), *Oxford Dictionary of National Biography* (Oxford: 2004).

6. THE SCOTIC DEBATE

1 Philip O'Sullivan Beare, *Historiae Catholicae Iberniae, Compendium* (Lisbon: 1621). An edition of this work was published in Dublin (1850) by Matthew Kelly under the same title. The sole manuscript witness to the *Tenebriomastix* is Poitiers: Bibliothèque de la Ville, MS 259 (97). For biographical information on O'Sullivan Beare see Hiram Morgan's article in this volume.

2 Giraldus Cambrensis, *Topographia Hiberniae* and *Expugnatio Hibernica* (c. 1189). Editions: William Camden (ed.), *Anglica, Hibernica, Normannica, Gambrica, a*

veteribvs scripta ex quibus Asser Meneuensis, anonymus de vita Gulielmi Conquestoris, Thomas Walsingham, Thomas de la More, Gulielmus Gemiticensis, Giraldus Cambrensis: plerique nunc primùm in lucem editi, ex bibliotheca Gvilielmi Camdeni (Frankfurt: 1602); J.S. Brewer (ed.), *Giraldi Cambrensis Opera* (London: 1861–91); A.B. Scott and F.X. Martin (editors and translators), *Expugnatio Hibernica* (Dublin: 1978).

3   Richard Stanihurst, *De Rebus in Hibernia Gestis* (Antwerp: 1584).

4   Paulo Giovio, *Descriptio Britanniae, Scotiae, Hyberniae et Orchadum* (Venice: 1548), p. 34: 'Verum inculta gens, ignara luxus'(Truly a race without culture, ignorant of luxury).

5   Peter Lombard, *De Regno Hiberniae Sanctorum Insula Commentarius* [written 1600], first published posthumously (Louvain: 1632); David Rothe, *Analecta Sacra* (Cologne: 1617); Rothe (under the pseudonym D.R.E.O.V.H.), *Brigida Thaumaturga* (Paris: 1620); Rothe, *Hibernia Resurgens* (Rouen: 1621); Rothe, *Tractatulus praeambularis de nominibus Hiberniae*, in Thomas Messingham's *Florilegium Insulae Sanctorum* (Paris: 1624); Philip O'Sullivan Beare, *Zoilomastix* (Uppsala: MS 248), written c. 1626; Stephen White, *Apologia pro Hibernia adversus Cambri calumnias* [written c. 1615], edited under the same title by Matthew Kelly (Dublin: 1849); idem, *Apologia pro innocentibus Ibernis* (Poitiers: Bibliothèque de la Ville, MS 276 (260)), written c. 1638.

6   Cf. O'Sullivan, *Compendium,* vol. I fol. 55; idem, *Zoilomastix*, Books 3 and 5. See also Clare Carroll, 'Irish and Spanish Cultural and Political Relations in the Work of O'Sullivan Beare', in H. Morgan (ed.), *Political Ideology in Ireland, 1541–1641* (Dublin: 1999), pp. 229–53, at p. 234.

7   Thomas Innes, *A Critical Essay on the Ancient Inhabitants of the Northern Parts of Britain or Scotland* (London: 1729). The text used here is the reprint, published Edinburgh, 1885, p. 110.

8   Monsieur de C. [identified as John O'Brien, bishop of Cloyne and Ross], 'Mémoire de Monsieur de C. à Messieurs les Auteurs du Journal des Sçavans, au sujet des Poëmes de M. MacPherson', *Journal des Sçavans*, May–Dec. 1764. For the identification of 'Monsieur de C.', see Diarmuid Ó Catháin, 'An Irish Scholar Abroad: Bishop John O'Brien of Cloyne and the Macpherson Controversy', in *Cork History and Society: Interdisciplinary Essays on the History of an Irish County* (Dublin: 1993), pp. 512–13.

9   O'Sullivan's own early Christian pedigree would appear to be impeccable. One of his ancestors rejoiced in having his foot pierced by St Patrick – an incident recounted in Jacobus de Voragine's *Golden Legend*. See Philip O'Sullivan Beare, *Tenebriomastix*, p. 94; also idem, *Patriciana Decas* (Lisbon: 1629), p. 46. For O'Sullivan's known ancestry, see Thomas O'Donnell (ed.), *Selections from the Zoilomastix* (Dublin: 1960), p. iv.

10 See Grosjean, S.J., 'Un Soldat Irlandais au service des "Acta Sanctorum"' in *Analecta Bollandiana*, vol. 81, fasc. III–IV (Brussels: 1963), pp. 418–30.

11 *Tenebriomastix*, pp. 1, 6.

12 The Scottish Catholic, David Chambers or *Camerarius*, who published *Davidis Camerarii Scoti: De Scotorum Fortitudine, Pietate, et Doctrina* (Lyon: 1631).

13 John Pinkerton, *An Enquiry into the History of Scotland*, 2 vols (Edinburgh: 1814), vol. ii. pp. 223–46: 'That the name of Scotia or Scotland originally belonged to Ireland and continued to belong to that country, alone, till a late period, begins now to be acknowledged even by the most prejudiced Scottish writers. This fact clearly appears from the following numerous authorities, while that the names Scoti, Scotia were ever applied to the present Scots and Scotland, before the reign of Malcolm II or the beginning of the eleventh century, not one satisfactory authority can be produced.' See also Wilhelm Wattenbach, 'Die Kongregation der Schottenklöster in Deutschland', in *Zeitschrift für christliche Archäologie und Kunst*

(1856), published as 'The Irish Monasteries in Germany', edited and translated by William Reeves in *Ulster Journal of Archaeology* 1859, pp. 227–47 and 295–313: 'We must not, indeed, understand Scotchmen by the *Scoti*, but the inhabitants of Ireland.' In an editorial note, Reeves comments: 'The voice of all antiquity pronounces Ireland to have been *Scotia*' (p. 227).

14 See *The Catholic Encyclopedia s.v.* Duns Scotus.

15 The term *Scotti* is first mentioned (AD 380–90) in Ammianus Marcellinus' *History* (27, 5). See also J.F. Kenney, *The Sources for the Early History of Ireland: Ecclesiastical. An Introduction and Guide* (New York: 1929) (reprint, Dublin: 1997), p. 136, n. 85, for the possible candidature of 'Hegesippus', for this title. Isidore of Seville is first to mention *Scotia*, in his *Etymologiae* or *Origines*, completed *c.* 600 (14, 6: *de insulis*).

16 William F. Skene, *Celtic Scotland: A History of Ancient Alban*, 3 vols (Edinburgh: 1886), vol. 1, p. 1.

17 ibid., p. 40. The *Caledonii* are first mentioned by Lucan in AD 65 (*Pharsalia*, vi. 67); *Caledonia*, by Pliny the Younger, *c.* AD 113 (*Epistulae*, iv. 30).

18 Skene, *Celtic Scotland*, vol. 1, p. 1.

19 Pinkerton, *An Enquiry*, p. 231. See also Skene, *Celtic Scotland*, vol. i, p. 40.

20 The name *Pictavia* is also found, being mentioned by Notker Balbulus (*c.* 895) in his *Martyrologium* (*v. Idus Junias*).

21 The Emperor Sigismund in 1422 speaks of the 'Monasterii Scotorum sive Hibernorum de Maiori Scotia in Ratisbona'. See O'Brien, 'Mémoire', p. 278, footnote.

22 Skene, *Celtic Scotland*, vol. 1, p. 5.

23 In the Anglo-Saxon Chronicle (for the year 937) mention is made of 'Yraland'. See Benjamin Thorpe (editor and translator), *'The Anglo-Saxon Chronicle' according to several original Authorities*, 2 vols (London: 1861) (Rolls Series), p. 5. See also *Tenebriomastix*, p. 127.

24 See Peter Lombard, *Commentarius de Regno Hiberniae, Insula Sanctorum* (Louvain: 1632), pp. 134–5.

25 Paul Grosjean, 'Un Soldat Irlandais', p. 444, refers to one such work by James Tyrie, S.J. (alias George Thomson), *De Antiquitate Religionis apud Scotos* (Rome and Douai: 1594) as '*un opuscule semblable à nos modernes brochures de propagande, pour soliciter des aumônes en faveur du Seminaire écossais de Pont-à-Mousson*'. Tyrie's work was later published in Antonio Possevinus' *Bibliotheca Selecta* (Cologne: 1607) and as 'The Antiquity of the Christian Religion among the Ancient Scots' in *Miscellany of the Scottish History Society*, vol. 2 (Edinburgh: 1904), pp. 130–2.

26 Rothe mentions this in two passages: (1) *Hib. Res.* [Epistola Dedicatoria]: '*Ut expositis maiorum facinoribus, Seminaristae nostri ad pietatem amplectendam et doctrinam imbibendam ardentius inflammarentur*' (So that, when the deeds of their ancestors have been related, our seminarians might be the more ardently moved to embrace piety and imbibe instruction); and (2) ibid., p. 24: '*Placuit auditoribus, dissertationem in lucem dari, ut nostris tyronibus stimulum adderet ad sectanda sanctorum vestigia*' (Those who heard the treatise [on St Brigit] resolved to have it published, in order that it might provide an incentive to our young men to follow closely in the footsteps of the saints).

27 John Leslie was busy in this regard in 1578, and the Benedictine, Ninian Winzet, became abbot of the Irish monastery of St James at Ratisbon in the same year; later, John Whyt obtained possession of the Irish monastery at Würzburg in 1595. See Wattenbach, 'Schottenklöster in Deutschland', p. 312; also O'Brien, 'Mémoire', p. 546.

28 This was published as *Brigida Thaumaturga* under the acromym D.R.E.O.V.H. at Paris in 1620. The initials stand for 'David Rothe Episcopus Ossoriensis Veridicus Hibernus'.

29 Thomas Dempster, *Scotorum scriptorum nomenclatura . . . ex Historia lib. XIX. eiusdem excerpta* (Bologna: 1619). This work was itself a response to Henry Fitzsimon's authoritive *Catalogus praecipuorum sanctorum Hiberniae* (Rome: 1611).

30 Thomas Dempster, *Scotia Illustrior* (Lyon: 1620); David Rothe (under the pseudonym Donatus Roirk), *Hibernia Resurgens* (Rouen: 1621); David Rothe (under the pseudonym G.F. Veridicus Hibernus), *Hiberniae, sive antiquioris Scotiae Vindiciae adversus immodestam Parechbasim Thomae Dempsteri* (Antwerp: 1621).

31 See the Roman *Index Librorum Prohibitorum* (1623).

32 David Chambers, *Davidis Camerarii Scoti: De Scotorum Fortitudine, Pietate, et Doctrina* (Lyon: 1631).

33 Thomas Dempster, *Historia Catholica Gentis Scotorum* (Bologna: 1627).

34 Chambers, *De Scotorum*, pp. 222–34 and 235–41 respectively.

35 ibid., p. 212.

36 ibid., p. 214–15.

37 ibid., p. 241–2.

38 ibid., p. 243–4.

39 For the title of his work O'Sullivan may have been indebted to David Rothe, who used the term *tenebrio* several times to describe Dempster. See Rothe, *Hibernia Resurgens*, p. 173: '*Fuge tenebrio*: (Begone, you trickster!).

40 Henry Fitzsimon, *Catalogus Praecipuorum Sanctorum Hiberniae* (Rome: 1611), edited by Paul Grosjean (Dublin: 1940). For a discussion of the various recensions of this work, see Pádraig Ó Riain, 'The Catalogus Praecipuorum Sanctorum Hiberniae, Sixty Years On', in A.P. Smith (ed.), *Studies in Early and Medieval Irish Archaeology, History and Literature in Honour of Francis J. Byrne* (Dublin: 2002), pp. 396–430.

41 It is probable that O'Sullivan learned a form of scholastic rhetorical debate, or *disputatio*, as part of his early training in grammar and philosophy at Compostela.

42 For a discussion of the authorship of this work see H. Caplan, *Rhetorica ad Herennium*, Loeb edition (London: 1954), pp. vii–xiv.

43 *Tenebriomastix*, p. 3

44 ibid. p. 6

45 *Tenebriomastix*, p. 139.

46 The title begins, *Davidis Camerarii Scoti . . .*

47 See James Ware, *De Hibernia & antiquitatibus ejus disquisitiones* (London: 1654). The edition cited here is: Walter Harris (editor and translator), *The Antiquities and History of Ireland* (Dublin: 1705), p. 133. For Stephen White, see his *Scoto-Caledonica Cornix deplumanda ab avibus mundi*, Poitiers: Bibliothèque de la Ville, MS 258 (55), written *c*. 1639, 393.

48 *Tenebriomastix*, p. 144.

49 Chambers even has Julius Caesar put to flight by the Scots! See *De Scotorum*, p. 19; and, for O'Sullivan's response, *Tenebriomastix*, p. 229.

50 Rothe, *Hibernia Resurgens*, pp. 126–9.

51 In this regard, O'Sullivan cites a work by his former teacher, Michael Cantwell, S.J., *Relatio praesentis status Iberniae*. See *Tenebriomastix*, p. 333: '*Doctor Michael Cantuelius nostras in Relatione praesentis status Iberniae eorum gymnasiorum fundamenta iaciendi laudem Ibernis vendicat: "Duo," inquit, "monachi nostrates nomine Ioannes et Clemens sive Cladius in Gallia gymnasij Parisiensis celeberrimi et in Italia Ticinensis, sive Papiensis fundamenta iecerunt, Caroli Magni Imperatoris patrocinio ad rem tantam suscipiendam confirmati.*"' (Our own countryman, Doctor Michael Cantwell, in his *Relation of the Present State of Ireland* claims for the Irish the honour of laying the foundations of these [*sc.* Carolingian] colleges. He says, 'two of our countrymen, by the name of Ioannes and Clemens, or Cladius laid the foundations

of the very famous Parisian college in France, and that of Ticinum or Pavia in Italy, having been assured of the protection of the Emperor Charlemagne in undertaking such an important task').

52 *Tenebriomastix*, p. 273.

53 ibid., p. 410.

54 ibid., pp. 183–4.

55 ibid., p. 24.

56 ibid., p. 412.

57 From *c.* AD 550 (the arrival of Columba) to AD 1061 (O'Sullivan's earliest date for the adoption of the name *Scotia*).

58 *Tenebriomastix*, pp. 468–9.

59 John Capgrave, English Augustinian and historian (1393–1462) best known for the *Nova Legenda Angliae*, a history of English saints. See *Catholic Encyclopedia s.v.* Capgrave.

60 Chambers, *De Scotorum*, p. 212.

61 ibid.: *'Incipiamus a primo saeculo 3: Irlandiam non fuisse Scotiam . . . patet manifeste a Capgranio* [sic], *qui eodom tempore aut paulo post floruit'* (Let us begin from the third century: that Scotia was not Ireland appears clearly from Capgrave, who lived at the same time or soon afterwards).

62 *Tenebriomastix*, p. 479. For Donatus O'Rourke as David Rothe, see n. 30.

63 Vincent of Beauvais, *Speculum Maius* (Douai: 1624), p. 29.

64 Chambers, *De Scotorum*, p. 215. O'Sullivan is himself not averse to the occasional judicious editing of a text.

65 *Tenebriomastix*, p. 484.

66 O'Sullivan's defence of Stanihurst is, of course, provisional and tactical. Like most early modern authors, he often endorses *sententia* from authors whom he elsewhere attacks.

67 Cf. Book 5 of the *Zoilomastix*.

68 *Tenebriomastix*, p. 529

69 Cf. Stanihurst, *De Rebus*, p. 245.

70 Chambers, *De Scotorum*, p. 228

71 *Tenebriomastix*, p. 531.

72 This is Rothe's phrase, found in the dedicatory letter of the *Hibernia Resurgens*.

73 *Tenebriomastix*, p. 538.

74 *De Scotorum*, pp. 243–4: *Epistola authoris ad Hibernos Irlandicos*.

75 Quoted in *Tenebriomastix*, p. 665; the original text is to be found in S. Reiter (ed.), *S. Hieronymi Presbyteri Opera: In Hieremiam libri vi*, Corpus Christianorum Series Latina (Turnhout: 1960), vol. 74, p. 119.

76 *Tenebriomastix*, p. 665.

77 *Tenebriomastix*, pp. 665–6. MS: *ferat. 'ferant'* is my proposed emendation.

78 While the quality of Philip O'Sullivan's rhetorical works in general has already been considered by both myself and others, the *Tenebriomastix*, although possessing many of the characteristics of his earlier works, requires further research before it can adequately be evaluated. See Paul Grosjean, S.J., 'Un Soldat Irlandais', p. 433; T. O'Donnell (ed.), *Zoilomastix*, pp. xxxiv–xxxv; D. Caulfield, 'Don Philip Strikes Back', in G. Petersmann and V. Oberparleiter (eds), *The Role of Latin in Early Modern Europe: Texts and Contexts II* (Salzburg: 2006), pp. 65–81.

7. A CASE STUDY IN RHETORICAL COMPOSITION

1 For analysis of the reception of Giraldus' works, see Hiram Morgan, 'Giraldus Cambrensis and the Tudor Conquest of Ireland', in idem (ed.), *Political Ideology in Ireland, 1541–1641* (Dublin: 1999), pp. 22–44.

2 Aside from the other contributions in this volume, on Stanihurst see Colm Lennon, *Richard Stanihurst the Dubliner, 1547–1618* (Dublin: 1981); and John Barry, 'Richard Stanihurst's *De Rebus in Hibernia Gestis*' in Ceri Davies and John E. Law (eds), *The Renaissance in the Celtic Countries* (London: 2004), pp. 1–18.

3 For further biographical details see Edmund Hogan, 'Life of Father Stephen White, S.J., Theologian and Polyhistor', *Journal of the Waterford and South East of Ireland Antiquarian Society*, vol. III, no. 12, April, 1897, pp. 55–8.

4 White, *Apologia pro Ibernia*, ed. Matthew Kelly (Dublin: 1849), pp. 77–8. The published title is 'pro Hibernia' but this misrepresents White's distinctive spelling, 'Ibernia', which I employ to refer to his work..

5 Stephen White, *Apologia pro innocentibus Ibernis*, MS 260 (276), Médiathèque François-Mitterand, Poitiers, ff. 270r–v.

6 ibid., f. 280v.

7 ibid., f. 297r.

8 White, *Apologia pro Ibernia*, p. v.

9 *Rhetorica ad Herennium*, I.iii.4 and III.ix.16.

10 White, *Apologia pro Ibernia*, 240–1.

11 ibid., p. v.

12 ibid., p. 6.

13 ibid., p. ii.

14 ibid., p. i.

15 ibid., pp. i, v.

16 ibid., p. 238.

17 ibid., p. ii.

18 Tertullian, *Adversus Gnosticos*, 1 *fin*; Pliny, *Historia Naturalis*, pp. 21, 20, 84 §146.

19 White, *Apologia pro Ibernia*, p. v.

20 ibid., p. i.

21 ibid., p. v.

22 ibid., pp. 77–8.

23 White, *Apologia pro innocentibus Ibernis*, f. 358r.

24 ibid., f. 270r.

25 ibid.

26 ibid.

27 ibid., f. 270v. Stanihurst had already settled in London in 1575 (before he had published his historical works), and he fled from there to the Low Countries in 1581, probably in response to the arrest and impending execution of his friend and former teacher Edmund Campion. See Colm Lennon, *Richard Stanihurst the Dubliner 1547–1618*, pp. 40–1, and Chapter 3, this volume.

28 White, *Apologia pro innocentibus Ibernis*, f. 271r.

29 'Ibernus' is generally used as a substantive, 'Ibernicus' as an adjective, but Stanihurst seems to use the two interchangeably and White does so increasingly during the course of this text.

30 White, *Apologia pro innocentibus Ibernis*, f. 276v.

31 ibid.

32 ibid., f. 277v–288r.

33 ibid., f. 277r.

34 ibid., f. 369r.

35 ibid., f. 273v.

36 ibid., ff. 273v–274r.

37 ibid., f. 336v.

38 Matthew Paris and Matthew of Westminster, medieval commentators on the reign of Henry II of England.

39 White, *Apologia pro innocentibus Ibernis*, f. 273r.
40 ibid., f. 280r.
41 ibid., f. 340v.
42 ibid., f. 321v; see also ff. 329r and 352v.
43 Machiavelli is mentioned on ff. 341r and 355v; More is mentioned on f. 361v.
44 White, *Apologia pro innocentibus Ibernis*, f. 359r.
45 A particularly fine example is found on ff. 287v–288r: '*vt omittam dicere de temporibus postquam Stanihurstus scripserat, ab anno sal: 1584. vsque ad hunc diem in quo spacio, vel ipse haec scribens, possem numerare plusquam milia matrimonia contracta inter illos, ridicule dictos ab illo Anglo Ibernos, et genuine Ibernos tam Nobiles, quam Ciues, aut inferioris status etc. et vt omittam commemorare multos milliones vtriusque generis Ibernorum Richardi Stanihursti qui ante illum natum connubia inter se coniunxant*' (Not to mention the times after Stanihurst wrote, from the year of salvation 1584 up to the present day, during which period even I who am writing these things might count more than a thousand marriages contracted between those whom Stanihurst ridiculously calls Anglo-Irish and those who are genuinely Irish, both noblemen and burghers, or people of lower status, and so forth. I also need not mention the many millions of both of Richard Stanihurst's kinds of Irish who married one another before he was born).
46 Cicero, *Epistulae ad Quintum fratrem*, Book 2, letter 15.
47 *Rhetorica ad Herennium*, Book 1, Chapter xii.
48 White, *Apologia pro innocentibus Ibernis*, f. 309v.
49 ibid., f. 293r.
50 ibid., f. 338r.
51 Richard Stanihurst, *De Rebus in Hibernia Gestis* (Antwerp: 1584), p. 9: '*Quid ais? Totámne, amabo, ut alia omittam, sacram litteraturam? Quî potest? Etiámne vetus instrumentum? Magnum, imò verò incredibile opus. Evangelion aliquod integrum? Audio. Epistolas verò Pauli? Quàm vellem numerare eas posset. unam tandem? Nihil profectò minus. Jacobi, Petri, vel Judæ litteras? Utinam. Non Apocalypsim? risum moves. Quid ergo? Dic, oro te, celerius. Ain' tandem? igitur ausculta. Qui Episcopatum desiderat, Bonum opus desiderat. utrum hoc Petrus, vel Paulus scripserit, viderint Theologi. Hæc est summa totius doctrinæ, hoc tantùm Latinitatis habet, hanc sententiam mente sæpius agiturae, crebris sermonibus usurpare solet.*' For translation, see John Barry's article in this volume, p. 44.
52 White, *Apologia pro innocentibus Ibernis*, ff. 338v–339r.
53 White had use the adjective '*turcicus*' in the *Apologia pro Ibernia* – twice in discussing Giraldus' claim that the Irish indulged in acts worse than those practised by the Turks and Tartars (i.e. bestiality and sodomy), but also once to refer to the manner of the Norman invasion: '*more iureque plane Turcico irruerunt, invaserunt*' (they rushed in and invaded Turkish style, according to the law of the Turk), p. iii; and see p. 94.
54 White, *Apologia pro innocentibus Ibernis*, f. 355v.
55 ibid., ff.355v–356r.
56 ibid., ff. 364r–v.
57 ibid., f. 273r.
58 ibid., ff. 292r–v.
59 ibid., f. 276r.

8. LATIN INVECTIVE VERSE IN THE COMMENTARIUS RINUCCINIANUS

1 The *Commentarius Rinuccinianus* project is funded by the Department of Arts, Sport and Tourism of the Republic of Ireland and administered by the University of Ulster.

2 Cecile O'Rahilly, *Five Seventeenth-Century Political Poems* (Dublin: 1977 [1952]) p. 47. The poem is not translated by O'Rahilly. Unless otherwise stated, all translations are my own. It should be noted that the Latin translations in particular are not literal but are designed to communicate to non-classicists the polemical nature of the material and the tone of the original. The approach is therefore similar to that adopted by Hooper for priapic poems (Richard W. Hooper, *The Priapus Poems* (University of Illinois Press: 1999), p. 31ff). I take full responsibility for all translations but I am indebted to Roisin McLaughlin and Caoimhín Breatnach for their help in researching the material in Irish in this chapter; and to Anna Chahoud, Jason Harris and Keith Sidwell for their constructive comments on the Latin translations. I am also indebted to members of the Trinity College Dublin History Seminar in November 2005 and the audience at the panel of the American Association for Neo-Latin Studies at the American Philological Association meeting in Montreal in January 2006 for their useful suggestions.

3 Cf. Dáibhí Ó Bruadair's epigram '*Mairg atá gan béarla binn*' (Woe to him who cannot simper English), which MacErlean thought likely to have been composed after Ormond's return to Ireland in 1662: J. MacErlean, *Duanaire Dháibhidh Uí Bhruadair*, Irish Texts Society, 3 vols (Dublin: 1910, 1913, 1917), vol. I, pp. 18–19; and '*Is beáradh suain*' (The chaos which I see), vol. II, pp. 18–23, which is an invective from 1674 against the Planters by whom, as MacErlean summarizes (p. 19), 'learning and literature are despised' (vol. II, pp. 18–23).

4 O'Rahilly, *Five Seventeenth-Century Political Poems*, p. 42. For O'Rahilly's comment on the 'pedantic' character of the poem, see p. 35.

5 Stanislaus Kavanagh (ed.), *Commentarius Rinuccinianus*, vols. I–VI (Dublin: 1932–49).

6 I am indebted to Billy Kelly, Tadhg Ó hAnnracháin, Éamonn Ó Ciardha and Leon O'Doherty for information on the historical background to the verse in the *Commentarius*.

7 The research into the classical pedigree of the diction in the verse of the *Commentarius* was facilitated by a period at the Fondation Hardt, Geneva, in 2004 during which the poetry was analysed with the aid of the *Bibliotheca Teubneriana Latina*.

8 *Commentarius*, vol. IV, part I, para. 611, ff. 1,981v–1,982. See also the annotated appendix to this chapter, which lists the other examples of verse contained in the *Commentarius*.

9 For biographical details on Inchiquin see Patrick Little, 'O'Brien, Murrough, first earl of Inchiquin (*c.* 1614–1647)', *Oxford Dictionary of National Biography* (Oxford University Press, 2004); hereafter, *Oxford DNB*.

10 Examples from Pindar include: Poseidon and Pelops (*Olympian* 1. 25, 40–4); Zeus and Ganymede (*Ol.* 1.44–5); Apollo and Cyrene (*Pythian* 9. 4–6). Examples from Ovid's *Metamorphoses* include: Juppiter and Ganymede (X.155–60); Juppiter and Io (I.584–600); Juppiter and Callisto (II.429–36); and Juppiter and Europa (846–75).

11 *Commentarius*, vol. VI (1949), pp. 21–2.

12 For example, Giambologna, *The Rape of the Sabine Women* (Florence: 1583); Gian Lorenzo Bernini, *Pluto and Proserpina*, Cardinal Ludovisi's Villa in Rome, 1621–2.

13 Jason McElligott, 'The Politics of Sexual Libel: Royalist Propaganda in the1640s', *Huntingdon Library Quarterly*, vol. 67, 2004, pp. 75–100, at p. 84.

14 Cynthia B. Herrup, 'Touchet, Mervin, second earl of Castlehaven (1593–1631)', *Oxford DNB*.

15 *Commentarius*, vol. VI, p. 221.

16 John T. Gilbert (ed.), *An Aphorismical Discovery of Treasonable Faction* published as *A Contemporary History of Affairs in Ireland, from 1641–1652*, 6 vols (Dublin: 1879), vol. 1, part 1, p. 74: 'Clanrickard . . . was the prime motor of this catostrophe,

Castlehaven now callinge to mind the execution of his father in London for buggery though enformer himself, or rather a patricide as aforementioned . . . Taaffe, a comon, cogginge gamster, a route banke and a temporizer fitt for any stampe; Diggby a publicke and knowen traytor against his Maiestie.'

17 The perceived moral danger of a Protestant upbringing underlies the following description of Ormond in the *Aphorismical Discovery* as: 'a younge man bred . . . in the bosome of Canterburie, a Puritant, Protestant or Atheiste' (Gilbert, *Contemporary History*, vol. 1, part 1, p. 144); the anonymous author later describes Ormond's men as a 'licentious Puritanicall armie' (vol. 2, part 1, p. 48). Cromwell was certainly not impressed with the end-product of this education, given that he is said to have described Ormond's appearance as 'more like a hunts-man than any way a souldier', which implies that Ormond was simultaneously predatory but inadequate: the author of the *Aphorismical Discovery* agreed with Cromwell and went on to say that his words were 'most true, and the very partie soe inclined by education and nature' (Gilbert, *Contemporary History*, vol. 2, part 1, p. 55).

18 Aidan Clarke, 'Atherton, John (1598–1640)', *Oxford DNB*. I am indebted to Jane Ohlmeyer for drawing the acquaintance of Inchiquin with Atherton to my attention.

19 Caesar Baronius, *Annales Ecclesiastici*, vol. XI (1606) p. 142 (ad ann. 1053).

20 *Commentarius*, vol. IV, part I, para. 38, ff. 1,758–1,759v

21 Vergil, *Aeneid* 6.789–97, *Eclogues* 4.1–30, *Georgics* 1.24–42; Ovid, *Metamorphoses* 15.745–61.

22 Cf. Ó Bruadair's reply to a panegyric on Ormond which was possibly composed on the occasion of Ormond's visit to Limerick in September 1666, 'A Shaoi re Gliogair' (Thou Sage of Inanity) in MacErlean, *Duanaire Dháibhidh Uí Bhruadair*, vol. I, pp. 196–207.

23 Catullus, 2.1, 3.4. On the 'deteriorating' tone of *deliciae* in classical Latin see James N. Adams, *The Latin Sexual Vocabulary* (London: 1982), pp. 170f., 196f. Even if O'Connell could ignore the reference to Catullus, he may have been equally aggravated to think of Suetonius' use of the phrase to describe the emperor Titus: '*amor ac deliciae generis humani*' (love and delight of the human race)' (Suetonius, *Titus*, p. 1).

24 The Edmund O'Meara in question was the son of Dermot O'Meara (see Chapter 4, this volume). Both father and son were doctors and grateful for the patronage of the 11th earl of Ormond. They were hostile to his successor, the 12th earl and 1st Duke of Ormond, who is depicted as the chief villain in the *Commentarius*. In fact, Dermot O'Meara had to flee to England to avoid a charge of high treason. Edmund became well known in Oxford as a result of his diatribes against the medical theories of Thomas Willis. It should be noted that his use of the epithet '*Ormoniensis*' (of Ormond) to describe himself in the title of his works is a mark of respect for his former patron, the 11th earl of Ormond, and not the 12th earl, who is the ultimate target of his verse: Kenneth Dewhurst, *Richard Lower's* Vindicatio: *A Defence of the Experimental Method* (Oxford: 1983), pp. xvi–xix.

25 Classical Latin diction and allusions in Blake's verses include the following: *ille dies*: Vergil, *Aeneid* 4.169, Horace, *Carmina* 2.17.8, 4.4.40; *sollicitusque timor*: cf. Lucretius, *De rerum natura* 5.46, Vergil, *Aeneid* 9.89; *Martis . . . horror*: Vergil, *Aeneid* 8.433–5; *imago tui*: cf. Vergil, *Aeneid* 2.369, 6.695, Tacitus, *Annales* 1.43.3; *Surgite*: Vergil, *Aeneid* 3.169, 8.59, 10.241; *proximus ardet/Ucalegon*: Vergil, *Aeneid* 2.310–11; *sparguntur sanguine campi*: cf. Vergil, *Aeneid* 11.188–92; *Tecta vorant flammae*: cf. Vergil, *Aeneid* 12.595–6, 12.656, Silius Italicus, *Punica* 14.312–13; *una dies*: Lucretius, *De rerum natura* 3.899, 5.95, 5.1000; *vernos . . . equos*: cf. Martial, *Epigrammata* 1.84.4; *pax ulla*: Ovid, *Epistulae ex Ponto* 3.1.7; *bella, horrida bella*: Vergil, *Aeneid* 6.86, 7.41; *consanguinea caede*: Statius, *Thebais* 4.436, cf. 11.57–61; *Parcite*

crudeles animae: cf. Vergil, *Aeneid* 6.847; *Saevas componite mentes*: cf. Silius Italicus, *Punica* 13.317; *saevior ira*: cf. Vergil, *Aeneid* 1.4; *Flos gentis*: cf. Vergil, *Aeneid* 8.499–500; *spes unica*: Livy, *Ab urbe condita* 3.26.8 et al., Silius Italicus, *Punica* 7.1; *salus populi*: Cicero, *De legibus* 3.8; *animi candor, honoris amor*: Ovid, *Tristia* 3.6.6–7; *ense caput*: Vergil, *Aeneid* 12.382, Ovid, *Metamorphoses* 5.104; *Bella paras*: cf. Vergil, *Aeneid* 3.248, 8.400, 11.18; *sors miseranda*: cf. Vergil, *Aeneid* 12.243. O'Meara's verses include the following examples of classical Latin diction and allusions: *sanctam . . . fidem*: Vergil, *Aeneid* 7.365; *Salutifer*: Ovid, *Metamorphoses* 2.642; *Septima . . . hyems*: Ovid, *Heroides* 7.88, Martial, *Epigrammata* 11.91.2; *flammam abiisse gelu*: cf. Lucretius, *De rerum natura* 2.515, 5.637–42; *Expertos belli*: Vergil, *Aeneid* 10.173; *imbellis, inops*: Tacitus, *Annales* 3.46.23; *Historiae* 4.23.4; *docta cohors*: cf. Statius, *Silvae* 5.3.91; *Pollentes opibus*: cf. Lucretius, *De rerum natura* 1.48, 2.650; *Sponte lacessitos*: Valerius Flaccus, *Argonautica* 4.207; *dura . . . compede*: Tibullus, *Elegiae* 1.7.42; *Arte . . . ingenioque*: Propertius, *Elegiae* 2.24b.7; *pondera rerum*: Lucan, *De bello civili* 3.337; *violare fidem*: Ovid, *Heroides* 7.57; *largas . . . opes*: Martial, *Epigrammata* 4.73.7, 5.25.4; *aemula laudis*: Ovid, *Metamorphoses* 6.86; *vultu prodente*: Horace, *Sermones* 2.5.104; *criminis auctor*: Propertius, *Elegiae* 2.6.19, Ovid, *Metamorphoses* 15.34; *examina*: Vergil, *Eclogae* 7.13; *O Patria*: Vergil, *Aeneid* 2.241, 5.632; *jubar*: cf. Vergil, *Aeneid* 4.130; *longi taedia belli*: Ovid, *Metamorphoses* 13.213; *Herba latet anguis in ista*: cf. Vergil, *Eclogae* 3.93; *toxica*: Propertius, *Elegiae* 1.5.4; *fatalis equus*: Vergil, *Aeneid* 6.515.

26 Gilbert, *Contemporary History*, vol. 1, p. vii.

27 Gilbert, *Contemporary History*, vol. 1, p. ix.

28 *Commentarius*, vol. IV, part II, para 281, ff. 2,142v–2,143.

29 The literal meaning of *Pseudo-pater* is 'false father' or 'false priest', which is a pun on the pseudonym *Philopater*, which means 'Father-loving'.

30 The last two lines of the above translation seek to reproduce some of the repetition in the original translation: a more literal translation would read: 'That book takes away your bad reputation from you. Why? I'll tell you: your bad reputation has been made very bad.'

31 Philopater Irenaeus used to be confused with Richard Bellings, to whom the work was attributed: Margaret Lantry, 'Cork Neo-Latin writers in the Early Modern Period', *Journal of the Cork Historical and Archaeological Society*, vol. 108, 2003, pp. 51–74, at p. 56. However, the catalogue in the National Library Dublin now gives the correct attribution.

32 John O'Callaghan, *Vindiciarum Catholicorum Hiberniae . . .* (Paris: 1650). I am indebted to Thomas O'Connor for providing information on the significance of the *Vindiciae*.

33 Patrick J. Corish, 'The Crisis in Ireland in 1648: The Nuncio and the Supreme Council: conclusions' (unpublished MA thesis: UCD 1952), p. 138. I am indebted to Meidhbhín Ní Úrdail for drawing my attention to material in this thesis. Cf. *Commentarius*, vol. V, part IV, para. 91, f. 2,513: '*Ormonistarum causa de facto pessima longe peior ibi habita fuerit*' (The cause of the Ormondists, which was actually in a very bad way, was far worse there).

34 It should be noted that the prefix *pseudo-* is ubiquitous in the *Commentarius*. Its use in the phrase *pseudo-Comitiorum prolocutor* (Speaker of the pseudo-Assembly) in the introduction to the poem by Blake quoted above shows how the word is associated with the illegitimate use of power and authority: the Assembly is always referred to as *pseudo*.

35 The book is 75mm in width and 125mm in height. It has been classified by some libraries as sextodecimo and others as duodecimo, but in any event is very small indeed. I am indebted to Máire Kennedy of Dublin City Archives for this information.

36 Lantry, 'Cork Neo-Latin Writers', p. 56.

37 *Commentarius*, vol. IV, part I, para. 588, f. 1,972.

38 There is a double meaning here, as the Latin noun for *pledge* (*obses*) is connected with the Latin verbal form which means *to besiege* (*obsidere*).

39 Homer, *Odyssey* 9.371–4; Vergil, *Aeneid*, 3.630–3. Morever, the Cyclops is emblematic of both foul and sacrilegious behaviour since early Latin satire, as Cicero recalls in *De Natura Deorum* 1.63 (= Lucilius, 1312–13 Marx).

40 *In Marcum Antonium Oratio Philippica Secunda*, 63 [25]. The original image in the Latin quoted above is of a gladiatorial physique, which would have been considered inappropriate for an upper-class Roman. As the original image could be misunderstood by non-classicists as being complimentary, I have substituted the image of a body-building lager lout. Mark Anthony's 'vomitory' style of public speaking made him an easy target for Cicero: Anthony Corbeill, *Controlling Laughter: Political Humor in the Late Roman Republic* (Princeton: 1996), p. 178. Compare the metaphorical incontinence of *Commentarius*, vol. III, para. 1,100, f. 1,601v: '*Ad vomitum rediere omnes*' (All resumed their spewing). There is also the biblical image of vol. II, part III, para 313, f. 1,159: '*impiam animam momento eructavit*' (he vomited out in an instant his unholy soul). Cf. *Leviticus* 18. 28 and *Revelation* 3.16.

41 Bede, *Ecclesiastical History*, 2.1. The source of the poem is *Commentarius Rinuccinianus*, vol. V, part IV, paras 164–5, ff. 2,549v–2,551.

42 Dáithí Ó hÓgáin, 'Nótaí ar Chromail i mbéaloideas na hÉireann', *Sinsear* 2, 1980, pp. 73–83, at p. 79 (English summary at 80–1). I am indebted to Michéal Ó Siochrú for details of secondary sources on Cromwell.

43 Alan Smith, 'The Image of Cromwell in Folklore and Tradition', *Folklore*, vol. 79, 1968, pp. 19–39, at p. 20; Ó hÓgáin, 'Nótaí', p. 79; ibid., pp. 74–6.

44 Vergil, *Aeneid*, 6.416–23.

45 Smith, 'The Image of Cromwell', p. 33; cf. the description of Ormond in the *Aphorismical Discovery* as a 'monstrous chicken' with his, presumably mutant, brood of heretic chicks (Gilbert, *Contemporary History*, vol. 1, part 1, p. 283). The treacherous nature attributed to Cromwell in the phrase '*callidus ingenio*/congenitally calculating' (p. 43) is also attributed throughout the *Commentarius* to Ormond (e.g. '*callidissimus hereticus*'/'most cunning heretic' (vol. IV, part I, para. 16, fo. 1,738)).

46 *Homo Bellua Tyrannum egit et monstrum* (30): cf. Pliny's *Panegyric*, where Trajan's predecessor Domitian is described as *immanissima belua* (52.3).

47 *Commentarius*, vol. I, part II, para. 98 , 313v.

48 Fergus Kelly, *A Guide to Early Irish Law* (Dublin: 1988), p. 18; cf. Kim McCone, 'A Tale of Two Ditties', in Donnchadh Ó Corráin, Liam Breatnach and Kim McCone (eds), *Sages, Saints, and Storytellers* (Maynooth: 1989), pp. 122–43, and *Pagan Past and Christian Present in Early Irish Literature* (Maynooth: 1990), pp. 84–137.

49 Kelly, *Early Irish Law*, p. 138.

50 ibid., p. 44.

51 The first instance of the refrain, which recurs throughout the poem, is at line 17.

52 *Odes* 4.15.4–5; cf. *Odes* 4.5.17–20.

53 For example, *Olympian* 1.12–13; *Pythian* 9.7.

54 Robert O'Connell, *Historia Missionis Hiberniae Minorum Capucinorum*, f. 562. I wish to thank the Capuchin order in Ireland for making their records and transcript of the *Historia* available; and the staff of Dublin City Archives, who have greatly facilitated my examination of the Capuchin typed copy of the Gilbert transcript of the Holkham transcript of the *Commentarius*; and the staff of the National Library for their assistance with research on the *Historia*.

55 *Commentarius*, vol. VI, p. 14.

56 Bibliothèque de Troyes, Cabinet de MSS, no. 706.

57 This Dublin manuscript (McEnery MSS, 1: Royal Irish Academy: 24 P 41 (1404)) was written by Tadhg mac Seaain mhic Thaidhg Uí Neachtúin. The verses at issue are to be found on f. 310 and are glossed in Latin as follows: *Gentis Hibernicae querelas hi versus Hibernici exprimunt* (These verses in Irish give expression to the laments of the Irish race). In addition to the material in Irish and of Irish interest in English or Latin, the same manuscript also includes material of interest to classicists: for example, f 91 'The Quest for the Golden Fleece'; 306: 'You Latin poets and you Greek forebear', 2 ll. Headed: 'The Lord Mount Garret on an Irish Poet'; 307 Latin quotations from the *Life of Cathaldus*, from Claudian, Ovid, and the Italian jurist Andrea Alciato, author of the famous *Emblemata* (1531) (Kathleen Mulchrone and Elizabeth Fitzpatrick, *Catalogue of Irish Manuscripts in the Royal Irish Academy*, 2 vols (Dublin: 1948)).

58 *Commentarius*, vol. VI, p. 20.

59 Eleanor Knott, *The Bardic Poems of Tadhg Dall Ó hUiginn*, Irish Texts Society, 2 vols (London: 1922–26), vol. 1, pp. liii–liv. Cf. the use of apple imagery in the erotic context of Sappho fr.105a (Voigt) and *Song of Songs*, 2.3. The earliest use of the image of an apple on a wave identified so far is its occurrence in *Cáin Adamnáin*, an Old Irish text dated to before the ninth century (Kuno Meyer (ed.), *Cáin Adamnáin: An Old-Irish Treatise on the Law of Adamnáin* (Oxford: 1905), para. 13, p. 8: *ubull for tuind*). Its use in the Old Irish text is comparable to that in the *Historia*, in that it occurs in the context of a description of the helpless and hopeless state of an individual.

9. Ussher and the collection of manuscripts in early modern Europe

1   Narcissus Marsh to Thomas Smith, 16 October 1680, Bodl. MS Smith 45, fol. 19.

2   Nicholas Bernard, *The Life and Death of the Most Reverend and Learned Father of our Church, Dr. James Usher, Late Arch-Bishop of Armagh, and Primate of all Ireland* (London: 1656), p. 7.

3   Constantine L'Empereur to Ussher, 16 November 1633: Charles Elrington, *Ussher's Works*, 17 vols (Dublin: 1847–64)(hereafter *UW*), vol. XV, pp. 576–7; John Buxtorf the Younger to Ussher, 26 August 1633: Elrington, *UW*, vol. XV, p. 566. I am grateful to Dr David Money for his translations of the Latin letters in the forthcoming critical edition of Ussher's correspondence, which I am currently preparing.

4   Andrew G. Watson, *The Library of Sir Simonds D'Ewes* (London: 1966), p. 57.

5   It must also be remembered that Marsh was focusing specifically on Greek manuscripts.

6   Watson, *Sir Simonds D'Ewes*, p. 22.

7   Bernard gives us a graphic account of the situation at Drogheda in 1641: Bernard, *Life*, pp. 93–4.

8   Richard Parr, *The Life of the Most Reverend Father in God, James Usher, late Lord Arch-Bishop of Armagh, Primate and Metropolitan of all Ireland. With a collection of Three Hundred Letters, between the said Lord Primate and most of the Eminentest Persons for Piety and Learning in his time, both in England and beyond the Seas* (London: 1686), Preface.

9   Bernard, *Life*, p. 101.

10 ibid., p. 100.

11 Richard Parr, *Life of Ussher*, p. 102, states that while at Dublin Castle, 'many of the Books, and most of the best Manuscripts were stolen away, or else imbezeled by those who were entrusted with them'. Dr Toby Barnard questions this, arguing that many works were returned: T.C. Barnard, 'The Purchase of Ussher's Library in 1657', *Long Room*, no. 4, 1971, p. 13.

12 The earliest catalogue of Ussher's books and manuscripts is TCD MS 793, f. 170r–
186v. This includes a number of manuscripts among the predominantly printed
books but, nevertheless, gives an indication of Ussher's early collecting habits. In
all, eight manuscripts are mentioned: 1) Boston of Bury's *Scriptorum Catalogus*,
which is joined to William de S. Amore's *De Periculis Nouissimorum Temporum* (f.
170r, f. 172r) – this work is referred to by Ussher in his letter to Camden, dated 30
October 1606: Elrington, *UW*, vol. XV, 18; 2) Augustine's *Opuscula* and the *Lamen-
tatio* of Petrus cardinalis tit. S. Marcelli (now TCD 218); 3) *Of Loue out of the
Canticles* – Richard Rolle's *Ego dormio*; 4) R. Wimbledon's *Sermon upon Redde
rationem*; 5) English Hymns; 6) Walden's *Fasciculus zizanorum*. Richard Maydeston's
Protectorium Pauperis, Determinationes aduersus Johannem Ashwarb i. . . *Confessio
Johannis Wiccliffe*; 7) Giraldus Cambrensis, *History of the Conquest of Ireland* trans-
lated by James Yong into English; 8) *Acta contra Henricum Crompe monachum de
Baltinglass a Joanne Langton descripta.*

13 Three copies of a manuscript catalogue of Ussher's manuscript collection exist: BL
Harl. MS 694, f. 63r–83r: 'Bibliotheca Usseriana Dublinii'; TCC MS 1319, fols 81–
121: 'Bibliotheca Usseriana' and TCD MS 7/2: 'Liber Collegii'. The latter includes all
those listed in the Harleian copy but is a later text (*c.* 1670) since it also includes a
good many accessions. It seems likely, as William O'Sullivan argues in his notes on
Ussher's catalogues, available in the Manuscripts Department of Trinity College
Dublin, that all three copies are recensions from an original text, most probably
drawn up by James Ware, shortly after the library came to Dublin. Certainly by
1661 provision had been made by the Irish House of Commons for such a catalogue to be compiled: *Journal of the House of Commons of Ireland* (Dublin: 1796) vol.
1, p. 400. The current manuscript catalogues in TCD divide descriptions of Ussher
manuscripts between a number of catalogues, usually separated into language
groups: a general catalogue of manuscripts by T.K. Abbott, *Catalogue of the manuscripts of the Library of Trinity College, Dublin* (Dublin: 1900); M.L. Colker's *Trinity
College Library Dublin: Descriptive Catalogue of the Mediaeval and Renaissance Latin
Manuscripts*, 2 vols (Aldershot: 1991), which includes a useful introduction by
William O'Sullivan as well as an appendix which gives notes on Ussher's transcripts
from European collections; T.K. Abbott and E.J. Gwynn, *Catalogue of the Irish Manuscripts in the Library of Trinity College, Dublin* (Dublin: 1921); Unpublished 'Grey
catalogues' by William O'Sullivan: 'Late Latin Manuscripts Unfinished *c.* 1980'.
This method ensures that different sections of individual manuscripts are cata-
logued but unfortunately many manuscripts belonging to Ussher either remain
uncatalogued or are only cursorily covered. By combining all the individual list-
ings, coupled with the shelfmarks said to be 'original' Ussher shelfmarks, the
overall figure of Ussher manuscripts in TCD comes to 371, with two manuscripts
formerly in Ussher's possession now in the library of the Royal Irish Academy – the
Books of Ballymote and Lecan – and two other manuscripts in Irish, 'Nomina' and
'Keating's history', missing. It should be said, however, that this figure is a notional
one since a number of manuscripts are included on the basis of annotations by
Ussher. The problem with this is that it is likely that Ussher may also have annotated manuscripts belonging to the library of TCD. It should also be remembered
that not all of these manuscripts were in Ussher's possession at the time of his death
– some he had already given to the college (see f. 1r of TCD MS 609), others subsequently found their way back there. The issue of tracking Ussher manuscripts is
fraught with difficulties: for instance, BL. Harl. 694, f. 63r–83r lists 518 manuscripts – to which O'Sullivan adds 27 manuscripts which were added as accessions
to MS 7/2, thus giving an overall number of 547, but since many of the items mentioned in Harl MS 694 were inevitably rebound this no longer correlates to the

overall figures now in TCD. It is likewise clear from looking at the 'original' Ussher shelfmarks alone (most likely to be Ware's shelfmarks) that a number of manuscripts are missing. Much work remains to be done in this area.

14 TCC MS 1319 is a partial catalogue and was evidently written by a careless transcriber as there are numerous infelicities throughout the work. While some of the broader general categories are now impossible to trace due to constant rebinding it is however instructive to look at these early catalogues since they provide vital insights into Ussher's collection. Throughout the catalogue in MS 1319 we find a number of poems, usually sacred in nature, which are not differentiated in other catalogues. Equally it is important to realize the strong contingent of material dealing with the political vicissitudes of mid-seventeenth-century England – in other words, this catalogue presents a slightly more politically aware Ussher than we generally find.

15 Colker says that John Lyons rebound nearly half of the Latin collection: Colker, *Latin Manuscripts I*, p. 29. On Sir Robert Cotton's almost compulsive rebinding of material see Colin G.C. Tite, *The Manuscript Library of Sir Robert Cotton. The Panizzi Lectures 1993* (London: 1994), pp. 104–5. Tite makes the important point that one reason Cotton engaged in this practice was because he wished to arrange an archive – he bound both originals and transcripts on similar subjects together: 57.

16 This is but one example of a number available in the concordances of call-numbers of Ussher's manuscripts which were drawn up by William O'Sullivan and which are still present among the catalogue collection of the Manuscript Department of Trinity College Dublin.

17 Parr, *Life of Ussher*, p. 102, states that the army in Ireland not only bought Ussher's collection of printed books, but also all his manuscripts 'which were not of his own handwriting'. In fact, a number of manuscripts in Ussher's hand were sent to Dublin but other Ussher manuscripts were undoubtedly kept by his chaplains, Bernard and Parr, who hoped to (and in some cases did) publish them. Parr gave a number of Ussher manuscripts into the hands of Archbishop William Sancroft and his collection was later sold to Thomas Tanner and Richard Rawlinson – whose collections in turn found their way to the Bodleian. We know that his immediate family retained a number of manuscripts, some of which were later given to the Bodleian: Ussher's grandson, James Tyrrell, gave eight volumes of Ussher's manuscripts to the Bodleian in 1707 (now Bodl. Additional MSS 27,610–17). It is clear, however, that the family retained a number of volumes after this date since some were later put on the market in the nineteenth century: see, for example, TCD MS 454 and TCD MS 943. Thomas Barlow, the mid-seventeenth-century librarian of the Bodleian, also acquired a number of manuscripts which were later given by him to the Bodleian: Bodl. Additional MS 6421 and 6436.

18 The Ussher correspondence contains a number of pleas from owners of manuscripts for their long-overdue return. On the St Donat incident see Parr, *Life of Ussher*, p. 61.

19 Brian Twyne's note at the end of Allen's catalogue, following the latter's death, certainly sounds damning: 'Mr Richard James of Corpus Christi College Comminge afterwardes into Mr Allen's acquayntance gott away many of those manuscripts from ye good old man and conveyed them awaye to London to Sir Robert Cotton's studie': Andrew G. Watson, 'Thomas Allen of Oxford and His Manuscripts', in Andrew G. Watson, *Medieval Manuscripts in Post-Medieval England* (Aldershot: 2004), p. 300. The monks of Corbey Abbey accused De Thou of smuggling out manuscripts in barrels during the temporary use of the abbey by royal troops during the French civil wars: Edward Edwards, *Libraries and Founders of Libraries* (London: 1864), p. 50.

20 Henry Bourgchier, writing to Ussher on 24 November 1624: Elrington, *UW*, vol. XV, p. 227.
21 Bernard Meehan, 'The Manuscript Collection of James Ussher', in Peter Fox (ed.) *Treasures of the Library, Trinity College, Dublin* (Dublin: 1986), pp. 97–110.
22 William O'Sullivan, 'Ussher as a Collector of Manuscripts', *Hermathena*, vol. 88, 1956, pp. 34–58.
23 Parr, *Life of Ussher*, p. 34. It should also be remembered, as Colin G.C. Tite reminds us in his seminal '"Lost or Stolen or Strayed": A Survey of Manuscripts formerly in the Cotton Library', in C.J. Wright (ed.), *Sir Robert Cotton as Collector. Essays on an Early Stuart Courtier and His Legacy* (London: 1997), p. 269: that some of the manuscripts of Henry Savile of Banke came to Ussher via the mediation of Sir Robert Cotton. Certainly this seems to be true of TCD MS 215 and MS 189. Equally, a manuscript formerly belonging to Camden had found its way to Ussher via Cotton: TCD MS 497.
24 Elrington, *UW*, vol. XV, pp. 225–6. William O'Sullivan discusses some of the issues raised by Davies, especially the difficulties involved in locating manuscripts and shipping them home to Ussher: O'Sullivan, 'Ussher as a Collector', pp. 45–8. In all, seven letters from Davies to Ussher are extant, dated between 29 August 1624 and 29 July 1628. Davies was not the only person Ussher employed in the Levant – in 1639 he engaged the services of Christian Rave who had travelled to Constantinople. Ussher agreed to pay him £24 per annum and in return Rave would, hopefully, locate sources for him. Ussher's wish-list of manuscripts in his letter to Rave of 12 November 1639 is impressive but perhaps overly optimistic: '*Libri quos pro me requiri velim, hi sunt: Vetus Testamentum Syriacum, non ex Hebraeo factum (illud enim jam habeo) sed ex Graeco versum, atque obelis et asteriscis distinctum. Polycarpi et Ignatii Epistolae Syriace conversae. Eusebii (non Historia ecclesiastica quae passim prostat) Chronicum Graecum, vel etiam Syriace versum. Si quid etiam versionum Symmachi, Aquilae et Theodotionis reperiri possit. Julii Africani Chronicon. Hegesippi Historia Ecclesiastica. Clementis Alexandrini Hypotyposeon libri, et de Paschate libellus Anatolii. Aniani et Panodori computi Paschales. Georgii Syncelli Graecum Chronicon. Apollodori Graecum Chronicon. Phlegon de Olympiadibus. Diodori Siculi, Polybii, Dionysii Halicarnassei, Dionis Cocceiani libri illi, qui apud nos desiderantu.*' (The books which I would like to be sought out, on my own behalf, are these: a Syriac New Testament, not made from Hebrew (for I have that already) but translated from Greek, and marked with obelisks and asterisks. The letters of Polycarp and Ignatius translated into Syriac. Eusebius (not his Ecclesiastical History, which is readily available), but his Greek Chronicle [or, Chronology?], or the same also translated into Syriac. Also anything that can be found of versions of Symmachus, Aquila and Theodotio. Julius Africanus' Chronology. Hegesippus' Ecclesiastical History. Clement of Alexandria's books of epitomes, and the little book of Anatolius on Easter. Anianus' and Panodorus' Easter calculations. George Syncellus' Greek Chronology. Apollodorus' Greek Chronicle. Phlegon on the Olympiads. Those books of Diodorus Siculus, Polybius, Dionysius of Halicarnassus, and Dio Cocceianus, which we lack. Hipparchus' Astronomy, in Greek): Elrington, *UW*, vol. XVI, pp. 53–4.
25 BL MS Add. 22905, f. 103r. Significantly this is a list of manuscripts still on loan at the time of his death: G.J. Toomer, *Eastern Wisedome and Learning. The Study of Arabic in Seventeenth-Century England* (Oxford: 1996), p. 205.
26 ibid.
27 Thomas Davies to Ussher, July 1625: Elrington *UW*, vol. XV, p. 285.
28 On Ussher's purchase of Waldensian manuscripts in the 1630s see J.H. Todd, *The Books of the Vaudois: The Waldensian Manuscripts Preserved in the Library of Trinity College, Dublin* (London: 1865). The manuscripts in question are TCD MSS 265,

266, 267 and 268. TCD MS 269 contains material on Cathars. There are also excerpts from trials of Waldensians in TCD MS 236, f. 220r–236r and material on Waldensians in TCD MS 260. W.S. Gilly, quoted in Todd's work on the Waldensian Manuscripts of Trinity College Dublin, says that Ussher paid £22 for them. In a letter of 11 October 1641, Ussher mentions to Jean de Laet his purchase of some books from the library of Francis Gomar: BL Add. MS 6395 f. 136r. It is, however, unclear whether this refers to books and/or manuscripts.

29 Constantine L'Empereur to Ussher, 16 November 1633: Elrington, *UW*, vol. XV, p. 577.

30 The diplomat Sir William Boswell (†1650) is mentioned in a number of letters in this capacity: Louis De Dieu to Ussher, 4 May 1636 mentions Boswell as a contact between the two correspondents: Elrington, *UW*, vol. XVI, p. 13. See also Constantine L'Empereur to Ussher, 25 December 1636: Elrington, *UW*, vol. XVI, pp. 32–3, and Isaac Gruter to Ussher, 16 July 1649: Elrinton, *UW*, vol. XVI, p. 136. Another diplomat mentioned in connection with collecting is Sir Thomas Roe: Sir Henry Bourghier complains to Ussher that though he has brought home from Constantinople a 'rare collection of Coyns and Medals', he has not brought any books home, except one for Charles I: Elrington, *UW*, vol. XV, p. 436.

31 Ussher to De Dieu, 14 September 1636: Elrington, *UW*, vol. XVI, p. 19.

32 Ward to Ussher, 2 January 1625: Elrington, *UW*, vol. XV, p. 229.

33 Watson, *Library of Sir Simonds D'Ewes*, p. 88 fn 230 relates the story of an unfortunate scholar attempting to gain access to the Parker collection in Corpus Christi College, Cambridge in 1659. This involved locating three different academics, each of whom held one of the three necessary keys. On gaining admittance, however, he was aghast to learn that he was not allowed to consult the manuscripts since he had neglected to obtain the permission of the Master and Fellows.

34 Watson, ibid., p. 40. Ussher's correspondence with Samuel Ward includes an example of Ussher mistaking a reference: Ward's letter to Ussher of 3 August 1625 says that though Ussher wanted 'to have a Book out of *Trinity Colledg* library, which you entitle, *Psalterium Gallicum, Romanum, Hebraicum MS. in magno Folio.* There is no such Book there, as the Master telleth me': Elrington, *UW*, vol. XV, p. 288. Edward Brownker, writing to Ussher from Wadham College, had a similar tale to tell on 11 September 1620: 'As for the Manuscripts you desire to hear of, neither one nor the other is to be found: It is true, according unto Dr. *James* his Catalogue, there was one *Gildas* in *Merton* Colledge Library, but he was *Gildas Sapiens*, not *Gildas Albanius*, whom *Pitts* says was the Author of the Book entitled, *De Victoria Aurelii Ambrosii*; neither is that *Gildas Sapiens* now to be seen in *Merton* Colledge, he hath been cut out of the Book whereunto he was annexed': Elrington, *UW*, vol. XV, p. 153.

35 Peter Beal, *In Praise of Scribes: Manuscripts and Their Makers in Seventeenth-Century England* (Oxford: 1998), p. 2.

36 Ussher to Arnold Boate, 29 November 1651: Elrington, *UW*, vol. XVI, p. 202.

37 Ussher to William Camden, 8 June 1618: Elrington, *UW*, vol. XV, p. 135.

38 On the 'Feathery Scribe' see Beal, *In Praise of Scribes*, p. 58ff. The Feathery Scribe's hand may be found in a disquisition of Sir John Davies in Ussher manuscript TCD MS 845.

39 Joseph Mede to Ussher, 4 May 1630: Elrington, *UW*, vol. XV, p. 496.

40 Ussher to Sir Robert Cotton, 4 May 1625: Elrington, *UW*, vol. XV, p. 276.

41 Thomas Lydiat to Ussher, undated letter, early 1619: Bodl. MS 313, f. 88r.

42 Elrington, *UW*, vol. XVI, p. 193.

43 ibid., pp. 193–4.

44 TCD MS 454, f. 200v.

45 Elrington, *UW*, vol. XVI, p. 54.

46 Parr, *Life of Ussher*, p. 99.

47 Raymond Gillespie and Bernadette Cunningham investigate one such network in: 'James Ussher and his Irish Manuscripts'.

48 Thomas Strange to Ussher, 31 October 1639: Bodl. Rawl. MS Letter 89, f. 106r–107r. While it is clear that some Roman Catholic scholars were on easy terms with Ussher it is significant that his contacts with Luke Wadding, and indeed other Roman Catholic scholars such as David Rothe, the Roman Catholic bishop of Ossory, tended to be via intermediaries. Wadding's codename for Ussher, referred to in Strange's letter, 'Mr Turrcremata', speaks volumes of the sometimes uneasy nature of this scholarly relationship. On Ussher's contacts with David Rothe see William O'Sullivan, 'Correspondence of David Rothe and James Ussher, 1619–23', *Collectanea Hibernica*, vol. 36–7, 1994–5, pp. 8–49.

49 Samuel Ward to Ussher, 25 September 1622: Elrington, *UW*, vol. XV, p. 177.

50 *Epistolae Sarrauii*, 1654 edition, p. 244.

51 Petrus Scavenius to Ussher, 26 March 1650: Elrington, *UW*, vol. XVI, p. 143.

52 On Peiresc as a collector see Peter N. Miller, *Peiresc's Europe. Learning and Virtue in the Seventeenth Century* (New Haven: 2000).

53 Ussher to Sir Henry Spelman, 1 April 1628: BL Add. MS 25384, f. 15r.

54 Ussher to Sir Henry Spelman, 26 August 1634: *Catalogue of the Collection of Autograph Letters and Historical Documents formed between 1865 and 1882 by Alfred Morrison* (1892), vol. 6, pp. 287–8. Ussher continued to ask Spelman to follow up on this in a letter dated 15 June 1638: 'When I sent the first part of my book de Primordiis unto you; by my letter I entreated you to procure certaine things for my use from Nicol. Fabricius Peirescius: from whom if you have received any answear, I should be very glad to heare of it': RIA MS SR 3.D.8. 30 (3192). Evidently Ussher had not heard of the death of Peiresc in 1637.

55 On De Thou see Samuel Kinser, 'An Unknown Manuscript Catalogue of the Library of J.A. De Thou', *Book Collector*, vol. 17, 1968 ,pp. 168–76; Antoine Coron, 'Ut prosint aliis'. Jacques de Thou et sa bibliothèque', in Claude Jolly (ed.), *Histoire des bibliothèques francaises: Les bibliothèques sous l'Ancien Régime 1530–1789* (Paris: 1988), pp. 101–25 (this includes a note on De Thou's manuscripts by Marie-Pierre Laffitte).

56 Bernard, *Life*, p. 43, states that 'The *Puteani Fratres* in *Paris*, two learned men helped him with many transcripts out of *Thuanus* and others, between whom and him many letters passed.' Unfortunately none of these letters are extant.

57 Elrington, *UW*, vol. XVI, p. 30.

58 TCD MS 197, f. 1r–7v.

59 For material on Faustus of Riez see TCD MS 197, in which may be found Paulinus' letter to Faustus: f. 22r–23r; and a number of letters from Faustus himself: f. 23r–38v. TCD MS 239 predominantly consists of material from Hincmar of Reims, Ratramnus of Corbey, Rabanus Maurus of Fulda and Prudentius of Troyes.

60 Ussher writes of his intention to Dr Samuel Ward, Master of Sidney Sussex College, Cambridge, on 10 December 1630: 'I have out of Corbey-Abbey, in France, two confessions written by Gotheschalcus himself, which as yet have not been printed. If we could obtain Rathramnus his treatise of the same argument, written unto the emperor Charles the same time: I doubt not but it would give us a great contentment . . .', see Elrington, *UW*, vol. XV, p. 541.

61 James Frey to Ussher, 25 June 1635: Elrington, *UW*, vol. XVI, p. 524.

62 On this point see Coron, 'Ut prosint aliis', p. 101 (full details in n. 55).

63 Tite, *The Manuscript Library of Sir Robert Cotton*, p. 12.

64 Watson, *Library of Sir Simonds D'Ewes*, p. 24.

65 Ussher to William Laud, bishop of London, 30 June 1631: CSPIre 63/252/1978.

66 A.G. Watson, 'Sir Robert Cotton and Sir Simonds D'Ewes: An Exchange of Manuscripts', *British Museum Quarterly*, vol. XXV, 1962, pp. 19–24.

67 Ussher to Sir Henry Spelman, 1 April 1628: BL Add. MS 25384, f. 15r.

68 Ussher to Arnold Boate, 5/15 July 1650: Elrington, *UW*, vol. XVI, p. 153.

69 Ussher to Patrick Young, 27 August 1639: Bodl. MS Smith 75, pp. 105–8.

70 Ussher to Arnold Boate, 27 September 1650: Elrington, *UW*, vol. XVI, p. 159.

71 Ussher to Sir Robert Cotton, 12 July 1625: Elrington, *UW*, vol. XV, p. 283.

72 Henry Fetherston writing to Ussher on 30 April 1628 outlines the scale of the collection: 'May it please your Grace, having occasion of furnishing of a note of ordinary vendible books sent unto mee from one Mr. Preston, although unknowne, by my good frend Mr. Fleming, the bearer hereof, I make bould to take occasion to signefie to your Grace that I have now coming, besides my Franckford books, an extraordinary large furniture from Venice, where amongst other rare books my factor writes that hee hath almost gone through for a Library of Greeke Manuscripts. I have given him tyme enough, and therefore, he doth not only ransack Venice, but also Padua, Bononia, Florence, and Rome itselfe, and intends to visite Naples in going up one way, and returning another, I thought it my duty to acquaint your Grace with soe much, by reason I have advices that I have already 40 great Chests at Sea, and if it please God to send them hither safe, to print a Catalogue of them and to send your Grace one.' Elrington, *UW*, vol. XVI, p. 466.

73 Ussher to William Herbert, 3rd earl of Pembroke, 22 January 1629: Elrington, *UW*, vol. XV, p. 421. Pembroke had been chancellor of Oxford since 1617 and Ussher no doubt hoped that if he could not induce the king to purchase the collection Pembroke might himself decide to buy it for his university. This Pembroke duly did.

74 Archibald Hamilton gives us the background of the alleged Carew bequest to TCD in his letter to Ussher dated 8 April 1629: 'The Earl of *Totnes* departed this Life some ten days since, his Corps is not yet buried: Soon after his decease, I went and made enquiry after that Press of Books and Manuscripts which only concern *Ireland*, and asked whether he had left them as a Legacy to our Colledg, as your Lordship heretofore moved him, and as he himself lately promised (to Sir *Fra. Annesly* and my self) that he would: whatsoever the good Man intended, or whatsoever direction he gave, I cannot learn, but the Colledg is not like to get them': Elrington, *UW*, vol. XV, pp. 433–4. It should be stated, however, that Ussher did manage to snaffle a few Carew manuscripts for himself: O'Sullivan, 'Ussher as a Collector', p. 42, suggests that TCD MSS 1432–7 are probably from the Carew collection. These include a couple of manuscripts in Irish on medicine. The conduit for this sale may well have been Sir Henry Bourghier, who wrote to Ussher on 26 March 1629 telling him of his intention to buy Carew's 'Irish Books and Papers': Elrington, *UW*, vol. XV, p. 430. On Carew as a collector, see Jason Dorsett, 'Sir George Carew: The Study and Conquest of Ireland', unpublished D. Phil. thesis, University of Oxford, 2000.

75 ibid., Elrington, *UW*, vol. XV, p. 434.

76 Elrington, *UW*, vol. XV, p. 451.

77 ibid.

78 Ussher to De Dieu, 9 June 1632: Elrington, *UW*, vol. XV, pp. 552–3. This was a very lengthy list indeed: '*Arabici Psalterii tria habui exemplaria, satis antiqua: quorum unum D. Londinensi episcopo, academiae Oxoniensis dignissimo cancellario, cum antiquam multis aliis codicibus MSS. nuper a me donatum est: alterum quod D. Gulielmo Bedwello commodaveram, eo jam vita functo, vix est ut recuperari a me posse sperem: bibliotheca mea terium adhuc conservat. Habeo et Genesim Arabice ex Graeco versam, et*

amplo commentario explicatam: Arabicas quoque homilias in sacrae historiae partem, a Josepho incipientes. Eadem lingua Chrysostomi conciones quadragesimales habeo, quae in nostris desiderantur libris, et Graecis et Latinis. Arabicum quoque Nomocanonem possideo; in quo veterum synodorum canones ad certos titulos reducti continentur. E Syriacis Ephraemi, praeter tractatum quem habes de amore sapientiae, hymni apud me sunt de humilitate, rescipiscentia, fine seculi, Gog et Magog, monachis et eremitis; nocturna meditatio contra ebrietatem et crapulam: et praecationum liber. Item hymni varii alphabetici. Habeo et Syriacum in quatuor Evangelia commentarium: et in universa fere biblia alterum Thesauri Secretorum titulo praenotatum: cui et quatuor tabulae chronologicae sunt insertae. 1. Patriarcharum, ab Adamo ad Mose. 2. Judicum, a Josua ad Samuelem. 3. Regum a Saule ad Sedechiam. 4. Imperatorum exterorum a Nebuchadnetsare ad Vespatianum usque. librum sermonum in dies festos his addas licet: et Syriacum grammaticam absolutissimam. Samaritica vero scripta, praeter Pentateuchum, quae nactus sum omnia ad communem amicum nostrum D. Johannem Seldenum transmisi: a quo, quod contineant poteris resciscere: et de nostris quidem hactenus' (I had three quite old copies of the Arabic Psalter: one of which was recently given by me to the lord bishop of London, the most worthy chancellor of Oxford University, with quite a number of other manuscript codices; and another of which I had lent to Mr William Bedwell, who has now passed away, and I can scarcely hope to get it back: my library still preserves the third. I also have a Genesis translated into Arabic from the Greek, and explained by an ample commentary: also Arabic homilies on part of the sacred history, beginning from Joseph. In the same language I have the Lent sermons of Chrysostom, which are wanting in our books (both Greek and Latin). I also possess an Arabic 'Canon of Law', in which the canons of the old synods are contained, reduced to certain titles. In Syriac, I have (besides the tract which you have on love of wisdom) Ephraim's hymns on humility, repentance, the end of the age, Gog and Magog, monks and hermits; a nocturnal meditation against drunkenness and intoxication; and a book of prayers. Also various alphabetic hymns. I have also a Syriac commentary on the four Gospels; and another on almost the whole Bible marked by the title 'Treasury of Secrets' (in which four chronological tables are inserted: (1) of Patriarchs, from Adam to Moses; (2) of Judges, from Joshua to Samuel; (3) of kings, from Saul to Zedekiah; (4) of foreign emperors, from Nebuchadnezzar continuously up to Vespasian). You may add to these a book of sermons on festival days: and a very complete Syriac grammar. As for Samaritan writings, apart from the Pentateuch, all that I obtained I sent across to our mutual friend Mr John Selden: from whom you can find out what they contain).

79   Ussher to De Dieu, 14 September 1636: Elrington, *UW*, vol. XVI, p. 19.
80   Bodl. Rawl. MS C. 850, f. 65v.
81   De Dieu to Ussher, 4 May 1636: Elrington, *UW*, vol. XVI, p. 14.
82   Isaac Basire to Ussher, 8 February 1648: *UW*, vol. XVI, p. 121, and Ussher to Christophe Justel, 12 February 1648: Elrington, *UW*, vol. XVI, pp. 110–11.
83   Isaac Gruter to Ussher, 26 February 1650: Elrington, *UW*, vol. XVI, p. 141.
84   Henri de Valois to Ussher, 3 December 1654: Elrington, *UW*, vol. XVI, pp. 298–9.
85   Ussher to Henri de Valois, 20 December 1654: Elrington, *UW*, vol. XVI, p. 300.
86   James Ussher, *Veterum epistolarum hibernicarum sylloge quae partim ab Hibernis, partim ad Hibernos partim de Hibernis vel rebus Hibernicis sunt conscriptae. Iacobvs Vsserivs* (Dublin: 1632).
87   Thomas Gataker to Ussher, 18 March 1617: Elrington, *UW*, vol. XV, p. 93.
88   John Hanmer to Ussher, 28 May 1627: Elrington, *UW*, vol. XV, p. 378.
89   Meric Casaubon to Ussher, 21 October 1650: Elrington, *UW*, vol. XVI, pp. 165–6.
90   John Greaves to Ussher, 19 September 1644: Elrington, *UW*, vol. XVI, p. 74.
91   John Bainbridge to Ussher, 3 October 1626: Elrington, *UW*, vol. XV, p. 352.

92   John Evelyn, commenting on his visit to Ussher in August 1655, says that Ussher told him 'how great the losse of time was to study much the Eastern languages, that excepting *Hebrew*, there was little fruite to be gathered of exceeding labour; that besides some *Mathematical* bookes, the *Arabic* itselfe had little considerable'. G.J. Toomer, *Eastern Wisedome and Learning: The Study of Arabic in Seventeenth-Century England* (Oxford: 1996), p. 85.

93   Parr, *Life of Ussher*, p. 101.

94   ibid. On D'Ewes's interest in Anglo-Saxon studies see Watson, *The Library of Sir Simonds D'Ewes*, p. 10.

95   Gerard John Vossius to Ussher, 11 January 1632: Bodl. MS Rawl. Letters 83, f. 67r–68v.

96   Ussher to Gerard John Vossius, 10 June 1632: Elrington, *UW*, vol. XV, p. 556. Ussher had already intimated to Samuel Ward his intention to hand over his work on the Marianus Scotus project as soon as he learned of Vossius' interest: Ussher to Ward, 15 March 1630: Elrington, *UW*, vol. XV, p. 481.

97   ibid. Ussher to Vossius, 10 June 1632: Elrington, *UW*, vol. XV, p. 556.

98   ibid.

99   Ussher to Sir Robert Cotton, 12 July 1625: Elrington, *UW*, vol. XV, p. 284.

100 Ussher to Sir Robert Cotton, 22 March 1629: Elrington, *UW*, vol. XV, p. 428.

101 Ussher to De Dieu, 7 July 1637: Elrington, *UW*, vol. XVI, p. 28

102 Ussher to Thomas James, 23 April 1608: Bodl. MS Ballard 44, f. 138r.

103 Thomas Morton, bishop of Chester, to Ussher, 20 April 1618: Elrington, *UW*, vol. XVI, p. 351.

104 William Eyre to Ussher, 17 August 1617: Elrington, *UW*, vol. XV, p. 124.

105 Ussher explains this to William Camden in a letter dated 28 April 1614: 'I know it will be accounted a great disgrace unto the worke, that forbearing (as much as might be) mine own style, I have sett down the wordes of mine authors in that barbarous kinde of speech which in their age was esteemed very elegant. But I could not helpe it: my Lord of Canterbury would have it so; that by that means all occasion of quarrelling might be taken away from the adversarye. And in very truthe, when the matter is meerlye historicall, and the dispute of that nature where I have no libertye to use mine owne invention, but simplye to produce what I finde delivered by them that went before me; (as in this argument it fell out to be my case:) I do not see how the matter would be better carried otherwise; and herein I am right of Velserus his judgment.': Elrington, *UW*, vol. XV, pp. 77–9.

106 Ussher to John Selden, 30 November 1627: Elrington, *UW*, vol. XV, p. 380.

107 Significantly, Ussher viewed his work on Gottschalk as something which was relevant to both the situation of the Church of England and also that of European Calvinism. Writing to De Dieu on 9 June 1632 he says that he is sending 'the history of the controversy over predestination (which so troubles your churches)': Elrington, *UW*, vol. XV, pp.553–4.

108 Parr, *Life of Ussher*, p. 100.

109 ibid. See also Bernard, *Life*, p. 8, quoting Alexandre Morus. Bernard in particular stresses this point, citing a number of authors in support: 9: 'Dr. *Prideaux* (late Bishop of *Worcester*) calls him, "The most rich Magazine of solid learning, and of all Antiquity."'

Index

237